Fighting Machines

Pennsylvania Studies in Human Rights
Bert B. Lockwood, Series Editor
A complete list of books in the series is available from the publisher.

FIGHTING MACHINES

Autonomous Weapons and Human Dignity

Dan Saxon

PENN

UNIVERSITY OF PENNSYLVANIA PRESS

PHILADELPHIA

Published by
University of Pennsylvania Press
Philadelphia, Pennsylvania 19104-4112
www.upenn.edu/pennpress

Printed in the United States of America on acid-free paper
10 9 8 7 6 5 4 3 2 1

Library of Congress Cataloging-in-Publication Data
Names: Saxon, Dan, author.
Title: Fighting machines : autonomous weapons and human dignity / Dan Saxon.
Description: Philadelphia : University of Pennsylvania Press, [2022] | Series: Pennsylvania studies in human rights | Includes bibliographical references and index.
Identifiers: LCCN 2021015345 |
ISBN 978-0-8122-5355-9 (hardcover)
Subjects: LCSH: Autonomous weapons systems—Moral and ethical aspects. | Autonomous weapons systems (International law) | Respect for persons. | Dignity. | International law—Moral and ethical aspects.
Classification: LCC KZ5645.5.A98 S29 2022 | DDC 341.6/3—dc23
LC record available at https://lccn.loc.gov/2021015345

For Bruce

CONTENTS

Introduction

> God himself . . . gave a mind to the human soul. . . . Has not human ingenuity discovered and exploited all our numerous and important techniques . . . ? And is it not this mental, this rational drive, even when it seeks satisfaction in things superfluous, nay more, in things dangerous and suicidal, a witness to the excellence of its natural endowment . . . ? What marvellous, stupendous results has human industry achieved . . . ! Against even human beings all the many kinds of poison, weapons, engines of war!
>
> —Saint Augustine, *The City of God Against the Pagans*

This book addresses the relationship between lethal autonomous weapon systems, human dignity, and international law. Its central thesis is that the delegation of human responsibility for moral judgments to lethal autonomous weapon systems erodes human dignity and, consequently, international law.

Weapon systems "are as old as warfare."[1] The Chinese, for example, presumably invented the simple but innovative foot stirrup in the fifth century A.D., and it was carried to western Europe by the eighth. Prior to the introduction of the stirrup, warriors sat precariously on their horses and risked a fall from their mount each time they slashed or lunged at their enemy.[2] The stirrup permitted a powerful new system of horse, rider, and the sword, spear, or lance that he carried.[3] The new technology provided additional lateral support to the person in the saddle and bonded horse and rider into a fighting unit capable of unprecedented violence: "The fighter's hand no longer delivered the blow; it merely guided it. The stirrup thus replaced human energy with animal power, and immensely increased the warrior's ability to damage his enemy. Immediately, without preparatory steps, it made possible mounted shock combat, a revolutionary way of doing battle."[4] The introduction of this "alien military technology" in Europe also led to dramatic social changes, such as the development of feudalism and "the seeds of chivalry."[5]

Like a mounted warrior from premedieval times, a modern foot soldier is also a "weapon system."[6] "Rifles," for example, "are as good as the men who pull the triggers. Each soldier must consider his weapon in the same light as he considers his right arm; together they are a team."[7] As rifle technology advances, soldiers change their tactics so that the system functions more effectively.[8]

Historically, "battle" for the common soldier and the system that he represented was often a series of myopic, small-scale scenarios that were fought by their own rules.[9] Infantry actions, for example, were "the sum of many combats of individuals—one against one, one against two, three against five."[10] Thus, as part of a vivid description of the efforts by U.S. Marines to occupy the island of Iwo Jima during the Second World War, military historian Max Hastings observed that "all battles break down into a host of intensely personal contests."[11]

During the nineteenth and twentieth centuries, however, that truism already had begun to change. The development of the machine gun "put into the hands of one man the fire-power formerly wielded by forty."[12] New kinds of heavy artillery, "perhaps the decisive weapon on the battlefield"[13] in World War I, made long-range shelling a crucial part of combat strategy. Prior to the start of the Battle of the Somme on 1 July 1916, for example, U.K. and French forces had fired 1.5 million artillery shells during a seven-day (and night) bombardment of the German lines, before the first infantry soldiers climbed over their trench tops and into no-man's land.[14] As time progressed, with the development of increasingly mechanized armored forces during World War II and the Cold War, the common soldier experienced a steep "reduction of his status to that of a mere adjunct to machinery, the software"[15] in the system.

Today, in the twenty-first century, this trend continues and at a faster pace. The U.S. Department of Defense treats the virtual and anonymous environment of cyberspace as a new domain of warfare, subject to offensive and defensive military operations.[16] By congressional mandate, today at least one-third of essential U.S. military aircraft and ground vehicles deployed should be unmanned[17] and "military robots"—controlled by computer software code that we call "artificial intelligence"—may outnumber manned weapons systems by 2030.[18] The F-35, the latest-generation jet fighter plane, "almost certainly will be the last manned strike fighter aircraft the [U.S.] Department of the Navy will ever buy or fly."[19] The increasing computerization and impersonalization of the modern battlespace relegates many soldiers and commanders to mere adjuncts to the software.[20]

For the purposes of this book, an "autonomous weapon system" is a "weapon system that, once activated, can select and engage targets without further intervention by a human operator."[21] "The key distinction" between autonomous and nonautonomous weapons is that "the machine self-initiates the attack."[22] This monograph addresses autonomous weapon systems that have the capacity to inflict lethal force because the use of autonomous weapons to target human beings presents the most complex and contentious legal and moral issues.[23] Today lethal autonomous weapon systems (LAWS) are important tools of modern warfare.[24] The great challenge for weapons developers, military professionals, government officials, and lawyers for the remainder of this century will be to ensure that the design and use of LAWS are in accord with international law.[25]

With respect to new weapon technologies, one commentator observed that "we are at a point in history where we can see into the future of armed conflict and discern some obvious points where future technologies and developments are going to stress the current law of armed conflict."[26] This book, therefore, primarily is what Immanuel Kant called "a history of future times, i.e. history."[27] As a predictive legal history, it attempts to define the international legal contours (i.e., the *lex lata*) of the use of new generations of autonomous weapon technologies.[28]

The obligation to protect human dignity is the starting point for the interpretation and application of international law.[29] International law then creates normative frameworks and rules for resolving the moral issues subsumed by concerns about human dignity. In light of its intended role, law should serve these broader normative purposes rather than be a slave to scientific or technological inevitability.[30] True, international life constantly evolves, and international law, to remain relevant, must be a reflection of that life.[31] But it is also true that international law, to preserve its capacity to adjust rights and responsibilities between states, and between states and individuals, must ensure the preeminence of the principle of human dignity.

Thus, the foundational notion of human dignity in international law provides a broader theoretical framework for this book. The following chapters explore whether humans legally may "delegate" to autonomous weapons their "responsibilities" for judgments that require assessments of competing legal and moral values, most importantly decisions to take human life. To be clear, I do not refer to a literal delegation of legal or moral responsibility to machines, because machines cannot possess responsibility. Rather this book addresses the transfer of human powers for the decisions to take human life to the artificial intelligence that controls LAWS.

As the swiftness of LAWS increases, however, the opportunities for human involvement and intervention in such decisions inevitably will decrease. Thus, the speed of LAWS and not their autonomy per se presents an additional challenge for the protection of human dignity, and the duties imposed by international law. Therefore, to preserve the principle of human dignity and ultimately international law, the book recommends that the design of LAWS *ensure* teamwork and interdependence between humans and the computer software that directs these weapon systems.

All law, both international and domestic, is based on the allocation of responsibility.[32] Therefore, as part of a review of the challenges for the application of treaty and customary law to these new weapons, this book examines whether humans should retain their duty to think and reason about complex value-based decisions. I conclude that humans should maintain responsibility for decisions that require moral judgments, for example, decisions that define what our values are, decisions that compel us to weigh competing and contradictory values, and decisions that likely will remain on our conscience and within our consciousness: in other words, decisions that test and build our humanity.

The decision to take a human life, or to spare it, is the supreme expression of morality and humanity. This decision, this use of judgment, requires the assessment and balancing of profound—and very different—moral values. Professional soldiers and officers train for years to develop sufficient knowledge and judgment to make decisions implicating the loss of human life. The ability and responsibility to make these judgments constitute an essential part of soldiers' and officers' identity, that is, their humanity. Replacing the human bearers of responsibility for such decisions with artificial intelligence removes the moral agency and autonomy that lie at the core of the personalities of these men and women. That stripping of responsibility, therefore, damages human dignity.

The Current Debate: LAWS, Human Dignity, and International Law

Today, much of the debate about LAWS focuses on the question whether it is lawful (and moral) to develop and deploy autonomous weapon systems that will exercise lethal force without human involvement or oversight.[33] At least thirty states have called for a ban on such weapons.[34] Human Rights Watch and the International Human Rights Clinic (IHRC) at Harvard Law School argue strenuously that LAWS should be banned because they will be unable to fulfill the requirements of international humanitarian law[35] and international human rights law[36] and, when they fail to fulfill these requirements, will create a lacuna in the ability to hold individuals accountable for violations of international law.[37]

In response to Human Rights Watch and the IHRC, Michael Schmitt and Jeffrey Thurnher argue that a ban of LAWS "is unsupportable as a matter of law, policy and operational good sense."[38] Schmitt and Thurnher contend that nothing in international humanitarian law per se supports a ban on LAWS, and that a ban on these weapons would deprive militaries of a valuable tool for compliance with the law.[39] Similarly, William Boothby concludes that, depending on the capacity of the technology, the employment of LAWS will be lawful, at least in certain situations.[40]

Past and present officials of the International Committee of the Red Cross (ICRC) acknowledge possible advantages in the development and use of (lethal) autonomous weapon systems. When he was president of the ICRC, Jakob Kellenberger observed that a "robot could be programmed to behave more ethically and far more cautiously on the battlefield than a human being."[41] Furthermore, Marco Sassóli, no stranger to situations of armed conflict, notes that "weapon systems which do not base the use of force upon an ad hoc human decision offer the advantage of a greater possibility of respecting international humanitarian law."[42]

In addition to issues of compliance with international legal rules, some lawyers and philosophers make moral arguments that human dignity is violated when an autonomous weapon (i.e., a machine) takes a human life. Peter Asaro, for example, explores the moral question, "whether computer, machine or automated process ought to make these decisions of life and death at all."[43] He contends that it is immoral to kill without the involvement of human reason, judgment, and compassion.[44] To enjoy dignity, persons must receive respect, and respect includes there being a reason or reasons for the rights of persons to be violated. Because autonomous weapons will kill in response to mathematical algorithms rather than reason(s), Asaro argues that when we permit a machine to make decisions about the taking of human life, we violate the target's dignity.[45]

The late Christof Heyns, the former United Nations special rapporteur for extrajudicial and summary executions, likewise contends that the "flipside of living a dignified life is dying a dignified death."[46] For Heyns, death with dignity, whether in an armed conflict or in a law enforcement situation, required some degree of human thought in the determination of whether to exercise lethal force: "Machines cannot fathom the importance of life, and the significance of the threshold that is crossed when a life is taken."[47]

Humans "deliberate"—Aristotle's term for the process of thinking and reasoning—about matters that are in their power.[48] Autonomous technology, however, forces persons to relinquish this power of deliberation and decision to a machine.[49] But the whole of our common morality, observed Isaiah Berlin, presupposes the notion of responsibility.[50] The crucial question, therefore, about the design, development, and employment of LAWS is not whether a human or a machine should make the decision to use lethal force. The essential question is whether there are certain responsibilities of human reasoning that we should not delegate to machines.[51]

Throughout this book, I argue it is correct that the use of LAWS to take human life constitutes a violation of human dignity, but I do not focus my concerns on the dignity of the victims of the use of lethal force. Instead, it is important to observe that as the technology advances, LAWS will engage in hostilities and law enforcement activities at speeds measurable in milliseconds. As the velocity of autonomous machine actions and reactions increases, the role of artificial intelligence will expand as the space for human thought declines. Humans—even those ostensibly "in-the-loop" or "on-the-loop"—will be unable to discern the development of bad "decisions" by autonomous machines and, crucially, to intervene to change those decisions.[52] This dynamic will obstruct the development of sound human judgment and moral agency that arises from opportunities for human reflection on one's own experience and that of others. Renaissance writers commonly understood man's unique ability to understand ideas and to act on his judgment as his "real dignity."[53] The evolutionary retreat represented by the use of LAWS is an implicit rejection of the moral agency and autonomy of the living human person, which constitutes a violation of human dignity.

This book illustrates several propositions. First, as autonomous weapons operate at increasingly greater speeds, their use will undermine the opportunities for, and the value of, human reasoning and judgment. Second, by transferring responsibility for reasoning and judgment about the use of lethal force to computer software, the use of LAWS violates the dignity of the soldiers, commanders, and law enforcement officers who historically have made such decisions and, therefore, breaches international law. Third, weapon designs that facilitate teamwork between humans and these autonomous systems are necessary to ensure that humans and autonomous weapons can operate interdependently so that individuals can fulfill their obligations under international law—including the preservation of their dignity—and ensure that human reasoning and judgment are available for cognitive functions better carried out by humans than by machines.

CHAPTER 1

Elements of Lethal Autonomous Weapon Systems

Weapons technology is outpacing law,[1] and, like the fog of war, a "fog of technology"[2] exists that can cloud how human beings apply the law. Without an understanding of the technical attributes and capacities of lethal autonomous weapon systems (LAWS), debates about the capacity of LAWS to operate consistently with international law occur in a partial vacuum.

Thus, this chapter describes several basic concepts and elements of LAWS as well as important technical characteristics and capacities of specific systems. I describe how states are developing weapon systems with faster and more autonomous functions, including the capacity to identify targets and destroy them with lethal force. I argue that efforts to fit these systems into fixed categories of human involvement such as "in-the-loop," "on-the-loop," "semi-autonomous," "fully autonomous," and the like fail to encompass the complexities of the systems and the fluid realities of modern armed conflict and law enforcement activities. Instead, states that develop autonomous weapon systems should prioritize a design that ensures human-machine interdependence and teamwork so that human reasoning and judgment are not discarded at critical phases of warfighting and police actions, including decisions to use lethal force.

As explained in the Introduction, for the purposes of this monograph, a LAWS is a "weapon system that, once activated, can select and engage targets without further intervention by a human operator." Depending on how one interprets technical specifications, arguably such weapon systems have been in use for decades. For example, the navies of many nations operate the Phalanx Close-In Weapons System on their ships against urgent air warfare threats such as planes and missiles. The U.S. Navy describes Phalanx as "the only deployed close-in weapon system capable of autonomously performing its own search, detect, evaluation, track, engage and kill assessment functions."[3] In addition, South Korea has deployed sentry robots along its demilitarized zone with North Korea whose sensors can detect approaching soldiers or infiltrators and respond with lethal force.[4] More than thirty countries possess similar "defensive supervised autonomous weapons" designed for situations where "the speed of engagement is too fast for humans to respond."[5]

The crucial distinction lies in the amount of freedom of maneuver delegated to the weapon system. For example, "Wide-Area Loitering Munitions," such as Israel's Harpy, are missiles designed to patrol large areas of terrain or ocean from the air, detect enemy radar defense installations, and destroy them.[6] Thus, the last human decision is a determination to launch the missile rather than a targeting judgment. In 2013, Christof Heyns singled out Harpy as a robotic weapon system "currently in use" with a degree of autonomy and lethality.[7] Paul Scharre goes further and identifies Harpy as "a fully autonomous loitering munition."[8] Israel Aerospace Industries, the manufacturer of Harpy and its successor, Harpon, asserts nonetheless that "there is always a man-in-the-loop in all target acquisition processes" and that the loitering mode of the system does not exist in current systems.[9] Publicly available promotional material about the Harpy system from Israel Aerospace Industries, however, indicates that such autonomous loitering and targeting technology has existed in weapon systems for several years: "Harpy operates autonomously, detecting, engaging and destroying emitting enemy radar. Harpy is ground launched and navigates autonomously to and in the target area. Harpy loiters for many hours, detecting and attacking emitting targets. . . . Multiple Harpies are deployed to autonomously suppress and destroy the enemy radar systems in a wide area."[10]

States that field LAWS will experience an increase in their sense of military confidence and superiority over their enemies. Conversely, new autonomous weapons technology looms as a threat to all who lack it.[11] Furthermore, after conflict, "there is a tendency for those who lose to imitate the victors."[12] These dynamics will drive a continuing race to develop LAWS because no one wants to be left behind in the race for better military technology: "In the end, we want to prevent our enemies from leaping ahead of us. There is a risk associated with investing a lot of money and a risk to not doing anything. You have allies and potential threats that are moving forward with robotics. We have to acknowledge conditions on the battlefield in 2025 will include robotics whether we invest in it or not."[13]

Unsurprisingly, therefore, the focus of the design and development of certain autonomous weapons (and particular semi-autonomous weapons) is not directed to the creation of opportunities for human reasoning or the protection of human dignity. Instead, the focus—and quite logically from a military perspective—is on the creation of faster, more autonomous, and more overwhelming weapons.[14] This trend helps to illustrate why it is far from certain that human beings will have the ability to apply international law to LAWS in the future.

Autonomous Weapon Technologies

Preliminarily, it is important to distinguish between "automatic" and "autonomous" weapon systems. "'Automatic' systems are fully preprogrammed and act repeatedly and independently of external influence or control."[15] By contrast, "autonomous" weapon systems are self-directed as they choose their behavior to achieve a human-determined goal. Unlike automatic systems, autonomous weapons can make an independent decision and then act on it.[16] LAWS, therefore, are capable of a higher level of performance compared to systems operating in a predetermined manner.

Autonomous weapon systems contain multiple components (for guidance, communication, targeting, etc.) that are directed and coordinated by computer programs (or "software" or "code"). The term of art for the sophisticated software that guides autonomous systems is "artificial intelligence." The U.S. Department of Defense defines the term artificial intelligence as "the ability of machines to perform tasks that normally require human intelligence—for example, recognizing patterns, learning from experience, drawing conclusions, making predictions, or taking action—whether digitally or as the smart software behind autonomous physical systems."[17] In the future, the United States anticipates "a focus on developing artificial intelligence systems that have the ability to reason as humans do, at least to some extent."[18]

Hannah Arendt perceived that "the main characteristic of mental activities is their invisibility."[19] A slight paradox, therefore, underlies the term "artificial intelligence" as all intelligence—including human intelligence—has an artificial, unreal quality because the processes of thinking and reasoning are intangible and invisible. Artificial intelligence, however, in the form of computer code, can be planned and programmed, checked after events, redesigned and reprogrammed.[20] In that sense, "artificial" intelligence is more tangible and real than human reasoning.

Historically, artificial intelligence software comprised a series of instructions, expressed in mathematical terms, that computers follow to achieve certain tasks. These mathematical statements are known as "algorithms," and they function at "blinding speed."[21]

Intelligence, however, is more than following a series of instructions or procedures for dealing with known problems.[22] It is also the ability to adapt to new situations. Thus, in addition to deductive, conventional algorithmic-based code, more contemporary artificial intelligence relies on "machine learning" algorithms.[23] Machine learning software involves the computation of probabilities in large data sets such as collections of words or images. The software "learns" to predict outcomes—such as identification of a target—by inductively recognizing patterns and associations in data and computing the statistical probabilities of when they occur.[24] The more times the system attempts a task it has been designed to do, the more accurately it can predict the outcome. By attempting a task billions of times, some systems make predictions so accurate that they execute the same task as well as humans, and sometimes outperform them, "even though the machine is still only guessing."[25]

Thus, in addition to the important pieces of mechanical equipment of an autonomous weapon system, the different software/artificial intelligence systems also are critical components of the weapons platform. However, because software usually is a detailed expression of mathematical statements, it does not fail in the same sense that a mechanical system does.[26] Software does not "break"; instead it fails in a conceptual sense. Moreover, besides failures caused by mistakes in the computer code, software can also function unpredictably because of design errors that lead to poor interaction between different systems.[27]

Autonomy is a dynamic state. Contemporary writers, however, often frame debates about human supervision, if any, of autonomous weapon systems in the deceptively simply phraseology of "semi-autonomous weapon systems" versus "fully autonomous weapon systems" versus "man-in-the-loop" systems versus "man-on-the-loop" systems.[28]

The U.S. military uses a category called "semi-autonomous" weapon systems: a "weapon system that, once activated, is intended to only engage individual targets or specific target groups that have been selected by a human operator."[29] Modern fighter planes, for example, often operate essentially as "semi-autonomous" weapons systems. During aerial missions where targets have been preselected and their coordinates preprogrammed into avionic software, fighter pilots approaching their targets verify that their weapons contain the right coordinates and that the weapons appear to be functioning correctly and then simply drop their bombs.[30] Similarly, cruise missiles, after launch, fly for great distances and hit targets that have been identified, selected, and approved by a human chain of command.[31]

The U.S. Defense Department is developing what it calls "System of Systems Integration Technology and Experimentation" (SoSITE), which will link together a network of manned and numerous unmanned aerial vehicles to enhance mission effectiveness and reduce risk to pilots. The unmanned systems will enter enemy territory with weapons, electronic warfare systems, and so on, while the manned platforms will "control" the unmanned systems using information fused by the technology. The pilot of the manned aircraft will "command" the group of unmanned vehicles, but he "is relieved of control burdens through the use of advanced distributive battle management aids." Prior to the pilot's decision to engage a target, "only a limited amount of information" will be transmitted from the unmanned systems to the pilot." Thus, "the planning of the engagement, selection and programming of weapons and generation of a targeted solution again [will be] conducted with minimal pilot burden."[32]

Progressively, the categorization of "semi-autonomous" versus "autonomous" is becoming a distinction without a difference as the line between the two becomes more difficult to discern.[33] For example, at present, flying an airplane is now a secondary or tertiary task of fighter pilots.[34] The onboard digital flight computer controls steering and the plane's stability. Similarly, a digital control system adjusts the power level of the engine within set limits, based on the pilot's input. This technology reduces the pilot's workload tremendously, and he or she can focus on other tasks, such as engaging with targets. Nevertheless, the pilot of older jets such as the F-16 must "fuse" (i.e., interpret) different information provided by the aircraft's sensors and electronics that indicate whether an approaching object is an enemy fighter or a "friendly" plane.[35] The new, more technologically advanced F-35 fighter jet, however, fuses the different data and then presents the best information to the pilot, thereby removing this "judgment call" from the pilot's responsibility.[36] "Whether it's correct or not, I don't know," observed one Netherlands Air Force pilot. "At least I don't have to spend time assessing information from multiple sources and worry about it."[37] In such situations, attempts to classify the F-35 as a semi-autonomous or autonomous weapon system are artificial as the pilot's real participation in targeting decisions can vary significantly.[38]

Similarly, the phrase "man-in-the-loop" refers to a design whereby the weapon system is supervised by human beings and has no independent decision-making ability.[39] "Man-on-the-loop" refers to weapon systems with sufficient autonomy to operate and make decisions independently, but which also allow for humans to monitor their behavior and either confirm or veto the machine's decisions; in other words, exercise human judgement over the behavior of the weapons platform.[40] Although the F-35, in a technical sense, can be called a "man-in-the-loop" weapon system, the human-machine interface, particularly at supersonic speeds when the pilot is so dependent on "fused" information from his avionic suite, suggests a more autonomous system.

The difficulty with such labels and categories is that they reveal little about the challenges faced by persons and machines in comprehending their environment, particularly during the stress of armed conflict and law enforcement activities. "To understand the world," writes Amartya Sen, "is never a matter of simply recording our immediate perceptions. Understanding inescapably involves reasoning. We have to 'read' what we feel and seem to see, and ask what these perceptions indicate and how we may take them into account without being overwhelmed by them."[41]

In "man-in-the-loop" systems, such as remote-controlled "drones," one of these challenges is simple boredom while, for example, intelligent and highly trained personnel must watch a house for many hours until an individual appears outside. The tedium of such tasks can result in complacency, leading to missed tactical opportunities or "unintended engagements" that produce civilian casualties.[42]

Furthermore, it is important to recognize that degrees of "autonomy" should change as conditions in the battlespace evolve.[43] Increased autonomy, such as the so-called man-on-the-loop system, empowers a single operator to monitor multiple robots while performing other tasks requiring coordination and complex decision making. However, the cognitive capacity necessary to monitor multiple weapons platforms can exceed that of a single human operator, even with higher levels of automation and autonomy.[44] Thus, different kinds and different amounts of human reasoning and judgement are necessary depending on the circumstances of the autonomous weapon systems and its human operators.[45]

Decades ago, T. B. Sheridan developed a list of at least ten different levels of machine/computer autonomy based on an interface between a single human being and a single computer.[46] Today, advances in technology permit additional and much more complex variations of autonomy. A single autonomous weapon system, however, may contain multiple computer subsystems, each with its own degree of autonomy. For example, a navigation subsystem may direct the autonomous weapon to change location because of bad weather, while the weapon subsystem simultaneously decides to launch an attack.[47]

Furthermore, models of a single autonomous weapon system actually represent a simplified version of modern warfare. Large military operations often are "a system of systems" with the autonomous weapon platform forming only one portion of the overall system.[48] An autonomous weapon system, for example, may function in coordination with manned weapon systems,[49] satellites that are crucial for maintaining communications, sensors, radars, and additional forms of technology such as (autonomous) cyberweapons. The autonomous weapon system may detect and report about its own position and condition, as well as about moving objects such as unknown vehicles, noncombatants, allied or cooperating autonomous weapons systems, and identifiable targets and threats. It might also detect and report about stationary objects such as targets and topographic obstacles.[50] Moreover the armed forces from different states may also integrate their systems so as to carry out joint operations.[51] Additional human factors will affect the use of autonomous weapons at different moments, such as the intent, orders, and influences expressed by commanders at different levels.[52]

These scenarios will only become more complex with the ongoing development of "swarm" technologies that permit large numbers of robotic weapon systems to operate cooperatively and communicate rapidly among themselves.[53] Swarm technologies developed from the combined efforts of engineers and social scientists to create a relatively simple algorithm that mimics the behavior of animals in nature, such as flocks of birds or schools of fish.[54] Over time, and as was important for later work on swarms of autonomous weapons, the developers modified and adjusted their algorithm to model this kind of social behavior, "which is multidimensional and collision-free."[55]

The ability to cooperate in the midst of uncertainty will be crucial to the success of any swarm. Consequently, the design of contemporary, multialgorithm swarm weapon systems requires consideration of many factors such as ease of use, workload of the human operator, information flow between individual robots (including random communication interruptions) and between individual robots and the operator, the speed of individual robots as well as the speed of the swarm, whether individual robots will perform single tasks or multiple tasks (and how these tasks will be updated), and software and hardware maintenance.[56] Furthermore, when deciding whether to perform a current task, the artificial intelligence of individual vehicles in a swarm must consider "what future tasks are possible in order to maximize the expected performance of the entire team."[57]

Swarm technology can be adapted for all weapons platforms in all battlespace domains. For example, future operations of the Israeli Defense Forces will include swarms of autonomous land, air, and sea weapon systems, including networks of miniature and nanotechnology platforms.[58] The U.S. Air Force is already testing Perdix, a swarm of microdrones that can be released from manned or unmanned aircraft to perform intelligence, surveillance, and reconnaissance missions and overwhelm enemy infrastructure. "Due to the complex nature of combat, Perdix are not preprogrammed synchronized individuals, they are a collective organism, sharing one distributed brain for decision-making and adapting to each other like swarms in nature. Because every Perdix communicates and collaborates with every other Perdix, the swarm has no leader and can gracefully adapt to drones entering or exiting the team."[59]

In addition, the U.S. Defense Department is testing Gremlins, a swarm of unmanned, recoverable, and reusable aerial vehicles launched from larger, manned aircraft. Like Perdix, Gremlins will perform surveillance and reconnaissance. They could also be used as low-cost missiles. Equipped with high-explosive warheads, swarms of Gremlins might fly to the suspected location of enemy surface-to-air missile sites, cooperatively locating, bombing, and recording evidence of the target's destruction—all without involving manned aircraft and with minimal supervision.[60]

Logically, larger and faster swarms of robots are more difficult for humans to monitor and control. To add to the complexity, in armed conflict scenarios, much of this autonomous behavior must occur in the face of opposition from enemy forces, including enemy swarms.

The introduction of "swarm" technology represents a "tipping point" for autonomous weapon technology. The use of larger and faster swarms of autonomous weapon platforms will make it impossible or nearly impossible to maintain human reasoning as part of the "system." The shrinking spaces for human reasoning in the operation of these weapons means that at best, humans will be "programmers of the law." That is a poor substitute for the foundational role of law and reasoning in human life. Limitations on autonomous functions, therefore, are necessary to maintain human-machine teamwork and interdependence, and thus, the role of human reasoning in warfare.

Arguably, similar military scenarios, albeit involving human commanders and units of human soldiers, existed throughout history. For example, during the Second World War, commanders in the United Kingdom, the United States, the Soviet Union, Germany, and Japan monitored and supervised military units spread over several continents and oceans (including submarines and aircraft).[61] A distinguishing characteristic of current and future autonomous weapon systems, in addition to their independence, is the speed with which these machines communicate information and execute decisions.[62] This quality will generate opportunities for significant military advantages. It will also, however, further limit capacities for human command and control, that is, the exercise of human reasoning and judgment.[63]

Schmitt and Thurnher argue that humans are never really "out of the loop" because "humans will decide when and where to deploy the [autonomous weapon] system and what parameters to embed within it."[64] However, when autonomous weapons react to events and use force (as they already do in certain cases) at speeds that effectively prohibit human influence or intervention, soldiers, operators, and commanders are, effectively, "out of the loop."[65]

The borders between automation and autonomy, however, need not be static. To improve the effectiveness of human-machine teamwork, new engineering designs such as "adjustable autonomy" and "adaptive automation" permit the roles of humans and computers to change within dynamic environments.[66] For example, the algorithms in Automated Planners make adjustments—without human intervention—to the tasks of autonomous vehicles at the tactical level while human operators periodically update algorithms that guide the autonomous vehicles at the strategic level.[67] Because of the speed of communications between individual vehicles, the tactical adjustments occur at a faster rate than updates from the human operator.[68] This design could assist operators of swarms of autonomous weapons in moderating their workload and thereby avoiding mistakes.[69]

The common denominator of the new autonomous weapon systems described below is a desire to achieve or maintain military superiority. As a matter of strategy and common sense, armed forces prefer not to go into battle at a disadvantage, or on an equal footing with their enemy.[70] These more autonomous weapon systems extend the offensive and defensive reach of armed forces.[71]

From a purely technical perspective, the objective of designing manned and unmanned systems should be to devise the most efficient means of conducting activities, "with human intelligence operating in the most effective location."[72] By using a "coactive" or teamwork-based design, as autonomous technologies improve, the interdependence between humans and machines will *increase*.[73] Paul Scharre argues that "the real future of combat—in the air and elsewhere—is human-machine teaming: physical teaming between 'manned' and 'unmanned' vehicles, and cognitive teaming that blends automation and human decision-making."[74] More advanced interdependent weapon systems with autonomous functions will create opportunities to accomplish more complex tasks more efficiently.[75] Determinations as to which kinds of cognitive activities are most appropriate for computers and artificial intelligence and which are better left to humans will form a crucial aspect of weapons design and warfare itself.[76]

When weapons developers submit options to the military for new weapon systems, however, the key question for the individuals making procurement decisions is: "Will it enhance my ability to carry out my strategic, military objective?"[77] Military interests require timely decision making,[78] and even with the best training of human operators, the challenge of maintaining meaningful or appropriate levels of human judgment and human-machine collaboration and teamwork will become increasingly difficult as decision-making cycles of autonomous weapon systems shrink to microseconds. Indeed, it is not difficult to envision future generations of autonomous weapon systems that will communicate between each other much more quickly than with humans and respond to threats faster than a human pilot.[79] As one computer scientist observes, as machines can function so much more quickly than humans, "'man-in-the-loop' means you lose."[80]

Thus, common sense suggests that in situations where lives depend on the fastest possible actions and reactions, the likelihood that human supervisors and operators will intervene with autonomous weapons systems will be reduced.[81] Decisions about the design and development of new automated and autonomous technologies are really "about speed of service. The better the automated system, the faster we can accomplish the mission. That is not the only consideration, but it is the main one."[82] Consequently, legal or abstract standards to govern the use of LAWS are unlikely to be effective substitutes for the exigencies of armed conflict.[83] A danger exists, therefore, that opportunities to achieve standards such as "appropriate levels of human judgment over the use of force" or "meaningful human control" or "coactive design" eventually will be reduced to very little or nothing. When we reach that moment, the capacity of humans to guide the conduct of LAWS will be in question.

Decisions made today in terms of research and development affect military capability decades in the future.[84] Accordingly, to preserve the relevance of human reasoning, validation and verification human-machine interdependence of LAWS as well as the capability to use them in compliance with international law must occur at the design phase of the weapon.[85]

Examples of Ground-Based LAWS

In addition to the Korean ground-based lethal autonomous weapons mentioned above, the Russian military is developing an autonomous version of the Taifun-M, a robot capable of guarding strategic missile sites and detecting and destroying stationary or moving targets.[86]

The Israeli Defense Forces deploy the Guardium Unmanned Ground Vehicle. Designed for reconnaissance and for leading troop movements, this weapon system possesses remote-controlled weapons as well as the capability for "autonomous decision making."[87] Israel has also developed Iron Fist, a defensive autonomous weapon system mounted on tanks, armored personnel carriers, and the like to protect them from rocket, grenade, or missile attacks. The Iron Fist's sensors detect an approaching munition and launches a countershell that destroys it in midair.[88]

Examples of Air-Based LAWS

The Brimstone is a missile developed for the Royal Airforce of the United Kingdom with "human-in-the-loop capability to meet restrictive rules of engagement."[89] Fired from a fighter jet, a helicopter, or a naval vessel, the missile seeks enemy targets at long range. In "direct mode," the pilot uses an onboard targeting system to identify the target prior to missile release.[90] In "indirect mode," the missile is programmed to search a defined area and autonomously identify, track, and strike targets.[91] Brimstone missiles (used to date in missions over Afghanistan, Iraq, Syria, and Libya) provide the ability to engage multiple targets simultaneously, including fast-moving and fast-maneuvering vehicles, tanks, and "swarming" naval vessels in "a cluttered battlespace."[92]

One autonomous weapons expert, Paul Scharre, argues that Brimstone is a semi-autonomous system that "doesn't quite cross the line to a 'LAWS'" because the human operator "instructs" the missile system to search for particular targets and because Brimstone missiles cannot "loiter" over its designated "kill box," where the human operator believes targets might be present.[93] Nonetheless, once launched in indirect mode, Brimstone missiles identify and engage targets without human input, placing the system within the definition of LAWS used by the U.S. Defense Department and adopted in this book.

Similarly, the U.S. Air Force's Golden Horde system of swarms of unmanned air vehicles will use autonomy "to confuse and overwhelm our adversaries." In a nuanced effort to keep the development of Golden Horde swarms within the parameters for autonomy set by the Defense Department, the U.S. Air Force explains that the "weapons would be semi-autonomous or [like Brimstone] only able to engage targets or groups of targets that a human chooses beforehand."[94]

The U.S. Navy has developed LOCUST, a system of swarming autonomous aerial vehicles that can overwhelm an enemy. The relatively inexpensive individual weapons share information and work collaboratively in order to find and attack targets. Moreover, they will force adversaries to concentrate on responding to the swarm.[95] A large group of airborne vehicles carrying explosive payloads, for example, could substitute for a more expensive antiship missile to attack an important enemy surface vessel.[96] U.S. Navy officials state that "there will always be a human monitoring the mission, able to step in and take control as desired."[97] This commitment, however, may be premature. The U.S. Air Force suggests that the means to control large numbers of autonomous systems coordinated with manned assets requires further development.[98] And "[t]he swarm idea inherently drives you toward autonomy. The whole idea of a swarm is not just that it's a lot of them, but a lot of them working together, sharing information across the swarm."[99]

The U.S. Air Force and Army launch the "small diameter bomb" (SDB) from aircraft and from the ground, respectively, to engage fixed, relocatable, or moving targets at any time of day or night and in adverse weather conditions.[100] The SDB has "autonomous stand-off attack capability."[101]

In addition to the Harpy loitering missile discussed above, Israel also operates the Spyder ground-to-air missile system, which seeks out, identifies, and destroys enemy aircraft and munitions.[102] A human operator may launch the Spyder, or the missile may launch autonomously in response to a perceived threat.[103] Similarly, the Israeli-made Hero-400EC airborne loitering munition system can engage a range of stationary or moving targets. The system can engage targets autonomously or under the direction of a human operator.[104]

Israel also produces the Spice Bomb, a "stand-off autonomous weapon system" that can be launched from modern jet fighters such as the F-15, F-16, and the F-35. The weapon can search for up to one hundred optional stationary and mobile targets[105] (and "track" the moving targets).[106] Rather than flying to preprogrammed Global Position System coordinates, each autonomous Spice Bomb compares "real time" images to "reference images" that have been stored in the weapon's computer.[107] After it performs "the scene-matching process," Spice "acquires the target automatically."[108]

Examples of Sea-Based LAWS

The U.S. Navy recently conducted a successful test of a swarm of thirteen autonomous boats that can defend friendly vessels and deter and attack enemy ships at sea. Each individual boat is directed by artificial intelligence software—originally developed for the Mars Rover—called Control Architecture for Robotic Agent Command and Sensing (CARACAS), which allows it to function autonomously as part of a swarm, and react to a changing environment.[109] Israel has developed a similar system, called Protector.[110]

More importantly, the development of systems of lethal swarms is just beginning. During the 2020s, the Chinese Navy is expected to deploy unmanned submarines that can position themselves at areas where enemy vessels are likely to pass to ambush targets.[111] South Korea, Turkey,[112] and Russia[113] intend to produce swarms of unmanned airborne vehicles. EUROSWARM and SPIDER are two recent European Defense Agency research projects dedicated to the use of swarm technology in military roles.[114] The U.K. will deploy swarm squadrons capable of confusing and overwhelming enemy air defenses."[115] To maintain military superiority, the scale of swarm weapon systems inevitably will increase. "You have maybe 100 or 1,000 surface-to-air missiles," explains a U.S. Air Force officer, "[b]ut we're going to hit you with 10,000 [small drones]."[116]

* * *

This chapter demonstrates that states are developing weapon systems with faster and more autonomous functions, including the capacity to identify targets and destroy them with lethal force. Furthermore, as the speed of autonomous weapon systems increases, particularly with the advent and use of swarm technology, efforts to fit these systems into fixed categories such as "in-the-loop," "on-the-loop," "semi-autonomous," "fully autonomous," and so on fail to encompass the complexities of the systems and the fluid realities of modern armed conflict. In order to ensure the continued participation of humans in the use of lethal force, militaries and manufacturers should take care at the design phase of autonomous weapon systems to ensure that they operate as partners of humans rather than as substitutes. States that develop LAWS, therefore, should prioritize a design that ensures human-machine interdependence and teamwork so that human reasoning and judgment is not discarded at critical phases of warfighting and law enforcement activities.

Weapons designers and developers, therefore, must ensure that the design of LAWS be based on an interdependent design in order to reduce the speed of autonomous weapon systems to a velocity where humans can: (i) effectively apply reasoning and law (in particular international humanitarian law and international human rights law) during their operation, and (ii) ensure that human reasoning and judgment is available for cognitive functions better carried out by humans than by machines.

CHAPTER 2

Human Dignity and Its Role in International Law

Dignity is a principle of law and morality.[1] The concept of dignity is intimately connected to law—as the foundation of many constitutions and statutes, as part of the content of legislation, as well as in the interpretation and application of laws.[2] In this chapter, I argue that a legal obligation to protect and preserve human dignity arises from human dignity's special role as a point of departure for the formation and interpretation of international law. Human dignity, grounded in treaties and customary international law, is a legal starting point, a guiding concept that states must use to operationalize the other norms and values that underlie their existence as independent societies. More specifically, the notion of human dignity helps to define the rights and obligations existing between individuals and between individuals and states. Thus, the starting point of human dignity helps to make law and also provides a barrier against the abuse of law. In the chapters that follow, I describe how the concept of human dignity speaks to the lawful design and use of lethal autonomous weapon systems (LAWS).

A Definition of Human Dignity

Finding a consensus on a single, accepted concept of dignity is more difficult than mapping its presence in international law. "Dignity" derives from the Latin word *dignus* "which means worthy of esteem and honor, due a certain respect, of weighty importance."[3] Early considerations of human dignity and its relationship to law can be traced to Aristotle, who wrote of law that "is based on nature."[4] Aristotle believed that "there is in nature a common principle of the just and unjust that all people in some way divine, even if they have no association or commerce with each other."[5] Writing at the border of the Middle Ages and the Renaissance, Thomas Aquinas believed that "it is proper to justice, as compared with the other virtues, to direct man in his relations with others because it denotes a kind of equality. . . . Hence it is evident that right is the object of justice."[6] For Aquinas, nothing in human affairs should violate "natural justice," which emanates from the "Divine right," that is, *human rights* bestowed by God: "For the Divine Law commands certain things because they are good, and forbid others, because they are evil, while others are good because they are prescribed, and others evil because they are forbidden."[7]

Human beings, Immanuel Kant explained in the eighteenth century, possess a dignity (an absolute inner worth) by which they exact respect for themselves from all other rational beings in the world.[8] Every human being is, in turn, bound to respect every other. Absent this mutual respect, humans lose their autonomy—their moral agency—which grounds "the dignity of a human and of every rational nature."[9] Thus, the moral worth of a person's life is tied directly to the possession and fulfillment of his or her moral autonomy and duty to respect the value and moral agency of others.[10]

For Kant, dignity is an important component in the making of law, that is, "universal law" and morality.[11] All rational beings are bound by the universal law that each must treat itself and all others never as a means but always as an end.[12] Only rational beings, *human* beings, enjoy the capacity to take action in conformity with law and morals, and that is how persons by necessity represent their own existence.[13] Dignity, therefore, arises from the efforts of individuals to reason and conduct themselves according to morality and universal law.[14] Persons who live a moral life use their dignity to create and support law.[15]

Today, unsurprisingly, definitions of human dignity vary dramatically across societies, but many descriptions reflect Kant's influence.[16] Michael Walzer, without mentioning the phrase "human dignity," succeeds as well as any other modern thinker to capture dignity's essence: "Individual rights (to life and liberty) underlie the most important judgments that we make about war. How these rights are themselves founded I cannot try to explain here. *It is enough to say that they are somehow entailed in our sense of what it means to be a human being.* If they are not natural, then we have invented them, but natural or invented, they are a palpable feature of our moral world."[17]

Michael Rosen explains that dignity arises from the "unconditional and intrinsic moral value"[18] possessed by every human as a moral agent. John

Finnis concludes that persons can be autonomous—that is, enjoy the "dignity" of being "responsible agents"—only if they are not made to live their lives for the convenience of others but are allowed to create their own identities.[19] Thus, in totalitarian societies, realization of human dignity will be difficult, if not impossible, as the "self-coercion" imposed by totalitarian logic destroys individuals' capacity for experience and thought as well as their capacity for action.[20]

Similarly, in Latin America, twentieth-century Catholic doctrine contained references to human initiative and responsibility as aspects of the concept of "the dignity of man." "In our continent, millions of men find themselves marginalized from society and impeded from achieving their true destiny, whether due to the existence of inadequate and unjust structures or due to other factors such as selfishness and insensitivity."[21] Fundamentally, dignity secures the capacity for self-direction and freedom from certain forms of control and manipulation.[22]

Linking these concepts of human dignity is the importance Kant placed on moral agency. Conceptual differences and real or perceived ambiguities in definitions of human dignity do not reduce the benefits or the challenges that dignity poses to our moral lives.[23] On the contrary, human dignity is the value that does the "moral work" for societies.[24] Humans "are thinkers and agents,"[25] and humans have dignity because we are capable of giving "the moral law to ourselves."[26] Should persons lose their capacity to make moral judgments, they lose their moral autonomy and responsibility and, consequently, a large measure of their dignity. The importance of the connected values of dignity, rights, judgment, and morality find expression in article 1 of the Universal Declaration of Human Rights: "All human beings are born free and equal in dignity and rights. They are endowed with reason and conscience and should act towards one another in a spirit of brotherhood."[27] Although an aspirational document rather than a formal source of law, the declaration helps to establish human dignity's importance in international law.

Sources of International Law: Treaties, Customary Law, General Principles, and Jus Cogens

Formal sources of international law include international conventions or treaties, customary international law (as evidence of a general practice of states accepted as law), general principles of law, and, as a subsidiary means for determining rules of law, judicial decisions and the writings of respected publicists.[28] The particular status in international law awarded to the concept of human dignity can be traced to treaty obligations, customary law, general principles of law, and even peremptory norms.

International Conventions or Treaties

A "treaty" or "convention" is an "international agreement concluded between states in written form and governed by international law."[29] The right to enter into international agreements "is an attribute of state sovereignty."[30] Accordingly, the law of treaties is grounded in two essential principles. First, as a corollary to the notion of state sovereignty, treaties must be based on the free consent of state parties.[31] Second, parties to a treaty in force must perform in good faith.[32] Thus, it follows that states have a duty to act consistently with their treaty obligations[33] and must refrain from acts that would defeat the object and purpose of the treaty.[34] State parties, therefore, must interpret treaties in good faith in accordance with the ordinary meaning to be given to the terms of the convention in their context and in light of the document's object and purpose.[35] Finally, treaties need not be static. Drafters can design treaties, such as the Convention on Certain Conventional Weapons, that provide for the addition of protocols, annexes, or further covenants.[36]

Customary International Law

The creation of customary international law requires a combination of state practice and *opinio juris*.[37] The first element, which can be demonstrated by a range of sources, must reveal consistent and uniform state actions over time.[38] The second, subjective element is proven by evidence that states act out of a belief that the law obliges them to do so.[39] The required number of instances of state practice, the space of time in which the practices should occur, and the characteristics of the countries that exhibit practice combined with *opinio juris* will depend on the particular activities and states involved.[40]

Scholars typically refer to the "traditional" and "modern" (or "contemporary") doctrines for the creation and determination of custom.[41] "Traditional custom" focuses primarily on state practice while *opinio juris* is a secondary consideration.[42] Traditional customary law develops through an "evolutionary" process whereby, through inductive reasoning, general custom is derived from specific examples of state practice.[43] The traditional process, however, has evolved "in adapting itself to changes in the way of international life."[44] Thus, modern customary law, by contrast, emphasizes statements of *opinio juris* rather than state practice.[45] Modern custom develops more rapidly than traditional customary law because it is deduced from multilateral treaties and the statements of international bodies such as the United Nations General Assembly.[46] Judges of the International Court of Justice have recognized this "acceleration in the process of formation of customary international law."[47]

Scholars have criticized both the inductive and the deductive methods of formation and identification of customary law. Professor Talmon, for example, describes both forms of reasoning as "subjective, unpredictable and prone to law creation" by the International Court of Justice.[48] Professors Simma and Alston preferred the slower but "hard and solid" customary laws derived from inductive reasoning to the "self-contained exercise in rhetoric," the phrase they used to describe the faster, deductive process.[49] The risk Simma and Alston perceived was the creation of "a sort of "instant" customary international law of dubious relationship to the actual behavior and interests of states."[50] The late Jonathan Charney, however, defended the modern method as more suitable for contemporary international society, given the existence of multilateral forums permitting state expressions regarding new international law.[51] In this sense, Charney appeared to view modern forms of customary lawmaking as more democratic, given that, from his perspective, customary law traditionally was made by a few interested states for all.[52]

It is important to remember that the development of international treaty and customary law are not mutually exclusive. For example, the ratification of a treaty may demonstrate *opinio juris* for the purpose of the creation of customary law.[53] Treaty provisions can obtain the status of customary law[54] and, thus rules codified in treaties may bind nonstate parties as a duty of customary international law.[55]

General Principles of Law

Article 38 of the Statute of the International Court of Justice refers to "the general principles of law recognized by civilized nations" as a source of international law.[56] General principles of law are broad, and general notions within legal systems that underlie the various rules of law can be applied to a variety of circumstances.[57] They extend to the fundamental concepts of all branches of law, "as well as to law in general," so far as the community of states recognizes these principles.[58]

The notion of "general principles of law" inherently includes elements of natural law.[59] These principles of law, therefore, do not depend on positivist forms of law and may or may not be accepted de facto, or practiced, within a particular legal system.[60] When a principle is accepted, however, it does not remain at the margins "but constitutes an intrinsic element which must be harmonized and adapted along with the other 'general principles' of the system."[61] We will consider this dynamic with respect to the general principle of human dignity below.

"General principles" of law are a recognized part of international humanitarian law,[62] international human rights law,[63] and international criminal law.[64] Thus, for example, the law of war principles (discussed in Chapter 4) assist practitioners in interpreting and applying specific treaty and customary rules, provide general guidelines for behavior during armed conflict when no specific rule applies, and serve as interdependent and reinforcing parts of a coherent system.[65] Conversely, when many international conventions express a particular rule, "it can be deemed an incontestable principle of law at least among enlightened nations."[66] Similarly, state parties to international treaties accept the important principles expressed and implied therein.[67]

Jus Cogens Norms

Peremptory norms create fundamental obligations for states.[68] Jus cogens are peremptory norms of international law accepted and recognized by the international community as norms from which no derogation is permitted, and which can be modified only by a subsequent norm of international law possessing the same character.[69] Moreover, because jus cogens norms "constitute the pinnacle of the hierarchy of sources of international law," "they bind states whether or not they have consented to them."[70] Professor Bianchi observes that jus cogens norms reflect "the inner moral aspiration"[71] of international law.[72] Given their special status, a comparatively small number of norms qualify as peremptory.[73]

Locating the Concept of Human Dignity Within the Sources of International Law

Human Dignity as an Obligation of Treaty Law

The preamble to the United Nations Charter ("the Charter") "sets forth the declared common intentions" of the member states.[74] In the preamble, the member states specifically reaffirmed their "faith in fundamental human rights, [and] in the dignity and worth of the human person."[75] Article 2 (4) of the Charter requires states to comply with the purposes of the United Nations,[76] which encompass respect for human rights and human dignity.[77]

Thus, as early as 1948, Professor Jessup concluded that: "[i]t is already the law, at least for Members of the United Nations, that respect for human dignity and fundamental human rights is obligatory. The duty is imposed by the Charter, a treaty to which they are parties. The expansion of this duty, its translation into specific rules, requires further steps of a legislative character."[78] The obligation to protect human dignity, therefore, constitutes "fundamental Charter law."[79]

In the years since the drafting of the United Nations Charter, the realization of human dignity has informed the objectives of numerous bilateral[80] and multilateral treaties.[81] During the drafting conference of the Convention on the Prevention and Punishment of the Crime of Genocide, for example, Mr. De L'A Tournelle, the French representative to the General Assembly, "on behalf of Europe," warned against making a mockery of the preamble to the Charter and the language affirming "faith in fundamental human rights, and the dignity and worth of the human person."[82] France was determined, De L'A Tournelle affirmed, to make "the greatest efforts to speed the progress of international law in a sphere which touches so nearly on the destinies and dignity of human society."[83] Similarly, Mr. Katz-Suchy, the Polish representative to the United Nations Economic and Social Council (ECOSOC), argued that a prohibition of the crime of genocide "was only part of the great struggle for human dignity."[84]

The protection and preservation of human dignity grounded in the Charter provides the foundation for much of international law, including, and as is important for this book, treaties and declarations codifying international humanitarian law and human rights law. The reference to dignity, as opposed to specific rights, in article 1 of the Universal Declaration of Human Rights is intended to explain *why* persons have rights to begin with.[85] Human dignity as a legal norm, therefore, is the "fountain of all rights"[86] and many human rights can be understood as incidents of that norm.[87] For example, the International Covenant on Civil and Political Rights and the International Covenant on Economic, Social and Cultural Rights illustrate that the notion of human dignity is separate from,[88] and indispensable for, the defense of human rights,[89] "which derive from the inherent dignity of the human person."[90] Consequently, the European Court of Human Rights observes that "[a] person should not be treated in a way that causes a loss of dignity, as "the very essence of the [European Convention for the Protection of Human Rights and Fundamental Freedoms] is respect for human dignity and human freedom."[91]

Human dignity then, serves as a thread connecting and reinforcing all human rights recognized in international law,[92] and states must demonstrate their recognition of the value of human dignity in everything that they do, or choose not to do.[93] For example, all contemporary international human rights instruments prohibit states from using torture as well as inhuman or degrading treatment or punishment.[94] Judgments of regional human rights courts and commissions invoke human dignity as a basis for redress for victims of myriad forms of state human rights violations such as poor detention conditions,[95] forced body cavity searches of family members of detainees,[96] discrimination against transsexuals,[97] failure to protect an indigenous community's right to property,[98] and racial violence.[99]

Similarly, modern humanitarian law conventions follow the principles of protection that emanate from the inherent dignity of persons, that is, from the foundation of the Charter:[100]

> The essence of the whole corpus of international humanitarian law as well as human rights law lies in the protection of the human dignity of every person, whatever his or her gender. The general principle of respect for human dignity is the basic underpinning and indeed the very raison d'être of international humanitarian law and human rights law; indeed in modern times it has become of such paramount importance as to permeate the whole body of international law. This principle is intended to shield human beings from outrages upon their personal dignity, whether such outrages are carried out by unlawfully attacking the body or by humiliating and debasing the honor, the self-respect or the mental well-being of a person.[101]

This narrative of human dignity in international treaties illustrates states' recognition, grounded in the Charter, that they bear a duty to prioritize human dignity in their treatment of citizens. "No other ideal," opined Oscar Schachter, "seems so clearly accepted as a universal social good."[102] Obviously the Charter preamble's expressed determination to reaffirm faith in, inter alia, the dignity and worth of the human person is different from the more specific rules and agreements usually expressed in a treaty.[103] Indeed, fifty years ago, the International Court of Justice held that the preambular sections of the Charter constitute "the moral and political basis" for the specific legal rules set out in the treaty.[104] But the border between law and morality is indeterminate at best, and certain concepts, such as human dignity, rest in both systems.[105] Simply put, it would be illogical to reject the normative legal power of a value incorporated into numerous international covenants, including operative articles of those conventions, as well as the vast majority of national legal systems.

Human Dignity and Customary International Law

In addition to the commitments of states to promote and protect human dignity expressed in treaty law, a majority of nations have expressly incorporated the value of human dignity into their constitutions. For example, research by Shultziner and Carmi reveals that, as of 2012, nearly 85 percent of countries use the term "human dignity" in their constitutions.[106] Every one of the forty-nine constitutions enacted between 2003 and 2012 include the term, whether in the preamble, in sections containing "fundamental principles," in specific articles, or in some combination.[107] The constitutions of some states, such as South Africa and Hungary, treat dignity as a separate right, and South African jurisprudence recognizes the right to human dignity as "a right concomitant to life itself."[108]

While the use of "human dignity" in preambles and fundamental principles may take the form of broad, overarching expressions of human dignity as a value,[109] its inclusion in operative constitutional articles serves to guide the implementation of those provisions.[110] For example, specific articles may protect the dignity of persons imprisoned or detained,[111] address the dignity of labor conditions and compensation,[112] use dignity as a guide for guarantees concerning vulnerable groups such as the elderly, children, and persons with disabilities,[113] and so on.

When the term "human dignity" is absent from the text of a national constitution, the concept can still imbue legal reasoning of the courts of that state. While the U.S. Bill of Rights, for example, does not specifically refer to "human dignity," its use in U.S. jurisprudence is "intuitive."[114] Accordingly, fundamental liberties enumerated in the Bill of Rights extend to personal choices central to individual dignity and autonomy, such as decisions concerning marriage or the use of contraceptives.[115] Similarly, although the Canadian Charter of Rights and Freedoms does not mention the value expressly, the specific rights guaranteed therein "are inextricably tied to the concept of human dignity."[116] Hence, the majority of modern domestic legal systems expressly or implicitly mandate respect for human dignity.[117]

In spite of these national commitments, it is trite to observe that no consistent state practice protecting and respecting human dignity exists; on the contrary, examples of serious violations of human dignity around the world are common. Thus, under the traditional analysis of customary law development, certainly no rule of customary law obliging respect for human dignity exists.

Adherents to the "modern" view of customary law formation, however, might argue that respect for human dignity has become a duty of customary international law, given the many state expressions in national constitutions[118] of the necessity to protect and promote this value. Widespread state ratification of international treaties and other documents that acknowledge the importance of human dignity constitute additional evidence of *opinio juris*. The validity of this claim, however, depends on whether interested parties accept the modern, deductive method of customary law formation. Indeed, any assertion that a rule of customary law exists is problematic when that claim turns solely on choices between diverging doctrinal perspectives.

Yet the discussion should not end there because state practice and *opinio juris* do demonstrate a more nuanced rule of customary law concerning human dignity. The overwhelming international and domestic practices of states, and their expressions of obligation, evidence a minimal legal duty *to commit themselves* to the protection and promotion of human dignity. Customary international law has evolved to this point, at least.

Finally, even absent a rule of customary international law pertaining to the protection of human dignity, courts (and other national institutions) may still look to this value for assistance in interpretation and application of domestic law.[119] Barriers exist "that democracy cannot pass, even if the purpose that is being sought is a proper one."[120] Human dignity, as a legal point of departure, is a constant reminder that rights, to be meaningful, must be respected.

Human Dignity and General Principles of Law

In the mid-twentieth century, Giorgio Del Vecchio argued that an obligation to protect human dignity exists as a "general principle" of international law. Del Vecchio argued that in an effective legal system, "directive ideas and the informative principles of the entire system take precedence over the particular rules."[121] The most important legal principles are those that give expression and respect "to the absolute import of the human personality,"[122] that is, dignity. Concurrently, the general principle of respect for human dignity cannot be divorced from other logically complementary principles, a dynamic that requires the coordinated application of legal precepts in a single regime.[123] Justice, for example, is an essential, complementary obligation for governments that strive to preserve human dignity among its constituents.[124]

While, from a progressive perspective, Del Vecchio's ideas may seem compelling, his interpretation appears to "force" the broad concept of human dignity into the same, smaller box of more precise, and more consistently defined, general legal principles incorporated by states, such as the presumption of innocence or *nullem crimen nulla poena sine lege*.[125] Essentially, however, "[h]uman dignity is based upon a generality."[126] If the development and respect for human dignity bear "absolute import," human dignity would seem to enjoy a higher and wider power than the norms commonly considered "general principles of law." Indeed, South African courts recognize the notion of human dignity as a "supreme"[127] and "foundational"[128] value that inspires and grounds the more specific rights enumerated in the South African Bill of Rights.[129] It does a disservice to the importance and scope of human dignity if we attempt to clothe it with the label of a "mere" general principle of law accepted by states.[130]

Human Dignity and Jus Cogens

Similar problems arise when we try to fit human dignity within the realm of preemptory or jus cogens norms. The concept of human dignity is much broader than individual preemptory norms, and the breach of a preemptory norm actually constitutes an attack on the foundational value of human dignity, which underlies and reinforces the norm. For example, "human trafficking" "is a new form of slavery that violates the value of human dignity."[131] Thus, many of these preemptory norms—such as the prohibitions on slavery, torture, and aggression—are more susceptible to precise definitions (and obligations) than the foundational notion of human dignity.[132] Indeed, the real value of preemptory norms is their ethical power as norms for the *recognition* of human dignity.[133]

The Unique Place of Human Dignity

That leaves the almost universally accepted,[134] broad concept of human dignity with a different role in international (and domestic) law. Essentially, human dignity serves as a *guiding* legal concept for the creation and application of more specific legal norms and rules.[135] This analysis illustrates that human dignity is a starting point rather than a precise treaty or customary rule, a general principle of law, or a peremptory norm reasonably susceptible to (consistent) definition.[136] The moral ideal of human dignity is an overarching legal point of departure, based in treaty and customary law, from which the majority of the world's governments navigate the conflicting interests, rights, beliefs, and values inherent to communities and societies. The modern system of public international law is not a mere body of rigid rules, but an entire decision-making process,[137] and for at least the past seventy years, human dignity has constituted an obligatory foundation for the evolution of the legal conscience of the community of nations.[138] Human dignity must, therefore, serve as the starting point for the design and use of LAWS as the community of states attempts to clarify the application of more precise rules of international law to these weapon systems.[139]

* * *

Critics of international law's reliance on "human dignity" argue that it is a vague and vacuous term lacking a stable definition.[140] Others see it as an aspiration rather than a right.[141] Nonetheless, human dignity represents an ideal that serves as the foundation of many decades of progress in international law and international relations. While the definition of human dignity may vary, the reliance of statesmen and stateswomen on this principle to forge bridges between different peoples and cultures suggests that it is very real.[142] As a starting point and guiding principle, human dignity plays important roles: it grounds the importance of moral agency for persons, it helps to define humanity, and it creates the opportunity for a discussion on the limits of human power.[143] Far from dogma, human dignity's very strength lies in its interpretive capacities within a changing world.[144]

In the next chapter, I will demonstrate why the use of LAWS in some circumstances, by restricting moral agency, will violate the human dignity of the groups and persons who operate them. In Chapters 4, 5, and 6, I examine how the value of human dignity informs the application of the principles and rules of international humanitarian law, international human rights law, and international criminal law to the design and employment of LAWS. In the last chapter, I will examine how the concept of human dignity should guide the assessment of the responsibility of states and arms manufacturers for the design and use of LAWS, as well as the harm caused by them.

CHAPTER 3

Lethal Autonomous Weapon Systems and Human Dignity

In Chapter 2, we saw that humans, to enjoy dignity, must have the capacity for moral agency. When individuals and communities perform "moral work," they possess and protect human dignity. Conversely, when persons lose their capacity to make moral judgments, they lose their moral autonomy and responsibility and their dignity. In this chapter I review the impact of the use of LAWS on the human dignity of soldiers and commanders who fight our wars. I illustrate how, in the short term, LAWS may preserve human dignity by reducing the loss of life on the battlefield and the overall suffering caused by war. In the long term, however, LAWS reduce the moral agency of warfighters, leading to a loss of their human dignity. This long-term loss of dignity carries an additional risk: the gradual abdication of human capacity for the expression of empathy and other moral values in circumstances when they are most needed. This devolution of humanity is the greatest danger presented by LAWS.

The Contradictions of Human Dignity and LAWS

Karl Marlantes, who has written extensively about his combat experience as a Marine officer in Vietnam, understands the moral challenges of warfare: "You can't be a warrior and not be deeply involved with suffering and responsibility. You're *causing* a lot of it. You *ought* to know why you're doing it. Warriors must touch their souls because their job involves killing people. Warriors deal with eternity."[1]

Marlantes' wisdom does much to explain why the decision to take a human life, or to spare it, is the supreme expression of morality and humanity. This use of human judgment requires the assessment and balancing of profound—and very different—moral values. Soldiers and commanders train for years to develop sufficient knowledge and judgment to make decisions implicating the loss of human life. The capacity and responsibility to make these judgments constitute an essential part of their identity, that is, their *humanity*. Replacing the human bearers of responsibility for such decisions with artificial intelligence removes the moral agency and autonomy that lie at the core of the personalities of these men and women. That stripping of moral and legal responsibility damages human dignity.

As described in more detail in the next chapter, in order to reduce the suffering caused by armed conflict, soldiers and commanders in modern, professional armies are trained to act rationally and in compliance with the laws of war. They know—or should know—that they are accountable for mistakes and crimes committed in violations those laws. The development of capacities such as rationality and accountability are crucial for human dignity as they assist individuals to be fully moral agents.[2] Thus, individuals—like soldiers—whose professions require them to make hard choices bear a duty to "touch their souls," to nurture their abilities to reason and consider moral norms, and thereby be accountable for their actions.[3]

If human dignity essentially is the enjoyment of moral agency, it would be the antithesis of human dignity to create structures that encourage the delegation of responsibility for the exercise of moral work. "Responsibilities, as well as rights, enhance the dignity and integrity of the person,"[4] and the fulfillment of responsibilities deepens our belief in our own dignity, that is, in our moral agency. Importantly, individuals—including soldiers and commanders—bear "judgmental responsibility" for acts or omissions if their conduct is assessed against performance standards.[5] The development of this form of responsibility is a process without an end as persons attempt to integrate their life experiences and their moral, ethical, and political values.[6]

Thus, the dignity of many rightsholders arises from the acknowledgement of the capacity of the person to bear the responsibility implicit in the right.[7] In democratic societies, for example, political leaders assume personal responsibility for their actions and omissions. They cannot transfer this responsibility.[8] Similarly, in a number of countries all citizens must, under the law, exercise their duty to vote in elections.[9]

It is significant that history is replete with examples of collective efforts to secure greater human responsibilities, rather than initiatives to discard them.[10] For example, the seeds of the eighteenth century war of independence fought by the North American colonies against British rule lay in the principle of "no taxation without representation," that is, without some measure of responsibility in the process of governance.[11] After extensive campaigns, women were granted the right to vote in the United States in 1920 and in the United Kingdom in 1928.[12] During the twentieth century, national liberation movements in countries such as Vietnam and Mozambique sought to wrest political control from colonial powers.[13] The 1993 Interim Constitution of South Africa for the first time accorded black citizens all duties, obligations, and *responsibilities* of South African citizenship.

These examples illustrate that the ultimate objective of a democratic state is to make persons free to develop their abilities.[14] Thus, "the greatest menace to freedom [and dignity] is an inert people,"[15] and governments that arbitrarily restrict the rights of their citizens to make free choices, form their identities, and become moral agents violate human dignity.[16] Writing in the mid-nineteenth century, John Stuart Mill foresaw the moral contradictions inherent in technological advancement:

> Among the works of man, which human life is rightly employed in perfecting and beautifying, the first in importance surely is man himself. Supposing it were possible to get houses built, corn grown, *battles fought*, causes tried, and even churches erected and prayers said, by machinery—by automotons in human form—it would be a considerable loss to exchange for these automotons even the men and women who at present inhabit the more civilized parts of the world, and who assuredly are but starved specimens of what nature can and will produce. Human nature is not a machine to be built after a model, and set to do exactly the work prescribed for it, but a tree, which requires to grow and develop itself on all sides, according to the tendency of the inward forces which make it a living thing.[17]

Indeed, "there are many truths of which the full meaning *cannot* be realized until personal experience has brought it home,"[18] and dignity, therefore, carries an obligation for individuals to retain their personal autonomy.[19] This implies a duty of self-respect: "[e]ach person must take his own life seriously; he must accept that it is a matter of importance that his life be a successful performance rather than a wasted opportunity."[20] Anything less would render human dignity a dead letter.

Consequently, a "basic good" of life is the ability to "bring one's own intelligence to bear effectively on the problems of choosing one's actions and lifestyle and shaping one's own character."[21] The "great power" (John Locke's term for the human capacity to think and reason), in particular about matters involving values and judgment, is a fundamental part of human identity and moral agency.[22] Over time, our powers of reason evolve and provide new alternatives for addressing complex problems, demonstrating qualitative changes in human thought.[23] This "great power" is the engine of moral responsibility, and, indeed, Ronald Dworkin described "judgmental responsibility" as "the weft of all moral fabric."[24]

But these long-term concerns for the preservation of human dignity ignore the potential deleterious effects to dignity in the short term. The day will come (it may already have arrived) when the use of LAWS will save lives; when they function much better than human soldiers in combat; when robots driven by artificial intelligence are faster, more accurate, better able to make tactical decisions, and less likely to harm civilians or cause such suffering as results from fighting men and women who are exhausted, confused, angry, or afraid. Arguably, "humans would be making progress"[25] in these circumstances as lives are preserved and human dignity protected.

Simultaneously, however, humans, in particular members of professional armed forces, would regress as they lose their ability—and their desire—to demonstrate the kinds of moral growth, courage, and empathy that humans can exercise in armed conflict.[26] The violence of war is brutal and often degrading[27] and usually requires the suppression of much in our nature that is human and humane.[28] Nevertheless, during warfare, the suppression of humanity,[29] identity,[30] and meaning[31] by human combatants occasionally is offset by (often irrational) expressions of compassion and illogical, even irresponsible acts of courage.[32] Consequently, examples of soldiers declining to use all their powers of violence—their "moral force"[33]—during wartime are common.[34] One U.S. veteran of the Iraq War described his experience in nearly mystical terms: "Combatants bear witness to all aspects of the human condition. It reveals the darkest parts of the human soul while residing side by side with the most exalted characteristics: nobility, honor, valor and God's grace. . . . I am complete for having experienced that kind of sacrifice."[35] This ability to empathize with human beings, whether soldier or civilian, would be absent from robotic weapons.[36]

Humans, via experience, develop instincts (our "sixth sense"), which often assist them in navigating difficult situations where strict rules may not suffice. For example, human soldiers can enter an environment and "get a feeling about it" that often is correct. Machines cannot do that.[37] This "ultimate test of experience" provides an essential contribution to the human realm of ideas[38] and, consequently, moral agency. Furthermore the development of "good" human judgment often requires divergence from absolute values to find solutions to value-based problems.[39] Instead of using our ability to deliberate about matters of importance, however, the employment of autonomous technology compels humans, to different degrees, to transfer this power to a machine.[40] When a reasoned and complex decision to use deadly force shifts from the political and military officials in whose name it is done, to a computer, the individuals "cease to be moral agents: people who take a decision and assume responsibility for it."[41]

Nonetheless, it is stating the obvious that human soldiers in combat often fail these "tests of experience" and respond to opportunities to demonstrate empathy with indifference or violence. The "sixth sense" of a combatant may be wrong or influenced by numerous factors that would belie the dispassionate analysis of data performed by artificial intelligence.[42]

Thus, when the development of artificial intelligence arrives at a point where the use of LAWS rather than human soldiers will save lives, then we must choose between *different dignities*: one short term—human life, including its inner worth; and one long term—humanity, including the continued moral agency of persons. This contradiction demonstrates why human dignity cannot always be a "trumping value"[43] with respect to the debate about LAWS. From a moral, if not legal, perspective, the most important part of this debate is the capacity to weigh the harm of one prospective dignity violation against another.[44] If we cannot make that calculation, arguably our only recourse is to redefine what it means to be human and possess human dignity.

The problem, however, is more nuanced because the concept of moral agency cuts both ways. While the essence of human dignity is the enjoyment of moral agency, future soldiers and commanders may view LAWS as simply another tool to be a more successful "agent" in combat. And rather than constitute a surrender of "moral autonomy," decisions to employ LAWS in certain circumstances may serve as demonstrations of "moral humility," that is, affirmations of human dignity because they acknowledge the possibility that the artificial intelligence driving the system may perform more effectively than individuals.[45] Moreover, some persons might choose not to become soldiers precisely because they do not wish to make the kinds of complex decisions that soldiers often have to make in combat. Arguably, in this sense, the act of relinquishing one's agency in given situations may serve as *expressions* of moral agency and dignity.

Human dignity, therefore, has a "perplexing capacity" to pull in several directions.[46] For example, in the context of artificial intelligence, a tension exists between the necessity to conserve our powers of thought and reason to make decisions as part of our human dignity, and the encouragement of the uniquely human capacity for "great achievements" as another manifestation our dignity.[47] The development of autonomous technologies for military and civilian use represents a dramatic leap in computer science, engineering, and robotics. Restrictions on the use of this technology, however, can discourage further research, the realization of more "great achievements," and, consequently, humankind's advancement toward the full realization of its abilities.[48] Nevertheless, this risk to "human potentiality"[49] is limited by the dual use nature of autonomous technologies. The vast number of potential civilian applications of this technology ensures continued challenges and accomplishments for scientists and other professionals.[50]

One also might argue that humans already delegate important responsibilities for certain tasks to machines with autonomous functions. For example, many commercial airplanes operate extensively on "autopilot," where the pilot does not physically control the plane. Manufacturers are testing autonomous automobiles on public roads in the United States. Developers of Google's so-called self-driving car expect that, eventually, it will be self-sufficient without human-machine interdependence.[51] In 2015, the unmanned New Horizons spacecraft flew autonomously for several hours, at thirty-one thousand miles per hour, three billion miles away from Earth, pursuant to a computer program.[52] There is a major qualitative difference, however, between autonomous technology programmed to comply with "mechanical" rules that under normal circumstances require little human thought—such as altitude levels for airplane autopilots, or speed limits for autonomous cars, or receiving scientific data—and autonomous technology that is "programmed" to apply complex and sometimes contradictory principles and values in fluid circumstances, resulting in the destruction of life and infrastructure.

It is also obvious that in certain difficult and complex situations, many human beings may prefer to delegate decision-making responsibilities to other persons or to computers:

> The yearning that lies in men for clear vision, and a doubt-free knowledge of right and wrong, cannot be suppressed, though it may be assuaged for a time by the promise of early fulfilment. But for the most part, deep perplexities seem to be the price of awareness of our situation; and even when the perplexities are endured, judgment still remains tortured by uncertainty. The temptation is strong to run to easier courses which dispense with the need for understanding, which keep the task of adjusting human claims from men's conscious decision, submitting it with resignation to some blind impersonal force.[53]

The transfer of certain powers and decisions to artificial intelligence during the stress of combat may protect the moral integrity of soldiers and commanders. Persons who suffer trauma—such as soldiers compelled to make decisions concerning life and death in the battlespace—often "try, usually in vain and at great expense of energy, to banish what has happened to them from their minds."[54] For instance, writing in his World War I diary of life in the trenches of France, a British corporal recorded that he had "a slight fit about 12 o'clock (fists clenched, felt a desire to kill someone, and collapsed) Rested all day after."[55] Primo Levi observed that it is "easier to deny entry to a memory than to free oneself from it after it has been recorded."[56] The use of LAWS has the potential to reduce the exposure of soldiers to violence and the responsibility to make decisions when all options are bad, helping to prevent "the anguish of memory,"[57] and the bitter and violent excesses that often result from such trauma.[58] During armed conflict, LAWS could reduce the suffering and loss of dignity to combatants and civilians alike.[59]

Even if the employment of LAWS in certain situations might preserve human dignity, that does not alter the potentially transformative impact of delegating decisions to take human life to machines. Transfer of this extraordinary responsibility to LAWS represents a sea change in the notion of what it means to be "human." No longer will "judgmental responsibility" and accountability necessarily serve as natural standards for human behavior or as expressions of human dignity. Instead, the transfer of our most difficult moral work and responsibilities to artificial intelligence creates a different kind of human and new perspectives on the value of moral agency and integrity. If humans transfer our moral agency in war to machines, we lose the quality known as our "moral compass." And the related qualities of integrity and "moral courage" cease to exist because these are *human* qualities, not the characteristics of machines or software.

Therefore, as science advances, the principle of human dignity compels us to consider the scope and meaning of our humanity, particularly with respect to transformations of this humanity brought about by technological change.[60] "The question is really whether we foresee that human kind will cause less harm to itself and coming generations by relying on machines or relying on humans and their judgment. This is where we need to converge our opinions further."[61]

Some scholars argue that the rights and dignity of humans will be disrespected when machines take their lives because computers cannot "reason" the way humans can about such important decisions.[62] This argument actually misses a finer point. Although human reasoning is often malevolent and immoral and one day artificial intelligence may equal or surpass the capacity of humans, the increasing speed of autonomous weapon systems will lead to a de facto absence of "reasons" for lethal force. In a practical and strictly legal sense, if high-speed algorithms make the "right" decisions under the law, no harm is done. The great speed, however, will make it impossible for humans to comprehend the development of "bad reasoning" by autonomous machines as it occurs and to intervene to stop the lethal exercise of that reasoning. Even worse, although in retrospect humans may review electronic records and data to observe the basis for a machine's "decision," the meaning of that "decision" is lost. The limited information that it conveys ceases "to suggest ideas, or suggest[s] only a small portion" of the concepts and beliefs originally employed to shape the decision.[63] That loss of opportunity for human thought, when it arrives, will diminish the dignity of persons (be they operators of autonomous weapon systems or surviving victims of the use of force) that underlies international law.

In an effort to ensure that LAWS function with a component of human reasoning, states, institutions, and scholars have called for a requirement of certain levels of human control over their use. Recommended standards to determine the lawful and moral use of autonomous weapon systems frequently are expressed as the exercise of "meaningful human control" or "appropriate levels of human judgment" over the use of force by these weapons.[64]

These are welcome efforts to develop standards for the design and operation of LAWS in compliance with international law. Nonetheless, numerous efforts to establish a consensus on clear definitions of these standards have been unsuccessful as these constructions are open to multiple interpretations.[65] For example, the government of Israel has observed: "Delegations have made use of various phrases referring to the appropriate degree of human involvement in respect to lethal autonomous weapon systems. Several states mentioned the phrase 'meaningful human control.' Several other states did not express support for this phrase. Some of them thought that it was too vague, and the alternative phrasing 'appropriate levels of human judgment' was suggested. We have also noted, that even those who did choose to use the phrase 'meaningful human control,' had different understandings of its meaning."[66]

Disagreements about the "meaning" of "meaningful human control" are not difficult to surmise. A too-restrictive approach to "meaningful human control" requiring direct human involvement in "every detailed action" of an autonomous weapon system would vitiate the entire concept of autonomy and could lead to ineffective and unsafe systems suitable for only a limited range of tasks and conditions.[67] The reliability and predictability of the LAWS could also condition acceptable levels of human control.[68] For example, the most reliable and predictable LAWS might employ the capacity to redefine their mission or objective without human intervention.[69] Other operational constraints, such as limits to taskings and permissible targets, as well as restrictions on the operational environment(s) or the time frame of autonomous operation, could inform the application of this standard in particular cases.[70]

Overly broad interpretations of "meaningful human control" would also lead to perverse outcomes. For example, in 2015 the government of Poland suggested that the undefined concept of "meaningful human control" should be extended to include "meaningful state control," that is, evaluating "meaningful human control" "from the standpoint of state's affairs, goals and consequences of its actions."[71] Such an open-ended framework would permit each state to make unilateral assessments of "meaningful human control" based on its own self-interest, thereby circumventing concerns about the legality and morality of LAWS.

Merel Ekelhof explains that in military practice, "discretion is typically distributed."[72] She argues that meaningful human control is better described as "distributed control" spread across a range of individuals and technologies operating in various parts of the targeting cycle. Similarly, the United Kingdom calls for a "technology-agnostic" approach to the concept of meaningful human control, where, throughout the life cycle of a weapons system, humans collaborate to enable human control tailored to the demands of specific tasks and operational environments.[73]

"Distributed control" or "technology-agnostic" approaches to human supervision of LAWS leave great discretion to operators of weapon systems—and potentially to the LAWS themselves—and do little to pinpoint accountability for the (mal)functions of an autonomous weapon system. The ICRC has proposed a more precise definition of meaningful human control, suggesting that LAWS be under constant supervision by a human operator who has the ability, through physical or communication links, to intervene and deactivate the system at any time.[74]

Part of the difficulty in finding consensus on the definition of "meaningful human control" over LAWS is the fluid nature of autonomy itself. Autonomy is a continuum;[75] some systems, or components of systems, will have greater autonomous capacities than others, and not every task carried out by an "autonomous" system need be free of human control.[76] This fluidity makes agreement on a single form or degree of human supervision for all systems much more difficult.

Nonetheless, LAWS bear the crucial ability to make the final decision to take human life. Any definition of "meaningful human control" over autonomous weapon systems, therefore, must include the ability—at any moment—for humans to intervene and make the ultimate decisions to use or forego lethal force. Anything less would vitiate human dignity and the essence of international law. In 2019 the International Committee for the Red Cross provided a similar—if awkwardly phrased perspective: "[i]n the ICRC's view, the core issue is ensuring meaningful/effective/sufficient/appropriate human control over decisions to select and attack targets, independent of the technical sophistication of the weapon system."[77] Human control cannot be meaningful if a machine, rather than a human being, makes the decision to take human life.

Human dignity speaks to the realization and fulfillment of the human condition. Reflection about our actions is a significant feature of human life,[78] and in a moral sense, if we do not think, we are not fully alive.[79] "We think about which acts to perform and when to perform them."[80] Absent extraordinary circumstances such as the "capture or kill" scenario discussed in Chapter 5, the long-term cost of delegating important decisions concerning the use of lethal force to autonomous weapon systems is intolerable. The wholesale transfer of the responsibility—the moral agency—to think and reason about deeply moral choices to machines is an unacceptable surrender of human dignity that devalues the human person.[81] Over time, it disables the moral agency and abilities to address difficult problems and exercise rights, which is the antithesis of a democratic society. International law's foundational requirement for the protection of human dignity demands that limits be set to this transfer of responsibility from humans to LAWS.

Given the challenges and contradictions described above, how can LAWS be designed so as to most effectively preserve human dignity in its different iterations? One strategy is to design autonomous weapon systems that facilitate teamwork between humans and these systems to ensure that humans and LAWS operate interdependently so that *individuals* fulfill their obligations under international law—including the preservation of their dignity—and ensure that human reasoning and judgment are available for cognitive functions better carried out by humans than by machines.

* * *

The decisions to have children, to create human life, and to take it, are the most essential expressions of moral agency and human dignity. Karl Marlantes, a father and a soldier who has killed, succinctly describes the importance of the latter responsibility: "It's the future killing that counts now. All any of us can do is wrestle with our own noble and ignoble intentions so that when we are asked to consider life-and-death issues, we'll do it honestly."[82] There is something deeply human—and valuable—in the moral "wrestling" process that Marlantes advocates for. As the use of LAWS becomes more common, as decisions about killing become the province of algorithms and machine learning software, we implicitly accept the loss of dignity that comes with this lost responsibility.

Neither the autonomy of new weapons technology nor its use per se undermines human dignity. The increasing delegation of responsibility and opportunity, however, for human thinking about important values that lie at the heart of the use of force will reduce moral agency and thereby undermine human dignity. Nevertheless, the greater speed offered by autonomous functions offers strategic, operational, and tactical advantage for armies. Moral and legal arguments about human dignity may be insufficient to override the most basic criteria of military necessity: the simple need of soldiers and armies to survive.[83]

Thus, the priority of speed over time for measured human "reasoning" or "control" or "judgment" will tilt the balance between necessity and humanity that is the foundation of international humanitarian law. Accordingly, the next chapter addresses the employment of autonomous weapon systems within the framework of the laws of war and whether an interdependent design for humans and machines will permit greater autonomy as well as compliance with international law.

CHAPTER 4

Lethal Autonomous Weapon Systems and International Humanitarian Law

During armed conflict, soldiers must conduct combat according to norms entrenched in both international and domestic law, so that military activity does not take place in a normative void.[1] Although "violence is appropriate to war,"[2] for many generations writers have advocated that "it is worthy of civilized nations . . . 'to restrain the destructive force of war, while recognizing its inexorable necessities.'"[3] Lord Wright, who edited *The Law Reports of Trials of War Criminals* following the Second World War, observed that the laws of war attempt "to diminish the evils of war so far as military requirements permit."[4] Thus, law cannot serve as a substitute for war.[5] It can, however, constrain the conduct of hostilities to reduce the suffering that occurs during armed conflict.

In this book, I use the phrases "international humanitarian law," "the law of armed conflict," and "the law of war" synonymously. The efforts of international humanitarian law (as well as international human rights law) to promote the "humanization of war" intuitively presuppose that war's protagonists and decision makers—soldiers, military commanders, civilian superiors, and insurgents—are human.[6] Concurrently, however, the growing use of technology by armed forces has driven the development of the laws of war.[7] As we saw in Chapter 1, increasingly, war is and will be fought by machines—and virtual networks linking machines—which, to varying degrees, are controlled by humans.

In this chapter, I describe the development of international humanitarian law, its basic principles, and the rules of targeting, which are particularly relevant to the design and employment of LAWS. I argue that (1) efforts to comply with the rules of targeting in international humanitarian law are intrinsically linked to the concept of human dignity, (2) the duty to protect human dignity obligates human soldiers and commanders, to the greatest extent possible, to make final decisions regarding the taking of human life, and (3) this obligation limits armed forces and organized armed groups to the use of autonomous weapon systems with interdependent designs that permits collaborative autonomy for decisions to use lethal force.

The Development and Applicable Principles and Rules of Modern International Humanitarian Law

The Development of Modern International Humanitarian Law

Dutch jurist Hugo Grotius, writing in the seventeenth century, was a catalyst for new thinking about the importance of law during armed conflict. Grotius explained that his objective was to decide "how far the power of lawfully destroying an enemy, and all that belongs to him, extends," and he introduced the principle that the lawful exercise of force during warfare is not unlimited.[8] He argued that "the power of the sword must be *restrained* from inflicting promiscuous death."[9] Grotius linked this notion of restraint with the importance of "moderation and humanity" in the conduct of war and foreshadowed how commanders might be held accountable should they fail to adhere to these principles.[10] Similarly, a century later, Emer (Emmerich) de Vattel contended that the right to use violence during armed conflict "goes hand in hand *with necessity* and the exigency of the case, but never exceeds them."[11] This connection between the exercise of force and necessity, de Vattel claimed, is part of Natural Law.[12] Thus, hostile acts by armed forces that are necessary to overpower the enemy's resistance and attain the end of a lawful war are lawful under international law.[13]

Just a few years after de Vattel's treatise appeared, Jean-Jacques Rousseau advanced the same nexus between necessity and lawful conduct: "[w]ar gives no right which is not necessary to the gaining of its object."[14] Rousseau also drew a distinction between the treatment of persons taking part in hostilities and those who did not, arguing that once persons lay down their arms, they should not be subject to attack.[15]

These Enlightenment doctrines eventually developed into the proscriptive and empowering rules of modern international humanitarian law, which is divided generally into two categories: Hague Law and Geneva Law. Hague Law[16] generally encompasses rules for the conduct of hostilities, while Geneva Law[17] addresses the protections enjoyed by civilians who are not directly participating in hostilities as well as combatants who find themselves hors de combat.[18]

With respect to Hague Law, the so-called Lieber Code, drafted by Professor Francis Lieber at the request of U.S. president Abraham Lincoln during the increasingly vicious American Civil War, constituted the first single set of instructions for soldiers and officers in the field pertaining to the laws and customs of war. Lieber was a realist, a tough humanitarian who believed that war should be waged vigorously.[19] "Blood," he once wrote to the general in chief of the Union armies, "is occasionally the rich dew of history."[20] Thus, although the Lieber Code proscribes acts of inhumanity ("[m]ilitary necessity does not admit of cruelty, that is, the infliction of suffering for the sake of suffering or for revenge"),[21] it does so pragmatically to facilitate the return to peace.[22] Moreover, the code sanctions and provides a framework for "all direct destruction of life or limb of armed enemies" and other persons who suffer incidental but unavoidable injury as a consequence of war.[23]

In addition to the Lieber Code's regulation of the conduct of hostilities, the 1868 Declaration of Saint Petersburg was the first formal international agreement that prohibited the use of certain weapons. The declaration prohibited the use of bullets that explode on impact and reiterated the principle suggested by Grotius, de Vattel, and Rousseau that "the only legitimate object which States should endeavor to accomplish during war is to weaken the military forces of the enemy."[24] Accordingly, the declaration banned the use of weapons that would needlessly aggravate the sufferings of persons, or render their death inevitable, a rule that is now part of customary international humanitarian law, as well as treaty law.[25]

A number of the tenets expressed in the Lieber Code and the Declaration of Saint Petersburg became part of the 1899 Regulations Concerning the Laws and Customs of War on Land and the 1907 Regulations Concerning the Laws and Customs of War on Land (the 1899 and 1907 Hague Regulations).[26] For example, articles 22 and 23 of both the 1899 and the 1907 regulations echo the Lieber Code's admonition that there are limits to the lawful exercise of violence during armed conflict. The comprehensive rules codified in the regulations address important areas of the conduct of hostilities including (1) the qualifications of lawful combatants, (2) the treatment of prisoners of war, (3) legal and illegal means and methods of warfare, (4) the status and treatment of spies during armed conflict, (5) flags of truce, capitulations, and armistices, and (6) military occupation of enemy territory.[27]

In addition, the preamble to the 1899 regulations contains the Martens Clause, an umbrella provision intended to encompass circumstances not specifically addressed in the regulations: "Until a more complete code of the laws of war is issued, the High Contracting Parties . . . declare that in cases not included in the Regulations adopted by them, populations and belligerents remain under the protection and empire of the principles of international law as they result from the usages established between civilized nations, from the laws of humanity and the requirements of the public conscience."

The development of Geneva Law began after Henry Dunant's experience tending to the wounded and dying survivors of the Battle of Solferino.[28] Dunant's proposals for reducing the kinds of suffering that he had witnessed led to the drafting of the Geneva Convention for the Amelioration of the Condition of the Wounded in Armies in the Field and, gradually, the development of the International Committee of the Red Cross.[29] A Second (more comprehensive) Convention for the Amelioration of the Condition of the Wounded in Armies in the Field was promulgated in 1906.[30] In 1929, a diplomatic conference drafted the Third Geneva Convention Relative to the Treatment of Prisoners of War.[31]

The disastrous events of the Second World War revealed significant gaps in Geneva Law. In many areas, the law was vague.[32] Furthermore, even with respect to provisions that were relatively clear and precise, breaches of the law demonstrated the need for more effective rules to monitor compliance and hold violators accountable. Consequently, a diplomatic conference produced the four 1949 Geneva Conventions (the 1949 Conventions). The First, Second, and Third 1949 Conventions significantly broadened the protections due to wounded and sick combatants as well as prisoners of war. Perhaps most important, the 1949 Geneva Convention IV Relative to the Protection of Civilian Persons in Time of War was the first treaty devoted exclusively to the protection of civilians during armed conflict.[33]

The 1949 Geneva Conventions share several common articles pertaining to the scope of the treaties. Common Article 2 provides that the Conventions apply to any armed conflict (whether formally declared or not) between two or more state parties. Thus, the four Conventions apply to international armed conflicts. Common Article 2 also invokes the power of the Conventions over situations of partial or total occupation of the territory of a state party, even when the occupation meets with no armed resistance. Common Article 3 compels parties to a non-international armed conflict occurring in the territory of a state party to treat persons taking no active part in hostilities humanely.

Additional gaps in Geneva Law (in particular concerning the protection of civilians and the status and treatment of prisoners of war) were identified during the post–World War II conflicts of decolonization as well as the Korean and Vietnam Wars.[34] Hence, in 1977, another diplomatic conference promulgated two Additional Protocols to the four 1949 Geneva Conventions.[35] As noted above, in addition to filling gaps in Geneva Law and obliging state parties to review the legality of new means and methods of warfare,[36] Additional Protocol I (API) includes more precise rules regarding the conduct of hostilities, including provisions that codify the rules of targeting.[37] Important for Chapter 6, "Autonomous Weapon Systems and International Criminal Law," API also obliges state parties to hold accountable persons who commit grave breaches of the 1949 Conventions and API, as well as commanders who fail to prevent or punish subordinates for violations of the laws of war.[38]

Many of the provisions of Hague Law and Geneva Law embody rules of customary international humanitarian law[39] and, thus, also bind states that are not parties to the treaties and conventions.[40] Indeed, the International Court of Justice has concluded that the fundamental rules expressed within the Hague Regulations and Geneva Conventions "constitute *intransgressible* principles of international customary law."[41] The Geneva Conventions have achieved almost universal application[42] although this is not yet the case for the Additional Protocols.[43] Nonetheless, many rules of customary international humanitarian law apply in both international and non-international armed conflicts.[44]

Basic Principles and Rules of Modern International Humanitarian Law

The application of modern international humanitarian law is an attempt to achieve an equitable balance between humanitarian requirements and the demands of armed conflict,[45] for example, between the principles of humanity and military necessity.[46] The principle of "humanity"—the heart of international humanitarian law[47]—prohibits the infliction of suffering, injury, or destruction not actually necessary for the accomplishment of a legitimate military purpose. This tenet is based on the concept that once a military purpose has been achieved, the further infliction of suffering is unnecessary.[48]

"These considerations are based upon the rights of the individual, and his [human] dignity."[49] For example, when civilians are present in a combat zone, their human dignity must be protected during military operations.[50] The humanitarian character of the principles of the law of armed conflict applies to all forms of warfare and all kinds of weapons, including future weapons.[51]

Francis Lieber defined "military necessity" as "the necessity of those measures which are indispensable for securing the ends of the war, and which are lawful according to the modern law and usages of war."[52] The U.K. armed forces use a more nuanced definition that mirrors the principle of humanity: "Military necessity is now defined as "the principle whereby a belligerent has the right to apply any measures which are required to bring about the successful conclusion of a military operation and which are not forbidden by the laws of war. Put another way a state engaged in an armed conflict may use that degree and kind of force, not otherwise prohibited by the law of armed conflict, that is required in order to achieve the legitimate purpose of the conflict, namely the complete or partial submission of the enemy at the earliest possible moment with the minimum expenditure of life and resources."[53]

Evident in both of these legal principles is the presence and influence of the concept of human dignity. The humanity principle's goal to reduce the suffering caused by war demands the (feasible) respect for human rights during armed conflict. In parallel, military necessity's limits on permissible use of force demands the same regard for human rights. Accordingly, humanity and military necessity are an expression of the interplay of human dignity and human rights within international humanitarian law.[54]

In addition to humanity and military necessity, two "crucial"[55] principles determine the effectiveness of modern international humanitarian law. First, the principle of distinction establishes that belligerents must always distinguish between enemy combatants and civilians and never intentionally target civilians or civilian objects.[56] Consequently, indiscriminate attacks, that is, those that are of a nature to strike military objectives and civilians without distinction, as well as the use of weapons that are indiscriminate, are unlawful.[57] Second, belligerent parties may not employ means and methods of warfare in a manner that causes superfluous injury or unnecessary suffering.[58] The phrase "means of combat" generally refers to the weapons used while "methods of combat" generally refers to the way in which weapons are used.[59] This constraint reflects the "most fundamental customary principle"[60] of the law relating to the conduct of hostilities: that the right of belligerents to adopt means of injuring the enemy, including the choice of weapons, is not unlimited.[61]

No rule of international humanitarian law specifically addresses LAWS, which is unsurprising given the state of technology in 1977, when the 1949 Geneva Conventions were last revised. Nevertheless, activity that is not specifically prohibited in treaty law is not necessarily lawful,[62] and article 1 (2) of API contains a revised version of the Martens Clause: "In cases not covered by this Protocol or by other international agreements, civilians and combatants remain under the protection and authority of the principles of international law derived from established custom, from the principles of humanity and from the dictates of public conscience." The Martens Clause itself is a rule of customary international law.[63]

The practical effect of the dynamic principles of "considerations of humanity" and "dictates of public conscience" varies depending on the means and method of warfare at issue,[64] and these phrases from the Martens Clause do not usually, by themselves, delegitimize weapons and methods of war.[65] Modern human rights law, including the United Nations Charter, informs interpretations of these principles.[66] Thus, the doctrinal basis of human dignity underlying the Charter and other international conventions instructs our application of the "considerations of humanity" and "dictates of public conscience" language of the Martens Clause to means and methods of warfare. The "dictates of public conscience" with respect to the development and use of LAWS are still evolving.[67] Nevertheless, the requirement of "considerations of humanity" must inform the current discussions about autonomous weapons. This new technology, by removing decisions about the use of lethal force from the responsibility of humans, forces us to reassess the concept of humanity.

The Law of Targeting: The Use of Force During Armed Conflict

In order to understand how the development and employment of LAWS impacts the exercise of force, it is necessary to review the process(es) professional armed forces undertake to plan and execute attacks. In modern warfare, the process of selecting and engaging targets can be extraordinarily complex, involving multiple stakeholders, interests, and values, and includes a mix of human thinking, automation, and autonomy. Essentially, the targeting process identifies resources that the enemy can least afford to lose or that provide him or her with the greatest advantage. Subsequently, targeters identify the subset of those targets that must be neutralized to achieve success.[68]

According to U.S. military doctrine, valid targets are those that have been vetted as "[a] part of target development that ensures all vetted targets meet the objectives and criteria outlined in the commander's guidance and ensures compliance with the law of armed conflict and rules of engagement."[69]

Four general principles guide the targeting process. First, it should be focused; that is, every target proposed for engagement should contribute to attaining the objectives of the mission. Second, targeting should be "effects-based,"[70] that is, it attempts to produce desired effects with the least risk and least expenditure of resources. Third, it is interdisciplinary in that targeting entails participation from commanders and their staffs, military lawyers, analysts, weaponeers,[71] and "other agencies, departments, organizations, and multinational partners."[72] Finally, targeting should be systematic: a rational process that methodically analyses, prioritizes, and assigns assets against targets.[73] A single target may be significant because of its particular characteristics. The target's real importance, however, "lies in its relationship to other targets within the operational system"[74] of the adversary.

There are two general categories of targeting: deliberate and dynamic. Deliberate targeting shapes the battlespace and addresses planned targets and efforts, this is, beyond the next twenty-four hours. Dynamic targeting manages the battlespace and refers to decisions requiring more immediate responses, usually within the current twenty-four-hour period.[75] Targets have temporal characteristics in that their vulnerability to detection, attack, or other engagement varies in relation to the time available to engage them.[76] Targets that are especially time sensitive present the greatest challenges to targeting personnel, who must compress their normal decision cycles into much shorter periods.

As mentioned above, targeting decisions must satisfy law of war obligations. In this context, targeting personnel bear three essential responsibilities. First, they must positively identify and accurately locate targets that comport with military objectives and rules of engagement. Second, they must identify possible concerns regarding civilian injury or damage to civilian objects in the vicinity of the target.[77] Finally, they must conduct incidental damage estimates with due diligence and within a framework of the accomplishment of "mission objectives, force protection, and collateral damage mitigation."[78]

In U.S. military doctrine, the methodology of collateral damage estimation "is a balance of science and art."[79] U.S. military personnel must consider five essential questions when performing collateral damage estimates: (1) Is the target positively identified? (2) Are there protected or collateral objects, civilian or noncombatant personnel, involuntary or unwitting human shields, or significant environmental concerns within the effects range of the weapon recommended to attack the target? (3) Can the damage to those collateral concerns be mitigated by striking the target with a different weapon or with a different method of engagement, yet still accomplish the mission? (4) If not, what is the estimate of the number of civilians and noncombatants that will be injured or killed by the attack? (5) Are the expected collateral effects of the attack excessive in relation to the expected military advantage gained, and should this decision to attack the target be addressed by the next level of command based on the rules of engagement (ROE) in effect?[80]

Targeting personnel must use their combined expertise, experience, and current intelligence to apply the science to the conditions of the operational environment. In addition to the potential for collateral damage and other law of war considerations, commanders may weigh and balance many other factors into their decision making such as operational and strategic objectives, rules of engagement, target characteristics, political risks, and risks to friendly forces and the mission itself.[81]

After targets are engaged, commanders must assess the effectiveness of the engagement.[82] "Direct" effects are the immediate consequences of military action, while "indirect" effects are the delayed or displaced second-, third-, or higher-order consequences, resulting from intervening events or mechanisms. Effects can "cascade," that is, ripple through a targeted system and effect other systems.[83] The assessment process is continuous and helps commanders adjust operations as necessary and make other decisions designed to ensure the success of the mission.[84]

Finally, the work of targeting is increasingly an automated (if not autonomous) process. "Targeting automation is decision support technology."[85] It refers to the use of computer applications to speed up the accurate development and use of information that matches objectives with targeting, and facilitates the assessment of effects. Military doctrine of the United States holds that while automation increases the speed of the targeting process, "it is not a replacement for human thinking or proactive communications,"[86] and personnel must "fully comprehend foundational targeting concepts."[87] The next section describes the most important targeting rules of international humanitarian law with respect to LAWS.

Applicable Rules of Targeting in International Humanitarian Law

The international humanitarian law provisions prescribing how belligerents should conduct targeting—that is, articles 48–59 of API—integrate the principles of military necessity and humanity. "The question who, or what, is a legitimate target is arguably the most important question in the law of war."[88] The targeting rules (perhaps the most important in international humanitarian law) attempt to delineate the parameters for the use of force during armed conflict and therefore are the most relevant to a discussion of the development and use of LAWS.

Articles 48 and 52 enshrine the customary law duty of parties to an armed conflict to distinguish between the civilian population and combatants and between civilian objects and military objectives, and thus they direct operations against only combatants or other military objectives such as enemy installations, equipment, and transport.[89] Consequently, military necessity will not provide a basis for derogation from this prohibition.[90] Article 51 (4) expresses the rule of customary international humanitarian law that prohibits indiscriminate attacks, which include:

(a) those that are not directed at a specific military objective;[91]
(b) those that employ a method or means of combat that cannot be directed at a specific military objective; and
(c) those that employ a method or means of combat the effects of which cannot be limited as required by API.[92]

Article 57 addresses the precautions that "those who plan or decide upon" an attack must exercise to avoid or minimize civilian casualties. Planners and executors of attacks must do everything feasible to verify that the target of the attack is a military objective and that the provisions of API do not forbid the operation.[93] Furthermore, belligerent forces must "take all feasible precautions in the choice of means and methods of attack"[94] to avoid and minimize incidental injury to civilians and damage to civilian objects.[95] "Feasible precautions" are precautions that are practicable or practically possible considering all circumstances ruling at the time, including humanitarian and military considerations.[96] Thus, this duty does not require an attacker to be certain that the target of the attack is lawful.[97] Instead the obligation is to act with due diligence and in good faith.[98]

According to U.K. military doctrine, when considering the means or methods of attack to be used, a commander should consider the importance of the target and the urgency of the situation; available intelligence about the use of the proposed target; the characteristics of the target itself; weapons available to the commander; their range, accuracy, and radius of effect; conditions affecting the accuracy of targeting, such as terrain, weather, and time of day; factors affecting incidental loss or damage, such as the proximity of civilians or civilian objects in the vicinity of the target; and the risks to his or her own troops present in the various options open to him or her .[99]As technology develops, however, the scope of what is "practicable," and therefore legally necessary, may expand accordingly.[100]

The rule of proportionality, expressed in articles 51 (5) (b) and 57 (2) (a) (iii), is the most challenging obligation within the realm of "precautions-in-attack." This rule requires parties to armed conflict to "refrain from deciding to launch any attack which may be expected to cause incidental loss of civilian life, injury to civilians, damage to civilian objects, or a combination thereof, which would be excessive in relation to the concrete and direct military advantage anticipated."[101] This duty requires consideration and balancing of at least three abstract values: "*excessive* incidental injury to civilians and/or damage to civilian objects," "concrete and direct," and "military advantage."[102]

The adjective "excessive" is important because, as Yoram Dinstein observes, incidental civilian damage during armed conflict is inevitable owing to the impossibility of keeping all civilians and civilian objects "away from the circle of fire in wartime."[103] However, the term does not lend itself to empirical calculations as it is impossible to prove, for example, that a particular factory is worth a certain number of civilians.[104] A variety of relevant military, moral, and legal concerns may inform an assessment of what is "excessive" such as the importance of the military objective, and the number of civilians at risk from the attack, as well as the risks to friendly forces and civilians if the attack does not occur.[105] Furthermore, calculations of *expected* incidental damage to civilians (whether excessive or not) will always be approximations[106] "to help inform a commander's decision making."[107]

Proportionality analyses, often made during the stress of military operations, are notoriously difficult and require a degree of subjectivity on the part of military commanders.[108] "It is much easier to formulate the principle of proportionality in general terms than it is to apply it to a particular set of circumstances because the comparison is often between unlike quantities and values. One cannot easily assess the value of innocent human lives as opposed to capturing a particular military objective."[109] Accordingly, military commanders must use their common sense and good faith when they weigh up the humanitarian and military interests at stake.[110]

The requirements of the article 57 rules concerning precautions in attack (as well as the other targeting rules codified in API) reflect elementary considerations of humanity and the international humanitarian law principle that civilians and civilian objects shall be spared, as much as possible, from the effects of hostilities.[111] Similarly, these rules speak to military necessity and the need of armed forces for disciplined soldiers who will fight effectively and facilitate the reestablishment of peace.[112] Thus, this dual proscriptive and permissive approach—based in the value of human dignity—runs through the laws and customs of war from the writings of Grotius, de Vattel, and their contemporaries to modern-day treaty and customary international humanitarian law.

Given the complexities of combat and the battlespace, the general principles of article 57 do not give rise to specific rules that particular types of weapons must be used in a specific case.[113] Instead, parties to armed conflict "retain considerable discretion to prioritize military considerations and the framework of operational requirements, and not simply humanitarian constraints."[114] Targeting assessments, therefore, often entail a degree of subjectivity.[115]

Nevertheless, the targeting rules of international humanitarian law apply to the use of LAWS (like any other weapon systems). Professional armies must "expect military commanders employing a system with autonomous functions to engage in the decision-making process that is required by international humanitarian law."[116] Logically, it is impossible for commanders to *direct* weapons at specific military objectives, as required by article 51 (4) (b) of API, without a proper understanding of the weapon. Thus, deployment of LAWS without a proper understanding of how the system works will constitute an indiscriminate attack and be subject to criminal sanction, at least in jurisdictions that recognize the *dolus eventualis* standard for mens rea.[117]

Moreover, prior to deploying an autonomous weapon, the superior must ensure one of two criteria: (1) once programmed, the artificial intelligence software controlling the autonomous weapon system has the robust capacity to comply with article 57, or (2) deployment of the autonomous weapon system is itself an expression of a "feasible precaution in the choice of means and methods of attack" within the meaning and spirit of the law.[118] By definition, once the commander deploys an autonomous weapon platform, he or she may lose the ability to take additional feasible precautions as well as make proportionality judgments. During the Clinton administration, for example, after U.S. armed forces under his command launched automated cruise missiles against the headquarters of Saddam Hussein's intelligence service in Baghdad, President Clinton was aghast to learn that the missiles neither had cameras mounted on them, nor could be "turned back" prior to striking their targets.[119]

LAWS and Compliance with the Laws of Targeting

As the laws of targeting are effects based, nothing in international humanitarian law per se makes the application of these targeting rules by LAWS unlawful, *provided* that the artificial intelligence of the autonomous functions is capable of compliance with the rule(s).[120] Currently, the limited powers of artificial "vision" and object recognition severely restrict the capacity of autonomous technologies to comply with the principle of distinction.[121] Thus, deployment of a LAWS programmed to seek out and attack an enemy (and only that enemy) would be lawful exclusively in remote areas such as deserts or the high seas, where the likelihood of the presence of civilians is extremely low and more complex assessments, such as proportionality, are unnecessary.[122] Even this restricted scenario contains additional challenges. Article 41 of API, for example, prohibits the targeting of individuals who clearly express an intention to surrender. Although this assessment can be difficult for human soldiers, sailors, and pilots as well,[123] the launch of an autonomous weapon system without this recognition capability would be unlawful.[124]

Indeed, the ability to make the difficult moral judgments often present in complex proportionality analysis (as well as other precautions in attack) probably presents the greatest cognitive challenge to the lawful operation of LAWS.[125] The data-processing strengths of modern computers miss the qualitative ability to assess the competing human priorities of military advantage and the protection of civilians. This reflective capacity, the presence of accumulated knowledge, experience, instinct,[126] and common sense, resides, at times, in the human mind.[127] Given the present state of artificial intelligence, without human-machine teamwork in situations where proportionality evaluations and other value-based decisions are necessary, the deployment of LAWS would be illegal pursuant to the targeting rules of international humanitarian law.

Nevertheless, as the technology improves, it is possible to envisage scenarios where a LAWS can fulfil targeting obligations more successfully than humans.[128] Tests of new "machine-learning" systems[129] demonstrate that machine-learning artificial intelligence often exhibits better judgment than humans in response to certain situations.[130] For example, the term "tactical patience" refers to the ability to permit a combat situation to develop to ensure that actions taken (such as attacks) are appropriate and lawful.[131] Unburdened by stress and fatigue and capable of processing more data, more quickly, than human soldiers, machines—in some situations—will exhibit more tactical patience and, potentially, more accuracy when distinguishing between civilian and combatants.

Similarly, LAWS could provide opportunities for greater precautionary measures—including more accurate proportionality analysis—than human soldiers planning and executing an attack. A LAWS, unworried about its own survival, can delay the use of force, thereby reducing doubt about the nature of a target. It can also use less force, including nonlethal force, when engaging the enemy, and so put civilians at lesser risk.[132] Consequently, the use of these autonomous systems may, in some situations, impact the process of balancing military necessity and humanity embodied in proportionality analysis, including, as lex ferenda, the importance of minimizing risk to *combatants*.[133] For example, in certain circumstances, particularly when capture is possible, there may be little military advantage to be gained from the use of lethal force by LAWS against, or in the vicinity of, human soldiers. Indeed, the introduction of LAWS to the battlespace may alter the meaning and scope of the necessity and humanity principles as new technology affects the ways wars are fought and social perceptions of acceptable human suffering change.[134]

LAWS, the Law of Targeting, and Human Dignity

Many of the tasks involved in the targeting process(es) do not require specific considerations about the act of killing. The gathering of data, calculations of expected damage to nonhuman military objectives and civilian objects, even the fusion of information for the identification of objects and persons as friendly or enemy are illustrative of subprocesses more efficiently performed by autonomous or automatic technology.

Conversely, final decisions concerning feasible precautions combine subjective and objective judgments involving the principles of military necessity and humanity. Evaluation of what is necessary in war is a difficult and subjective process, and, consequently, different persons frequently assess military necessity differently.[135] Commanders making these assessments may consider the broader imperatives of winning the armed conflict in addition to the demands of the immediate circumstances. Considerations of military necessity that encompass only immediate situations "could prolong the fighting and increase the overall suffering of the war."[136] Therefore, in addition to knowledge and experience, interpretations of "everything feasible" and "all feasible precautions" are "a matter of common sense and good faith."[137]

Delegation of these decisions to artificial intelligence directing LAWS would remove a great deal of pressure from soldiers and their commanders. This short-term gain, however, creates a long-term disadvantage. As discussed in Chapters 2 and 3, the ability to think and communicate about difficult concepts and values reflects the core of moral agency. Conveyance of this responsibility to machines is a transfer of human value; nothing could damage human dignity more. The onus for taking the precautionary measures described in article 57 of API, therefore, should remain with the human commanders and operators who have the capacity to exercise their judgment over, and interact with, LAWS.

Some commentators might respond that the human reasoning process for these decisions is simply shifted from the human commander or soldier to the person who programs the artificial intelligence software for each weapon.[138] For example, William Boothby observes that it "may sometimes be possible at the mission planning stage for a human being to determine that in all foreseeable circumstances programmed attacks will always comply with these evaluative rules."[139] With respect to an autonomous aerial weapon system, the person planning the mission inter alia will specify the area to be searched, the objective to be targeted, the munitions to be carried, the associated target recognition technology required for the mission, and the necessary quality of recognition.[140]

The unpredictability of warfare, however, makes this argument unsatisfactory. The moral and legal reasoning involved in these planning decisions only brings the LAWS to the entrance of the battlespace. It is impossible to foresee all the changing circumstances that result from the fluidity and violence of armed conflict. Consequently, it would be impossible for an operator of a LAWS to program the machine to address every contingency. The human planner—whether intentionally or simply by default—leaves many other issues to the artificial intelligence software.

In addition, one can argue that my perspective on the protection of human dignity will lead to a counterproductive "normative drift"[141] in international humanitarian law. By using concerns about human dignity to limit the use of LAWS, the international humanitarian law goal of reducing the suffering of war is "turned on its head." For example, robotic swarms of autonomous weapons are designed to quickly overwhelm an opponent, resulting in sharp but short wars. The fielding of these LAWS, therefore, has the potential to reduce human casualties of the attacking forces, and possibly avoid civilian injuries as well. Consequently, the employment of LAWS, consistent with the principle of military necessity, could accelerate and facilitate the return to peace.[142]

Open-ended claims about threats to human dignity, consequently, apart from skewing the balance between military necessity and humanity, could lead to greater violations of international humanitarian law. Kenneth Anderson and Matthew Waxman argue that in such circumstances, "the moral value of dignity . . . has to give way":[143]

> [T]he protection of civilians in war and reduction of the harms of war are "not finally about the promotion of human virtue and the suppression of human vice" as ends in themselves; human moral psychology is simply a means to those ends, and so is technology. If technology can further those goals more reliably and lessen dependence upon human beings with their virtues but also their moral frailties—by increasing precision; taking humans off the battlefield and reducing the pressures of human soldiers' interests in self-preservation; removing from battle the human soldiers' emotions of fear, anger, and desire for revenge; and substituting a more easily disposable machine—this is to the good.[144]

Clearly the availability of new tools that permit greater fulfillment of the principles of international humanitarian law represents an advance in the application of this body of international law to warfare. Nonetheless, "human moral psychology" is not a means; it is an end. It is precisely by delegating our moral responsibilities to artificial intelligence that we devalue it to a means. And if human dignity underlies and guides the application of all branches of international law, using LAWS to increase compliance with the laws of war may perversely, over the long term, vitiate the importance and function of international law.

Thus, the concept of human dignity can inform assessments of military necessity and humanity in multiple, nuanced ways, depending on the circumstances.[145] For example, autonomous machines can still replace humans in many important functions during the conduct of hostilities—thereby reducing the suffering caused by war—while human soldiers and commanders continue to make complex moral decisions more effectively. Boothby, for example, describes how, if humans plan an autonomous weapon attack in a "relatively depopulated area," or "within an exclusively military area," then precautions taken in the premission planning may address legal concerns adequately for the duration of the mission,[146] while minimizing risk to human soldiers. This outcome would support the principles of military necessity and humanity, as well as the overarching value of human dignity. In addition, autonomous weapon systems might neutralize, more quickly and accurately than would human soldiers, an armed group that is mistreating prisoners of war or civilians. A similar situation might arise where the only soldiers available to a commander for deployment have a history of disrespect for the rules of international humanitarian law or human rights law. In those particular situations, concerns about law and human dignity arguably would demand the use of LAWS.

The Law of Targeting, Human Dignity, and the Design of LAWS

International humanitarian law facilitates "the difficult moral and legal choices that require human judgment in order to preserve human dignity and life to the greatest degree possible in light of the military mission."[147] As autonomous technology for warfare continues to develop within the framework(s) of international law, the importance of preserving human dignity compels the use of interdependent design of autonomous technology and human-machine teamwork. Moreover, an emphasis on teamwork between human and computer protects the principles and obligations enshrined in international humanitarian law *and* encourages the development of more advanced technologies: "the U.K. position is that [international humanitarian principles], and the requirement for precautions in attack, are best assessed and applied by a human. Within that process a human may of course be supported by a system that has the appropriate level of automation to assist the human to make informed decisions. This is . . . *intelligent partnership*."[148]

An interdependent design of LAWS permits flexibility in the degree of human-to-machine supervision in the face of the uncertainties of armed conflict.[149] Humans can provide "high-level direction" while machines autonomously perform complex computations for specific tasks according to predetermined rules.[150]

Tension will arise, however, between the methodical practice of "deliberate" targeting to assure compliance with the law of war and the ever-increasing speed of autonomous weapon technology.[151] The extent to which a state prioritizes the safety of its armed forces is the "fault line of compliance" with the obligation to take precautionary measures.[152] A danger exists that in battlespace environments where reaction cycles are measured in microseconds, the obligation to take "feasible" precautionary measures may be swallowed by the velocity of the opponent's weapon systems.

This reality (which arguably provides more weight to the priorities of military necessity than to concerns about humanity) reflects the possibility that autonomous weapons technology will one day operate at such speeds that *all* threats will be immediate and the notion of "deliberate" target assessments impossible or suicidal. Professor Sassóli observes that "[a]s the weapons actually delivering kinetic force become increasingly quicker and more complex, it may be that humans become simply too overwhelmed by information and the decisions that must be taken to direct them."[153] The growing development of autonomous swarm technology represents the clearest trend toward this state of affairs. Decisions made literally at the speed of light by machines will obliterate opportunities for reasoned reflection and gradually reduce human involvement in the application of the law.[154]

Law should steer the development of new weapons technologies.[155] It is crucial to consider how the design of LAWS should be adapted to the targeting rules of International Humanitarian Law. Article 36 ("New Weapons") of API admonishes that "[i]n the study, development, acquisition or adoption of a new weapon, means or method of warfare, a High Contracting Party is under an obligation to determine whether its employment would, in some or all circumstances, be prohibited by this Protocol or by any other rule of international law applicable to the High Contracting Party."[156] The purpose of article 36 is to prevent the use of weapons that violate international law in all circumstances and to impose limits on the use of weapons that violate international law in some circumstances. Article 36 requires states to determine their lawfulness before the new weapons are developed, acquired,[157] or otherwise incorporated into the state's arsenal.[158]

This rule has not yet acquired the status of customary law[159] as only a relatively small number of states have acknowledged that they have established formal review processes under article 36.[160] However, one of those countries, the United States, is perhaps the leading developer of autonomous weapon systems. Therefore, it is worthwhile to examine the appropriate contours of a legal review for these systems.

Preliminarily, as William Hays Parks observes, "no single model for compliance with Article 36 exists."[161] It is important, in the context of LAWS, to consider what must be reviewed during an article 36 process. Legal reviews address the general legality of a weapons system as such, not its use in a specific situation. A weapon system includes the weapon itself—the device that is designed to kill or injure persons or damage property—and other components necessary for the weapon's operation.[162] Logically, a legal review of a LAWS must evaluate the weapon or weapons designed for the intended use of the system as well as the artificial intelligence hardware and software that will control targeting processes.[163]

For states that produce LAWS for their own use or for export, legal reviews should commence at the concept or design phase and continue through the development, testing, and acquisition periods. This policy will compel researchers and developers to focus their efforts, at the earliest possible stage, on ensuring that the results of their work will comply with the demands of international humanitarian law.[164] It also ensures that human dignity will maintain its place as the point of departure for this legal analysis. Moreover, after LAWS are deployed to the battlefield, they should be subject to regular review based on their technical performance.[165]

As new technologies emerge and are applied to weapon systems, participants in legal reviews must have a reasonable understanding[166] of how the systems work, or will work, or possess the ability to obtain this knowledge.[167] The complexities of LAWS will require a multidisciplinary approach, with computer scientists, robotics engineers, and other specialists assisting the military lawyers conducting the review.[168] Given the speed at which autonomous technologies are changing and advancing, complete records of each legal review of each new system, and each new modification of a system, are necessary to ensure consistency.[169]

For the reasons described above, legal reviews of the designs of new LAWS must ensure that the system will function consistently with international humanitarian law. In order to preserve human dignity over the long term, reviewers should insist that each new system employ an interdependent design that permits the participation of military personnel in tactical and operational decisions to take human life.[170] Tactical and operational decisions should not be conflated with the programming of artificial intelligence software before a LAWS is deployed. Where exceptions to this policy occur, they should document the particular circumstances in which the LAWS might use lethal force without human involvement. This policy should continue as legal reviews of the same system(s) are completed at the development, testing, and acquisition phases.

* * *

In international humanitarian law, the "hard cases are those which are in the space between the extreme examples."[171] In order for the use of LAWS to comply with the rules of this body of law, *including* international law's underlying precept of human dignity, armed forces should ensure that final decisions to take human life remain—to the greatest possible extent—with military personnel. At the same time, states should not abandon autonomous technologies that assist soldiers and commanders in doing their jobs more effectively within legal limits. Designs of autonomous weapon systems that guarantee human-machine interdependence during targeting processes will help to ensure compliance with international humanitarian law, including the concept of human dignity.

Nevertheless, continued pressure for faster weapon systems and "systems-in-systems" to increase "military effectiveness" (i.e., military advantage over opponents) will work against efforts to maintain teamwork between human warfighters and their machines.[172] Fundamentally, this condition will impede the exercise of human reasoning and judgment in decisions during armed conflict, weakening moral agency and the value of human dignity as a starting point for compliance with the law.

CHAPTER 5

Lethal Autonomous Weapon Systems and International Human Rights Law

In the preceding chapter, I demonstrated that during armed conflict, LAWS potentially have the capacity to comply with the rules governing the conduct of hostilities. Nevertheless, humans should continue to make decisions concerning the use of lethal force. Anything less would result in violations of human dignity, which is the foundation and guide of all international law.

In this chapter, I explain that international human rights law is most relevant to the use of LAWS in two sets of circumstances: (1) in law enforcement/antiterrorist situations where state authorities use lethal force, and (2) during armed conflict, where international human rights law applies concurrently with international humanitarian law. As autonomous technology advances, LAWS may have the capacity to fulfill particular requirements of international human rights law. However, consistent with my arguments in Chapter 4 concerning international humanitarian law, I demonstrate that the use of LAWS to take human life in law enforcement situations violates human dignity.

This chapter begins with a brief review of the sources of international human rights law. I then describe the capacity of LAWS to protect these human rights during law enforcement/antiterrorist operations. Subsequently, I review the interplay between international humanitarian law and international human rights law during armed conflict and explain when the use of LAWS during law enforcement/antiterrorist operations and during armed conflict can comport with the principle of human dignity. Finally, I conclude that an interdependent design of LAWS provides the best option for this new technology to fulfill the objectives of international human rights law.

The Sources of International Human Rights Law

Unlike international humanitarian law, which strives to find a balance between the imperatives of military necessity (i.e., the use of violence) and the value of humanity, the basic assumption of human rights law is a commitment to the universal principle of human dignity.[1] Logically then, this ubiquitous, bedrock principle must inform all interpretations of human rights law.[2] Dignity is a source, as well as a product, of fundamental human rights because "[h]uman rights flow from, and are necessary for, the recognition of human dignity."[3] Thus, in the context of international human rights law, violations of the value of human dignity take on a nearly primordial significance.[4]

Writing in the seventeenth century, British political philosopher John Locke observed that human beings cannot alienate their fundamental rights, which, for Locke, emanated from natural law.[5] An early (but limited) Western expression of these rights can be found in the Bill of Rights of 1689, which provided members of the English Parliament with certain rights and protections against abuses of power by their sovereign.[6] One hundred years later, the National Assembly of France attempted to codify "in a solemn declaration the natural, unalienable, and sacred rights of man."[7] Moreover, beginning in 1791 and continuing into the twentieth century, a number of these rights were adopted or extended in the Bill of Rights attached to the Constitution of the United States.[8]

The genesis of the "detailed tapestry"[9] of modern international human rights law lies in the United Nations Charter of 1945.[10] In the preamble, state parties "reaffirm faith in fundamental human rights, in the dignity and worth of the human person, in the equal rights of men and women and of nations large and small."[11] Moreover, one of the purposes of the United Nations is to promote and encourage respect for human rights and fundamental freedoms without distinction as to race, sex, language, or religion.[12] Concurrently, however, article 7 constrains international intervention to protect human rights as it reaffirms the sovereign power of states to address matters arising within their domestic jurisdiction.

Following the adoption of the U.N. Charter, a large and comprehensive body of international and regional human rights conventions (and corresponding monitoring and judicial mechanisms) was produced. The Universal Declaration of Human Rights (Universal Declaration), ratified on 10 December 1948, was drafted as a nonbinding,[13] aspirational document, and the arguable development of its provisions into customary international law will be discussed below. The United Nations General Assembly adopted the Convention on the Prevention and Punishment of the Crime of Genocide (Genocide Convention) just one day before the ratification of the Universal Declaration. The contracting parties to the Genocide Convention accepted the duty to undertake to prevent and punish the crime of genocide.[14]

States enacted a number of international and regional human rights treaties and conventions during the last half of the twentieth century; the two most prominent are the International Covenant on Civil and Political Rights (ICCPR)[15] and the International Covenant on Economic, Social and Cultural Rights (ICESCR).[16] These two covenants, together with the Universal Declaration, are referred to as the International Bill of Rights.[17] In addition to their substantive provisions expressing international human rights norms, the ICCPR, the ICESCR, and other "core" international human rights treaties[18] establish monitoring bodies (or "treaty bodies") that review state party compliance with their obligations and provide guidance (General Comments) on the nature and scope of these duties.[19] These treaty bodies may also conduct inquiries into well-founded reports and complaints of serious violations of the relevant convention by a state party.[20]

Moreover, a number of human rights rules expressed in these conventions, such as the prohibitions of slavery, torture, and genocide, have been described as part of jus cogens,[21] the class of elevated rights invoked as moral and legal prescriptions for derogations from human rights. Indeed, Professor Bianchi observes that there "is an almost intrinsic relationship between jus cogens and human rights."[22]

Furthermore, several regional human rights conventions such as the European Convention for the Protection of Human Rights and Fundamental Freedoms (ECHR) and its fourteen additional protocols, the American Convention on Human Rights (ACHR), and the African Charter on Human and Peoples' Rights (ACtHPR)—and the human rights judicial systems they created—have led to the development of a large body of international human rights jurisprudence.[23] Indeed, in 1994, two commentators concluded that the "achievements" of the European Convention on Human Rights "have been quite staggering, the case-law of the European Commission and Court of Human Rights exerting an ever deeper influence on the laws and social realities of the State parties."[24]

Determinations of the customary status of international human rights obligations are complex given the frequent disparity between state expressions of their human rights obligations and the common occurrence of gross human rights violations around the world; in other words, the dichotomy between *opinio juris* and state practice.[25] Professor Chinkin notes, for example, that "many commentators" believe that the contents of the Universal Declaration of Human Rights have become customary law.[26] Simma and Alston, however, strongly rejected this view, arguing that it is impossible to elevate the Universal Declaration and other documents to the status of customary international law "in a world where it is still customary for a depressingly large number of states to trample upon the human rights of their nationals."[27]

In addition, the development of international human rights law may occur over time through forms and expressions of "soft law."[28] Examples would include the work of the "treaty bodies" mentioned above and other human rights mechanisms,[29] as well as the vast body of United Nations General Assembly and Security Council resolutions that pronounce on human rights issues,[30] reports of United Nations special rapporteurs and special experts,[31] the Universal Periodic Review process conducted by the United Nations Human Rights Council,[32] reports by international commissions of inquiry,[33] and more.

Finally, while obviously the development of this large body of international human rights law and its associated structures and enforcement mechanisms create enormous potential for furthering the rule of law, primary responsibility for its implementation lies with national governments and courts.[34]

The Right to Life

According to the ICCPR, "[e]very human being has the inherent right to life. This right shall be protected by law. No one shall be arbitrarily deprived of his life."[35] The European Convention for the Protection of Human Rights and Fundamental Freedoms (ECHR), the American Convention on Human Rights (ACHR), and the African Charter on Human and Peoples' Rights (ACHPR) also prohibit the arbitrary deprivation of life.[36]

The right to life is a condition precedent for the realization of other rights and, when disrespected, "all the other rights lack meaning."[37] Thus, Professor Benvenisti refers to the norm that every human being has the inherent right to life as "the premise that permeates human rights law."[38] States, therefore, must take "all appropriate measures" to ensure the creation of conditions required to avoid violations of inalienable human rights.[39] In the context of the right to life, these steps include all necessary measures, not only to prevent and punish deprivation of life as a consequence of criminal acts, in general, but also to prevent arbitrary executions by its own security agents.[40] This positive, proactive obligation applies to legislators and all state institutions, in particular those who must protect security, that is, their police and armed forces.[41]

At the same time, circumstances may compel constraints on the right to life, particularly when the cost to other rights is too high. Thus, international human rights law permits states or their agents to take life via the use of force that is no more than absolutely necessary:

(a) in defense of any person from unlawful violence;
(b) in order to effect a lawful arrest or to prevent the escape of a person lawfully detained;
(c) in action lawfully taken for the purpose of quelling a riot or insurrection.[42]

Thus, in certain circumstances, the use of lethal force by state security forces in peacetime may be justifiable.[43] However, because of the fundamental nature of the right to life, the scope of circumstances justifying its deprivation is construed narrowly.[44] For example, when state agents use lethal force with the aim of protecting persons from unlawful violence, deadly force must be "absolutely necessary"[45] to achieve one of the three purposes listed above. In other words, the force used must be "strictly proportionate" to the achievement of the permitted aims.[46] In the context of human rights law (in contrast with international humanitarian law), "necessity" means that force must be used only as a last resort and that, in such circumstances, states should use a graduated approach.[47]

Consequently, during law enforcement and antiterrorist operations, government authorities must plan and control activities so as to minimize, as much as possible, recourse to lethal force.[48] Police may not use lethal force, for example, against a fleeing burglar who poses no immediate danger, although the burglar will escape, because the preservation of property rights does not justify the intentional taking of life.[49] Force should be used against a person only if that person poses an imminent threat of violence "normally implying a matter of seconds or even split-seconds."[50] Accordingly, authorities should minimize to the greatest extent possible recourse to lethal force in circumstances of arrest and detention.[51] For example, where it is known that a person escaping from lawful detention poses no threat to life or limb and is not suspected of having committed a violent offence, recourse to deadly force does not meet the "absolutely necessary" standard.[52]

Moreover, protection of the right to life requires states to ensure that their agents do not perform unregulated and arbitrary actions involving the use of lethal force.[53] Thus, governments must create a framework of rules and safeguards to guard against the arbitrary exercise of force.[54] This framework should include modern and effective laws regulating the use of weapons by state agents in peacetime,[55] as well as systems for planning and controlling law enforcement and antiterrorist operations so as to minimize, as much as possible, resorting to lethal force.[56] In circumstances where the risk to innocents is great, the primary aim of such operations should be to protect lives from unlawful violence.[57]

Finally, the obligation to protect the right to life implicitly requires an effective form of official investigation when citizens die as a result of the use of force by state agents.[58]

The Use of LAWS and the Protection of the Right to Life

LAWS and the Protection of the Right to Life

The jurisprudence of regional human rights courts requires states to plan and control law enforcement and antiterrorist activities "so as to minimize, to the greatest extent possible, recourse to lethal force."[59] To achieve that objective, authorities must take all feasible precautions in the choice of means and methods of security operations.[60] "[T]he more predictable a hazard, the greater the obligation to protect against it."[61] Thus, if the deployment of an autonomous weapon system—even one with lethal capabilities—can feasibly minimize the necessity of lethal force, international human rights law should require the use of the weapon.

However, as discussed above, international human rights law provides that during peacetime, states may use lethal force only in three situations: (1) to defend persons from unlawful violence; (2) to effect a lawful arrest or to prevent the escape of a lawfully detained person; or (3) in lawful actions to quell riots or insurrections.[62] Moreover, a state's use of lethal force must be "absolutely necessary and proportionate,"[63] which substantially reduces the incidence of lawful lethal force in law enforcement situations. The current generation of autonomous machines, however, cannot make such complex, values-based judgments, and, as Christof Heyns observed, "there is significantly less room" for the use of LAWS "in law enforcement, where it will be difficult to outperform human beings."[64] Indeed, it is precisely those decisions *not* to use force that often require the most sophisticated and courageous forms of thinking and reasoning.[65] Thus, the contemporary use of LAWS during law enforcement or antiterrorist operations will violate international human rights law.

Will this situation change, however, when artificial intelligence capabilities advance? Might the use of more advanced autonomous weapon systems in some situations reduce recourse to lethal force? Threats to the life and safety of law enforcement officials are a threat to the stability of society as a whole.[66] Thus, police officers and other state agents rightly can consider their own security when evaluating whether the use of lethal force is "absolutely necessary" to save a third party, to apprehend a fleeing detainee, or to control a riot or insurrection.[67] Therefore, where it is known that a person facing arrest or escaping from lawful detention poses an imminent threat to the arresting officer, recourse to deadly force may meet the "absolutely necessary" standard. But where the same suspect or detainee confronts an autonomous weapon, the presence of the autonomous weapon system should *preclude* the use of lethal force—which will not be absolutely necessary—unless the suspect poses an immediate danger to third parties in close proximity. In these circumstances, the use of LAWS rather than police officers would result in reduced loss of life.

Legislators and other state institutions, in particular security forces, have a positive obligation to regulate (1) the deployment of LAWS in law enforcement and antiterrorist situations, and (2) the degrees of force that these systems may employ.[68] Accordingly, states will need new laws that regulate the use of LAWS during law enforcement and antiterrorist activities.[69] For example, as in the case of military operations, fast decisions and actions are important for successful police efforts to apprehend criminals, protect third parties, control riots, and so on.[70] Nevertheless, the speed of decisions by LAWS is inversely proportional to the degree of human judgment available to guide or override the machine. A balance must be struck, therefore, between faster LAWS and systems that permit the influence of human judgment over law enforcement decisions to take human life. Therefore, law enforcement agencies should deploy interdependent human-machine systems that ensure full compliance with human rights law.

One might argue that options exist for police officers or soldiers to avoid the loss of dignity that accompanies their abdication of moral agency to artificial intelligence software. Police officers, after all, can refuse to follow orders or use certain weapons and can resign their positions. Indeed, in states where "volunteer" armies are the norm, no one need put him- or herself in a position whereby he or she might have to cede responsibilities to a machine. While this claim may be true, it misses the point. The result still will be that human beings will not develop the ability to perform the kinds of moral and legal reasoning necessary to make the most difficult decisions during armed conflict and law enforcement operations. This narrowing of thousands of years of human thinking is plainly inconsistent with the norm of human dignity and, therefore, the essence of human rights law.

Others might contend that the use of autonomous weapon systems simply creates new forms of thinking and new methods to address moral and legal questions. Yet this seems to be a disingenuous and illogical argument. One cannot abdicate opportunities for moral and legal reasoning, and then call it "new forms of reasoning." Similarly, as described in Chapter 4, the reasoning applied to orders to deploy LAWS, or the act of programming onboard computers, ignores many of the moral and legal balancing processes inherent to the law of targeting and the use of lethal force in war and peacetime. When human beings leave these processes to software, whether as a matter of policy, for strategic or tactical reasons, or simply out of convenience, the result is a restriction of human dignity.

The Interplay of International Human Rights Law and International Humanitarian Law

As discussed in Chapter 4, during armed conflict international humanitarian law protects certain categories of persons from deliberate targeting by belligerents. Conversely, under the same body of law, the intentional killing of enemy combatants and civilians directly participating in hostilities is lawful. However, international human rights law prescribes standards for the use of lethal force that are more rigorous than the laws of war. This section examines the application of international human rights law during armed conflict and its relationship with international humanitarian law. It foreshadows how the development and use of LAWS can shape this relationship.

Although international humanitarian law and international human rights law are distinct bodies of law, they protect similar principles and interests,[71] and, as explained in the previous chapter, in a normative sense, modern international humanitarian law has roots in international human rights law. For example, the principle of humanity in international humanitarian law and related rules such as the duty to distinguish between combatants and civilians and the obligation to treat prisoners and wounded combatants decently are linked to fundamental human rights such as the right to life, the right to be free of torture and cruel and inhuman treatment, and so on.[72] Indeed, the Geneva Conventions contain certain norms that can be regarded as jus cogens.[73]

Thus, "humanitarian law also contains a prominent human rights component,"[74] and human rights law continues to apply during armed conflict.[75] According to the International Court of Justice, international humanitarian law is the *lex specialis* designed to regulate the conduct of hostilities, while international human rights law continues to function as the *lex generalis*.[76] Consequently, some circumstances in armed conflict may conform only to matters of international humanitarian law; others may speak exclusively to international human rights law; and others may implicate both branches of international law.[77] In its judgment in the *Case Concerning Armed Activities on the Territory of the Congo*, for example, the court ruled that Ugandan forces, as the occupying power of parts of the Democratic Republic of Congo, were obliged to secure respect for the applicable rules of international humanitarian law *and* international human rights law.[78]

In some situations, therefore, international human rights law can inform (if not control) the scope of law of war obligations. For example, the ability of persons interned during armed conflict to appeal the restrictions on their freedom provides the protected persons a stronger guarantee of fair treatment[79] and layers the application of international humanitarian law with responsibilities imposed by international human rights law. The human right to fair legal procedures also resonates in article 84 of Geneva Convention (III) Relative to the Treatment of Prisoners of War, which provides that "a prisoner of war shall be tried only by a military court. . . . In no circumstances whatever shall a prisoner of war be tried by a court of any kind which does not offer the essential guarantees of independence and impartiality." These "essential guarantees," and others, are enshrined, inter alia, in article 14 of the ICCPR.[80] Thus, parties holding prisoners of war should look to international human rights instruments when they initiate proceedings under article 84.

Conversely, as mentioned above, relevant provisions of international humanitarian law instruments serve as guides for the interpretation of international human rights law.[81] For example, article 9 (1) of the ICCPR provides that "[e]veryone has the right to liberty and security of person. No one shall be subjected to arbitrary arrest or detention. No one shall be deprived of his liberty except on such grounds and in accordance with such procedure as are established by law." During international armed conflicts the Fourth Geneva Convention grants occupying powers the authority to intern protected persons "for imperative reasons of security."[82] Thus, in these circumstances, allegations of violations of article 9 (1) should be viewed through the lens of the Fourth Geneva Convention.

In important ways, "the standards of human rights law, at least as applied by the [European Court of Human Rights], are probably more rigorous than those of international humanitarian law."[83] For example, international humanitarian law permits combatants to kill their enemy in situations where capture might be an alternative.[84] The European Court of Human Rights, on the other hand, requires that every use of lethal force be "no more than absolutely necessary" to achieve the desired aim.[85] As Françoise Hampson observes: "The key distinction between an international humanitarian law analysis and a human rights law analysis is that the former allows targeting by reference to status. That means that a person can be targeted on account of their membership of a group, whether that is opposing armed forces or an organized armed group in which the individual exercises a continuous combat function. Generally speaking, a human rights paradigm only allows targeting based on the behavior of the individual targeted."[86]

The precise contours, however, of the application of international human rights law during armed conflict, and its interplay with international humanitarian law, remain a matter of debate. Preliminarily, there is no single applicable rule that controls the relationship between the two regimes.[87] Professor Jinks makes an articulate argument that international humanitarian law "is best understood as a floor of humanitarian protection—but the application of this law does not require the level of legal protection down to this floor. . . . [T]he inference that the [Geneva] Conventions displace much, if not all, of international human rights law is unwarranted."[88]

The European Court of Human Rights takes a similar view. In *Hassan v. the United Kingdom*, the court concluded, first, that international human rights law continues to apply during international armed conflict, "albeit interpreted against the background of the provisions of international humanitarian law."[89] In the words of the majority, relevant provisions of international human rights covenants "should be accommodated, as far as possible" with the relevant laws of war.[90] Thus, when circumstances arise where conflicting rules of both regimes apply, preference can be given (implicitly) to the rules of international humanitarian law. In *Hassan*, the applicant was an Iraqi citizen detained, "screened," and released by British forces in April 2003. The court observed that Hassan's capture and detention were consistent with the rules prescribed in the Third and Fourth Geneva Conventions.[91] Accordingly, the court ruled that Hassan's detention conformed with the essential purpose of article 5 (1) of the European Convention of Human Rights, which is to protect the individual from arbitrary detention.[92]

Perhaps no aspect of the interplay between international humanitarian law and international human rights law is more controversial today than the "kill or capture" debate emanating from the *Interpretive Guidance on the Notion of Direct Participation in Hostilities Under IHL* (*Interpretive Guidance*),[93] published by the International Committee of the Red Cross (ICRC). In part 9 of *Interpretive Guidance*, the ICRC opined: "In addition to the restraints imposed by international humanitarian law on specific means and methods of warfare, and without prejudice to further restrictions that may arise under other applicable branches of international law, the kind and degree of force which is permissible against persons not entitled to protection against direct attack must not exceed what is actually necessary to accomplish a legitimate military purpose in the prevailing circumstances."[94]

Effectively, the ICRC suggests that international law prohibits (or should prohibit) soldiers from killing enemy combatants when the possibility of capture or other nonlethal means to neutralize the enemy exists.[95] This constraint is consistent with the "absolutely necessary" standard for the use of lethal force under human rights law reflected in the jurisprudence of the European Court of Human Rights. The language of the more recent *Hassan* judgment, directing states to accommodate, "as far as possible" relevant provisions of international human rights law with the rules of international humanitarian law, echoes *Interpretive Guidance*.[96]

Part 9 of the ICRC's *Interpretive Guidance* has been the subject of sustained and forceful criticism, in particular from international humanitarian law experts with military expertise,[97] who contend that the ICRC incorrectly imposes international human rights standards into the norms and obligations of the law of war. Indeed, the capture-if-possible standard proposed in *Interpretive Guidance* is absent from the ICRC's extensive study and formulation of rules of modern customary international humanitarian law.[98] Furthermore, the ICRC position contradicts a 2003 NATO policy that "[t]here is no legal obligation to resort to non-lethal force when lethal force is authorized and today there is no foreseeable reason why this may change in the future."[99]

Time will tell whether states will adopt *Interpretive Guidance*'s more restrictive approach to the use of lethal force during armed conflict. Hitoshi Nasu contends that the power to kill or capture debate should be seen as a possible *future* legal approach to weapons law, "heralding a new humanitarian law era in which questions concerning 'humane' ways to attack lawful targets may be more fully explored, rather than an argument that reflects lex lata."[100]

The increasing use of LAWS could facilitate the development of state practice and *opinio juris* in this direction. The availability of LAWS with the capacity to make these "capture or kill" judgments puts fewer human soldiers at risk from enemy combatants and reduces the dangers of efforts to capture the enemy (i.e., the dangers of accommodating international human rights law).[101] Thus, by fielding sophisticated LAWS, belligerent parties reduce the number of situations where the use of lethal force is "actually/absolutely necessary," thereby changing the balance between military assessment and humanity. Consequently, modern armed forces that follow the ICRC's standard and deploy LAWS will have to assess whether it is inappropriate (if not illegal) to use lethal force instead of capturing enemy combatants.

Artificial intelligence software has not yet advanced to a level whereby computers can make complex determinations as to the "actual/absolute necessity" of using lethal force against enemy targets to serve "a legitimate military purpose" in the "prevailing circumstances." However, should *Interpretive Guidance*'s *lex ferenda* standard for the use of lethal force one day become an obligation under customary international humanitarian law, the fielding of LAWS lacking this capacity will violate the law's prohibition of means and methods of warfare designed to cause unnecessary suffering. Under the same standard, use of these weapons to exercise lethal force potentially would violate international human rights law's proscription of arbitrary deprivations of the right to life.

The analysis should not end, however, when the artificial intelligence driving LAWS possesses the capability to make the assessments necessary to fulfill *Interpretive Guidance*'s rigorous standard for the exercise of lethal force. It must be determined whether, under international human rights law, the delegation of power and responsibility to make such decisions from humans to machines comports with the rights to freedom of thought and expression and, by extension, human dignity.

LAWS, Human Dignity and the Interplay of International Humanitarian Law and International Human Rights Law

In Chapter 4, we saw how the delegation of responsibility for the use of lethal force from persons to LAWS during armed conflict violates human dignity. Norms with sufficient importance to apply during wartime—in particular the value of human dignity—ought to apply during peacetime as well.[102] The exercise of lethal force by autonomous weapon systems is not wholly inconsistent with the obligation to protect human dignity because the use of force may be necessary to secure rights against persons intending to violate them.[103] Furthermore, in some situations, the use of LAWS might be more effective at saving innocent lives than men and women conducting security actions for the state. If that premise is correct, then, in such cases, LAWS will protect the fundamental right to life and the value of human dignity more successfully.

I explained previously that, when state agents use lethal force with the aim of protecting persons from unlawful violence, deadly force must be absolutely necessary. "Necessity" requires that (proportionate) force be used only as a last resort and that, in such circumstances, states should use a graduated approach. The precondition of a graduated approach in the use of force in law enforcement or antiterrorist environments completely vitiates one of the primary reasons to field LAWS: the ability to act with exceptional speed. It would be illogical, therefore, to employ such weapons and undermine human dignity when the use of conventional weapons could achieve the same result.

That leaves two legal arguments in support of the premise that human rights law demands the employment of LAWS in law enforcement and antiterrorist operations. First, circumstances could arise both during armed conflict and in peacetime where the use of LAWS could reduce (at least in the short term) human rights violations. For example, in one scenario LAWS might neutralize, more quickly and accurately than human soldiers or police, an armed group that is detaining and mistreating civilians. In such situations, concerns about law and human dignity arguably would demand their use. A similar situation might arise where the only available soldiers or police officers available to a commander have a history of disrespect for the rules of international humanitarian law or human rights law.

Second, as described above, in certain law enforcement situations, the presence of LAWS should preclude the use of lethal force—which will not be absolutely necessary—unless an alleged criminal poses an immediate danger to third parties in close proximity. In these circumstances, the availability of LAWS will reduce the use of "absolutely necessary" lethal force and place fewer state agents in harm's way. If, as discussed above, state officials must plan and control activities during law enforcement and antiterrorist operations so as to minimize, as much as possible, recourse to lethal force, human rights law (and the underlying value of human dignity) seems to require the use of LAWS.

These arguments, however, actually support the claim that the *systematic* use of LAWS vitiates human dignity. If a military commander or a law enforcement officer has the ability to identify those situations where LAWS can be used legally, he or she will do so based on his or her background, experience, and accumulated knowledge.[104] These qualities of reason and reflection that inform the commander's moral agency will not develop (much less be used) when the employment of LAWS becomes the norm rather than the exception.

Moreover, laws are means to ends, and states deserve a margin of appreciation as regards the means to strike a balance between the protection of different rights.[105] Indeed, where human rights are "pitted against each other," "'respect for human freedom and human dignity' may prevail."[106] Accordingly, as discussed in Chapters 3 and 4, if dignity is to be a meaningful concept in international law, it can receive greater weight in some cases than the right to life.

For example, a number of countries qualify the right to life by permitting terminally ill persons to receive lethal drugs or the assistance of physicians to end their lives[107] and their "constant and unbearable physical or mental suffering."[108] The Canadian Supreme Court held that bans on "physician-assisted dying" *violated* the right to life because "the prohibition deprives some individuals of life, as it has the effect of forcing some individuals to take their own lives prematurely, *for fear that they would be incapable of doing so* when they reached the point where suffering was intolerable."[109] In addition, the court concluded that Canada's ban violated the rights to liberty and security of the person, which includes a person's dignity and autonomy.[110] Therefore, compliance with the law (in this case the right to protection of life) is self-defeating if compliance implies harmful consequences for the spirit and purpose of the law.

"If the burdens [of protecting life] surpass the benefits, then the state's obligation may, in appropriate cases, cease."[111] A duty on states to use LAWS rather than human agents to protect life in armed conflict or law enforcement situations would severely limit the expression of moral agency and human dignity. Reason and persuasion—thought and expression—rather than force, are the pillars of democracies.[112] The loss of human dignity and erosion of democratic skills and processes emanating from such a duty represents an intolerable burden to freedom and human rights.[113] Over the long term, these consequences outweigh any potential benefits to the protection of human rights derived from the employment of LAWS by state authorities during and outside of armed conflict.

International Human Rights Law and the Design of LAWS

The preceding discussion demonstrates, again, the logic and advantages of an interdependent design for LAWS when employed during law enforcement and antiterrorist activities, as well as during armed conflict. The "graduated approach" for the use of force by state agents required by international human rights law usually negates the advantage of speed offered by LAWS. An interdependent design permits human-machine teamwork, which preserves the moral agency required for the complex decisions inherent to the use of lethal force by states. Such teamwork also protects against dynamics where human or computer errors are "locked in" to weapon systems, resulting in greater violations of international law.[114] This design permits states to achieve a reasonable balance between their duty to protect human life and the obligation to preserve the fundamental value of human dignity.

* * *

Paradoxically, the deployment of LAWS by states outside of armed conflict potentially can reduce the frequency of the exercise of deadly force by state agents. Moreover, during wartime, should state practice and *opinio juris* adhere to the *lex ferenda* position expressed in chapter 9 of the ICRC's *Interpretive Guidance*, customary international human rights law and humanitarian law will compel the use of LAWS to increase opportunities for the capture, rather than killing, of enemy belligerents.

Conversely, the widespread use of LAWS carries a serious cost to human dignity, as the delegation to machines of the decision(s) to apply lethal force, as well as determinations about whether arrest or capture is more appropriate, restricts the exercise of moral agency inherent in these decisions. The long-term reduction of human dignity that will result when LAWS regularly make these decisions outweighs the benefits because expressions of humanity are too essential to be outsourced to machines. "Protection of the right to life must be implemented in a way that respects the human dignity of the protected individuals *and of those called upon to protect them*."[115] Thus, human-machine interdependence for decisions about the use of lethal force presents the best option for effectively balancing rights enshrined in international human rights law and the value of human dignity itself.

CHAPTER 6

Lethal Autonomous Weapon Systems and International Criminal Law

The goal of international criminal law is to proscribe serious violations of international law and to hold those persons who participate in such conduct criminally responsible.[1] The fundamental legal principle of individual responsibility, however, stipulates that persons are responsible only for their own acts or for those of their agents.[2] This chapter will discuss whether international criminal justice mechanisms provide an adequate and effective system of accountability for violations of the laws of war and gross violations of international human rights law perpetrated with LAWS.

Preliminarily, if, as I argued previously, human dignity serves as a legal point of departure for our decision making, we see that exclusive reliance on criminal prosecutions as a method of accountability for the use of LAWS is a poor strategy. International criminal law (generally) looks backward.[3] Efforts to hold persons responsible for crimes occur *after* the tragic events—and their concomitant violence and human suffering—have occurred. A more effective model would use the rules of state responsibility in international law (discussed in the following chapter) to complement efforts to achieve accountability and individual criminal responsibility. This more proactive approach serves the interests of human dignity by reducing the levels of criminal conduct using autonomous weapon systems.

"Accountability" refers to the duty to account for the exercise of power.[4] This value is a moral derivative of human dignity because accountability arises from the moral agency of persons: "Only people, intentional agents with the potential to act, can do wrong and violate expectations of what they owe each other."[5] Accountability is important for soldiers because it imposes a duty on them to take moral and legal responsibility for their actions and decisions. Thus, when crimes or accidents occur during or because of the use of LAWS, the actions and decisions of human commanders and operators must form part of any accountability analysis. But by transferring power for moral and legal decisions in warfare to machines, we reduce the moral agency of the warfighter and undermine his or her capacity for accountability.

In criminal law, evidence of the accused's intent, the mental element or mens rea, during the commission of the crime is a crucial pillar of any prosecution.[6] The underlying rationale for the mens rea requirement is that a sense of personal blame is absent if the accused did not in some way intend his or her action or omission. However, once the speed of autonomous technology reaches levels that preclude effective human supervision and control, proof of the existence of the mens rea, may be illusory or impossible to establish. Arguably, this could result in an "accountability gap" when crimes occur during the employment of LAWS.

But concerns about "accountability gaps"[7] for particular crimes or modes of criminal responsibility reflect only part of the problem. If our overarching goal is to promote and protect human dignity, then logically "accountability" for the (mis)use of LAWS means something more than individual punishment for violations of narrowly defined rules of treaty and customary law. The fact that a particular autonomous weapon functions within the "black letter" prescriptions of international law is secondary if the human designer, operator, commander, or other involved person can transfer his or her moral agency in favor of artificial intelligence. "Accountability" in this sense includes a commitment by states and nonstate actors to ensure that humans will not transfer their responsibility for decisions implicating the taking of human life to LAWS. By adopting an interdependent design, for example, we better ensure that "accountability" encompasses the full protection of human dignity, and not "only" the important exercise of holding individuals responsible for serious violations of customary and treaty law after they occur.

I argue that the use of interdependent designs for LAWS permits teamwork between humans and autonomous technologies that can result in lower levels of criminality and higher levels of accountability when crimes occur. This policy serves to preserve the human dignity of all members of society, including participants in armed conflict and law enforcement operations.

This chapter begins with a brief review of the sources of international criminal law followed by an analysis of the relationship of human dignity to this body of law. It continues with a discussion of the theories of individual criminal responsibility relevant to the use of LAWS. It reviews how the deployment of these weapons will simultaneously facilitate and complicate efforts to ensure accountability for serious violations of international law, and it describes the effect of these dynamics on the preservation of human dignity. Finally, this chapter explains why an interdependent design of LAWS provides greater opportunities to hold individuals criminally responsible for the misuse of these weapon systems while simultaneously preserving the dignity of the operators of these machines.

Sources of International Criminal Law

While the concept of "international crimes" has existed for centuries,[8] sources of modern international criminal law include special agreements of states (or special agreements between states and international institutions such as the United Nations and the European Union), international treaties, the Security Council's exercise of its powers under the United Nations Charter, customary international law, and other bodies of law such as international humanitarian law and international human rights law. This section briefly reviews each of these sources of international criminal law.

Agreements of States

At the close of World War II, the victorious powers created the Nuremberg and Tokyo courts by the 1945 London Agreement for the International Military Tribunal, and the 1946 Special Proclamation by General MacArthur for the Tokyo Tribunal, respectively.[9] Each agreement was supplemented by a charter that defined the constitutional powers and responsibilities of the court, such as their jurisdiction and the fair trial rights of the accused.[10] More recently, the government of Kosovo, at the "urging" of the European Union and the United States, established a special war crimes court that will prosecute former members of the Kosovo Liberation Army for international crimes committed in Kosovo between 1998 and 2000.[11]

International Treaties

International conventions are also important sources of international criminal law. For example, the 1919 Versailles Treaty stipulated that the Allied powers could prosecute persons responsible for violations of the laws and customs of war.[12] The 1948 Genocide Convention on the Prevention and Punishment of the Crime of Genocide confirms that genocide is a crime under international law, which the state parties must undertake to prevent and punish.[13] Moreover, the Convention Against Torture obliges state parties to ensure that all acts of torture (as well as attempted acts and complicity in torture) are offenses under their criminal law.[14] The Rome Statute to the International Criminal Court (ICC) codifies a comprehensive list of crimes that are punishable under international law.[15]

The United Nations Security Council

Pursuant to its powers under chapter 7 of the United Nations Charter, the United Nations Security Council has established several international or "hybrid" criminal tribunals. In 1993 and 1994 respectively, the Security Council established the International Criminal Tribunal for the Former Yugoslavia (ICTY) and the International Criminal Tribunal for Rwanda (ICTR).[16] Moreover, in 2005, the Security Council established an Independent International Investigation Commission (IIIC) tasked with investigating the terrorist attack that killed former Lebanese prime minister Hariri in February 2005.[17] Subsequently, pursuant to its chapter 7 powers and an agreement between United Nations and the government of Lebanon, the Security Council created the Special Tribunal for Lebanon in 2007.[18]

Customary International Law and Other Bodies of Law

The post–Second World War international criminal tribunals expressed a number of principles that have become part of customary international criminal law.[19] The seven "Nuremberg Principles"[20] are reflected, for example, in the statutes of modern international criminal tribunals such as the ICTY, ICTR, and the ICC. In addition to identifying specific crimes, fair trial rights of the accused, and the existence (or not) of particular defenses, customary law also informs the modes of individual liability for criminal behavior.[21]

As a matter of customary law, serious violations of international humanitarian law constitute war crimes.[22] Furthermore, the international humanitarian law rules and principles concerning means and methods of warfare during international armed conflicts have gradually extended to civil wars.[23] Thus, customary international law criminalizes violations of the laws or customs of war whether committed in international or non-international armed conflicts.[24]

International criminal law also addresses serious violations of international human rights law. For example, international criminal law concerning crimes against humanity generally is predicated on human rights law.[25] Furthermore, at the ICC, human rights law guides the application and interpretation of law:[26] "Human rights underpins the Statute; every aspect of it, including the exercise of the jurisdiction of the Court."[27]

Judicial Decisions as a Subsidiary Source of International Criminal Law

Judicial decisions (as well as the teachings of highly qualified publicists) are useful in determining applicable rules of international law.[28] Jurisprudence is particularly helpful in defining and clarifying rules of international criminal law. In addition to defining elements of substantive crimes,[29] the case law of modern international criminal tribunals has clarified the components of different forms of individual criminal responsibility such as ordering[30] and superior responsibility.[31]

Human Dignity and Individual Criminal Responsibility

A central argument of this book is that the use of LAWS to take human life will violate human dignity. When humans delegate power for these decisions to machines, they abdicate an important part of their value as persons: their moral agency.

If, as I demonstrate in Chapters 2 and 3, human dignity is the foundation and starting point of international law, it must also be the foundation and point of departure of international criminal law.[32] From a Kantian perspective, when individuals use other persons (or society as a whole) merely as a means to their own ends, they violate human dignity,[33] and society, consequently, is justified in imposing a penalty.[34] Thus, the use of so-called criminal hate speech, for example, by self-interested politicians and other leaders is a discriminatory form of aggression that destroys the dignity of the members of the group under attack. "It creates a lesser status not only in the eyes of the group members themselves but also in the eyes of others who perceive and treat them as less than human."[35]

Accordingly, the preamble to the Rome Statute of the ICC—a significant expression of the aspirations and goals of global society—affirms "that the most serious crimes of concern to the international community must not go unpunished." Punishment for such crimes must express the international community's condemnation of the behavior and demonstrate that it will not tolerate serious violations of international humanitarian and human rights law.[36] On a more micro level, punishment counteracts the power of the criminal over the victim and seeks to restore the dignity that predated the crime.[37] Thus, international criminal law serves to protect the dignity of society and its members by holding perpetrators *fully* accountable for their misdeeds.[38] Forms of "civil responsibility," therefore, limited to fines or other kinds of economic penalties, are insufficient, by themselves, to redress these particularly egregious wrongs.[39]

Conversely, a failure to address past crimes leaves open the wounds in a community[40] as "the failure to punish implies continuity of the criminal's dominance over the victim."[41] The existence of impunity, therefore, serves as an affirmation and renewal of this loss of dignity.[42] Indeed, the goal of reducing or ending impunity, often voiced as an objective of this body of law,[43] is another dimension of the protection and restoration of human dignity.[44]

Thus, international criminal law sources often refer to the violated dignity of victims and the need to punish those responsible.[45] However, this body of law also speaks to the dignity of *perpetrators* and others allegedly responsible for crimes or the actions of subordinates.[46] Antony Duff argues that criminal trials should engage accused in a communicative enterprise. By calling them to account for the wrongs committed, society treats defendants as responsible agents and "members of the normative community of humanity."[47] In addition, mechanisms for "restorative" criminal justice, in addition to returning some measure of dignity lost to victims of crimes and their survivors, can renew the human values of decency and respect for others that perpetrators discard when they commit their offences.[48] Similarly, an emphasis on rehabilitation in sentencing decisions reflects society's belief that criminals can and should rebuild their personalities—the manifestation of their human dignity.[49]

Furthermore, international criminal law arguably preserves the human dignity of both perpetrators and victims via its (aspirational) goal of the prevention and deterrence of crime.[50] Although there is a great deal of overlap between these concepts, the two terms are not synonymous. "Deterrence" refers to the processes within criminal justice systems that result in a rational cost/benefit analysis by potential offenders who decide that the expected costs of punishment are likely to surpass the possible benefits of the crime.[51] Stated more simply, deterrence rests on the premise that the fear and pain of punishment discourages crime in potential offenders.[52] "Prevention" is a much broader, systemic concept, which, while it includes deterrence, also spans the generational processes of education, economic progress, lawmaking, and institutional development that can lead to reduction of crime.[53] If one or both processes reduce the incidence of crime, the result is the conservation of dignity.

Moreover, international criminal law supports another dimension of human dignity. As explained in Chapters 2 and 3, one facet of human dignity is the ability of persons to express their moral agency, including the capacity to fulfill their responsibilities. Members of the armed forces of states, organized armed groups, and law enforcement authorities must comply with the obligations of customary international humanitarian law and customary international human rights law, as well as international treaties.[54] International criminal law expresses and codifies the duty of individuals to assume their responsibilities under international law.[55] Consequently, courts can find individuals to be criminally liable should they fail to exercise their duties.

Therefore, a functioning system of international criminal law reinforces the social and professional expectations that commanders, combatants, and members of state security forces will take responsibility and hold themselves accountable for their actions related to war and law enforcement actions.[56] The same principle applies to members of nonstate organized armed groups.[57] Conversely, by failing to perform their duties to uphold the law, law enforcement (and military) officials can legitimize criminal conduct by others.[58]

Hence, international criminal law works to preserve the human dignity of potential perpetrators by compelling them to fulfill the responsibilities accorded to them by their governments and international law. During his closing address to the International Military Tribunal at Nuremberg, at the end of the case against the indicted organizations, British prosecutor David Maxwell Fyfe reminded the judges that, when confronted with moral problems "[g]reat captains are not automata to be weighed against a rubber stamp."[59] At a deeper level, Maxwell Fyfe was referring to the importance of moral agency.

Freedom "makes us accountable for what we do,"[60] and so moral agency would be an empty shell if it were unaccompanied by responsibility.[61] Consequently, the legal obligations of soldiers and members of security forces exist even in times of turmoil or armed conflict where they find themselves "torn between different views of right and wrong."[62] It is precisely at those moments where the values of personal autonomy and responsibility combine to strengthen human dignity.

Theories of Individual Criminal Responsibility for Unlawful Attacks with LAWS

This section continues with a discussion of the modes of individual criminal responsibility most relevant to holding perpetrators accountable for the misuse of autonomous weapon systems. It describes how the deployment of these weapons simultaneously facilitate and complicate efforts to ensure accountability for serious violations of international law and protect the value of human dignity.

Theories of Individual Criminal Responsibility for Unlawful Attacks with LAWS

Preliminarily, two general kinds of individual criminal responsibility may arise when soldiers or their commanders violate international humanitarian or international human rights law. First, "direct" responsibility arises from an individual's acts or omissions that contribute to the commission of crimes.[63] Second, "superior" or "command" responsibility emanates from the failure of military or civilian superiors to perform their duty to prevent their subordinates from committing such crimes, or the failure to fulfill the obligation to punish the perpetrators thereafter.[64] Thus, in the "Čelebići" case, the ICTY Appeals Chamber held that the superior "would be tried for failure to act in respect of the offences of his subordinates *in the perpetration of which he did not directly participate*."[65]

Moreover, each theory of individual criminal liability contains objective and subjective elements:[66] the actus reus—the physical act necessary for the offence—and the mens rea—the necessary mental element.[67] The principle of individual guilt requires that an accused can be convicted of a crime only if his or her mens rea comprises the actus reus of the crime.[68] A conviction absent mens rea would violate the presumption of innocence.[69] Thus, to convict an accused of a crime, he or she must, at a minimum, have had knowledge of the facts that made his or her conduct criminal.[70] Similarly, at the ICC conviction can occur "only if the material elements are committed with intent and knowledge."[71] This conjunctive approach requires the accused to possess a volitional element encompassing two possible situations: (1) the accused knows that his or her actions or omissions will bring about the objective elements of the crimes and undertakes such actions or omissions with the express intent to bring about the objective elements of the crime, or (2) although he or she does not have the intent to accomplish the objective elements of the crime, the accused is nonetheless aware that the consequence will occur in the ordinary course of events.[72]

Theories of Direct Responsibility

The use of LAWS for the perpetration of crimes can involve one of six modes of direct responsibility: commission, planning, ordering, instigation/inducement, aiding and abetting, or attempt.

Individual "commission" of a crime entails the physical perpetration of a crime or engendering a culpable omission in violation of criminal law.[73] The actus reus of this mode of criminal liability is that the accused participated, physically or otherwise directly, in the material elements of a crime, through positive acts or omissions, whether individually or jointly with others.[74] At the ad hoc tribunals, the requisite mens rea for commission is that the perpetrator acted with the intent to commit the crime, or with an awareness of the probability, in the sense of the substantial likelihood, that the crime would occur as a consequence of his or her conduct.[75] The Rome Statute of the ICC, however, excludes the application of the *dolus eventualis* standard, as well as the mens rea of recklessness.[76] Instead, the criminal mens rea exists if the accused means to commit the crime, or, if he or she is aware that by his or her actions or omissions, the crime will occur in the ordinary course of events.[77]

In addition, at the ICC, criminal responsibility may accrue when accused make an essential contribution to a plurality of persons acting with a common criminal purpose. The accused must be aware of his or her essential contribution and must act with the intention that the crime occur, or with the awareness that by implementing the common plan, the crime "will occur in the ordinary course of events."[78] At the ad hoc tribunals, culpable participation in a common criminal purpose is referred to as "joint criminal enterprise" and requires a significant contribution to the realization of the crime.[79]

At the ad hoc tribunals, the actus reus of "planning" requires that one or more persons design the criminal conduct constituting one or more statutory crimes that are later perpetrated.[80] It is sufficient to demonstrate that the planning was a factor substantially contributing to such criminal conduct.[81] The mens rea for this mode of responsibility is the intent to plan the commission of a crime or, at a minimum, the awareness of a substantial likelihood that a crime will be committed in the execution of the acts or omissions planned.[82]

Responsibility under the mode of "ordering" ensues when a person in a position of authority orders an act or omission with the awareness of the substantial likelihood that a crime will be committed in execution of that order, and, if the person receiving the order subsequently commits the crime.[83] Orders need not take a particular form, and the existence of orders may be established using circumstantial evidence.[84] Liability ensues if the evidence demonstrates that the order substantially contributed to the perpetrator's criminal conduct.[85]

The modes of liability of soliciting and inducing fall into the broader category of "instigation" "or "prompting another to commit a crime," in the sense that they refer to conduct by which a person influences another to commit a crime.[86] The instigating acts or omissions must clearly contribute to the conduct of the persons who subsequently commit the crimes.[87] Proof must also exist that the defendant intended to provoke or induce the commission of the crime, or was aware of the substantial likelihood that the commission of a crime would be a probable consequence of his or her acts.[88]

In recent years, the requirements of "aiding and abetting" have been a contested area of international criminal law. At the ICTY, Appeals Chambers have divided over the question whether this mode of criminal responsibility requires that assistance to perpetrators be "specifically directed" to the execution of specific crimes. In *Prosecutor v. Momčilo Perisić*, one chamber held that specific direction is an element of the actus reus of aiding and abetting.[89] Subsequently, however, a differently constituted chamber emphatically and "unequivocally" rejected the *Perisić* approach.[90] In *Prosecutor v. Šainović, et al.*, the majority held that, under customary international law, the actus reus of aiding and abetting is "practical assistance, encouragement, or moral support which has a substantial effect on the perpetration of the crime."[91] The mens rea is the knowledge that the acts assist the commission of the crime.[92] Likewise, at the Special Court for Sierra Leone, the Appeals Chamber also rejected any "specific direction" requirement as part of the actus reus of aiding and abetting.[93] Thus, it appears that (for now) the actus reus of aiding and abetting does not contain a "specific direction" component.

The Rome Statute of the ICC includes "attempt" as one mode of individual criminal responsibility.[94] An "attempt" occurs with the commencement of execution of a crime within the court's jurisdiction "by means of a substantial step."[95] The statutory term "substantial step" requires that the perpetrator's conduct reach a more definite and concrete stage beyond mere preparatory acts.[96] The adequacy of this conduct requires that, in the ordinary course of events, the accused's conduct would have resulted in the completion of the crime, had circumstances outside the accused's control not intervened.[97] The mens rea or *dolus* that embodies an attempt is the same as the mens rea that embodies the consummated act.[98]

The Theory of Superior Responsibility

When crimes occur because of the misuse of LAWS, the theory of superior responsibility also may be appropriate to hold commanders accountable. The superior-subordinate relationship lies at the heart of the doctrine of a commander's liability for the crimes committed by his or her subordinates. The role of commanders is decisive,[99] and it is the position of command over subordinates and the power to control their actions (and comply with international law) that form the legal basis for the superior's duty to act, and for his or her corollary liability for a failure to do so.[100] As a tenet of customary international law, the doctrine of superior responsibility applies to both international and non-international armed conflicts.[101]

In general terms, pursuant to the statute and jurisprudence of the ad hoc tribunals, a military or civilian superior may be held accountable if the superior knew or had reason to know that his or her subordinates were committing or about to commit criminal acts and failed to take necessary and reasonable measures to prevent the crimes or to punish the perpetrators.[102] The Rome Statute of the ICC alters the evidentiary thresholds for holding civilian and military commanders accountable under the theory of superior responsibility. In addition to the three elements found in the law of the ad hoc tribunals, prosecutors at the ICC must establish that the crimes committed by subordinates occurred as a result of the superior's "failure to exercise control properly over such forces."[103] In short, it is necessary to prove that the superior's omission increased the risk of the commission of the crimes charged.[104]

The Superior-Subordinate Relationship

A superior-subordinate relationship exists when a superior exercises effective control over his or her subordinates, that is, when he or she has the material ability to prevent or punish their acts.[105] Factors indicative of an accused's position of authority and effective control include the official position he or she held; his or her capacity to issue orders, whether de jure or de facto; the procedure for appointment; the position of the accused within the military or political structure; and the actual tasks that he or she performed.[106] The indicators of effective control are more a matter of evidence than of substantive law and depend on the specific circumstances of each case.[107] More than one superior may be held responsible for failure to prevent or punish crimes committed by a subordinate, regardless of whether the subordinate is immediately answerable to the superior or more distantly under his or her command.[108]

The Superior's Knowledge of the Criminal Acts of His or Her Subordinates

A superior's mens rea, that is, his or her knowledge that subordinates were about to commit or had committed crimes, may be actual knowledge or the availability of "sufficiently alarming" information that would put the superior on notice of these events.[109] Such knowledge may be presumed if the superior had the means to obtain the knowledge but deliberately refrained from doing so.[110] An assessment of the mental element (knowledge) required for superior responsibility must be performed in the specific circumstances of each case, "taking into account the specific situation of the superior concerned at the time in question."[111]

At the ICC, instead of requiring proof that the superior "had reason to know" that his or her forces were committing or had committed crimes, the court's "knowledge" standard for military commanders compels prosecutors to establish that he or she "should have known" about such crimes.[112] This standard requires the commander "to ha[ve] merely been negligent in failing to acquire knowledge" of subordinates' unlawful conduct.[113] The "knowledge" requirement for demonstrating liability of civilian superiors is higher: "the superior either knew, *or consciously disregarded* information which clearly indicated that the subordinates were committing or about to commit such crimes."[114]

Necessary and Reasonable Measures to Prevent the Crimes or Punish the Perpetrators

"Necessary" measures are the measures appropriate for the superior to discharge his or her obligation (showing that the superior genuinely tried to prevent or punish) and "reasonable" measures are those reasonably falling within the material powers of the superior.[115] A superior will be held responsible if he or she failed to take such measures that are within the superior's material ability and the superior's explicit legal capacity to do so is immaterial provided that he or she had the material ability to act.[116]

"The determination of what constitutes 'necessary and reasonable measures' is not a matter of substantive law but of fact, to be determined on a case-by-case basis."[117] This assessment depends on the superior's level of effective control over his or her subordinate(s).[118] Depending on the circumstances of the case, "necessary and reasonable" measures can include carrying out an investigation, providing information in a superior's possession to the proper administrative or prosecutorial authorities, issuing orders aimed at bringing unlawful conduct of subordinates in compliance with the international humanitarian law and securing the implementation of these orders, expressing criticism of criminal activity, imposing disciplinary measures against the commission of crimes, reporting the matter to the competent authorities, and insisting before superior authorities that immediate action be taken.[119]

Application of the Theories of Individual Criminal Responsibility to the Design and Use of LAWS

Application of Theories of Direct Responsibility

In cases involving deliberate, unlawful attacks with the use of LAWS, proof of a commander's individual criminal responsibility under the direct modes, inter alia, of commission, planning, and ordering will be relatively simple.

For example, if, during armed conflict, a tactical commander[120] intentionally employs a LAWS in circumstances where the system's capabilities for compliance with international humanitarian law are inadequate (such as within a densely populated urban area where civilians are known to be present), and death and injuries to civilians occur, that commander is culpable for the commission of a war crime.[121]

In addition, as mentioned above, at the ICC, under the mode of "commission," criminal responsibility may accrue when the accused makes an essential contribution to a plurality of persons acting with a common criminal purpose.[122] Thus, a commander can make an essential contribution to a common criminal design by, for example, by providing a LAWS for use in the perpetration of crimes.

Similarly, if a tactical commander orders or plans the use of a LAWS in similar circumstances, with knowledge that the system's capabilities for international humanitarian law compliance are inadequate, and damage to civilian objects or injuries to civilians subsequently occurs, he or she incurs liability under these theories of responsibility.

Moreover, under the "reasonable commander" standard enunciated in international criminal law jurisprudence,[123] individual criminal responsibility should accrue when commanders and operators of LAWS clearly fail to consider relevant elements of the targeting rules or when they disregard the necessity for human-machine interdependence for complex military tasks, or both, and serious violations of international law consequently occur. More limited autonomous technology, for example, will signal a demand for greater input of human judgment (as well as communication and accountability) during the mission. Conversely, ignorance of a system's capabilities cannot permit the avoidance of accountability. This principle does not imply a new, onerous duty for professional commanders: "As you deploy weapons as a commander, you're accountable. . . . There's no difference with autonomous weapon systems. So commanders won't take their reliability as a matter of trust. So there is no 'accountability gap.'"[124] Therefore, to avoid criminal culpability, a sound understanding of the function, capabilities, and limitations of the semi-autonomous and autonomous weapon technologies available to armed forces will become a prerequisite for command of modern military units that operate LAWS.[125]

These hypothetical scenarios represent relatively clear-cut examples where findings of direct criminal responsibility for employing LAWS to carry out unlawful attacks are possible. More complex issues arise, however, when the tactical commander conducts him- or herself reasonably in the selection of potential targets, in the choice of an appropriate autonomous weapon system, as well as in the programming of the system, yet the weapon nevertheless attacks civilians or performs outside the confines of international humanitarian or human rights law.[126] Given the lack of any criminal intent on his or her part, no criminal culpability accrues to the field commander.[127] Thus, the "close cases" involving hard moral, legal, and military choices by military commanders will not easily produce the culpable mens rea required for individual criminal responsibility.

In addition, the development of "moral remoteness" on account of increased reliance on computerized systems can create challenges to the establishment of criminal intent in military commanders. The tendency for human beings to depend on their computers at moments of stressful decision making can lead to "moral buffering" and a reduced sense of responsibility for the consequences of those decisions.[128] "Too much trust can lead to disastrous consequences,"[129] just as a skeptical attitude toward technology does not permit full exploitation of modern weapon systems.

As artificial intelligence computer software for LAWS improves, the risk increases that, subjectively, commanders will transfer their accountability for stressful decisions to the computer.[130] This risk will be particularly high if states follow an "appropriate level of human judgment" or other semantic standard for human interaction with lethal autonomous weapon systems as commanders and operators can "hide" behind such designated "levels" rather than taking responsibility for ensuring sufficient human oversight of the weapon in specific circumstances. That moral shift confuses efforts to determine the existence of a criminal mens rea, and, consequently, a legal basis for individual responsibility.[131]

An implied or express delegation of responsibility for decisions to take human life from a human superior to the artificial intelligence software of a LAWS reduces the human dignity of the superior as well as the victim of unlawful conduct. The superior forfeits his or her moral and professional accountability for actions, not to mention forfeiting his or her conscience. In *Bloody Constraint: War and Chivalry in Shakespeare*, Theodor Meron illustrates how this form of human reflection works as a powerful instrument for ensuring accountability, when we pay attention to it.[132] The victim, of course, loses the possibility of redress for the wrong suffered. Preservation of accountability—and human dignity—therefore, require human-machine interdependence for decisions implicating complex or contradictory values.

As the speed of autonomous weapon technologies increases, however, opportunities for interdependence will decline while, in parallel, perceptions of how a "reasonable commander" should perform in particular circumstances will change, and, perhaps paradoxically, may become more demanding. Computer technologies, especially those "linked to virtual information resources, are reshaping legal obligations related to overall attack planning."[133] For example, during proportionality assessments, many Western militaries utilize sophisticated "collateral damage modeling algorithms," which estimate anticipated damage by incorporating data on weapon guidance systems.[134] The scope of what is legally feasible has been altered by what is now operationally *required.*[135]

These scenarios will produce accountability dichotomies rather than "accountability gaps." The employment of interdependent LAWS, however, can reduce these contradictions by permitting (if not requiring) greater human-machine teamwork. For example, when systems are interdependent, it will be unreasonable for commanders to not consider whether a particular autonomous weapon system may provide a more discriminate or proportionate option when planning and executing attacks.

Application of Superior Responsibility

In certain scenarios, the theory of superior responsibility may be appropriate to hold military commanders and civilian superiors responsible for failing to prevent or punish crimes perpetrated with LAWS. For example, if a commander at the operational level becomes aware that a subordinate officer at the tactical level is using LAWS to perpetrate unlawful attacks, the operational commander has a duty to prevent further misconduct and punish his or her subordinate.[136] As long as evidence exists demonstrating the three essential elements of a commander's effective control over subordinates who commit crimes, the commander's knowledge, and a failure to take necessary and reasonable measures to prevent or repress[137] further crimes and punish the perpetrators, then criminal liability should ensue.

However, the advances in technology may require reassessments of the "knowledge" and "reasonable measures" pillars of superior responsibility. With respect to the "knowledge" element, at first blush, commanders of forces operating LAWS will not easily convince a court that they were unaware that their subordinates operated autonomous weapon systems unlawfully.[138] Any state or organized armed group with the resources and ability to field LAWS will also have the means and the communications technology to constantly monitor how these weapons are used. Furthermore, any competent commander utilizes all possible methods to observe the progress and operations of his or her subordinate units.[139] Indeed, to ensure compliance with international law, this full-time and real-time monitoring capability should be an obligatory aspect of every LAWS at the design and procurement stage.[140]

The availability of electronic records also will minimize the challenge that physical or temporal "remoteness" poses to the accountability of superiors.[141] Modern communications increasingly provide superiors with real-or-nearly-real-time access to circumstances and events, including combat occurring far from command centers and headquarters.[142] Furthermore, the internet and social media technology create virtual links between frontline areas and all parts of the world. These connections, combined with electronic records of commanders' decision-making processes, "shorten" the physical and temporal distances between a superior and events in the battlespace and reveal much about a superior's mental state. This evidence of the superior's intent and knowledge is far more relevant to individual criminal responsibility analysis than are concerns about temporal or geographic "remoteness."[143]

However, the vast and overwhelming amounts of data "available" to commanders will not guarantee a superior's actual or constructive knowledge of particular information concerning the conduct of his or her subordinates.[144] The ability of modern technology to acquire larger and larger amounts of data can, at times, compound the "fog of war."[145] As Professor Cummings (an engineer and former fighter pilot) has observed: "command and control technology have outpaced human reasoning capabilities and traditional command structures."[146] Thus, as we saw above in the section on direct theories of individual criminal responsibility, advances in technology may make it more difficult for commanders to be accountable for the misconduct of their subordinates.

The scope of "necessary and reasonable measures" to prevent further crimes and punish the subordinates involved in misconduct may vary when LAWS are used to carry out unlawful attacks. For example, the use of swarm technology will undoubtedly increase the tempo of military engagements.[147] The faster pace of combat—and unlawful conduct—will reduce a superior's opportunities to prevent crimes.

However, unlike human soldiers, it is possible to design LAWS so that they can be switched off.[148] Thus, measures available to a commander to prevent or repress unlawful attacks carried out with LAWS should include efforts to electronically deactivate the machines. Indeed, part of the procurement process, including legal reviews of new weapon technologies conducted pursuant to article 36 of API, should include a requirement for an "override" mechanism permitting superiors to stop their subordinates' misuse of LAWS by taking control of, or shutting down, the machines. Use of override systems will constitute "necessary and reasonable" measures to repress further unlawful conduct, and a commander's failure to make use of such mechanisms should result in criminal liability.

As Christof Heyns observed, however, "the power to override may in reality be limited because the decision-making processes of robots are often measured in nanoseconds and the information basis of those decisions may not be practically accessible to the supervisor. In such circumstances, humans are de facto out of the loop."[149] Nonetheless, that scenario still will leave the commander with the duty to deactivate or override a LAWS as soon as practicable after becoming aware of its misuse.

Human Dignity and Individual Criminal Responsibility in the Hard Cases

As outlined in the proceeding sections, situations will arise where establishment of individual criminal responsibility for events involving LAWS will be very difficult if not impossible. Geoffrey Corn has argued that, in situations where no fault for civilian injury or damage lies with soldier-operators, security forces, or commanders operating LAWS, the "Compliance Commander," that is, the officer in charge of the procurement process of the new autonomous weapon system, should bear criminal responsibility for the "misconduct" of the LAWS.[150] In Corn's view, standards for validation of new autonomous weapon systems should be high enough to ensure their consistent functioning within their foreseen use and capacity. When the "Compliance Commander" approves the new weapon system, the argument continues, he or she takes responsibility for ensuring that these standards have been met, and for failures that occur when the system does not operate according to these standards.[151]

Lex ferenda criminal responsibility for compliance commanders may be appropriate if evidence exists that he or she intentionally and knowingly approved the procurement of a flawed LAWS, or did so recklessly without first validating the systems capabilities, all possible failsafe mechanisms, all subsystems, and so on. Similarly, designers who deliberately create autonomous weapon systems that will fail to comply with international law should incur criminal liability.

However, if no such evidence of intentional malfeasance exists, there would appear to be no basis—absent a "strict criminal liability"[152] standard—for penal responsibility for the compliance commander or the weapon designer. Some commentators argue that strict criminal liability violates international human rights norms such as the rights to a fair trial, in particular the presumption of innocence.[153] Indeed, the ICTY Appeals Chamber implicitly rejected the use of strict criminal liability when it observed that the principle of individual criminal responsibility "requires that fundamental characteristics of a war crime be mirrored in the perpetrator's mind."[154]

Furthermore, the mens rea requirement common to criminal law makes an important contribution to the fulfillment of human dignity. Implicit in the requirement that conduct, to be "criminal," must be intentional is the importance that humans develop powers of self-restraint.[155] Part of moral agency is the ability to make independent, moral judgments about one's own conduct. Expansion of the strict liability doctrine to include conduct during armed conflict or civil strife will have the perverse result of undermining the sense of personal accountability that lies at the heart of international humanitarian and human rights law. "[P]rinciples of fundamental justice,"[156] as well as human dignity, therefore, militate against the application of a strict liability criminal standard to serious violations of international law.

Under the *lex lata*, therefore, cases will arise where assignment of individual criminal responsibility is impossible in the face of allegations of unlawful use of LAWS. For the reasons described at the start of this chapter, this "accountability gap"[157] is an affront to the dignity of victims of serious international crimes. To determine whether this accountability gap and loss of dignity is tolerable in a modern society, we must consider the consequences for the dignity interests of potential accused, that is, persons who design, procure, use, and program LAWS, if society lowers the standards for liability for crimes perpetrated with these weapons.

Preliminarily, in the face of insufficient evidence of mens rea or other elements of crimes, "the simplest way to overcome allegations of impunity is to over-extend individual responsibility."[158] Nevertheless, as discussed above in the context of "strict liability," measures that lower the bar for criminal liability increase the risk that the accused will be unable to fully exercise their rights, in particular the presumption of innocence.[159] Because of the potential for loss of liberty upon conviction, an accused "has at stake an interest of transcending value."[160] Thus, laws and legal proceedings that do not carefully protect the rights of accused are, by definition, unfair, and the conviction of innocents are gross violations of their dignity.[161]

In essence, when we respect important criminal law principles, such as *nullum crimen, nulla poena sine lege*, we tacitly acknowledge the impossibility that criminal law today will meet every possible future contingency[162] and accept that some individuals will not be held accountable for aberrant behavior.[163] That helps to explain why no democratic system of justice is 100 percent effective and why well-documented *absences* of criminal responsibility inevitably arise in modern warfare.[164] Without evidence of culpable mens rea for the field commander, the programmer, the compliance commander, or the designer, and absent a "strict criminal liability" standard, an "unlawful attack" perpetrated with the use of a LAWS will be analogous to other kinds of military incidents where there is no human criminal responsibility. A limited "accountability gap" is the price society pays to avoid a substantial "dignity gap."

The Design of LAWS and Accountability

Previously in this chapter I described how a functioning system of international criminal law protects the human dignity of persons who participate in armed conflict or law enforcement situations. The professional ethos of responsibility and accountability for one's actions—essential qualities of superiors in modern militaries[165]—helps to preserve the dignity of all actors in times of war and civil strife. Concurrently, international criminal law assists society to reaffirm and readjust the rights of its members following violations of international law.[166] The increasing use of LAWS presents advantages as well as challenges to systems of criminal responsibility.

Responsibility—in the sense of accountability for errors and criminal conduct—is also a development and design challenge.[167] High testing and validation standards should detect negligent or intentional "mis-programming" of component systems of autonomous weapon by computer programmers and designers of these weapon systems. Detection and correction of such mistakes before the LAWS reach the battlespace reduce concerns about how to hold scientists, engineers, computer programmers, and others accountable when the autonomous weapons systems that they help to design and manufacture subsequently are employed in violation of international law.

Once LAWS are deployed to the field, an interdependent design of lethal autonomous weapon systems advances efforts at accountability on two dimensions. First, "building in" human-machine teamwork for complex decisions forces human commanders and operators to conserve, rather than abdicate, their own sense of moral and legal responsibility and accountability for the results of attacks using these weapons. In doing so, it permits the development and use of "tactical patience" so that commanders may avoid mistakes and misconduct.[168] In addition, an interdependent design provides more opportunities for soldiers and commanders to adjust the behavior of autonomous technologies, including, for example, the ability to modify artificial intelligence software.[169]

Second, the violent and chaotic conditions of armed conflict and civil strife often reduce the quality and effectiveness of legal reviews of the conduct of soldiers and law enforcement personnel.[170] An interdependent design, however, increases the possibility that a functioning system of international criminal justice will hold accountable those commanders or operators who use LAWS for the commission of crimes. Moreover, situations arise, however, where judicial intervention is necessary while conflict is ongoing.[171] Absent an interdependent design, high-speed LAWS further limit the possibility for courts and lawyers to review compliance with international humanitarian law (and international human rights law) during hostilities.

A slower, interdependent design that permits human-machine teamwork will produce opportunities for more effective legal reviews of the use of force during conflict or civil strife and provide more opportunities for intervention when necessary. If legal interventions are effective, fewer violations of international law should occur, and, when they do, international criminal law mechanisms will be more successful.

Regardless of whether legal reviews occur during or subsequent to events, the electronic and virtual records of activities of LAWS should increase the accuracy and fairness of the accountability process. Although the location of proof—particularly of mens rea—always represents a challenge for prosecutors, one advantage of the sophisticated technology found in LAWS is that the systems can be designed to leave an electronic "footprint" of important decisions by commanders and programmers.[172] The more interdependent the weapon system's design, the larger the footprint. Thus, although a review may occur after the fact, an interdependent design facilitates the contemporaneous documentation of decisions and events that may constitute violations of international law.

To ensure compliance with international law, designers of LAWS must include a subsystem of electronic recording of commanders' operational and targeting decisions such as: (1) identity of target(s), (2) anticipated location of moving targets, (3), anticipated civilian injuries, (4) anticipated damage to civilian objects, (5) description of anticipated military advantage offered by neutralization of target, (6) precautionary measures (if any) taken to avoid civilian injuries and damage to civilian objects, (7) foreseeable capacities of the LAWS selected for use, and so on.[173] In addition to the evidentiary trail produced by such electronic records, the creation of an obligatory record of human decisions and evaluations of international legal obligations—and the possibility of accountability—will focus the minds of field commanders and law enforcement officers so as to avoid criminal conduct.

Decisions about design, therefore, are directly related to future findings of individual criminal responsibility for misdeeds committed with LAWS. The preservation of human dignity is the value that runs from the design phase of the weapon systems through to criminal prosecutions and other accountability mechanisms. The use of an interdependent design serves to protect and enhance the dignity of the users of these LAWS as well as that of the victims of their misuse.

* * *

"Combat involves both lawful and unlawful killing, injury, and destruction."[174] When armed forces, state security forces, and organized armed groups employ LAWS, an effective international criminal law structure ensures that (most) operators of these systems will fulfill their independent legal duties, and, therefore, preserve their dignity. Similarly, when crimes do occur, a functioning system of international criminal law serves to restore, to some degree, the dignity of victims and, possibly, that of the alleged perpetrators as well. Superiors and operators of LAWS, therefore, must be held accountable—to the greatest extent possible—if they use these machines intentionally or recklessly to commit serious violations of international humanitarian law or international human rights law. Given the different "dignity interests" at stake, limited situations where individual criminal responsibility is absent are tolerable, if not by public opinion, at least by international law.

Thus, the preservation of human dignity—for both potential and actual perpetrators as well as for victims—is an intrinsic part of international criminal law. The discussion in this chapter has demonstrated that the development and use of LAWS will not result in a dramatic new "accountability gap" for serious violations of international law. Indeed, thanks to the ability of advanced electronic technology to record the behavior of humans and weapons, employment of autonomous technologies may provide new evidentiary avenues for determining the individual criminal responsibility of operators and commanders. Nevertheless, this advance in accountability can be sustained only as long as interdependent designs for LAWS are the standard. As the speed of LAWS increases, however, and human-machine interdependence declines, it will be more difficult to use the value and process of accountability to protect the human dignity of combatants and victims of crimes.

CHAPTER 7

Lethal Autonomous Weapon Systems and the Responsibility of States and Arms Manufacturers

The introduction of LAWS into modern battlespace(s) creates new facts, scenarios, ideas, and questions in international life. In Chapters 4, 5, and 6, we saw that, at least in theory, these new weapons can be used in compliance with the treaty and customary rules of international humanitarian and human rights law and, at times, may improve the effectiveness of international criminal law. However, the possibility that states can use LAWS consistently with the rules of international law does *not* answer the question whether the use of such weapons is lawful; more general legal principles have to be consulted.[1]

In Chapter 2, I argued that the legal duty to protect human dignity is a foundational responsibility of states imposed by the United Nations Charter.[2] This chapter discusses primary and secondary rules of state responsibility relevant to the development and use of LAWS. Primary rules are those that define the content of the international obligations whose breach gives rise to responsibility. Secondary rules explain the conditions under international law where states are considered responsible for wrongful acts or omissions and the resulting legal consequences.[3]

Thus, an essential question is how nations use the concept of human dignity to guide the application of (international) legal rules to their LAWS. As the government of Ghana observed in 2015: "Our ultimate objective as States remains the preservation of human dignity and respect for basic sanctity of humanity at all times and, most especially, during armed conflicts. The laws of war must in this regard remain at the forefront of all our efforts and ahead of technological developments. Technology must not be allowed to overtake our commitment to these goals."[4]

Yet, in Chapter 3, I explained that the inevitable velocity of autonomous military engagements will obstruct the development of sound human judgment that arises from opportunities for reflection on questions and decisions involving the taking of human life. This dynamic will violate human dignity as the ability of humans to fully develop their moral agency—including the capacity to respect the rights of others—will inevitably diminish. Absent regulation, as national armed forces and police increasingly employ LAWS, a new, counterintuitive kind of "state accountability gap" emerges. I use the term "counterintuitive" because, by definition, the state responsibility regime normally facilitates only *interstate* accountability on the basis of positive legal rules.[5] Without an interdependent design that permits human involvement in decisions to use lethal force, the "victims" over time will be the *users and operators* of the weapons in addition to their targets.[6] This result will occur even when the artificial intelligence software directing the weapons "follows" the rules of international law.

The responsibility of states for the development and use of LAWS is important for another, related reason. As explained in Chapter 6, judgments about individual accountability, for example, findings of criminal responsibility for misuse of autonomous weapons, will be complex and difficult for most cases absent clear proof of the individual's intent to commit or contribute to crimes, or recklessness in committing or contributing to them. The easy cases will occupy the extremes, but most allegations of misconduct will fall within the gray area dominated by the fog of war, civil strife, terrorist activities, and the unforeseen reactions of artificial intelligence software to changing circumstances. Clarity and power of rules of state responsibility, as well as rules for nonstate actors such as arms manufacturers, therefore, are necessary to complement the processes of individual criminal responsibility, and, hopefully, to set standards for accountability that reduce the likelihood of violations of international law.

Thus, this chapter has two goals: (1) to explain how the concept of human dignity underlies the international legal responsibility of states to apply these theories to the design, development, and use of LAWS; and (2) to propose theories of legal responsibility for states and arms manufacturers for damage and injuries caused by LAWS. I argue that three mechanisms for attributing responsibility in international environmental law—the preventive principle, the precautionary principle, and the polluter-pays principle—can, by analogy, serve to determine responsibility for harm resulting from LAWS.

The Responsibility of States with Respect to Human Dignity and LAWS

The Duty of States to Protect Human Dignity

In Chapter 2, "Human Dignity and Its Role in International Law," I discussed the Charter-based obligation of United Nations member states to promote and protect human dignity, as well as the duty under customary law to (at a minimum) commit themselves to this task.[7] This section describes the three general mechanisms by which states can breach this duty: (1) through the affirmative act of violating international humanitarian law and international human rights law via the use of LAWS, (2) by producing and employing LAWS that do not permit human involvement in decisions involving the taking of human life, and (3) by failing to prevent the use of such LAWS by state and nonstate actors (i.e., the failure to exercise due diligence).

Affirmative Acts

International courts have defined the affirmative responsibility of states to protect the dignity and rights of their citizens as well as other persons. In its judgment in the case of *Democratic Republic of Congo (DRC) v. Uganda*, the International Court of Justice ruled that Uganda was "internationally responsible" for violations of international human rights law and international humanitarian law committed by members of its armed forces in the DRC, including a failure to comply with its obligations as an occupying power.[8] In addition, Uganda failed to fulfill its obligation to prosecute those responsible for grave breaches of international humanitarian law.[9] The international conventions violated by Uganda oblige states to conduct their relations in accordance with civilized behavior and modern values, *including respect for human dignity*.[10] Consistent with the principles of state responsibility in international law, Uganda had a duty to make full reparations to the DRC for the injuries caused by its conduct.[11]

Similarly, in the seminal case *Velásquez Rodriguez v. Honduras*, the Inter-American Court of Human Rights found that Honduras was responsible for the enforced disappearance of Manfredo Velásquez in 1981. The court held that the enforced disappearance of persons constituted a multiple and continuous breach of obligations of state parties to the American Convention of Human Rights.[12] The court noted that this practice had already received "world attention" from the United Nations and the Organization of American States as well as the Inter-American system of human rights.[13] Illustrating how the duty to protect human dignity limits the prerogative of sovereignty, the court concluded that "the power of the State is not unlimited, nor may the State resort to any means to attain its ends. The State is subject to law and morality. *Disrespect for human dignity cannot serve as the basis for any State action*."[14]

More recently, the European Court of Human Rights concluded that the practice by the Central Intelligence Agency (CIA) and European states of secret, incommunicado detention of persons violated the right to be free from arbitrary detention enshrined in the European Convention for the Protection of Human Rights and Fundamental Freedoms.[15] In addition, the court ruled that this practice also breached the state's duty not to interfere with the right to private and family life, which protects the right to personal development as well as the right to develop relationships with other human beings and the outside world.[16] Thus, states should not treat persons "*in a way that causes a loss of dignity*" as "the very essence of the Convention is respect for human dignity and human freedom."[17] When states violate these duties, they incur responsibility to redress their acts and omissions.[18]

These judgments confirm that one of the principal concerns of the contemporary international legal system is state protection of the human rights and dignity of every individual.[19] Accordingly, when states deliberately employ LAWS in the commission of serious violations of international law, they will be in affirmative breach of their international legal obligations.

Failure to Exercise Due Diligence

In addition to affirmative acts that violate human dignity, a failure to exercise due diligence in the design, procurement, and use of LAWS breaches the obligation to protect the dignity of individuals. The exercise of due diligence encompasses the reasonable preventive and precautionary measures that a well-administered government can be expected to exercise under similar circumstances.[20] For example, in the so-called *Iran Hostages Case*, the International Court of Justice ruled that Iran failed to perform its obligation to protect the premises, staff, and archives of the U.S. Embassy and consulates in Iran during the 1979 revolution.[21] These failures led to, inter alia, breaches of article 29 of the Vienna Convention on Diplomatic Relations,[22] which prohibits the arrest or detention of diplomatic agents "and any attack on his person, freedom *or dignity*"[23] as well as breaches of the principles of the United Nations Charter.[24]

The failure-to-exercise-due-diligence basis for state responsibility, however, provides a weaker theoretical basis for accountability than positive breaches of international rules. The objective analysis required by the due diligence doctrine creates greater intellectual space for states to test the boundaries of the legality (and illegality) of LAWS.[25] Nevertheless, the creation of due diligence obligations provides additional guidance for states and nonstate actors who develop and use this technology. In addition, the due diligence requirement provides an interpretive framework for assessing responsibility and compensation.

Indeed, international legal decisions have (implicitly or explicitly) recognized a duty of states to exercise due diligence and prevent harm with respect to the design, manufacture, and use of weapons. For example, in the so-called *Alabama* case, an arbitral tribunal determined that Great Britain did not exercise due diligence in the performance of neutral obligations when it failed to prevent the construction and armament of a warship intended for use by the Confederacy against Union forces during the American Civil War.[26] Moreover, in the *Corfu Channel* case, the International Court of Justice held that Albania was responsible for the deaths of U.K. sailors and damage to warships because it failed to notify the shipping industry of the existence of a new minefield in Albanian waters, and to notify the warships approaching the minefields of the imminent danger.[27] "In fact, nothing was attempted by the Albanian authorities to prevent the disaster."[28] This failure to prevent harm incurred the international responsibility of Albania.[29]

Furthermore, in 1996, the U.S. government agreed to pay nearly 132 million U.S. dollars to the government of Iran as compensation for the 1988 shoot-down of an Iranian passenger plane by a U.S. warship operating in the Strait of Hormuz.[30] The inadequate design of the ship's defense systems was an important contributing factor to the tragedy. The Aegis air and missile defense system on board the ship functioned as intended. However, the design of the human-machine interface did not permit certain crucial information at the time (whether the approaching plane was ascending or descending) to be displayed on the system's display console. Confusion about this matter contributed to the erroneous belief by the sailors on board the ship that the "target" was a military aircraft.[31]

Based on the "human dignity paradigm" that I have developed in this book, we can ascertain a nonexhaustive list of due diligence responsibilities of states vis-à-vis the development and use of LAWS. The absence of these due diligence measures encourages the delegation of human responsibility to computers for decisions to take human life during armed conflict and in periods of civil unrest. It limits the capacity of the individual to develop his or her own capacities for judgment and moral agency. Thus, when states fail to ensure compliance with one or more of these obligations by their actors,[32] they increase the risk that autonomous weapon systems will operate in ways that undermine the dignity of individuals, both the victims of attacks *and* the users and operators themselves.[33] All law depends on the fundamental principle of the dignity and worth of the human person.[34] If "the ultimate objective" of state responsibility is the preservation of human dignity, states cannot ignore their legal responsibility to control the development and use of LAWS. The next section describes several interpretive mechanisms for assessing the responsibility of states and arms manufacturers for harm caused by LAWS.

Theories of Responsibility for States and Arms Manufacturers for Harm Caused by LAWS

States incur international responsibility by acts imputable to them that violate a rule or rules of international law.[35] Today, states recognize that their responsibilities under international law extend to the use of LAWS by their actors.[36] As explored in more detail in the above section on state responsibility and human dignity, when state behavior constitutes deliberate unlawful acts or omissions, determination of state responsibility should be relatively straightforward.[37] The same should be true in situations of intentional, illegal use of LAWS. Nevertheless, owing to the complexity of these systems, situations will arise where autonomous weapons cause serious damage to life and property, yet fault—or even causation—cannot be assigned precisely.

Furthermore, harm from LAWS may arise, apart from the state, owing to misconduct or negligence of the arms manufacturer who produced the system. The status of nonstate actors such as corporations varies under international law.[38] For example, "persons," nongovernmental organizations, and groups of individuals may have "victim" status before the European Court of Human Right (ECtHR).[39] The European Court of Human Rights interprets the word "person" to include legal persons such as corporations.[40] Generally, however, under international law, the conduct of private enterprises is not attributable to states.[41]

At present, however, neither international humanitarian law, international human rights law, nor international criminal law[42] contains specific (primary or secondary) rules defining responsibility of private enterprises for harm caused by weapons manufactured by them. In particular circumstances, however, secondary rules may permit the attribution of responsibility for the (mis)conduct of private enterprises to states. For example, states cannot abdicate their international responsibilities to private enterprises. Hence, nations cannot circumvent the rules of state responsibility by transferring powers normally exercised by state officials, or by acquiescing the assumption of such functions, to private entities.[43] Similarly, if a person or group of persons acts under the instructions or control of a state, the conduct of the individual or group is considered an act of the state.[44]

Broad guidelines and other forms of "soft law" encourage principled and conscientious behavior. For example, the United Nations "Guiding Principles on Business and Human Rights" contains "principles" that explain what corporations should do to respect and protect human rights, including performing "human rights due diligence."[45] States should ensure that those affected by corporate failures have access to an effective remedy.[46] Nonetheless, these protocols and frameworks do not constitute legal rules or create legal duties.

A (future) system of accountability for nonstate actors is crucial because civilian entities play a leadership role in the development of autonomous systems.[47] Indeed, private entities may develop autonomous technologies for very benign reasons, only to see them "reincarnated" on the battlefield.[48]

To close these "gaps" in state and corporate responsibility, this section explores possible options for holding states and weapons manufacturers accountable in these hard cases. By analogy, I use three principles from international environmental law as potential mechanisms for holding states and corporations responsible for injury and damage caused by autonomous weapon systems: the preventive principle, the precautionary principle, and the polluter-pays principle.

The Preventive Principle

Where activity may cause significant harm to the environment, the international environmental law principle of prevention[49] obliges parties to prevent, or at least mitigate, the damage.[50] For example, the "ultimate objective" of the 1992 United Nations Framework Convention on Climate Change is to achieve "stabilization of greenhouse gas concentrations in the atmosphere at a level that would *prevent* dangerous anthropogenic interference with the climate system."[51] Similarly, one of the commitments in the convention is for state parties to cooperate in the development and diffusion of technology and practices that control, reduce, or prevent emissions of greenhouse gases resulting from human behavior.[52]

When activities in one state may impact the territory of others, states bear a duty of prevention of harm to other states and not merely of reparation for the harm caused.[53] Thus, the obligation to prevent requires vigilance and preventive action to be taken *before* damage has actually occurred,[54] and to respond appropriately when damage does occur.[55]

The duty to prevent environmental harm includes an obligation to act with due diligence with respect to all activities performed by a party, or that take place under its jurisdiction and control.[56] Due diligence does not require a guarantee of no harm, but it demands the best possible efforts by states.[57] As the risk level of activities rises, so will the expected amount of due diligence.[58] Indeed, "*activities which may be considered ultra-hazardous* require a much higher standard of care in designing policies and a much higher degree of vigor on the part of the State to enforce them."[59] Twenty years ago, one authority observed that part of the risk involved in the use of nuclear power plants was that the technology was so new that it "has not been given a chance to reveal its full potential for danger."[60] Today, the same can be said for LAWS. The use of new autonomous weapons, therefore, would fall within the "ultra-hazardous" category and would require the adoption of "ultra-prevention measures" to avoid harm.[61]

Moreover, owing to the relentless development of new technologies, perceptions of appropriate levels of due diligence can change over time.[62] Thus, the due diligence obligation requires states and manufacturers to keep abreast of scientific and technological advances concerning autonomous functions and to accept responsibility when they do not.[63] In the context of LAWS, Peter Margulies contends that as a matter of state responsibility, autonomous weapon systems must include mechanisms for the regular update of artificial intelligence software and the information databases on which the software relies. "The duty to update is arguably a state obligation under human rights law, which bars the arbitrary taking of human life."[64]

In the environmental context, the due diligence of states includes the exercise of administrative control over public and private entities.[65] This implies that domestic laws and measures must be consistent with guidelines and recommendations of international technical bodies.[66] Should an international technical body one day determine standards for the development and use of LAWS, compliance with such standards should form part of the due diligence practices of states and manufacturers.

In its advisory opinion concerning *Legality of the Threat or Use of Nuclear Weapons*, the International Court of Justice concluded that "[t]he existence of the general obligation of states to ensure that activities within their jurisdiction and control respect the environment of other states or of areas beyond their national control is now part of the corpus of international law relating to the environment."[67] It would be absurd to not extend a similar legal duty of due diligence to states in their development and use of other sophisticated weapons, particularly those with lethal autonomous functions.

Indeed, the preventive/due diligence principle already finds expression in international treaty law concerning weapons control. State parties to the Convention on Certain Conventional Weapons, for example, are "encouraged to take generic preventive measures aimed at minimizing the occurrence of explosive remnants of war."[68] Moreover, article 5 of the Protocol on Prohibitions or Restrictions on the Use of Mines, Booby-Traps and Other Devices requires state parties to take all feasible measures to prevent the unauthorized removal, destruction, or concealment of any system used to establish the perimeter of an area where antipersonnel mines are stored.[69]

Thus, in the context of international humanitarian law,[70] the preventive principle naturally demands a comprehensive "Article 36 legal review" of new LAWS and methods of warfare. States are not required to analyze or predict all possible misuses of a weapon, as nearly every weapon can be used unlawfully.[71] Nonetheless, failure to perform an adequate legal review will be grounds for a state's responsibility in case of damage ensuing from failure of the weapon.[72] But the duty of prevention should not stop at article 36 reviews. Given that autonomous weapon systems are actually "systems of systems," unexpected interactions of these complex systems are inevitable, resulting in a higher probability of accidents.[73] Thus, because of the extraordinary complexity of these weapon systems, the obligation must also include, inter alia, constant monitoring of the system(s) to ensure that the component systems interact with each other in appropriate ways[74] and that human-machine interfaces work effectively in the field. This duty to monitor is extremely important as new technologies may interact and produce results that their inventors did not predict or consider.[75]

Finally, the preventive principle also includes a duty to prevent harm within a state's own jurisdiction.[76] For example, article 24 of the African Charter on Human and Peoples' Rights requires state parties to "take reasonable and other measures to prevent pollution and ecological degradation."[77] In 2004, the Inter-American Court of Human Rights found that Belize was responsible for damage to Maya lands and communities because the state failed to adopt adequate safeguards and mechanisms regarding logging activities.[78] In addition, the state failed to ensure that it had sufficient personnel to make certain that logging in these areas would not cause further environmental damage.[79] Logically then, the preventive principle should also function as a theory of state responsibility for the application of international human rights law to the use of LAWS during law enforcement activities. Within national jurisdictions, the preventive principle, by analogy, should also impose due diligence requirements on manufacturers and exporters of LAWS to ensure that their products function as designed.

The Precautionary Principle

Scientific certainty about certain activities often arrives too late to design effective environmental responses. Respect for human dignity, however, requires that society develop "an account of precautionary reasoning" that is capable of managing the uncertainties that surround technological development without rendering us incapable of action.[80] Thus, the precautionary principle creates a duty to respond to potential environmental threats, instead of waiting for certain scientific proof.[81] Put differently, the precautionary principle requires that where scientific uncertainty exists about the impact of an activity, states and other entities must assess the situation "in the light of prudence and caution."[82]

The precautionary principle and the preventive principle are related and overlap.[83] For example, in the European Union, "[c]ommunity policy on the environment shall aim at a high level of protection taking into account the diversity of situations in the various regions of the Community. It shall be based on the precautionary principle and on the principles that preventive action should be taken."[84] Moreover, the state parties to the 1992 Climate Change Convention agreed to "take precautionary measures to anticipate, prevent or minimize the causes of climate change and mitigate its adverse effects. Where there are threats of serious or irreversible damage, lack of full scientific certainty should not be used as a reason for postponing such measures, taking into account that policies and measures to deal with climate change should be cost-effective so as to ensure global benefits at the lowest possible cost."[85]

In addition to extraterritorial matters, international human rights courts have recognized that the precautionary principle creates responsibilities for states within their national jurisdictions. In *Tatar v. Romania*, for example, a mining company used sodium cyanide to extract gold at a mine, and this process allegedly contaminated the environment and damaged human health. The European Court of Human Rights held that although the existence of a causal link between exposure to sodium cyanide and certain conditions was unproven, the state still bore a duty to assess the risks and to take appropriate measures to reduce them. Romania, therefore, breached the precautionary principle, "according to which the absence of certainty with regard to current scientific and technical knowledge could not justify any delay on the part of the State in adopting effective and proportionate measures."[86]

Furthermore, in *Giacomelli v. Italy*, the European Court of Human Rights concluded that the precautionary principle required states to perform appropriate investigations and studies "in order to allow them to predict and evaluate in advance the effects of those activities which might damage the environment and infringe individuals' rights and to enable them to strike a fair balance between the various conflicting interests at stake."[87] More recently, in *Di Sarno and Others v. Italy*, the same court concluded that the precautionary principle obliged states to establish regulations adapted to the features of the activity in question, particularly with regard to the level of risk potentially involved. "They must govern the licensing, setting-up, operation, security and supervision of the activity and must make it compulsory for all those concerned to take practical measures to ensure the effective protection of citizens whose lives might be endangered by the inherent risks."[88]

Similarly, in *Kaliña and Lokono Peoples v. Surinam*, the Inter-American Court of Human Rights ruled that before a state grants a concession to private entities to carry out activities in the territory of indigenous peoples, it must complete an environmental impact statement to assess "the possible damage or impact that a development project or investment might have on the property and community in question."[89] This reasoning is consistent with the precautionary principle.

The seven due diligence recommendations described above represent general preventive and precautionary measures relevant to the design, development, and use of LAWS. In addition to international legal obligations for states, these recommendations should be implemented in domestic legislation to ensure the exercise of due diligence on the part of arms manufacturers and exporters. The need for more specific measures would depend on the kinds of new autonomous technologies developed, their capacity, and their particular use in the field.

The Polluter-Pays Principle

This concept requires states to ensure that in cases where the environment has been or will be polluted, the responsible individual or entity bears the costs resulting from the prevention or removal of the pollution.[90] Allocating the costs of preventive or remedial actions to the polluters ensures that they incur a substantial incentive to avoid future conduct detrimental to the environment.[91] The polluter-pays principle is reflected in multilateral and bilateral instruments,[92] as well as in national jurisprudence.[93] The precise legal status of the precautionary principle remains uncertain. However, the principle contributes to the interpretation of international instruments so as to protect the environment in cases of scientific uncertainty with respect to the impact of a particular activity.[94]

In cases of environmental harm, the "polluter," of course, is often a private company as opposed to a state agent or institution.[95] In the context of LAWS, the arms manufacturer assumes the role of the private "third party" at fault for harm. Given the lack of international rules attributing responsibility to corporations for weapons malfunctions, the polluter-pays principle, by analogy, can fill this gap in international law to ensure that victims of harm attributable to corporate negligence or malfeasance in the design, development, and sale of LAWS receive compensation.

The complexity of modern weapon systems (actually "systems of systems") creates challenges for a proportionate distribution of fault under the polluter-pays principle. For example, the latest (and perhaps the last) generation of human-piloted fighter jet, the F-35, is developed by a "partnership of countries," including the United States, Great Britain, Italy, the Netherlands, Turkey, Canada, Australia, Denmark, and Norway.[96] Although the "Major Contractor" for the airplane is Lockheed Martin of the United States,[97] more than fourteen hundred suppliers from around the world provide the three hundred thousand individual parts that make up the plane.[98] During the final assemblage, robots assemble parts of the aircraft, adding another dimension of "autonomy" to the process, as well as further questions concerning the attribution of fault.[99] Situations may arise, therefore, where the identification of the component of a LAWS that caused a particular failure or an "unintended engagement"[100] is in dispute.

To ensure compensation to parties wrongfully injured by LAWS it will be most efficient to hold the major contractor liable for civil damages caused by its weapon system(s), and then permit the major contractor—through litigation—to assign fault more specifically to one of its suppliers. Nonetheless, given the complexity of LAWS, it would be inequitable to require that an injured party demonstrate a causal nexus between a specific (design or manufacturing) activity and the ensuing harm.[101] This policy lies close to the problematic concept of strict liability, discussed in Chapter 6 with respect to international criminal law. A system of strict liability for manufacturers of dangerous weapons, however, entails financial compensation as opposed to imprisonment and the restriction of an individual's liberty. Furthermore, the corporation can pass on these compensation costs to the consumers or other entities who purchase the weapon systems. Thus, a principle or rule that the "Major Contractor pays" for damages caused by LAWS will be within the realm of fairness and would encourage arms manufacturers to take greater care in their design and production of these systems.[102]

A number of states argue that the polluter-pays principle applies at the domestic level but does not govern relations or responsibilities between states at the international level.[103] This is a pragmatic approach, reflecting the concept's dual function as a lever of national economic policy, and as a legal principle.[104] However, when applied to damage or injury caused by LAWS, this interpretation should not per se prevent persons harmed by autonomous weapons in third countries from seeking compensation from the manufacturer or manufacturers of the system (as well as from a state, should fault lie with the state as well).

Application of These Principles to LAWS

LAWS are extraordinarily complex, and it is that complexity that magnifies their hazardous nature. Thus, by analogy, the essence of the preventive and precautionary principles and the polluter-pays principle should apply to LAWS. For example, when state-operated LAWS cause violations of international humanitarian law, such violations should be attributed to the state.[105]

In situations where state responsibility for damage or injury caused by LAWS is alleged, several questions should lie at the core of the dispute: (1) Did the state or its agents intentionally violate international law in its design, development, use, or sale of the weapon systems? (2) If the state or its agents did not intentionally violate the law, did the state and its agents take sufficient preventive and precautionary measures in order to ensure the safe operation of the weapon system? (3) Were these measures adequate and sufficient in the circumstances at the time? Similarly, applying the polluter-pays principle to manufacturers and exporters of LAWS, these enterprises can be held responsible for damage caused by a malfunctioning system.

To date, the most comprehensive state effort to define preventive and precautionary measures for autonomous weapon systems is U.S. Department of Defense Policy Directive 3000.09 (Directive 3000.09 or "the Directive"), entitled "Autonomy in Weapon Systems."[106] Directive 3000.09 "does not establish a U.S. position on the potential future development of LAWS—it neither encourages nor prohibits the development of such future systems."[107] Nonetheless, the document permits the production and employment of LAWS with the approval of three high-ranking Pentagon officials.[108]

The individuals who prepared and drafted Directive 3000.09 considered that four principles should guide the development and use of autonomous weapon systems. First, the system must be capable of accomplishing the military mission.[109] Second, the system must be robust against failures and hacking.[110] Third, the system must be capable of lawful use. Fourth, the system must employ the proper balance of autonomy and human supervision vis-à-vis other criteria such as military professionalism, ethics, and the public perception of such systems. The authors considered that the last principle should be applied more flexibly than the first three.[111]

One concern that led to the creation of Directive 3000.09 was that the absence of a clear U.S. policy concerning autonomous weapon systems might result in the development or deployment of weapon systems that are unsafe, illegal, or unethical.[112] For example, in any combat environment, professional and well-trained commanders are expected to maintain and exercise control over their subordinate units in order to preserve discipline, efficiency, and proper conduct. Fully autonomous weapon systems, therefore, would subvert the military need for commanders to monitor the progress of subordinates and maintain control.[113] Accordingly, the drafters of the Directive determined that the design of new autonomous weapon systems must permit commanders to retain control over the system.[114] Therefore, it requires that LAWS be designed with the capability to allow commanders and operators to exercise "appropriate levels of human judgment in the use of force" and to employ systems with appropriate care and consistent with international humanitarian law, applicable treaties, weapons system safety rules and applicable rules of engagement (ROE).[115]

Probably the most controversial—and undefined—element of the of the Directive is the standard requiring designs and modes of use that permit the exercise of *appropriate levels of human judgment over the use of force* by autonomous weapon systems. Absent in the Directive is a definition or explanation of this crucial guideline for the employment of LAWS. Nor does the Directive provide guidance as to how the appropriate levels of human judgment—if any—should be exercisable, and exercised, by military commanders and operators of LAWS before, during, and after the use of lethal force.

The authors of the Directive considered that this precautionary standard should be applied flexibly.[116] The drafters decided not to include an explicit definition of "appropriate levels of human judgment over the use of force" in the document; nor did they treat this language as a precise concept. They believed that the "appropriate" standard for levels of human judgment over the use of force requires the balancing of multiple interests, including military necessity. Colonel Richard Jackson, one of the authors of Directive 3000.09 and a leading international humanitarian law expert, explained after its publication that the drafters intended the language "appropriate levels of human judgment" to refer to the levels of supervision required to ensure compliance with the standards prescribed by the law of armed conflict, that is, "distinction," "proportionality," and whether the autonomous weapon system is, by its nature, an indiscriminate weapon. "We still expect military commanders employing a system with autonomous functions to engage in the decision-making process that is required by IHL."[117] Thus, determinations of the "appropriate" level of human judgment will vary according to the circumstances, such as the kind of weapon, the interaction between operators of weapon systems, the particular characteristics of the weapon and of the environment in which it is used, and the mission objectives of the weapon system.[118]

Colonel Jackson described the challenge of balancing the speed of new autonomous technologies with the policy of maintaining appropriate levels of human supervision as "a huge focus of our working group." The drafters sought to alleviate risks of "machine bias," that is, human overreliance on a computer's decision-making ability, by emphasizing proper training of operators as well as the strong "validation and verification approach" during the acquisition phase of new autonomous weapon systems: "These guidelines have been developed more broadly to make sure that we don't have the individual relying too much on the decision-making capability of the machine."[119]

Nonetheless, even with the best training of human operators, the challenge of maintaining "appropriate" levels of human judgment and human-machine collaboration and teamwork will become increasingly difficult as decision-making cycles of autonomous weapon systems shrink to microseconds. It is not difficult to envision future generations of LAWS that will communicate between each other much more quickly than with humans. Thus, it is important to recall that, depending on the conditions, the phrase "appropriate levels of human judgment over the use of force" exercised by commanders and operators of autonomous weapon systems can include the exercise of no human judgment at all.

Indeed, Mary Cummings, an engineer, former U.S. Navy fighter pilot, and expert on human-autonomous system interaction, bluntly observes that "[m]any controls engineers see the human as a mere disturbance in the system that can and should be designed out."[120] Thus, notwithstanding the Directive, at some point in the future, LAWS will likely inhabit the battlefield (and may eventually become the predominant players) and will make decisions that we now believe require human intervention.[121]

As a comprehensive national attempt to articulate preventive and precautionary standards for the development and use of LAWS, and by its emphasis on compliance with international law, the Directive represents "a demonstration of state responsibility to a degree that is unprecedented."[122] The Directive is a statement of policy, however, rather than an expression of legal obligation. To borrow a phrase from Jan Klabbers, it creates "twilight norms" (such as "appropriate levels of human judgment") that conserve flexibility for future developments and decision-making.[123] Such unilateral state efforts to define policies concerning LAWS, moreover, can clothe those countries with political legitimacy while simultaneously setting the agenda for legal interpretation(s).[124] Nevertheless, these national efforts, while reflecting self-interests of states, are a positive development because they illustrate an implicit acceptance of membership in an international "constitutional order" that demands, inter alia, deeper thinking and effective constraints on the development of new weapon systems.[125] More importantly, they place the issue of the legality and morality of LAWS squarely within this constitutional order.

In a legal sense, as an effort to develop preventive and precautionary measures and as an acknowledgment of state responsibility, Directive 3000.09 is a "glass that is half full." While it emphasizes that LAWS must have the capability to comply with international law, the Directive does not mention the phrase "human dignity." Nor (crucially) does this instruction address whether it is (legally and morally) acceptable to delegate (previously) human decisions about the taking of human life to computers. In that sense, Directive 3000.09 leaves to another day important discussions about the impact of LAWS on human dignity, and how the legal compass of human dignity influences the responsibility of states for the design and use of these weapons.

* * *

There must be limits to a state's power to serve its interests through science at the expense of the dignity and personality of human beings.[126] If, as I argue, human dignity is a Charter-based conceptual starting point of international law, then logically United Nations member states bear a responsibility to use human dignity as a guide to their application of international and national legal rules. The fact that states may differ as to the meaning and scope of the notion of human dignity does not alter their broader responsibility to assimilate the concept in their legal systems and decisions.[127] If my chosen definition of human dignity (the capacity to make moral judgments) is accurate, then the design and use of LAWS that restrict this development is inconsistent with the concept of dignity." This reality, consequently, obliges states and nonstate actors to ensure that their designs and use of LAWS permit the exercise of moral agency in decisions to take human life. Furthermore, in cases where harm caused by LAWS may not have been deliberate, three concepts common to international environmental law—the preventive, precautionary, and polluter-pays principles—provide a framework for attribution of responsibility to states and arms manufacturers.

Conclusion

The pursuit of values "is part of what it is to be a human being,"[1] and the basic value and dominant purpose of international law are the promotion of human welfare, dignity, and freedom.[2] Therefore, humans must, to preserve their moral agency and hence their dignity, retain their responsibility to think, reason, and express judgment in essential realms of life. Compliance with responsibility in international and domestic affairs, however, can be, appropriately, a "double-edged sword."[3] All autonomous technologies, including weapons technology, raise important questions about where humans should exercise their reason, judgment, and values. In this book, I have demonstrated that the delegation to LAWS of the human responsibility for decisions to take human life erodes human dignity and, consequently, international law. Indeed, this problem permeates each of the bodies of international law discussed in the preceding chapters.

Nevertheless, as the speed of swarm technologies and other autonomous machine actions and reactions inevitably increases in the future, the role of autonomy—and the artificial intelligence that drives it—will expand as the space for human reasoning declines. These conditions will increasingly violate human dignity as the ability of humans to exercise their moral agency progressively diminishes and as human judgment loses its relevance. Attempts to ameliorate this problem with standards for human involvement such as "meaningful human control" or "appropriate levels of human judgment over the exercise of force" may assist but will not resolve the fundamental problem of abdication of moral agency to software.

Fortunately, the use of an interdependent design of LAWS can serve as an effective buffer against risks to the development and preservation of human dignity. Human-machine teamwork at crucial moments in the application of, inter alia, international humanitarian law and international human rights law facilitate the development and expression of moral agency. This design thereby serves to protect the value of human dignity, and, on a more practical level, it also ensures the exercise of human reasoning and judgment for cognitive functions better carried out by persons than by machines.

Accordingly, in the context of international humanitarian law, humans should make decisions to take human life during armed conflict except for rare situations where the use of LAWS would clearly reduce the suffering caused by war. Conversely, the need for human involvement is reduced in scenarios that require other kinds of "reasoning" such as the location and fusion of intelligence information.

With respect to international human rights law, the use of LAWS in exceptional law enforcement situations warranting the exercise of lethal force constitutes a relinquishment of moral agency in exchange for greater speed in the application of force. In the short term, delegation of the power to take human life to machines may save lives, thereby preserving dignity. Over time, however, relinquishment of such decisions to artificial intelligence undermines the moral agency that enables human beings to exercise their human rights in the first place. Therefore, to protect human dignity over the long term, in circumstances outside of armed conflict, human beings should maintain the capacity to intervene in decisions to take human life.

By maintaining human-machine corroboration at such crucial moments, interdependent designs of LAWS help to strengthen accountability and, thereby, the effectiveness of international criminal law. Greater accountability means greater dignity for all parties. With each increment in the speed of LAWS, however, the underlying tactical benefits of human-machine teamwork begin to recede.

Even the most sophisticated and "flawless technology of man"[4] can produce unforeseen injury to humankind. In the case of LAWS, however, we can *perceive* the damage that will be done to human dignity by the use of these weapons. Yet, as weapons technology rapidly becomes more automated and autonomous, the evolution of law concerning the proper design and use of these weapon systems lags behind. As one expert puts it, "I imagine the technology will move so quickly our policies are going to have a hard time catching up to it."[5] The resulting "legal lacunae" presents a significant threat to human dignity and, therefore, to the integrity of our system of international law.[6]

In international law, the well-being of individuals takes priority over the well-being and freedom of states.[7] Accordingly, states bear a responsibility to ensure that their employment of LAWS complies with international obligations to promote and protect human dignity. Furthermore, in cases where the attribution of fault for harm caused by LAWS is problematic, international courts and arbiters should use the international environmental law principles of prevention, precautionary measures, and polluter pays by analogy to determine the responsibility of states and arms manufacturers. Concurrently, the development of due diligence measures designed to reduce the likelihood of accidental harm caused by LAWS, and to minimize that harm when it occurs, will make the application of these principles more uniform.

LAWS will transform warfare and law enforcement operations.[8] To preserve and promote human dignity—the cornerstone and starting point of international law—this transformation compels reflection about what it means to be human and the significance of humanity.[9] These concepts evolve when technology changes the way wars are fought and as societal understandings of acceptable human suffering change.[10] As autonomous functions develop and dominate aspects of warfighting and crime control, men and women lose their moral agency, including the ability to apply judgment and law. This sacrifice of human dignity to machine autonomy and efficiency reduces "human" to a simple delegate or conduit, rather than a source, of responsibility for moral and legal decisions.

As the meaning of "human" narrows, however, the introduction of LAWS, paradoxically, can alter perceptions of humanity to allow for less use of violence during conflict and civil strife, rather than more. If "humanity," in the context of war and civil disturbances, refers to the reduction of suffering, then "humanity" (and human dignity) requires (at least in certain situations) the use of LAWS.[11] The paradox, and the challenge, is to operationalize this perception of humanity without altering and constraining human dignity.

Two essential questions emerge from this challenge: First, as the role of LAWS increases, can our current, dignity-based interpretation of international law coexist with this changing conception of "humanity"? If not, should we accept the legal and existential cost of outsourcing our responsibilities for the use of lethal force and other fundamental moral judgments to machines?[12] In this book I have tried to demonstrate that the answer, at least to the second question, is "no." The damage to human dignity wrought from the common use of LAWS to take human life represents a regression in humanity and, thus, is too high a price to pay for greater efficiency in the use of violence.[13]

The obligation to protect human dignity is the starting point for the interpretation and application of international law. International law then creates normative frameworks and rules for resolving the moral issues subsumed by concerns about human dignity.[14] In light of its moral, social, political, military, and economic role, law should serve these broader normative purposes rather than be a slave to scientific or technological inevitability.[15] It may be true that international affairs constantly evolve and that international law, to remain relevant, must reflect that evolution.[16] But it is also true that international law, to preserve its capacity to adjust rights and responsibilities between states, and between states and individuals, must ensure the preeminence of the principle of human dignity.

In the Introduction to this book, I described this work as a "predictive legal history" of the influence of LAWS on international law and vice-versa.[17] "But history," as Grotius observed, "is sometimes nothing more than a catalogue of actions marked with injustice, and ungovernable fury."[18] International law can and should play a determinative role so that the use of LAWS does not result in avoidable injustices and unnecessary violence. If and when individual, state, and civil responsibility exist for the design, development, and use of LAWS, then this "predictive" legal history becomes a present where autonomous weapon technologies can be employed without vitiating human dignity.

In the foregoing chapters, I have attempted to prove several propositions. First, as LAWS operate at increasingly greater speeds, their use will undermine the opportunities for, and the value of, moral agency. Second, when the value of moral agency is diminished, the killing of human beings by LAWS will violate human dignity and, therefore, international law. Third, interdependent designs of these weapon systems are necessary to ensure that humans and LAWS can operate collaboratively so that individuals can (1) fulfill their obligations under international law—including the preservation of their dignity—and (2) ensure that human reasoning and judgment are available for cognitive functions better carried out by humans than by machines.

Thus, this book explains several of the legal and moral problems raised by the use of LAWS. Some readers, naturally, may disagree with my proposed solutions. Nevertheless, the debate must address not only the impact of autonomous technology on warfare and security, but also its consequences for the preservation of human dignity and international law, and, ultimately, for what it means to be human.

NOTES

Introduction

Epigraph: Saint Augustine, *The City of God Against the Pagans*, William M. Green (trans.) (Cambridge, Mass.: Harvard University Press, 1972), vol. 7, book 22, pp. 327–29.

1. A. Roland, "Technology and War: A Bibliographic Essay," in M. Roe Smith (ed.), *Military Enterprise and Technological Change: Perspectives on the American Experience* (Cambridge, Mass.: MIT Press, 1985), p. 375.

2. Without the assistance of stirrups, riders needed extensive training in how to grip the sides of the animal with their thighs. V. Hanson, *A War Like No Other: How the Athenians and Spartans Fought the Peloponnesian War* (New York: Random House, 2005), p. 223.

3. L. White Jr., *Medieval Technology and Social Change* (Oxford: Clarendon, 1962), p. 2.

4. White, *Medieval Technology and Social Change*, p. 2.

5. White, *Medieval Technology and Social Change*, pp. 33 and 38, 28–38. Similarly, the introduction of firearms and artillery transformed interstate warfare, economic relations "and the capitalist organization of arms production." F. Braudel, *Capitalism and Modern Life: 1400–1800*, M. Kochan (trans.) (New York: Harper and Row, 1973), 291. For a discussion of the "underlying connections between military developments and social change," see M. Howard, *War in European History* (Oxford: Oxford University Press, 2009), pp. 94–115.

6. G. Corn, remarks at "Autonomous Weapon Systems—Law, Ethics and Policy" Conference at European University Institute, Academy of European Law, 24 April 2014.

7. J. Weller, *Fire and Movement: Bargain-Basement Warfare in the Far East* (New York: Crowell, 1967), p. 133.

8. Howard, *War in European History*, p. 102.

9. J. Keegan, *The Face of Battle* (New York: Penguin Books, 1976), p. 47.

10. Keegan, *Face of Battle*, p. 100.

11. M. Hastings, *Nemesis: The Battle for Japan, 1944–45* (London: Harper Perennial, 2007), p. 277. Similarly, writing in the nineteenth century, Prussian field marshal General Count Helmuth von Moltke observed that in war, "everything must be individual." "Letter, 11 December 1880," in T. Holland (ed.), *Letters to "The Times": Upon War and Neutrality with Some Commentary* (New York: Longmans, Green, 1914).

12. Keegan, *Face of Battle*, p. 232.

13. Howard, *War in European History*, p. 104.

14. Howard, *War in European History*, pp. 216 and 235. This extended artillery attack occurred despite the fact that the British and French enjoyed a 7–1 superiority in infantry numbers. M. Middlebrook, *The First Day on the Somme: 1 July 1916* (London: Penguin Books, 1984), pp. 75 and 78.

15. Keegan, *Face of Battle*, p. 340.

16. W. J. Lynn III and N. Thompson, "The Pentagon's New Cyberstrategy," *Foreign Affairs*, 1 October 2010, http://www.foreignaffairs.com/discussions/news-and-events/foreign-affairs-live-the-pentagons-new-cyberstrategy, accessed 15 August 2012.

17. J. Beard, "Law and War in the Virtual Era," 103 *American Journal of International Law*, 3 (2009), 409, 413. By 2013, the U.S. military operated over eight thousand remotely controlled unmanned aircraft systems and over twelve thousand unmanned ground systems. B. Hoagland, "Manning the Next Unmanned Air Force: Developing RPA Pilots of the Future," Policy Paper, Centre for 21st Century Security and Intelligence (August 2013), p. 1.

18. A. Krishnan, *Killer Robots: Legality and Ethicality of Autonomous Weapons* (Surrey: Ashgate, 2009), p. 88.

19. S. LaGrone, "Mabus: F-35 Will Be 'Last Manned Strike Fighter' the Navy, Marines 'Will Ever Buy or Fly,'" *U.S. Naval Institute News*, 15 April 2013, http://news.usni.org/2015/04/15/mabus-f-35c-will-be-last-manned-strike-fighter-the-navy-marines-will-ever-buy-or-fly.

20. The United States' 2018 National Defense Strategy observes that the Department of Defense will "invest broadly in military application of autonomy, artificial intelligence, and machine learning." Summary of the "2018 National Defense Strategy of the United States of America: Sharpening the American Military's Competitive Edge," https://dod.defense.gov/Portals/1/Documents/pubs/2018-National-Defense-Strategy-Summary.pdf.

21. A. Carter, "Autonomy in Weapons Systems," *Department of Defense Directive*, United States of America, Number 3000.09 (21 November 2012). This definition "includes human-supervised autonomous weapon systems that are designed to allow human operators to override operation of the weapon system, but can select and engage targets without further human input after activation" (13–14). The U.K. armed forces employ a more cognitive-based definition of "autonomy." According to U.K. military doctrine, an "autonomous system is capable of understanding higher level intent and direction. . . . As such they must be capable of achieving the same level of situational understanding as a human." "Joint Doctrine Note 2/11," *The U.K. Approach to Unmanned Aircraft Systems*, 30 March 2011, paras. 205–6 and 508, www.gov.uk/government/uploads/system/uploads/attachment_data/file/33711/20110505JDN_211_UAS_v2U.pdf. An "automated" or "automatic" weapon system, however, is one that, in response to inputs from one or more sensors, is programmed to logically follow a predefined set of rules in order to provide a predictable outcome.

22. The International Committee of the Red Cross (ICRC) distinguishes between weapon systems where humans choose the specific target at a particular point in time and at particular location, and weapon systems "where the exact timing, location and/or nature of the attack is not known to the user since it is self-initiated by the weapon, which is—in turn—triggered by the environment." Agenda Item 5 (c): "Characterization. The Importance of Critical Functions," ICRC Statement, CCW GGE "LAWs," 25 March 2019, p. 2, https://www.unog.ch/80256EDD006B8954/(httpAssets)/7EA110E50853887DC12583CC003032E7/$file/ICRC+GGE+LAWS+ICRC+statement+agenda+item+5c+25+03+2019.pdf, accessed 6 August 2020.

23. Labels such as "lethal" or "nonlethal" weapons actually create a distinction without a difference as any weapon can be lethal, depending how it is used.

24. For just one example, see B. Farmer, "Brimstone: British Missile Envied by the US for War on Isil," *Telegraph*, 1 October 2014, http://www.telegraph.co.uk/news/uknews/defence/11133680/Brimstone-British-missile-envied-by-the-US-for-war-on-Isil.html; "Brimstone," Royal Air Force, http://www.raf.mod.uk/equipment/Brimstone.cfm.

25. The president of the International Committee of the Red Cross described autonomous weapon systems and cyberweapons as "new territories" requiring engagement with states to determine how these weapons might be used. P. Mauer, remarks at Leiden University College, The Hague, 22 May 2014.

26. E. Talbot Jensen, "The Future of the Law of Armed Conflict: Ostriches, Butterflies, and Nanobots," 35 *Michigan Journal of International Law* 2 (2014), 253, 256.

27. I. Kant, "The Contest of Faculties," in Hans Reis (ed.), *Kant's Political Writings* (Cambridge, Mass.: Harvard University Press, 1970), 177. Although the word "history" most often refers to an account of past events, the term can also mean encompass "acts, ideas or events that will or can shape the course of the future; immediate but significant happenings." "History," Dictionary.com, http://dictionary.reference.com/browse/history. Indeed, as Professor (now Judge) Crawford noted: "history happens forwards. History happens day-by-day." *Maritime Dispute (Peru v. Chile)* (Verbatim Record) [14 December 2012] ICJ [12], http://www.icj-cij.org/docket/files/137/17230.pdf.

28. Study and analysis of challenges in international law with respect to changing weapon technologies are common. For reflections on the current and future law of autonomous weapon systems, see N. Bhuta et al. (eds.), *Autonomous Weapon Systems—Law, Ethics, Policy* (Cambridge University Press, 2016), Report of the 2019 session of the Group of Governmental Experts on Emerging Technologies in the Area of Lethal Autonomous Weapons Systems, Geneva, 25 September 2019, CCW/GGE/3, https://undocs.org/en/CCW/GGE.1/2019/3, and the Report of the 2018 session of the Group of Governmental Experts on Emerging Technologies in the Area of Lethal Autonomous Weapons Systems, 23 October 2018, CCW/GGE.1/2018/3, para. 23 (f), https://undocs.org/en/CCW/GGE.1/2018/3. In the context of cyberoperations, see M. Schmitt, "Rewired Warfare: Rethinking the Law of Cyber Attack," *International Review of the Red Cross* (2014); and P. Margulies, "Sovereignty and Cyber Attacks: Technology's Challenge to the Law of State Responsibility," 14 *Melbourne Journal of International Law* (2013), 496.

29. P. Jessup, *A Modern Law of Nations* (New York: Macmillan, 1948), 91. "No other ideal seems so clearly accepted as a universal social good." O. Schachter, "Human Dignity as a Normative Concept," 77 *American Journal of International Law* (1983), 848, 849.

30. *Prosecutor v. Dražen Erdemović*, Joint Separate Opinion of Judge McDonald and Judge Vohrah, IT-96-22-A, Appeals Chamber, 7 October 1997, para. 75 (observing that "the law should not be the product or slave of logic or intellectual hair-splitting, but must serve broader normative purposes in light of its social, political and economic role"). "Moral and political considerations are not alien to law but part of it." B. Simma, "The Responsibility of Individuals for Human Rights Abuses in Internal Conflicts: A Positivist View," 93 *American Journal of International Law* (1999), 302, 308. For a different view, see J. Goldsmith and E. Posner, *The Limits of International Law* (Oxford University Press, 2005), p. 185 (arguing that states have no moral obligation to follow international law).

31. *Corfu Channel Case*, Judgment of 9 April 1949, Separate Opinion of Judge Alvarez, ICJ Reports 1949, 41.

32. C. Droege, "Get Off My Cloud: Cyber Warfare, International Humanitarian Law, and the Protection of Civilians," 94 *International Review of the Red Cross*, 886 (Summer 2012), 533, 541.

33. M. Wagner, "Autonomy in the Battlespace: Independently Operating Weapon Systems and the Law of Armed Conflict," in D. Saxon (ed.), *International Humanitarian Law and the Changing Technology of War* (Leiden: Martinus Nijhoff, 2013), pp. 99–122; K. Anderson and M. Waxman, "Law and Ethics for Autonomous Weapon Systems: Why a Ban Won't Work and

How the Laws of War Can," *American University Washington College of Law Research Paper* No. 2013-11 (Jean Perkins Taskforce on National Security and Law).

34. "Stopping Killer Robots: Country Positions on Banning Fully Autonomous Weapons and Retaining Human Control," Human Rights Watch, 2020, p. 4, file:///Volumes/NO%20 NAME/HRW_Stopping%20Killer%20Robots%202020.pdf.

35. B. Docherty, "Losing Humanity: The Case Against Killer Robots," Human Rights Watch and International Human Rights Clinic (Harvard Law School, November 2012), 5, 30–36, and 46–48. Human Rights Watch is part of an international consortium of organizations dedicated to achieving a ban on "killer robots." See Campaign to Stop Killer Robots, http://www.stopkillerrobots.org/.

36. B. Docherty, "Shaking the Foundations: The Human Rights Implications of Killer Robots," *Human Rights Watch and International Human Rights Clinic* (Harvard Law School, May 2014), p. 25.

37. B. Docherty, "Mind the Gap: The Lack of Accountability for Killer Robots," *Human Rights Watch and International Human Rights Clinic* (April 2015), pp. 25 and 37.

38. M. Schmitt and J. Thurnher, "Out of the Loop: Autonomous Weapon Systems and the Law of Armed Conflict," 4 *Harvard National Security Journal* (2013), 231, 233.

39. Schmitt and Thurnher, "Out of the Loop," pp. 243–65.

40. W. Boothby, "How Far Will the Law Allow Unmanned Targeting to Go?" in D. Saxon (ed.), *International Humanitarian Law and the Changing Technology of War*, pp. 57–59 and 62.

41. J. Kellenberger, "Keynote Address," International Humanitarian Law and New Weapon Technologies, 34th Round Table on Current Issues of International Humanitarian Law, San Remo, 8 September 2011, https://www.unog.ch/80256EDD006B8954/(httpAssets)/F77AF42ED509F890C1257CD90025183F/$file/IHL+&+new+weapon+technologies_Sanremo.pdf. "Only humans can be inhuman and only human beings can deliberately choose not to comply with the rules they were instructed to follow." M. Sassóli, "Autonomous Weapons and International Humanitarian Law: Advantages, Open Technical Questions and Legal Issues to Be Clarified," 90 *International Law Studies* (2014), 308, 310.

42. Sassóli, "Autonomous Weapons and International Humanitarian Law," p. 311. This argument presupposes that it is possible to build autonomous weapon systems that are as accurate as the average soldier vis-à-vis the targeting rules of international humanitarian law.

43. P. Asaro, "On Banning Autonomous Weapon Systems: Human Rights, Automation and the Dehumanization of Lethal Decision-Making," 94 *International Review of the Red Cross*, 886 (Summer 2012), 687, 699.

44. Asaro, "On Banning Autonomous Weapon Systems," p. 708.

45. P. Asaro, "Human Dignity and Autonomous Weapon Systems," Presentation to Conference on Autonomous Weapon Systems—Law, Ethics, Policy, European University Institute, Academy of European Law, 24 April 2014.

46. C. Heyns, Presentation to Convention on Certain Conventional Weapons Meeting of Experts on Lethal Autonomous Weapon Systems, 16 April 2015, p. 6, http://www.unog.ch/80256EDD006B8954/(httpAssets)/1869331AFF45728BC1257E2D0050EFE0/$file/2015_LAWS_MX_Heyns_Transcript.pdf.

47. Heyns, Presentation to Convention on Certain Conventional Weapons, p. 6. Heyns also argued that if the decision to take human life is removed from the responsibility of military officers, their dignity as well is violated.

48. Aristotle, *Nichomachean Ethics*, W. D. Ross (trans.), book 3, p. 5. "[E]xcellence in deliberation involves reasoning" (book 6, p. 7).

49. Author interview with Gianfranco Visentin (Head), Automation and Robotics Section, European Space Research and Technology Centre, European Space Agency, Noordwijk, Netherlands, 4 November 2013.

50. I. Berlin, "My Intellectual Path," in *The Power of Ideas*, H. Hardy (ed.) (Princeton University Press, 2000), p. 20.

51. In this sense, "responsibility" refers not only to processes of accountability, but also to obligations "to act formatively toward society, when we have the responsibility for establishing, changing or taking steps to preserve particular forms of social order," including laws, agreements, institutions, and social arrangements that shape human relations. L. Fuller, "Freedom—a Suggested Analysis," 68 *Harvard Law Review* (June 1955), 1305, 1308.

52. Michael Schmitt and Jeffrey Thurnher suggest that "[f]uture combat may . . . occur at such a high tempo that human operators will simply be unable to keep up. Indeed, advanced weapon systems may well 'create an environment too complex for humans to direct.'" "Out of the Loop," p. 238 (citing P. Singer, *Wired for War: The Robotics Revolution and Conflict in the 21st Century* [New York: Penguin, 2009], p. 128; quoting Thomas Adams, Colonel [Ret.], U.S. Army).

53. H. Baker, *The Image of Man: A Study of the Idea of Human Dignity in Classical Antiquity, the Middle Ages, and the Renaissance* (New York: Harper and Row, 1961), p. 299. Pico della Mirandola, for example, warned that humans should never "through slothful inaction to lose our power of reason, that faculty by which the mind examines, judges and measures all things." G. Pico della Mirandola, *Oration on the Dignity of Man* (1486), A. Robert Caponigri (trans.) (Chicago: Henry Regnery, 1956), p. 29.

Chapter 1

1. L. Antebi, "Changing Trends in Unmanned Aerial Vehicles: New Challenges for States, Armies and Security Industries," 6 *Military and Strategic Affairs* (August 2014), 24. To put the growing demand for more unmanned military technology in perspective, today, more than seventy nations operate unmanned aerial systems, including platforms with autonomous functions. Unmanned aerial systems are manufactured on every continent with the exception of Antarctica, and as of 2012 nearly fifty countries were producing almost nine hundred different types of unmanned aerial systems. Israel alone has exported unmanned aerial systems to dozens of nations. Nonstate actors, such as Hezbollah, operate these systems for combat as well as intelligence purposes (pp. 23–28).

2. D. Hollis, "The Fog of Technology and International Law," Blog of the Italian Society of International Law and European Law, 15 May 2015, http://www.sidiblog.org/2015/05/14/the-fog-of-technology-and-international-law/, accessed 15 August 2018.

3. "Phalanx Close-In Weapons System (CIWS)," United States Navy Fact File, http://www.navy.mil/navydata/fact_display.asp?cid=2100&tid=487&ct=2, accessed 14 August 2018.

4. A. Velez-Green, "The South Korean Sentry—a 'Killer Robot' to Prevent War," Lawfare, 1 March 2015, https://www.lawfareblog.com/foreign-policy-essay-south-korean-sentry%E2%80%94-killer-robot-prevent-war, accessed 15 March 2020; "Future Tech? Autonomous Killer Robots Are Already Here," NBC News, 15 May 2014, https://www.nbcnews.com/tech/security/future-tech-autonomous-killer-robots-are-already-here-n105656, accessed 14 August 2018.

5. P. Scharre, *Autonomous Weapons and the Future of War* (New York: W. W. Norton, 2018), p. 4.

6. Israel Aerospace Industries describes the Harpy Loitering Weapon as "a 'Fire and Forget' autonomous weapon, launched from a ground vehicle behind the battle zone," http://www.iai.co.il/2013/16143-16153-en/IAI.aspx, accessed 30 June 2015; "IAI's MBT HARPY System," Israel Aerospace Industries, https://www.youtube.com/watch?v=AyKXUfOubH0, accessed 15 August 2018; "Weapons from Israel," Maccabean Online, March 2009, http://www.freeman.org/MOL/pages/march2009/weapons-from-israel.php, accessed 15 August 2018. The United States' "'Harpoon' Anti-Ship Missile" system has similar capabilities although more recent versions permit human control over the final attack on a target. "Harpoon," WeaponSystems.net, http://weaponsystems.net/weapon.php?weapon=HH10+-+Harpoon, accessed 15 August 2018.

7. "Report of the Special Rapporteur on Extrajudicial, Summary or Arbitrary Executions, Christof Heyns," A/HRC23/47, 9 April 2013, para. 45.

8. Scharre, *Autonomous Weapons and the Future of War*, pp. 47–48.

9. Electronic mail messages from Noga Nadler Mozes, Corporate Communications, Israel Aerospace Industries, 29 June 2015.

10. "IAI's MBT HARPY System," Israel Aerospace Industries, https://www.youtube.com/watch?v=AyKXUfOubH0, accessed 16 March 2020. Also see "Successful Flight Demonstrations for HAROP Loitering Munitions," Israel Aerospace Industries, http://www.iai.co.il/2013/32981-46464-en/MediaRoom_News.aspx, accessed 16 March 2020.

11. See M. McLuhan, *Understanding Media: The Extensions of Man* (Cambridge, Mass.: MIT Press, 1994), p. 344.

12. J. Weller, *Wellington in India* (London: Longman/Camelot, 1972), p. 296.

13. Lt. Colonel Matt Dooley, Chief, Lethality Branch, Army Capabilities Integration Centre (ARCIC), in J. Gould, "U.S. Army Readying Unmanned Systems Doctrine," *Defense News*, 8 April 2015, http://www.defensenews.com/story/defense/land/army/2015/04/08/us-army-readying-unmanned-systems-doctrine/25473749/, accessed 16 March 2020. The U.S. Army's request for robotics development funding rose from 38 million USD in 2018 to 115 million USD in 2020. M. Klare, "Pentagon Asks More for Autonomous Weapons," Arms Control Association, April 2019, https://www.armscontrol.org/act/2019-04/news/pentagon-asks-more-autonomous-weapons, accessed 16 March 2020. As of 2016, the research and manufacture of autonomous weapon technologies was a twenty billion USD industry in forty different countries. A. Kasperson, Head of International Security at the World Economic Forum, Remarks, "Private Sector Perspectives on the Development of Lethal Autonomous Systems," Geneva, 12 April 2016.

14. "In modern asymmetrical warfare, the number of [military] targets is increasing and the timeframe for engaging and killing each target is decreasing." "Aviation Defense Equipment Technology: Rafael Spice 250," AirRecognition.com, 14 January 2015, http://www.airrecognition.com/index.php/focus-analysis-photo-report-aviation-defence-industry/aviation-defence-industry-technology/1424-rafaels-spice-250-precision-guided-glide-bomb-undergoing-adaptation-test-on-iafs-fighters.html.

15. "Unmanned Systems Integrated Roadmap FY2011–2036," U.S. Department of Defense, p. 43, http://www.acq.osd.mil/sts/docs/Unmanned%20Systems%20Integrated%20Roadmap%20FY2011-2036.pdf. In a sense, even human soldiers exhibit automatic qualities because they are trained to act instinctively during basic combat functions such as shooting, moving, and communicating. Thus, "you want soldiers to be automated in terms of the technical aspects of fighting." However, when situations—such as changing conditions in the battlespace—arise

that require thinking and reasoning, the soldier must apply his or her contextual knowledge of the operating environment. Author interview with Allen Borelli, former U.S. Army Intelligence Specialist, The Hague, 15 July 2015. Conversely, soldiers in the field who hesitate often put themselves and those around them in great danger. M. Waxman, "Detention as Targeting: Standards of Certainty and Detention of Suspected Terrorists," 108 *Columbia Law Review* (2008), 1365, 1409.

16. L. Letendre, "Lethal Autonomous Weapon Systems: Translating Geek Speak for Lawyers," 96 *International Law Studies* (2020), 274, 278.

17. Summary of the 2018 Department of Defense Artificial Intelligence Strategy: Harnessing AI to Advance Our Security and Prosperity," p. 5, https://media.defense.gov/2019/Feb/12/2002088963/-1/-1/1/summary-of-dod-ai-strategy.pdf, accessed 18 March 2020.

18. Statement by Dr. Lisa Porter, Deputy Under Secretary of Defense for Research and Engineering, Before the House Armed Services Committee on Emerging Threats and Capabilities, on "Department of Defense's Artificial Intelligence Structures, Investments and Applications," 11 December 2018, https://docs.house.gov/meetings/AS/AS26/20181211/108795/HHRG-115-AS26-Wstate-PorterL-20181211.pdf, accessed 18 March 2020.

19. H. Arendt, *The Life of the Mind* (New York: Harcourt, 1978), p. 71.

20. E. Lubofsky, "A Smarter Undersea Robot: Engineers Seek to Correct a Curious Deficiency," *Oceanus*, 16 January 2015, http://www.whoi.edu/oceanus/feature/a-smarter-undersea-robot.

21. B. Gates, EdX Course CS50x3 (Computer Science 50), Harvard College, Week 1 2015.

22. J. Seabrook, "The Next Word," *New Yorker*, 14 October 2019, pp. 52, 59.

23. Author interview with Gianfranco Visentin, Head, Automation and Robotics Department, European Space Agency, Noordwijk, 4 November 2013.

24. Seabrook, "Next Word," pp. 52–57.

25. Seabrook, "Next Word," p. 59.

26. J. Lyons, ARIANE 5, Flight 501 Failure, Report by the Inquiry Board, 19 July 1996, https://www.ima.umn.edu/~arnold/disasters/ariane5rep.html.

27. Lyons, ARIANE 5; "Spy Plane Causes Air Traffic Chaos," BBC NEWS, 6 May 2014, http://www.bbc.com/news/technology-27292440. Given the potential for catastrophic results should computer programs in autonomous weapon systems be inadequate, designers and developers should assume that the software is faulty until the most rigorous testing methods prove otherwise. Lyons, ARIANE 5.

28. D. Akerson, "The Illegality of Offensive Lethal Autonomy," in D. Saxon (ed.), *International Humanitarian Law and the Changing Technology of War* (Leiden: Martinus Nijhoff, 2013), p. 71.

29. A. Carter, "Autonomy in Weapons Systems," Department of Defense Directive, United States of America, Number 3000.09, Part II, "Definitions," 21 November 2012, p. 13.

30. The burden to ensure that the pilot is bombing the correct target, in accordance with international humanitarian law and the rules of engagement, rests on the pilot's chain of command and the officer who approved the mission. Electronic mail message, General B. A. Fabio Giunchi, Commander of Air Cooperation School, Guidonia Airport, Italian Air Force, 16 February 2015. General Giunchi is a former fighter pilot and participant in the development of the F-35 Lightning II, the latest-generation stealth, multirole fighter jet now deployed by the NATO powers.

31. Carter, "Autonomy in Weapons Systems," p. 13.

32. "New Concept for Air Warfare," DARPA Advancing System-of-Systems Open Architectures for Airborne Assets," *AUVSI News*, 31 March 2015, http://www.auvsi.org/blogs/auvsi-news/2015/03/31/darpasos.

33. Author interview with Colonel Denny Traas, MSc, Chief Air Force Branch, Plans Directorate, Defense Staff, Netherlands Ministry of Defense, The Hague, 20 February 2015.

34. Author interview with Colonel Denny Traas.

35. Author interview with Colonel Denny Traas.

36. "Much of the F-35's electronic warfare and intelligence, reconnaissance and surveillance (ISR) capabilities are made possible by a core processor that can perform more than one trillion operations per second." Lockheed Martin, "Multi-Mission Capability for Emerging Global Threats," F-35 Lightning II, https://www.f35.com/about/capabilities.

37. Author interview with Colonel Denny Traas. See, for example, description of the M426S E-Scan IFF Interrogator, produced by SELEX ES, http://www.selex-es.com/-/m426s.

38. Modern fighter pilots are "automated" to rely on and react to the information provided to his instruments; "that's how he is trained." Author interview with Allen Borelli.

39. D. Akerson, "The Illegality of Offensive Lethal Autonomy," in D. Saxon (ed.), *International Humanitarian Law and the Changing Technology of War*, p. 71.

40. Akerson, "Illegality of Offensive Lethal Autonomy," pp. 71–72. Akerson also describes a system of "variable autonomy" where autonomous weapon systems could switch from "man-on-the-loop" mode to "man-in-the-loop" mode." Markus Wagner also describes three categories of autonomy: "remotely-controlled systems," "automated systems," and "autonomous weapons systems." "Autonomy in the Battlespace: Independently Operating Weapon Systems and the Law of Armed Conflict," in D. Saxon (ed.), *International Humanitarian Law and the Changing Technology of War*, pp. 103–5.

41. A. Sen, *The Idea of Justice* (London: Penguin, 2010), p. viii.

42. M. Cummings et al., "Boredom and Distraction in Multiple Unmanned Vehicle Supervisory Control," 25 *Interacting with Computers* (2013), 34–37.

43. F. Gao et al., "Teamwork in Controlling Multiple Robots," Proceedings of the Seventh Annual ACM/IEEE International Conference on Human-Robot Interaction (2012), pp. 81–88, http://web.mit.edu/aeroastro/labs/halab/papers/hri167-gao.pdf. Cf. "Vehicle Management," in VCS-4586 Capabilities Guide, Lockheed Martin, p. 4, http://www.lockheedmartin.com/content/dam/lockheed/data/ms2/documents/cdl-systems/VCS-4586%20CAPABILITIES%20GUIDE-August2013.pdf.

44. "Increasing complexity and speed of the battlespace means that the demands on combat decision-makers are outstripping the cognitive capacity of the unaided human." U.S. Air Force 2030 Science and Technology Strategy, p. 7, https://www.airforcemag.com/PDF/DocumentFile/Documents/2019/USAF%20Science%20and%20Technology%20Strategy.pdf, accessed 11 April 2020.

45. At the European Space Agency, for example, robotics scientists apply a gradient containing four separate levels of autonomy. The highest level of autonomy (known as "E4") could be further subdivided into additional degrees. Author interview with Gianfranco Visentin.

46. (1) The computer offers no assistance to its human supervisor(s); (2) the computer offers a complete set of alternatives to its human supervisor(s); (3) the computer narrows the selection to a restricted set of options and sends the reduced list to the human supervisor(s); (4) the computer sends a single option for action to its human supervisor(s); and (5) the computer executes that option if the human supervisor(s) approves; or (6) the computer allows the

human supervisor(s) to veto the action before automatic execution; or (7) the computer informs the human supervisor(s) after execution; or (8) the computer informs the human supervisor(s) after execution if he or she asks; or (9) the computer informs the human supervisor(s) after execution if it decides to; or (10) the computer decides everything without communication to the human supervisor(s). T. B. Sheridan et al. "Adapting Automation to Man, Culture and Society," 19 *Automatica*, 6 (1983), 605, 611.

47. Author interview with Gianfranco Visentin.

48. *Joint Doctrine Note 2/11*, paras. 104 and 513. Moreover, systems and the institutions that create and operate them "interact to form more embracing systems." T. Hughes, "Convergent Themes in the History of Science, Medicine and Technology," 22 *Technology and Culture* (July 1981), 550, 555.

49. Modern manned weapons platforms also represent "systems of systems." For example, the last-generation U.S. Navy fighter-bomber, the F-18, contains eleven different weapon systems to control different kinds of rockets, missiles, bombs, and guns. Aircraft Weapon Systems, 15–20, http://www.globalsecurity.org/military/library/policy/navy/nrtc/14313_ch15.pdf.

50. R. Bamberger Jr. et al., "Flight Demonstrations of Unmanned Aerial Vehicle Swarming Concepts," 27 *Johns Hopkins APL Technical Digest*, 1 (2006), 41, 49, http://www.jhuapl.edu/techdigest/TD/td2701/Bamberger.pdf.

51. General J. Shapland, lecture to Conference on Air Defense in the Modern Era, Institute for National Security Studies, 18 March 2014, http://www.inss.org.il/index.aspx?id=4479&categoryid=59.

52. For example, in a Tactical Directive issued in 2010 for members of the International Security and Assistance Forces (ISAF) in Afghanistan, General David Petraeus reminded his subordinates that "[s]trategic and operational commanders cannot anticipate every engagement. We have no desire to undermine the judgment of tactical commanders. However, that judgment should always be guided by my intent." "General Petraeus Issues Updated Tactical Directive: Emphasizes 'Disciplined Use of Force,'" ISAF News List, 2010-08-CA-004, 4 August 2010, http://www.isaf.nato.int/article/isaf-releases/general-petraeus-issues-updated-tactical-directive-emphasizes-disciplined-use-of-force.html.

53. D. Werner, "Drone Swarm: Networks of Small UAVs Offer Big Capabilities," *Defence News*, 12 June 2013, http://www.defensenews.com/article/20130612/C4ISR/306120029/. Israel's HARPY System can operate as a swarm of loitering autonomous missiles. "IAI's MBT HARPY System," Israel Aerospace Industries, https://www.youtube.com/watch?v=AyKXUfOubH0, accessed 30 June 2015.

54. J. Kennedy and R. Eberhardt, "Particle Swarm Optimization," Neural Networks, Proceedings, IEEE International Conference, pp. 1995, 1942–48, http://citeseerx.ist.psu.edu/viewdoc/download?doi=10.1.1.248.4138&rep=rep1&type=pdf.

55. Kennedy and Eberhardt, "Particle Swarm Optimization," p. 1945. There are five basic principles of swarm intelligence: (1) proximity: the population should be able to carry out simple space and time computations; (2) quality: the population should be able to respond to quality factors in the environment; (3) diverse response: the population should not commit its activities along excessively narrow channels; (4) stability: the population should not change its mode of behavior every time the environment changes; (5) adaptability: nevertheless, the population must be able to change its behavior when necessary (pp. 1946–47).

56. J. McLurkin, "Speaking Swarmish: Human-Robot Interface Design for Large Swarms of Autonomous Mobile Robots," *Association for the Advancement of Artificial Intelligence*

(2006), 1–4; E. Raboin et al., "Model-Predictive Asset Guarding by Team of Autonomous Surface Vehicles in Environment with Civilian Boats," 38 *Autonomous Robot* (2015), 261–63. Most of these factors also are relevant to the design and function of single autonomous weapon systems.

57. Raboin, "Model-Predictive Asset Guarding," p. 262.

58. Lt. General B. Gantz, "The IDF in 2025," Address to the Begin-Sadat Centre for Strategic Studies, 9 October 2013, http://besacenter.org/new-at-the-besa-center/idf-chief-staff-benny-gantz-speaks-besa-center/, accessed on 22 March 2020.

59. A. McCullogh, "The Looming Swarm," *Air Force Magazine*, 22 March 2019, https://www.airforcemag.com/article/the-looming-swarm/, accessed 22 March 2020.

60. K. Mizokami, "Gremlin Drone's First Flight Turns C-130 into a Flying Aircraft Carrier," *Popular Mechanics*, 21 January 2020, and DARPA, "Gremlins: Airborne Launch and Recovery of Unmanned Aerial Vehicles, https://www.popularmechanics.com/military/aviation/a30612943/gremlin-drone-first-flight/, accessed 28 March 2020.

61. B. H. Liddell Hart, *History of the Second World War* (New York: G. P. Putnam's Sons, 1970), pp. 99, 229, 235, 257, 259, 264, 269, 276, 329, 349, 438, and 684.

62. Werner, "Drone Swarm"; M. Zenne, "Death from a Swarm of Tiny Drones," *Daily Mail*, 20 February 2013, http://www.dailymail.co.uk/news/article-2281403/U-S-Air-Force-developing-terrifying-swarms-tiny-unmanned-drones-hover-crawl-kill-targets.html; P. Fiddian "UAV Swarm Technology Trial Success," *Armed Forces International News*, 7 August 2012, http://www.armedforces-int.com/news/uav-swarm-technology-trial-success.html.

63. U.K. Doctrine on unmanned aircraft systems notes that "practical methods to control swarming systems have yet to be fully developed and demonstrated" and refers to commentary "that suggests that the increasing speed, confusion and information overload of modern war may make human response inadequate." Joint Doctrine Note 2/11, paras. 316 and 520.

64. M. Schmitt and J. Thurnher, "Autonomous Weapon Systems and LOAC," 4 *Harvard National Security Journal* (2013), pp. 231, 280.

65. Colonel Shane Riza, a U.S. Air Force fighter pilot, explains that presently military "communication occurs at the speed of light" and recognizes that autonomous weapons systems permit "the speed of future decision cycles outpacing the human mind." M. Shane Riza, *Killing Without Heart: Limits on Robotic Warfare in an Age of Persistent Conflict* (Washington, D.C.: Potomac Books, 2013), p. 41.

66. A. Clare et al., "Assessing Operator Strategies for Real-Time Replanning of Multiple Unmanned Vehicles," 6 *Intelligent Decision Technologies* (2012), pp. 221, 222.

67. Clare et al., "Assessing Operator Strategies," pp. 222–23.

68. Clare et al., "Assessing Operator Strategies," p. 222.

69. Clare et al., "Assessing Operator Strategies," p. 230.

70. J. Wilson, "Interview with Brig. General Gary L. Thomas, U.S. Marine Corps Assistant Deputy Commandant for Aviation," Defense Media Network, 23 March 2012, http://www.defensemedianetwork.com/stories/interview-with-brig-gen-gary-l-thomas-u-s-marine-corps-assistant-deputy-commandant-for-aviation/3/.

71. "CARACAS (Control Architecture for Robotic Agent Command and Sensing)," Naval Drones, U.S. Office of Naval Research, Science and Technology, http://www.navaldrones.com/CARACAS.html. Conversely, as the control of human operators over these platforms increases, "the less autonomous those systems can be, which defeats the purpose." J. Borrie, "On Safety Aspects of Meaningful Human Control: Catastrophic Accidents in Complex Systems,"

Conference in Weapons, Technology and Human Control, United Nations Institute for Disarmament Research, New York, 16 October 2014.

72. C. Townes, "Report of the Task Force on Space," 8 January 1969, in J. Logsdon (ed.), *Exploring the Unknown: Selected Documents in the History of the U.S. Civil Space Program* (Washington, D.C.: 1995), vol. 1, *Organizing for Exploration*, p. 505, http://history.nasa.gov/SP-4407/vol1/intro.pdf.

73. C. Townes, "Report of the Task Force on Space," 505. Indeed, research has shown that with "more interactions that humans and robots have, they begin to develop their own language." L. Steels, "Ten Big Ideas of Artificial Intelligence," Remarks to 25th Benelux Conference on Artificial Intelligence, Delft Technical University, 8 November 2013.

74. "Yes, Unmanned Combat Aircraft Are the Future," *Centre for a New American Security*, 11 August 2015, http://www.cnas.org/opinion/yes-unmanned-combat-aircraft-are-the-future#.VhJzG03smdJ.

75. As several leading proponents of the coactive design model argue: "the property of autonomy is not a mere function of the machine, but rather a relationship between the machine and a task in a given situation." M. Johnson et al., "Beyond Cooperative Robotics: The Central Role of Interdependence in Coactive Design" (May–June 2011) IEEE Computer Society, p. 84.

76. Failure to carefully adhere to such allocations of function and responsibility can have catastrophic results. For example, one of the causes of the shoot-down of a civilian Iranian airliner in 1988 by the U.S. Navy vessel *Vincennes* was the crew's misreading of information, accurately provided by the ship's AEGIS Combat System, that the approaching airplane was ascending rather than descending. "Investigation Report," Formal Investigation into the Circumstances Surrounding the Downing of Iran Air Flight 655 on 3 July 1988, U.S. Department of Defense, 19 August 1988, p. 61.

77. G. Corn, remarks at Autonomous Weapon Systems—Law, Ethics and Policy Conference at European University Institute, Academy of European Law, 24 April 2014.

78. W. Boothby, *The Law of Targeting* (Oxford University Press, 2012), 122. Lockheed Martin, "F-35 Experience," Video in F-35's Capabilities: Multi-Mission Capability for Emerging Global Threats, https://www.f35.com/about/capabilities. "Every wasted minute of a senior leader . . . has real impacts on the battlefield." C. Fussell, former aide-de-camp to General Stanley McChrystal, *The Tim Ferriss Show*, http://fourhourworkweek.com/2015/07/05/stanley-mcchrystal/.

79. H. Lye, "Dr. Will Roper on AI and Autonomy in the U.S. Air Force," *Air Force Technology*, 3 December 2019, https://www.airforce-technology.com/features/dr-will-roper-on-ai-and-autonomy-in-the-us-air-force/, accessed 22 March 2020.

80. A. Fursman, Remarks, "Private Sector Perspectives on the Development of Lethal Autonomous Systems," Geneva, 12 April 2016.

81. "So many decisions on the battlefield are time-sensitive; to engage with the enemy and destroy them." Corn, remarks at Autonomous Weapon Systems—Law, Ethics and Policy Conference at European University Institute. NATO doctrine provides that, as part of the "battle rhythm" of NATO operations, coalition forces "should maintain a rate of activity greater than that of the opponent." AJP-3 (B), *Allied Joint Doctrine for the Conduct of Operations*, North Atlantic Treaty Organization, March 2011, para. 0424, http://www.cicde.defense.gouv.fr/IMG/pdf/20110316_np_otan_ajp-3b.pdf.

82. Col. John L. Haithcock Jr., TSM FATDS, Fort Sill, OK, Letter to the Editor, Field Artillery, January–February 2006, http://sill-www.army.mil/firesbulletin/archives/2006/jan_feb_2006/jan_feb_2006_full_edition.pdf.

83. Neither abstract concepts nor the law is an effective substitute for armed conflict. H. Lauterpacht, *The Function of Law in the International Community* (Oxford: Clarendon, 1933), p. 437.

84. B. Burridge, Air Chief Marshall (ret.), U.K. Army, "Military Capability Is Founded on a Body of Knowledge to Which Industry Is a Major Contributor," 2010, copy in author's possession.

85. Corn, remarks at Autonomous Weapon Systems—Law, Ethics and Policy Conference at European University Institute.

86. Defense and Security News—Russia, 23 April 2014, http://www.armyrecognition.com/april_2014_global_defense_security_news_uk/russian_army_to_use_unmanned_ground_robot_taifun-m_to_protect_yars_and_topol-m_missile_sites_2304143.html.

87. "Guardium Mark2 UGV: Field Proven UGV with Enhanced Combat Capabilities," GNIUS Unmanned Ground Systems, http://g-nius.co.il/pdf/brochures/GuardiumLS.pdf.

88. "Future Weapons Israel: Iron Fist APS," Discovery, https://www.youtube.com/watch?v=fI_cbAdCZCw, accessed 28 March 2020.

89. "Brimstone Precision Attack Weapon Data Sheet," MBDA Missile Systems, https://www.mbda-systems.com/product/brimstone/, accessed 28 March 2020.

90. Missile Defense Project, "Brimstone," *Missile Threat*, Center for Strategic and International Studies, published 6 December 2017, last modified 15 June 2018, https://missilethreat.csis.org/missile/brimstone/, accessed 28 March 2020.

91. The missile's "target seeker" produces high-resolution images for evaluation by the system's target recognition algorithms. Missile Defense Project, "Brimstone."

92. "Brimstone Precision Attack Weapon Data Sheet"; "Brimstone," *Missile Threat*, Center for Strategic and International Studies.

93. *Army of None: Autonomous Weapons and the Future of War* (New York: W. W. Norton, 2018), pp. 105–8.

94. R. Cohen, "Skyborg, Weapons Swarms, Satellites Chosen as First 'Vanguards,'" *Air Force Magazine*, 22 November 2019, https://www.airforcemag.com/skyborg-weapon-swarms-satellites-chosen-as-first-vanguards/, accessed 28 March 2020.

95. The LOCUST swarm can be launched from ground-based vehicles, ships. and planes. D. Smalley, "LOCUST: Autonomous Swarming UAVs Fly into the Future," America's Navy, 4 April 2015, http://www.navy.mil/submit/display.asp?story_id=86558://, accessed 28 March 2020.

96. J. Richardson, "The Coming Drone Swarm," *Defence Procurement International*, 16 February 2017, https://www.defenceprocurementinternational.com/features/air/drone-swarms, accessed 28 March 2020.

97. J. Richardson, "Coming Drone Swarm."

98. U.S. Air Force 2030 Science and Technology Strategy, p. 8, https://www.airforcemag.com/PDF/DocumentFile/Documents/2019/USAF%20Science%20and%20Technology%20Strategy.pdf, accessed 29 March 2020.

99. A. Gregg, "Swarming Drones Could Soon Be Real Weapons for the Military," *Washington Post*, 19 February 2019, https://www.latimes.com/business/la-fi-drone-swarms-20190219-story.html, accessed 4 April 2020.

100. Chairman of U.S. Joint Chiefs of Staff, Joint Publication 3-09, Joint Fire Support, 12 December 2014, III-8, https://www.jcs.mil/Portals/36/Documents/Doctrine/pubs/jp3_09.pdf, accessed 2 April 2020; "Ground Launched Small Diameter Bomb," *Army Technology*, https://www.army-technology.com/projects/small-diameter-bomb-glsdb/, accessed 2 April 2020.

101. Chairman of U.S. Joint Chiefs of Staff, Joint Publication 3-09.

102. "Future Weapons Israel Special Part V, Spyder ADS," Discovery, https://www.youtube.com/watch?v=YW8G-8uyqdA; "SPYDER-SR ADS Short Range Air Defense System," Rafael Advanced Defense Systems Ltd., http://www.rafael.co.il/Marketing/186-704-en/Marketing.aspx.

103. "Future Weapons Israel Special Part V, Spyder ADS." India's armed forces also operate the Spyder system. "India Buys Israeli 'SPYDER' Mobile Air Defense System," *Defense Industry Daily*, 19 August 2009, http://www.defenseindustrydaily.com/india-to-buy-israeli-spyder-mobile-air-defense-system-02702/.

104. "Hero-400EC Extended Range Loitering System," *Air Force Technology*, https://www.airforce-technology.com/projects/hero-400ec-extended-range-loitering-system/, accessed 29 March 2020.

105. A. Egozi, "Israeli F-35s to Use Spice Bomb Kits," F-16.Net, 13 March 2013, http://www.f-16.net/forum/viewtopic.php?t=23226, accessed 2 April 2020.

106. R. Hughes, "Rafael Enhances SPICE 250 with Advanced Automatic Target Recognition Capability," *Jane's Missiles and Rockets*, 10 June 2019, https://www.janes.com/article/89149/rafael-enhances-spice-250-with-advanced-automatic-target-recognition-capability, accessed 2 April 2020.

107. "Spice: Precision Guided Weapon Kit," Rafael Advanced Weapon Systems, http://www.rafael.co.il/Marketing/332-891-en/Marketing.aspx, accessed 2 April 2020.

108. "Spice: Smart, Precise-Impact and Cost-Effective Guidance Kits," Rafael: Smart and to the Point, http://www.rafael.co.il/marketing/SIP_STORAGE/FILES/4/924.pdf.

109. P. Tucker, "Inside the Navy's Secret Swarm Robot Experiment," *Defence One*, 5 October 2014, http://www.defenseone.com/technology/2014/10/inside-navys-secret-swarm-robot-experiment/95813/; accessed 4 April 2020; "Unmanned Boats Demonstrate Autonomous Swarm," *Defense Update*, 4 October 2014, https://www.youtube.com/watch?v=GGuMdJBpWdE, accessed 4 April 2020.

110. "Protector: USV, Unmanned Integrated Naval Combat System," Rafael Advanced Defense Systems," https://www.rafael.co.il/wp-content/uploads/2019/03/Protector.pdf, accessed 4 April 2020.

111. S. Chen, "China Military Develops Robotic Submarines to Launch a New Era of Sea Power," *South China Morning Post*, 22 July 2018, https://www.scmp.com/news/china/society/article/2156361/china-developing-unmanned-ai-submarines-launch-new-era-sea-power, accessed 4 April 2020.

112. D. Hambling, "Change in the Air: Disruptive Developments in Armed UAV Technology," *UNIDIR*, pp. 5–6, https://www.unidir.org/files/publications/pdfs/-en-726.pdf, accessed 4 April 2020.

113. "Russia Is Developing Artificial Intelligence for Military and Civilian Drones," *Tass*, 15 May 2017, https://tass.com/defense/945950, accessed 4 April 2020.

114. "Pilot Project EUROSWARM and SPIDER Completed," *European Defense Agency*, 23 February 2018, https://www.eda.europa.eu/info-hub/press-centre/latest-news/2018/02/23/pilot-project-euroswarm-and-spider-activities-completed, accessed 4 April 2020.

115. G. Williamson, "Defense in Global Britain," GOV.UK, 11 February 2019, https://www.gov.uk/government/speeches/defence-in-global-britain, accessed 4 April 2020.

116. Col. Travis Burdine, Air Force Division Chief for Unmanned Aircraft, in D. Hambling, "If Drone Swarms Are the Future, China May Be Winning," *Popular Mechanics*, 23 December 2026, https://www.popularmechanics.com/military/research/a24494/chinese-drones-swarms/, accessed 4 April 2020.

Chapter 2

1. J. Waldron, "Dignity, Rank and Rights: The Tanner Lectures on Human Values," delivered at University of California, Berkeley, 21–23 April 2009, p. 209, https://tannerlectures.utah.edu/_documents/a-to-z/w/Waldron_09.pdf, accessed 25 April 2020.

2. Waldron, "Dignity, Rank and Rights," p. 210.

3. J. Aguas, "The Notions of the Human Person and Human Dignity in Aquinas and Wojtyla," 3 *Kritike*, 1 (June 2009), pp. 40–41, n. 5, http://www.kritike.org/journal/issue_5/aguas_june2009.pdf, accessed 11 April 2020.

4. Aristotle, book 1, chapter 13, *On Rhetoric: A Theory of Civic Discourse*, G. Kennedy (trans.), 2nd ed. (New York: Oxford University Press, 2007), p. 97.

5. Aristotle, book 1, chapter 13, *On Rhetoric*, p. 97.

6. T. Aquinas, *The Summa Theologica*, II-II, question 57, art. 1, http://dhspriory.org/thomas/summa/SS/SS057.html#SSQ57OUTP1.

7. Aquinas, *The Summa Theologica*, II-II, question 57, art. 1.

8. I. Kant, *The Groundwork of Metaphysics of Morals*, M. Gregor and J. Timmermann (eds. and trans.) (Cambridge University Press, 2011), vol. 4, pp. 428, 429, and 436.

9. Kant, *Groundwork*, vol. 4, p. 436.

10. Kant, *Groundwork*, vol. 4, pp. 439–41.

11. Kant, *Groundwork*, vol. 4, pp. 421–24.

12. Kant, *Groundwork*, vol. 4, p. 433.

13. Kant, *Groundwork*, vol. 4, pp. 427–29.

14. Kant, *Groundwork*, vol. 4, pp. 434–35.

15. Kant, *Groundwork*, vol. 4, pp. 434–35. I am grateful to an anonymous reviewer for drawing my attention to this point.

16. R. Howard and J. Donnelly, "Human Dignity, Human Rights, and Political Regimes," 80 *American Political Science Review*, 3 (September 1986), pp. 801–2.

17. M. Walzer, *Just and Unjust Wars: A Moral Argument with Historical Illustrations* (New York: Basic Books, 1977), p. 54 (emphasis added).

18. M. Rosen, *Dignity: Its History and Meaning* (Cambridge, Mass.: Harvard University Press, 2012), p. 36.

19. J. Finnis, *Natural Law and Natural Rights* (Oxford: Clarendon, 1980), p. 272.

20. H. Arendt, *The Origins of Totalitarianism* (New York: Harcourt, 1968), p. 474.

21. "Conclusions," *The Church in the Actual Transformation of Latin America in Light of the Council*, II, Bogota, General Secretariat of Episcopal Conference of Latin America, 1968, p. 217, citing Paul VI, Enc. Populorum progressio, No. 30.

22. Finnis, *Natural Law and Natural Rights*, p. 273.

23. Suzanne Killmister, "Dignity: Personal, Social, Human," 174 *Philosophical Studies* (2017), 8, pp. 174, 2063, 2081.

24. Killmister "Dignity," p. 2065.

25. T. Baldwin, "Identity," in *The Oxford Handbook of Law, Regulation and Technology*, R. Brownsword, E. Scotford and K. Yeung (eds.) (Oxford University Press, 2017), p. 130.

26. Killmister, "Dignity," p. 2068 (citing Kant, *Groundwork*).

27. UNGA Res. 217 A (III), U.N. Doc. A/810, 10 December 1948. Again, I am grateful to an anonymous reviewer for drawing my attention to this point.

28. Art. 38 (1), Statute of the International Court of Justice.

29. Art. 1 (a), Vienna Convention on the Law of Treaties, 23 May 1969.

30. *Case of the S.S. Wimbledon* (Judgement) Permanent Court of International Justice 1923, p. 25.

31. J. Klabbers, *International Law* (Cambridge University Press, 2013), pp. 42–43. See *The Case of the S.S. Lotus* (Judgement) Permanent Court of International Justice Series A No. 10 1927, p. 18 (holding that the rules of law binding on states emanate, inter alia, from their own free will as expressed in conventions). Preamble, Vienna Convention on the Law of Treaties.

32. "Pacta sunt Servanda," art. 26, Vienna Convention on the Law of Treaties.

33. Klabbers, *International Law*, p. 30.

34. Art. 18, Vienna Convention on the Law of Treaties.

35. Art. 31, Vienna Convention on the Law of Treaties. Together with the context of the agreement, parties shall also take into account: (1) subsequent agreements between the states regarding the interpretation of the treaty or the application of its provisions, (2) subsequent practice in the application of the treaty that demonstrates the agreement of the parties concerning its interpretation; and (3) relevant rules of international law applicable to the relations between the parties.

36. A. Boyle and C. Chinkin, *The Making of International Law* (Oxford University Press, 2007), p. 241.

37. *North Sea Continental Shelf* (Judgment) ICJ Reports 1969, paras. 77–78.

38. H. Charlesworth, "Law-Making and Sources," in J. Crawford and M. Koskenniemi (eds.), *The Cambridge Companion to International Law* (Cambridge University Press, 2012), p. 193.

39. Charlesworth, "Law-Making and Sources," p. 193.

40. For example, in its judgment in *North Sea Continental Shelf*, the International Court of Justice noted, with respect to the creation of customary international law, that "even without the passage of any considerable period of time, a very widespread and representative participation" in a form of activity "might suffice of itself" to form new customary law, provided it included participation of states whose interests were specially affected. Para. 73. In some circumstances, expressions of governments and their officials can serve to illustrate both state practice and *opinio juris*. *The Paquette Habana*, 175 U.S. 677, 686–708 (1900). The majority ruled that customary international law prohibited one belligerent state from seizing the fishing vessels of an enemy state during wartime, unless the vessel was used in connection with the hostilities.

41. Charlesworth, "Law-Making and Sources," pp. 192–94.

42. A. Roberts, "Traditional and Modern Approaches to Customary International Law: A Reconciliation," 95 *American Journal of International Law* (2001), 757, 758.

43. Roberts, "Traditional and Modern Approaches," 758.

44. *South West Africa Case, Second Phase*, Judgment, Dissenting Opinion of Judge Tanaka, ICJ Reports 1966, p. 291.

45. Strong statements of *opinio juris* are important because they illustrate normative considerations about existing customs and emerging customs and can generate new customs. Roberts, "Traditional and Modern Approaches," 788. Professor (and Judge) Meron, for example, supports the modern method of identifying customary international humanitarian law through the practice of state incorporation of provisions of the 1977 Additional Protocols into the military manuals of their armed forces. T. Meron, *Human Rights and Humanitarian Norms as Customary Law* (Oxford: Clarendon Press, 1989), p. 78.

46. Roberts, "Traditional and Modern Approaches," 758. See, for example, the judgment of the International Court of Justice in the *Case Concerning Military and Paramilitary Activities in and Against Nicaragua*, where the court opined, without a discussion of the requirement of

state practice, that it could deduce *opinio juris*, and therefore customary international law, from the attitude of states toward "certain General Assembly resolutions." *Nicaragua v. United States of America* (Merits) 1986, paras. 188–94. Confusingly, the court reverted to a more traditional analysis later in its judgment: "[t]he existence in the opinio juris of states of the principle of non-intervention is backed by established and substantial practice," paras. 202 and 205–7.

47. R. Higgins, "Fundamentals of International Law," in *Themes and Theories: Selected Essays, Speeches, and Writings [of Rosalyn Higgins] in International Law* (Oxford University Press, 2009), p. 122; *South West Africa Case, Second Phase*, Dissenting Opinion of Judge Tanaka, p. 291.

48. S. Talmon, "Determining Customary International Law: The ICJ's Methodology Between Induction, Deduction and Assertion," 26 *European Journal of International Law* 2 (2015), 417, 432.

49. B. Simma and P. Alston, "The Sources of Human Rights Law: Custom, Jus Cogens, and General Principles," 12 *Australian Yearbook of International Law* (1988–89), p. 89.

50. Simma and Alston, "Sources of Human Rights Law," p. 97 (citing the Committee on the Formation of Customary International Law, American Branch of the International Law Association: "The Role of State Practice in the Formation of Customary and Jus Cogens Norms of International Law," 19 January 1989, p. 7). Similarly, Professor Roberts observes that the strongest "criticism of modern custom is that it is descriptively inaccurate because it reflects ideal, rather than actual, standards of conduct." Roberts, "Traditional and Modern Approaches," p. 769.

51. J. Charney, "Universal International Law," (October 1993) 87 *American Journal of International Law*, 4, 529, 543–48. As the deductive method of law creation that he supported reduced the reliance on state practice common to the inductive process, Charney proposed to label this new modern law "general international law" rather than customary international law. "Universal International Law," p. 546.

52. Charney, "Universal International Law," pp. 536–38.

53. *Prosecutor v. Blagoje Simić et al.*, Decision on the Prosecution Motion Under Rule 73 for a Ruling Concerning the Testimony of a Witness, IT-95-9, 27 July 1999, para. 74.

54. For example, most provisions of the Geneva Conventions are considered to be declaratory of customary international humanitarian law. *Prosecutor v. Blagoje Simić et al.*, Decision on the Prosecution Motion Under Rule 73, para. 48.

55. Art. 38, Vienna Convention on the Law of Treaties, North Sea Continental Shelf, para. 71; ICRC Introduction to *Convention (II) with Respect to the Laws and Customs of War on Land and its Annex: Regulations Concerning the Laws and Customs of War on Land*, The Hague, 29 July 1899, https://www.icrc.org/ihl/INTRO/150?OpenDocument; J. Kellenberger, "Foreword" to J. Henckaerts and L. Doswald-Beck, *Customary International Humanitarian Law*, vol. 1, *Rules* (Cambridge University Press, 2009), p. x.

56. Art. 38, Statute of the International Court of Justice, http://www.icj-cij.org/documents/?p1=4&p2=2. The old-fashioned (and condescending) term "civilized" commonly is interpreted to refer to the "community of nations," or at least those that possess a mature legal system. G. Boas, *Public International Law: Contemporary Principles and Perspectives* (Cheltenham: Edward Elgar, 2012), p. 105.

57. B. Cheng, *General Principles of Law as Applied by International Courts and Tribunals* (London: Stevens and Sons, 1953), p. 24; J. Klabbers, *International Law*, p. 34.

58. *South West Africa Case, Second Phase*, Dissenting Opinion of Judge Tanaka, pp. 295–98 (observing that the concept of human rights and their protection falls within the category of

"general principles of law" for the purpose of art. 38 [1] [c] of the Statute of the International Court of Justice). Hersch Lauterpacht called the general principles of law "a modern version of the laws of nature." *An International Bill of the Rights of Man* (1945) (Oxford University Press, 2013), p. 42.

59. *South West Africa Case, Second Phase,* Dissenting Opinion of Judge Tanaka, p. 298.

60. *South West Africa Case, Second Phase,* Dissenting Opinion of Judge Tanaka; G. Del Vecchio, *General Principles of Law,* F. Forte (trans.) (Boston University Press, 1956), p. 50. Thus, general principles of law are not limited to national statutory provisions. Indeed, some of the more abstract general principles that form part of international law ("good faith," "freedom of the seas," etc.) "have been accepted for so long and so generally as no longer to be *directly* connected to state practice." J. Crawford, *Brownlie's Principles of Public International Law,* 8th ed. (Oxford University Press, 2012), p. 37 (emphasis in original).

61. Del Vecchio, *General Principles of Law,* p. 50.

62. *Department of Defense Law of War Manual,* Office of General Counsel, U.S. Department of Defense, June 2015, paras. 2.1.1 and 2.1.2, http://www.defense.gov/Portals/1/Documents/pubs/Law-of-War-Manual-June-2015.pdf.

63. *Case of Khaled El Masri v. Federal Yugoslav Republic of Macedonia,* Judgment, European Court of Human Rights (ECtHR), 13 December 2012, para. 106 (referring to case law of the Court of Appeal of England and Wales holding that arbitrary detention of persons at Guantánamo Bay contravened fundamental principles of international law).

64. For example, the broad legal principle of the "presumption of innocence" imposes more specific obligations on criminal proceedings, such as laying the burden of proof on the prosecution to prove guilt beyond a reasonable doubt and the right of the accused to remain silent. W. Schabas, *An Introduction to the International Criminal Court,* 4th ed. (Cambridge University Press, 2011), p. 216. Professor Werle argues that the Rome Statute of the International Criminal Court represents "the high point of efforts at codification of general principles of international criminal law." *Principles of International Criminal Law,* 2nd ed. (The Hague: T. M. C. Asser, 2009), para. 365.

65. Department of Defense Law of War Manual, para. 2.1.2. Emmanuel Voyiakis argues that the distinction between customary international law and general principles of law is not very consequential. In his view, general principles of law constitute a distinct source of international law only in the sense that they extend "the database of existing legal material" used by international lawyers in support of their claims about international law. "Do General Principles Fill 'Gaps' in International Law?" in G. Loibl and S Wittich (eds.), 14 *Austrian Review of International European Law* (2009) (Leiden: Martinus Nijhoff, 2013), p. 254.

66. *The Paquete Habana,* 707 (citing Ignacio de Megrin, *Elementary Treatise on Maritime International Law* [1873]).

67. For example, the International Criminal Tribunal for the former Yugoslavia held that "the parties [to the Geneva Conventions] must be taken as having accepted the fundamental principles on which the ICRC operates, that is impartiality, neutrality and confidentiality, and in particular as having accepted that confidentiality is necessary for the effective performance by the ICRC of its functions." *Prosecutor v. Blagoje Simić et al.,* Decision on the Prosecution Motion Under Rule 73 for a Ruling Concerning the Testimony of a Witness, para. 73.

68. International Law Commission, *Draft Articles on Responsibility of States for Internationally Wrongful Acts, with Commentaries* (2001), Commentary to chapter 3, para. (7), http://legal.un.org/ilc/texts/instruments/english/commentaries/9_6_2001.pdf. In its Nicaragua judgment,

a majority of the International Court of Justice cited to authority that described jus cogens norms as fundamental or cardinal principles of customary law. *Case Concerning Military and Paramilitary Activities in and Against Nicaragua*, Judgment, para. 190, http://www.icj-cij.org/docket/files/70/6503.pdf. The court expressly recognized the concept of peremptory norms in its judgment in *Armed Activities on the Territory of the Congo* (New Application [2002]) (*Democratic Republic of the Congo v. Rwanda*) (Jurisdiction and Admissibility), ICJ Reports 2006, p. 52.

69. Art. 53, Vienna Convention on the Law of Treaties (VCLT), 23 May 1969. David Bederman describes jus cogens (rather glibly) as "simply entrenched customary international law"). *Custom as a Source of Law* (Cambridge University Press, 2010), p. 159.

70. Boyle and Chinkin, *Making of International Law*, p. 114.

71. A. Bianchi, "Human Rights and the Magic of Jus Cogens," 19 *European Journal of International Law* (2008) 3, 491, 495.

72. Bianchi, "Human Rights and the Magic of Jus Cogens," 491 and 495. This is because "human rights peremptory norms form the social identity of the group as well as one of the main ordering factors of social relations" (p. 497).

73. International Law Commission, Commentary to art. 40, paras. 4–7. Examples would include the prohibitions of aggression, slavery, discrimination, and torture, and the right to self-determination.

74. Department of Public Information, *Yearbook of the United Nations (1946–1947)* (Lake Success, N.Y.: United Nations Publications, 1947), p. 17 (citing Drafting Committee I/1).

75. Done at San Francisco 26 June 1945, entered into force on 24 October 1945, http://www.un.org/en/sections/un-charter/preamble/index.html.

76. *Legality of the Threat or Use of Nuclear Weapons*, Advisory Opinion, Dissenting Opinion of Judge Weeramantry, ICJ Reports 1996, p. 434, http://www.icj-cij.org/docket/files/95/7521.pdf.

77. *Legality of the Threat or Use of Nuclear Weapons*. Indeed, the dignity and worth of the human person is "the cardinal unit of value in global society" (p. 442).

78. P. Jessup, *A Modern Law of Nations* (New York: Macmillan, 1948), p. 91. Similarly, in the *South West Africa Case*, Judge Tanaka observed that the provisions of the United Nations Charter referring to "human rights and fundamental freedoms" imply that states bear an obligation to respect human rights and fundamental freedoms. (Dissenting Opinion: Second Phase) ICJ Reports 1966, p. 289.

79. *Legality of the Threat or Use of Nuclear Weapons*, Advisory Opinion, Dissenting Opinion of Judge Weeramantry, p. 507.

80. See the Maipú Treaty for Integration and Cooperation Between the Argentine Republic and the Republic of Chile, Buenos Aires, 15 June 2007 (declaring that this treaty is "an instrument honoring the commitment to raise the quality of life and dignity of their inhabitants"); the Framework Agreement on Cooperation in the Field of Immigration Between the Kingdom of Spain and the Republic of Mali, Madrid, 23 January 2007 (recognizing that illegal migration "must be fought effectively while ensuring full respect for the human rights and personal dignity of emigrants"); the Treaty Concerning Friendly Cooperation and Partnership in Europe Between Romania and the Federal Republic of Germany, Bucharest, 21 April 1992 (affirming that the parties "shall place the human person, with his or her dignity and rights, . . . at the center of their policy"); the Treaty Between Romania and the Italian Republic on Friendship and Collaboration, Bucharest, 23 July 1991 (agreeing that Romania and Italy shall develop their relations on the basis of trust, collaboration and mutual respect in keeping with, inter alia, the principle of human dignity).

81. Indeed, soon after the charter entered into force, and before Professor Jessup made this observation, the state parties to the United Nations Educational, Scientific and Cultural Organization (UNESCO) recalled that "the wide diffusion of culture, and the education of humanity for justice and liberty and peace are indispensable to the dignity of man and constitute a sacred duty which all the nations must fulfill in a spirit of mutual assistance and concern." Constitution of UNESCO, London, 16 November 1945, in the Royal Institute of International Affairs, *United Nations Documents, 1941–1945* (Oxford University Press, 1947), p. 225.

82. A/PV.123, 21 November 1947, General Assembly Hall, Flushing Meadow, N.Y., in H. Abtahi and P. Webb, *The Genocide Convention: The Travaux Préparatoires* (Leiden: Martinus Nijhoff, 2008), p. 449.

83. Abtahi and Webb, *Genocide Convention*, p. 450.

84. E/SR.218, General Statements on Draft Convention on the Crime of Genocide, 218th Meeting of ECOSOC, Paleis de Nations, Geneva, 26 August 1948, in Abtahi and Webb, *Genocide Convention*, p. 1234.

85. M. Glendon, *A World Made New: Eleanor Roosevelt and the Universal Declaration of Human Rights* (New York: Random House, 2002), p. 146.

86. Judgment, South African Constitutional Court, *The State v. T. Makwanyane and M. Mchunu*, Case No. CCT/3/94, 6 June 1995 at 172, Justice Mokgoro concurring.

87. Waldron, "Dignity, Rank and Rights," p. 212.

88. For example, the Preamble to the Charter of the United Nations begins: "We the Peoples of the United Nations Determined . . . to reaffirm faith in fundamental human rights, in the dignity and worth of the human person, in the equal rights of men and women and of nations large and small."

89. G. Kateb, *Human Dignity* (Cambridge: Harvard University Press, 2011), p. 42. In *Pretty v. United Kingdom*, the European Court of Human Rights held that "[w]here treatment humiliates or debases an individual, showing a lack of respect for, or diminishing, his or her human dignity, or arouses feelings of fear, anguish or inferiority capable of breaking an individual's moral and physical resistance, it may be characterised as degrading and also fall within the prohibition of Article 3." Judgment, Application No. 2346/02 (ECtHR, 2002) para. 52, http://hudoc.echr.coe.int/sites/eng/pages/search.aspx?i=001-60448.

90. Preamble, International Covenant on Economic, Social and Cultural Rights, 16 December 1966; cf. Preamble, International Covenant on Civil and Political Rights, 19 December 1966.

91. *Case of Husayn (Abu Zubaydah) v. Poland*, Judgment, European Court of Human Rights, ECtHR, Application No. 7511/13, 24 July 2014, para. 532 (citing *Pretty v. the United Kingdom*, Judgment, paras. 61 and 65).

92. D. Feldman, "Human Dignity as a Legal Value: Part 2," *Public Law* (2000), p. 5.

93. *S. v. Makwanyane*, Case No. CCT/3/94, Constitutional Court of South Africa, 6 June 1995, para. 144, Justice Chaskalson.

94. Preamble, Convention Against Torture and Other Cruel, Inhuman or Degrading Treatment or Punishment, 10 December 1984; art 7, International Covenant on Civil and Political Rights, 16 December 1966; art. 3, European Convention on Human Rights; art. 5, African Charter for Human and Peoples' Rights. Article 5 (2) of the American Convention on Human Rights creates a positive duty for states to treat all detained persons "with respect for the inherent dignity of the human person." Art. 5, Universal Declaration of Human Rights, 10 December 1948 (the Universal Declaration of Human Rights is an "aspirational" document rather than a treaty); art. 1, UNESCO Convention Against Discrimination in Education, Paris, 14 December 1960.

95. *Case of M.S.S. v. Belgium and Greece*, Judgment, EctHR, Application No. 30696/09, 21 January 2011, paras. 233, 253, and 263 (holding that conditions of detention for an asylum seeker in Greece damaged the victim's dignity and that official indifference to an applicant's circumstances can constitute a lack of respect for her dignity); *Case of Kuznetsov v. Ukraine*, Judgment, EctHR, Application No 39042/97, 29 April 2003, para. 126 (holding that conditions of detention for a convicted murderer diminished his human dignity).

96. *Ms. X v. Argentina* Case 10.506 Report No. 38/96 OEA/Ser.L/V/II.95 Doc 7. Rev. at 50, Inter-American Court of Human Rights (Inter-Am. Ct. H.R.), 1997, paras. 93, 96, and 100 (holding that requirement of vaginal searches of mother and daughter each time they visited their imprisoned relative violated their rights to dignity, privacy, honor, and family life).

97. *Case of Christine Goodwin v. the United Kingdom*, Judgement, ECtHR, Application No. 28957/95, 11 July 2002, para. 91 (holding that states can tolerate some inconvenience to enable persons to live in dignity in accordance with the sexual identity chosen by them).

98. *Case of the Mayagna (Sumo) Awas Tingni Community v. Nicaragua*, Judgement, Inter-Am. Ct. H.R., 31 August 2001, para. 140 (f) (citing the argument of the Inter-American Commission for Human Rights, 4 June 1998, that the community's land and resources are protected by, inter alia, the rights to dignity and property and the state must adopt measures to fully guarantee the community's rights to its lands and resources).

99. *Case of Nachova and Others v. Bulgaria*, Judgement, ECtHR, Application No. 43577/98, 5 July 2005, para. 145 (holding that racial violence—a violation of the prohibition of discrimination—is a particular affront to human dignity).

100. *Application of the Convention on the Prevention and Punishment of the Crime of Genocide (Bosnia and Herzegovina v. Serbia and Montenegro)* (Separate Opinion of Judge Weeramantry), ICJ Reports 2007, p. 645. On a smaller scale, in 2002, Argentina, Brazil, Paraguay, and Uruguay signed an "Agreement Regarding the Residence of Nationals of the States Parties to MERCOSUR." The accord was motivated, in part, by the importance of combating trafficking in persons, to reduce the incidence of "situations involving denial of their human dignity." *Treaty Series: Treaties and International Agreements Registered or Filed and Recorded with the Secretariat of the United Nations*, vol. 2541, United Nations, 2008, p. 118.

101. *Prosecutor v. Anto Furundija* (Judgment) IT-95-17/1-T (10 December 1998), para. 183, http://www.icty.org/x/cases/furundzija/tjug/en/fur-tj981210e.pdf.

102. O. Schachter, "Human Dignity as a Normative Concept," 77 *American Journal of International Law* (1983), 848, 849.

103. It is important not to assume that all treaty "rules" are necessarily specific. Indeed, less-than-precise language may serve as the best possible common denominator. As Philip Allott observed, a treaty "is a disagreement reduced to writing." "The Concept of International Law," 10 *European Journal of International Law* (1999) 31, para. 35.

104. *South West Africa Case, Second Phase*, para. 50.

105. In 1946, for example, the United Nations General Assembly declared that the crime of genocide is contrary to "moral law." "The Crime of Genocide," Resolution 96 (I), Fifty-Fifth Plenary Meeting, 11 December 1946. Indeed, it is impossible to separate law strictly from morality, politics, and culture. S. Marks et al., "Responsibility for Violations of Human Rights Obligations: International Mechanisms," in J. Crawford et al. (eds.), *The Law of International Responsibility* (Oxford University Press, 2010), p. 736. "Law" is a synonym for the phrase "moral rules." Macmillan Dictionary, http://www.macmillandictionary.com/thesaurus-category/british/moral-rules-and-rules-of-behaviour.

106. D. Shultziner and G. Carmi, "Human Dignity in National Constitutions: Functions, Promises and Dangers," p. 2 and related data, draft paper in author's possession.

107. Shultziner and Carmi, "Human Dignity in National Constitutions," pp. 7 and 18–28. Several South American constitutions refer to human dignity as a foundational norm, value, or purpose of the state itself. Art. 1 (iii), 1998 Constitution of Brazil (Rev. 2014), https://www.constituteproject.org/constitution/Brazil_2014.pdf; art. 1, 1991 Constitution of Colombia (rev. 2005), https://www.constituteproject.org/constitution/Colombia_2005.pdf; art. 1, 1992 Constitution of Paraguay (rev. 2011), https://www.constituteproject.org/constitution/Paraguay_2011.pdf?lang=en; art. (9) (2), 2009 Constitution of Plurinational State of Bolivia, https://www.constituteproject.org/constitution/Bolivia_2009.pdf. According to the Charter of Fundamental Rights of the European Union, the union is founded, inter alia, on the universal value of human dignity. 2000/C 364/01.

108. 2011 Constitution of Hungary, art. 2, 1996; Constitution of the Republic of South Africa, art. 10; *S. v. Makwanyane*, at para. 311, Justice Mokgoro concurring.

109. By enshrining human dignity in a "prime position," such as the preamble or set of fundamental principles, states make this concept the normative and theoretical source of all other constitutional rights, or a kind of "mother right." C. Dupre, *The Age of Dignity: Human Rights and Constitutionalism in Europe* (Oxford: Hart), 2015, p. 71.

110. Shultziner and Carmi, "Human Dignity in National Constitutions," pp. 22–23.

111. Art. 5, Constitution of New Zealand of 1852 (with revisions through 2014), https://www.constituteproject.org/constitution/New_Zealand_2014.pdf?lang=en.

112. Art. 32 (3), Constitution of South Korea of 1948, https://www.icrc.org/ihl-nat.nsf/162d151af444ded44125673e00508141/aba339f342ad7493c1256bc8004c2772/$file/constitution%20-%20korea%20-%20en.pdf.

113. Arts. 54 and 57, Constitution of Kenya (Rev. 2010), http://www.lcil.cam.ac.uk/sites/default/files/LCIL/documents/transitions/Kenya_19_2010_Constitution.pdf.

114. A. Barak, *Human Dignity: The Constitutional Value and the Constitutional Right* (Cambridge University Press, 2015), p. 206.

115. *Obergefell v. Hodges*, 576 U.S. 644, (2015), 10, 13, 21, and 28.

116. *R. v. Morgentaler*, [1988] 1 SCR 30, 164.

117. Del Vecchio, *General Principles of Law*, pp. 52 and 54.

118. For example, in Germany, "[h]uman dignity shall be inviolable. To respect and protect it shall be the duty of all state authority." Art. 1, Bundesministerium der Justiz, "Basic Law for the Federal Republic of Germany in the Revised Version Published in the Federal Law Gazette Part III," classification no. 100-1, as amended by the Act of 21 July 2010 (Federal Law Gazette I), 944, http://www.gesetze-im-internet.de/englisch_gg/englisch_gg.html#p0014; Judgment of the First Senate of 15 February 2006, 1 BvR 357/05, http://www.bundesverfassungsgericht.de/entscheidungen/rs20060215_1bvr035705en.html. Article 1 of the Constitution of Brazil states that Brazil is founded on, inter alia, "the dignity of the human person," http://www.wipo.int/wipolex/en/text.jsp?file_id=218270. The preamble to the Constitution of India assures the "dignity of the individual," http://lawmin.nic.in/olwing/coi/coi-english/Const.Pock%202Pg.Rom8Fsss(3).pdf. In Iran, the dignity of the individual is inviolate, except in cases sanctioned by law. Art. 22, Constitution of Islamic Republic of Iran, http://www.iranonline.com/iran/iran-info/government/constitution-3.html. In Kenya, one of the national values and principles of governance is human dignity. Art. 10 (b), Constitution of Kenya [Rev. 2010], https://www.kenyaembassy.com/pdfs/The%20Constitution%20of%20Kenya.pdf. In Nigeria, every "individual is entitled to

respect for the dignity of his person." Art. 34 (1), Constitution of the Federal Republic of Nigeria, http://www.nigeria-law.org/ConstitutionOfTheFederalRepublicOfNigeria.htm#Chapter_4. According to article 7 of the Swiss Constitution, "[h]uman dignity must be respected and protected," http://www.legislationline.org/documents/section/constitutions.

119. Meron, *Human Rights and Humanitarian Norms as Customary Law*, p. 9; E. Cameron, "Dignity and Disgrace: Moral Citizenship and Constitutional Protection," in Christopher McCrudden (ed.), *Understanding Human Dignity* (Oxford University Press, 2013), p. 474.

120. *Adalah v. Minister of Defence*, Judgment, President (Emeritus) A. Barak, HCJ 8276/05 [2006] (2) IsrLR 352, p. 377.

121. Del Vecchio, *General Principles of Law*, pp. 24–25.

122. Del Vecchio, *General Principles of Law*, pp. 52 and 54.

123. Del Vecchio, *General Principles of Law*, p. 54.

124. N. Schrijver and L. van den Herik, *Leiden Policy Recommendations on Counter-Terrorism and International Law*, Grotius Centre for International Legal Studies, 1 April 2010, para. 6. Similarly, early in the nineteenth century, the U.S. Supreme Court observed that international law is in part unwritten and in part conventional; to "ascertain what is unwritten we resort to the great principles of reason and justice." *Thirty Hogsheads of Sugar v. Boyle*, 13 U.S. 191, 198 (1815).

125. This norm prohibits prosecution of crimes that were not recognized as such at the time they were committed. W. Schabas, *An Introduction to the International Criminal Court*, 4th ed. (Cambridge University Press, 2011), p. 73.

126. *Adalah v. Minister of Defence*, Judgment, Barak, p. 159.

127. See *S. v. Makwanyane*, para. 57, citing with approval Justice Brennan's concurring opinion in *Furman v. Georgia*, 408 U.S. 238 (1972), p. 296 ("the dignity of the individual is the supreme value"). Similarly, human dignity is the supreme value of the state of Israel.

128. *National Coalition for Gay and Lesbian Equality v. Minister of Home Affairs*, Case No. CCT 10/99, Constitutional Court of South Africa, 2 December 1999, para. 42. "It is a value that informs the interpretation of many, possibly all other rights." *Dawood v. Minister of Home Affairs*, Case No. CCT 35/99, Constitutional Court of South Africa, 7 June 2000, para. 35.

129. *The Minister of Home Affairs v. Watchenuka*, Case No. 10/2003, Supreme Court of Appeal of South Africa, 28 November 2003, para. 26.

130. The drafters of the International Covenant on Civil and Political Rights (ICCPR) appeared to share this view that the concept of human dignity falls outside the scope of general principles of law. The drafters explained that the preamble of each human rights covenant "sets forth general principles *relating to* the inherent dignity of the human person." "Commission on Human Rights, 8th Session (1952), A/2929, Chap. III, Sec. 1" in M. Bossuyt, *Guide to the "Travaux Préparatoires" of the International Covenant on Civil and Political Rights* (Dordrecht: Martinus Nijhoff, 1987), p. 3 (emphasis added). What does constitute a "general principle" is the notion that human dignity is one of the foundations of freedom, justice, and peace (Bossuyt, *Guide to the "Travaux Préparatoires,"* sec. 4, p. 4).

131. 2010 Report on the Application of the EU Charter of Fundamental Rights, European Commission, p. 24, http://ec.europa.eu/justice/fundamental-rights/files/annual_report_2010_en.pdf.

132. Most jus cogens norms refer to factual situations or actions rather than to claims under international law. S. Talmon, "The Duty Not to 'Recognize as Lawful' a Situation Created by the Illegal Use of Force or Other Serious Breaches of a Jus Cogens Obligation: An Obligation

Without Real Substance?" in C. Tomuschat and J. M. Thouvenin (eds.), *The Fundamental Rules of the International Legal Order: Jus Cogens and Obligations Erga Omnes* (Leiden: Martinus Nijhoff, 2006), p. 104.

133. S. Schmahl, "An Example of Jus Cogens: The Status of Prisoners of War," in Tomuschat and Thouvenin, *Fundamental Rules*, p. 56.

134. Professor Schmahl argues that the "achieved 'common conscience of values' in the modern international legal order, especially regarding human dignity and the inherent and equal value of every human being, is not disputed anymore." Schmahl, "Example of Jus Cogens," p. 56.

135. Professor Tomuschat describes how the concept of human dignity, in addition to being a moral value, serves as a tool for legal analysis because the notion helps us to construe legal rules and to balance common interests against the rights and interests of individuals. C. Tomuschat, *Human Rights: Between Idealism and Realism* (Oxford University Press, 2014), p. 89.

136. Shultziner and Carmi, "Human Dignity in National Constitutions," 23. "[I]t is necessary not to confuse the moral ideal with the legal rule intended to give it effect." *South West Africa Case, Second Phase*, para. 52.

137. M. McDougal and N. Schlei, "The Hydrogen Bomb Tests in Perspective: Lawful Measures for Security," 64 *Yale Law Journal* (1955), p. 656.

138. *Reservations to the Convention on Genocide*, Advisory Opinion, Dissenting Opinion of Judge Alvarez, ICJ Reports (191), p. 51 (describing the "new international law reflecting the new orientation of the legal conscience of the nations").

139. Jan Klabbers argues that normative expressions should be presumed to have legal force, unless and until the opposite is proven. *International Law*, p. 39.

140. P. Carozza, "Human Dignity," in D. Shelton (ed.), *The Oxford Handbook of International Human Rights Law* (Oxford University Press, 2013), p. 1. Remy Debes notes that scholars have conceived dignity variously "as honor, rank, station, inherent worth, inalienable worth, equal worth, supreme worth, uniqueness, beauty, poise, gravitas, personality, integrity, bodily integrity, self-respect, self-esteem, a sacred place in the order of things [and] simply brute and questionable "specialness." Remy Debes, "Dignity's Gauntlet," *Philosophical Perspectives*, 23 (2009), 45, 45–46.

141. D Feldman, "Human Dignity as a Legal Value," Part 1, *Public Law*, 682 (1999). Feldman offers a particularly opaque definition of dignity: "an expression of an attitude to life which we as humans should value when we see it in others as an expression of something which give particular point and poignancy to the human condition" (p. 3).

142. In defense of the utility of the concept of human dignity, Paolo Carozza explains that the "capaciousness of the word 'dignity' allows it to represent an affirmation belonging to a wide array of different traditions." "Human Dignity," p. 3.

143. C. Byk, "Is Human Dignity a Useless Concept? Legal Perspectives," in M. Düwell et al. (eds.), *The Cambridge Handbook of Human Dignity: Interdisciplinary Perspectives* (Cambridge University Press, 2014), p. 364.

144. Byk, "Is Human Dignity a Useless Concept?" 364.

Chapter 3

1. K. Marlantes, *What It Is Like to Go to War* (London: Corvus, 2012), p. 44 (emphasis in original).

2. "As a rational being *he necessarily wills that all capacities in him be developed*, because they serve him and are given to him for all sorts of possible purposes." I. Kant, *Groundwork of the*

Metaphysics of Morals, M. Gregor and J. Timmerman (eds. and trans.) (Cambridge University Press, 2012), vol. 4, p. 423.

3. O. Ulgen, "Autonomous Weapons and Human Dignity," Lecture at Winter Academy on Artificial Intelligence and International Law, Asser Institute, The Hague, 22 January 2020.

4. *United States v. Windsor*, 570 U.S. 744 (2013), p. 22.

5. R. Dworkin, *Justice for Hedgehogs* (Cambridge, Mass.: Harvard University Press, 2011), p. 223.

6. Dworkin, *Justice for Hedgehogs*, pp. 107, 119, and 192–93.

7. J. Waldron, "Dignity, Rights and Responsibilities" (2011) 43 *Arizona State Law Journal* 1107, p. 1121.

8. Waldron, "Dignity, Rights and Responsibilities," at 1122 (citing M. Weber, *Politics as a Vocation* [1919]).

9. For example, Australia, Commonwealth Electoral Act 1918-Sect 245 (1), "Compulsory Voting," http://www.austlii.edu.au/au/legis/cth/consol_act/cea1918233/s245.html; Argentina, Codigo Electoral Nacional, Ley No. 19,495, capítulo 1, "Deber a Votar," artículo 12, http://infoleg.mecon.govar/infolegInternet/anexos/15000-19999/19442/texact.htm; Peru, Ley Orgánica de Elecciones, "Ejercício del Derecho al Voto," artículo 7, http://pdba.georgetown.edu/Electoral/Peru/leyelecciones.pdf. The U.S. Supreme Court has held that "[o]ther rights, even the most basic, are illusory if the right to vote is undermined." *Wesberry v. Sander*, 376 U.S. 1 (1964), p. 17.

10. Constitution of the Republic of South Africa Act 200 of 1993, chapter 2 (5), http://www.govza/documents/constitution/constitution-republic-south-africa-act-200-1993#Citizenship and Franchise.

11. D. McCullough, *John Adams* (New York: Simon and Schuster, 2001), p. 61.

12. Nineteenth Amendment to Constitution of the United States, https://www.congress.gov/constitution-annotated; "Equal Franchise Act 1928," http://www.parliament.uk/about/living-heritage/transformingsociety/electionsvoting/womenvote/parliamentary-collectionsdelete/equal-franchise-act-1928/.

13. M. Ishay, *The History of Human Rights: From Ancient Times to the Globalization Era* (Berkeley: University of California Press, 2004), p. 338.

14. *Whitney v. California* (Brandeis J. Concurring), 274 U.S. 357 (1927), p. 375.

15. *Whitney v. California* , p. 375.

16. P. Carozza, "Human Rights, Human Dignity and Human Experience," in C. McCrudden (ed.), *Understanding Human Dignity* (Oxford University Press/British Academy, 2013), p. 618.

17. J. Mill, "On Liberty," p. 61.

18. J. Mill, "On Liberty," p. 44.

19. J. Waldron, *Dignity, Rank and Rights* (Oxford University Press, 2012), pp. 140–41.

20. Dworkin, *Justice for Hedgehogs*, p. 203.

21. J, Finnis. *Natural Law and Natural Rights* (Oxford: Clarendon Press, 1980), pp. 88 and 100–101.

22. J. Locke, "Of Complex Ideas," in *An Essay Concerning Human Understanding*" (1690), chapter 12, para. 2, ftp://ftp.dca.fee.unicamp.br/pub/docs/ia005/humanund.pdf.

23. H. Simon, *Reason in Human Affairs* (Stanford University Press, 1983), p. 106.

24. Dworkin, *Justice for Hedgehogs*, p. 224.

25. J. Seabrook, "The Next Word: Where Will Predictive Text Take Us?" *New Yorker*, 14 October 2019, pp. 52, 63. Seabrook describes the development of artificial intelligence software that eventually may produce writing of higher quality than that of humans.

26. A. Srinivasan, "Busy Bodies: What Termites Are Teaching Us," *New Yorker*, 17 September 2018, pp. 26 and 31.

27. Many soldiers of the First and Second World Wars expressed "their sense of littleness, almost of nothingness, of their abandonment in a physical wilderness, dominated by vast impersonal forces from which even such normalities as the passage of time had been eliminated." J. Keegan, *The Face of Battle* (New York: Penguin Books, 1978), p. 328. Battlefield conditions "reduced [the soldier's] subjective role, objectively vital though it was, to that of a mere victim" (p. 328).

28. J. Hatzfeld, *A Time for Machetes: The Rwandan Genocide; The Killers Speak* (London: Serpent's Tail, 2008), pp. 98 and 136; J. Hatzfeld, *Into the Quick of Life: The Rwandan Genocide Survivors Speak* (London: Serpent's Tail, 2008), pp. 164–65.

29. Lt. Col. D Grossman observes that "there is within most men an intense resistance to killing their fellow man." *On Killing: The Psychological Cost of Learning to Kill in War and Society* (Boston: Little, Brown, 1996), pp. 4 and 39.

30. "[A]n identity—that is, dignity—is necessary in order to live." P. Levi, *The Drowned and the Saved* (New York: Vintage International, 1989), p. 128.

31. "Meaning came out of living." K. Marlantes, *Matterhorn* (London: Corvus, 2010), p. 664. "Man conceals mysterious reasons for wishing to go on surviving. The more we died, the more ready we were to die, and yet the faster we ran to gain an extra moment of life." Hatzfeld, *Into the Quick of Life*, p. 72.

32. See R. Chantler, "Translator's Introduction" to V. Grossman, *Life and Fate* (London: Flamingo, 1985), p. 12; D. Avery, *De Man Die Naar Auschwitz Wilde (The Auschwitz Volunteer)* (Antwerp: House of Books, 2011), pp. 162–63. Some philosophers argue that this may be reasoned, even obligatory behavior. Amartya Sen contends that "effective power" to assist others in need creates an obligation to at least consider taking action. *The Idea of Justice*, pp. 205–7, 270–71, and 372–76.

33. Keegan, *Face of Battle*, p. 280.

34. In December 1862, during the American Civil War, for example, after Confederate forces had repulsed the attacking Union army at Fredericksburg, Virginia, the Confederate forces declined to counterattack the weakened and vulnerable Union divisions. A Confederate officer who was present explained later that this decision had no basis in strategy or military necessity but rather, lack of appetite for further bloodshed. "We had no want of it." General G. Moxley Sorrel, *Recollections of a Confederate Staff Officer* (New York: Neale, 1905), p. 144. In 1871, Prussian forces invaded France and closed the entrances to Paris. When angry civilians demonstrated against these measures, Prussian commanders ordered their subordinates "to shoot in the last resort." This was a step too far for one officer, who recalled: "I did not care to give that order, and preferred to go out and give some blows with the flat of my sabre." U. Wilamowitz-Moellendorf, *My Recollections: 1848–1914* (London: Chatto and Windus, 1930), p. 144. During the Second World War, even hardened Nazi leaders recognized the value of compassion, albeit only for (certain) Germans. Writing on 16 December 1941, Reich-Commissar for the Coordination of Justice and Governor General of Poland Hans Frank stated: "[a]s a matter of principle we shall have pity only for the German people—and for no one else in the world." H. Shawcross, "Closing Speech," 27 July 1946, *The Trial of German Major War Criminals, Proceedings of the International Military Tribunal Sitting at Nuremberg, Germany*, part 19 (1949), p. 440. Near the end of the war, mourning the combat death of a friend and colleague, Joseph Goebbels wrote (apparently without a trace of irony) that he "shall treasure his memory. How much valuable blood has been spilt in

this war!" *Final Entries 1945: The Diaries of Joseph Goebbels*, H. Trevor-Roper (ed.) (New York: G. P. Putnam's Sons, 1978), p. 27 (entry of 2 March 1945).

35. Staff Sergeant David Bellavia, Induction into Pentagon Hall of Heroes, 26 June 2019, https://www.youtube.com/watch?v=zu3Gm5PGvRM, accessed 1 August 2020.

36. B. Docherty, "Losing Humanity: The Case Against Killer Robots," *Human Rights Watch and the International Human Rights Clinic of Harvard Law School* (November 2012), p. 38.

37. Author interview with Allen Borelli, former intelligence specialist, U.S. Army, The Hague, 15 July 2015.

38. H. Lauterpacht, *An International Bill of the Rights of Man* (1945) (Oxford University Press, 2013), p. 39.

39. H. Kelsen, "What Is Justice?" in *What Is Justice: Justice, Law and Politics in the Mirror of Science; Collected Essays by Hans Kelsen* (Berkeley: University of California Press, 1957), p. 10.

40. Author interview with Gianfranco Visentin, Head, Automation and Robotics Section, European Space Research and Technology Centre, European Space Agency, Noordwijk, Netherlands, 4 November 2013.

41. C. Heyns, "Comments to Informal Meeting of Experts on Lethal Autonomous Weapons: Convention on Conventional Weapons," 16 April 2015, p. 6, http://www.unog.ch/80256EDD006B8954/(httpAssets)/1869331AFF45728BC1257E2D0050EFE0/$file/2015_LAWS_MX_Heyns_Transcript.pdf.

42. I am grateful to Kevin Jon Heller for this insight.

43. S. Killmister. "Dignity: Personal, Social, Human" (2017) 174 *Philosophical Studies*, 8, pp. 174, 2063, 2080.

44. During the American Civil War, Abraham Lincoln, more famous for his service to humanity than for cold-blooded calculations, instituted policies directed to the victory of Union forces over Southern secessionists and for eventual racial justice for African Americans. One of Lincoln's policies was to condition continued prisoner exchanges with the Confederate army on the equal treatment of white and black soldiers, e.g., a commitment by the Confederacy to grant protected prisoner of war status to captured black Union soldiers. The Confederate army refused to accept Lincoln's terms, and the cost of his policy was extended and severe suffering and death for thousands of Union prisoners languishing in Southern camps. Lincoln, however, was compelled to balance "conflicting dignities," i.e., racial justice for freed slaves (and the participation of thousands of black soldiers in the Union effort) versus humane treatment for Union prisoners. J. Witt, *Lincoln's Code: The Laws of War in American History* (New York: Free Press, 2012), pp. 258–63.

45. "A Presumption of the Moral Equality of Combatants," in D. Rodin and H. Shue (eds.), *Just and Unjust Warriors: The Moral and Legal Status of Soldiers* (Oxford University Press, 2008), pp. 223–24.

46. D. Feldman, "Human Dignity as a Legal Value: Part 2," *Public Law* (2000), 3. The concept of freedom within society possesses similar contradictions, as some form of order (i.e., constraint) is often essential to freedom. L. Fuller, "Means and Ends," in Kenneth Winston (ed.), *The Principles of Social Order: Selected Essays of Lon L. Fuller* (Durham, N.C.: Duke University Press, 1981), p. 59.

47. George Kateb argues that great achievements, which may derive from individuals or collectives, "are the central manifestation of the partway separation of the human species from nature and thus help to substantiate the special kind of human uniqueness and hence human dignity." G. Kateb, *Human Dignity* (Cambridge, Mass.: Harvard University Press, 2011), pp. 115 and 123–31.

48. Writing in 1945 about the concept of natural rights, Professor Lauterpacht emphasized the importance of the state as the "absolute condition of the civilized existence of man and of his *progression toward the full realization of his faculties*." *An International Bill of the Rights of Man*, p. 16 (emphasis added).

49. Human potentiality is an important human trait. Kateb, *Human Dignity*, p. 124.

50. For example, the U.S. National Aeronautics and Space Agency (NASA) sponsors an annual robotic mining competition to encourage the design and development of mining robots that can traverse simulated Martian terrain. Teams fielding robots that demonstrate the most autonomy receive a special award. "RMC—about the Competition," 17 May 2015, http://www.nasa.gov/offices/education/centers/kennedy/technology/nasarmc/about. Furthermore, in the future, swarms of miniature autonomous submarines could one day assist in underwater search operations. E. Ackerman, "World's Largest Swarm of Miniature Robots," *IEEE Spectrum*, 5 May 2015, http://spectrum.ieee.org/automaton/robotics/artificial-intelligence/worlds-largest-swarm-of-miniature-robot-submarines. Autonomous ground and air vehicles one day may join humans and dogs in emergency search and rescue teams. E. Ackerman, "Emergency Response Teams Combine Mobile Robots, Drones and Dogs," *IEEE Spectrum*, 6 May 2014, http://spectrum.ieee.org/automaton/robotics/military-robots/emergency-response-teams-combine-mobile-robots-drones-and-dogs.

51. Electronic mail message from G. Santhanam, Senior Engineer at Google X, 31 May 2015. Google employees believe that humans are unreliable partners for a driverless car. D. Bohn, "Astro Teller: Google X 'Encouraged Too Much Attention' for Project Glass," *Verge*, 17 March 2015, http://www.theverge.com/2015/3/17/8235277/sxsw-astro-teller-google-x.

52. J. Achenbach, "After a Wait, Spacecraft Confirms That It Survived Its Close Pass of Pluto," *Washington Post*, 14 July 2015, http://www.washingtonpost.com/national/health-science/new-horizons-finally-makes-it-to-pluto-sees-craters-and-great-mounds/2015/07/14/9bcb0f04-2a1f-11e5-bd33-395c05608059_story.html?wpisrc=nl_evening&wpmm=1.

53. J. Stone, *The Province and Function of Law* (Sydney: Associated General Publications, 1946), p. 782.

54. W. Sebald, *On the Natural History of Destruction* (London: Hamish Hamilton, 2003), p. 153.

55. WWI War Diary Transcription of Acting Cpl. James Strangeway, S8922. No3 Section, 12th Platoon "C" Co. 2nd Battn. Rifle Brigade, https://www.forces-war-records.co.uk/library/document/1980/wwi-war-diary-transcription-of-acting-cpl-james-strangeway-s8922-no3-section-12th-platoon-c-co-2nd-battn-rifle-brigade/page-8/?searchCategory=war+diary&searchTag=wwi&searchPage=1&filterPagesOnSearchQuery=False&filterPagesOnSearchQueryExact=True.

56. Levi, *Drowned and the Saved*, p. 31.

57. Sebald, *On the Natural History of Destruction*, p. 153.

58. For example, during the Second World War and in Vietnam, "[s]oldiers who were inured to violence, numbed to the taking of human life, embittered over their own casualties and frustrated over the tenacity of an insidious and seemingly inhuman enemy sometimes exploded and at other times grimly resolved to have their revenge at the first opportunity." C. Browning, *Ordinary Men: Reserve Police Battalion 101 and the Final Solution in Poland* (New York: Harper Collins, 1992), p. 160.

59. However, it is also possible that the traumatic memories of warfare play a role in deterring additional armed conflicts. Surviving Japanese veterans of World War II argue that it

is their "generation's bitter experiences, and resulting aversion to war, that have kept Japan firmly on a pacifist path since 1945." M. Fackler, "Japanese Ace in World War II Is Pacifist Voice," *New York Times*, 4 April 2015, pp. A1 and A5.

60. C. Byk, "Is Human Dignity a Useless Concept? Legal Perspectives," in *The Cambridge Handbook of Human Dignity: Interdisciplinary Perspectives*, M. Düwell et al. (eds.) (Cambridge University Press, 2014), p. 364.

61. Concluding Remarks of Finland, 2015 Meeting of Experts on Lethal Autonomous Weapon Systems, Convention on Certain Conventional Weapons, 17 April 2015, http://www.unog.ch/80256EDD006B8954/(httpAssets)/06EE5826D66D6B58C1257E2D002C3ED4/$file/2015_LAWS_MX_Finland_W.A.pdf.

62. P. Asaro, "On Banning Autonomous Weapon Systems: Human Rights, Automation, and the Dehumanization of Lethal Decision-Making," 94 *International Review of the Red Cross*, 886 (2012), pp. 687 and 708; C. Heyns, "Autonomous Weapon Systems and Human Rights Law," Presentation Made at Informal Expert Meeting Organized by the State Parties to the Convention on Certain Conventional Weapons, Geneva, 13–16 May 2014, p. 6; and C. Heyns, "Autonomous Weapon Systems: Living a Dignified Life and Dying a Dignified Death," in *Autonomous Weapon Systems—Law, Ethics, Policy*, N. Bhuta et al. (eds.) (Cambridge University Press, 2016).

63 Mill, "On the Liberty of Thought and Discussion," pp. 36–40 (describing the dangers of accepting what one is told as "truth" and the absence of free discussion). Similarly, computational models leave out a great deal of information. "What we are really doing, most or all of the time with computations, is *approximating* the world." P. Asaro, "Determinism, Machine Agency, and Responsibility," 2 *Politica & Societa*, 2 (2014), pp. 265 and 273 (emphasis added).

64. Professor Beard uses the phrase "effective exercise of human judgment." J. Beard, "Autonomous Weapons and Human Responsibility," 45 *Georgetown Journal of International Law* (2014), pp. 617, 621.

65. Jason Millar, an engineer and ethicist, observes that the active involvement of human beings in the direction of autonomous systems will not necessarily equate to "meaningful human control." Presentation to Convention on Certain Conventional Weapons Meeting of Experts on *Lethal Autonomous Weapon Systems*, 15 April 2015, p. 5, http://www.unog.ch/80256EDD006B8954/(httpAssets)/F483D421E67D230FC1257E2F0033E690/$file/Jason+Millar+-+Meaningful+Human+Control+and+Dual-Use+Technology.pdf.

66. Government of Israel, 2015 Meeting of Experts on Lethal Autonomous Weapons, 15 April 2015, http://www.unog.ch/80256EDD006B8954/(httpAssets)/AB30BF0E02AA39EAC1257E29004769F3/$file/2015_LAWS_MX_Israel_characteristics.pdf.

67. "Agenda Item 5 (b): Characterization of the Systems Under Consideration in Order to Promote a Common Understanding on Concepts and Characteristics Relevant to the Objectives and Purposes of the Convention," submitted by the United Kingdom, Group of Governmental Experts on Emerging Technologies in the Area of Lethal Autonomous Weapon Systems, Geneva, 25–29 March 2019, p. 2, https://www.unog.ch/80256EDD006B8954/(httpAssets)/A969D779E1E5E28BC12583D3003FC0D9/$file/20190318-5(b)_Characterisation_Statement.pdf, accessed 6 August 2020.

68. "Autonomy, Artificial Intelligence and Robotics: Technical Aspects of Human Control," submitted by International Committee of the Red Cross, Group of Governmental Experts on Emerging Technologies in the Area of Lethal Autonomous Weapon Systems, CCW/GGE.1/2019/WP.7, Geneva, 20 August 2019, paras. 3 and 8, https://www.unog.ch/80256EDD006B8954/

(httpAssets)/0F149C84EF8D36CEC125845C0051F592/$file/CCW_GGE.1_2019_WP.7.pdf, accessed 6 August 2020.

69. "Food for Thought Paper," submitted by Belgium, Ireland, and Luxembourg, Group of Governmental Experts on Emerging Technologies in the Area of Lethal Autonomous Weapon Systems, CCW/GGE.1/2019/WP.4, Geneva, 28 March 2019, para. 3, https://www.unog.ch/80256EDD006B8954/(httpAssets)/F3A850205D48D5A4C125841E00351CD7/$file/CCW_GGE.1_2019_WP.4.pdf, accessed 6 August 2020.

70. "Agenda Item 5 (c): Characterization: The Importance of Critical Functions," ICRC Statement, CCW GGE "LAWs," 25 March 2019, p. 2, https://www.unog.ch/80256EDD006B8954/(httpAssets)/7EA110E50853887DC12583CC003032E7/$file/ICRC+GGE+LAWS+ICRC+statement+agenda+item+5c+25+03+2019.pdf, accessed 6 August 2020.

71. Presentation of Poland to Convention on Certain Conventional Weapons Meeting of Experts on Lethal Autonomous Weapon Systems, 14 April 2015, http://www.unog.ch/80256EDD006B8954/(httpAssets)/16BDFE48306133F6C1257E31002BA329/$file/2015_LAWS_MX_Poland_characteristics.pdf.

72. "Autonomous Weapons: Operationalizing Meaningful Human Control," ICRC Humanitarian Law and Policy Blog, Autonomous Weapons Series, Conduct of Hostilities, Law and Conflict, New Technologies, 15 August 2018, p. 6, https://blogs.icrc.org/law-and-policy/2018/08/15/autonomous-weapons-operationalizing-meaningful-human-control/, accessed 6 August 2020.

73. "Agenda Item 5 (b): Characterization of the Systems Under Consideration in Order to Promote a Common Understanding on Concepts and Characteristics Relevant to the Objectives and Purposes of the Convention," submitted by the United Kingdom, p. 2.

74. "Agenda Item 5 (c): Characterization: The Importance of Critical Functions," p. 2.

75. K. Anderson and M. Waxman, "Debating Autonomous Weapon Systems, Their Ethics, and Their Regulation Under International Law," in *The Oxford Handbook of Law, Regulation, and Technology*, R. Brownsword et al. (eds.) (Oxford University Press, 2017), 1097, 1101–2.

76. I am grateful to Paul Scharre for this insight. Electronic message, 8 June 2020.

77. ICRC Statement "Agenda Item 5 (c): Characterization: The Importance of Critical Functions," 25 March 2019, p. 2.

78. C. Frith, "The Role of Metacognition in Human Social Interactions," *Philosophical Transactions* (August 2012), http://www.ncbi.nlm.nih.gov/pmc/articles/PMC3385688/, accessed 2 August 2020.

79. Arendt, *The Life of the Mind* (New York: Harcourt, 1978), p. 191.

80. Frith, "Role of Metacognition in Human Social Interactions."

81. Frith, "Role of Metacognition in Human Social Interactions."

82. Marlantes, *What It Is Like to Go to War*, p. 58.

83. M. Schmitt, "The Interpretive Guidance on the Notion of Direct Participation in Hostilities: A Critical Analysis," 1 *Harvard National Security Journal* (2010), p. 6.

Chapter 4

1. *The Public Committee Against Torture in Israel v. The Government of Israel*, Separate Opinion of President D. Beinisch, HCJ 769/02, 11 December 2005.

2. L. White Jr. *Medieval Technology and Social Change* (Oxford: Clarendon Press, 1962), p. 103.

3. Preface, *The Laws of War on Land*, Institute of International Law, Oxford, 9 September 1880, citing Baron de Jomini, https://www.icrc.org/applic/ihl/ihl.nsf/ART/140-80005?OpenDocument.

4. Foreword, vol. 15, Digest of Laws and Cases, *Law Reports of Trials of War Criminals*, London, United Nations War Crimes Commission, 1949, xiii, http://www.loc.gov/rr/frd/Military_Law/pdf/Law-Reports_Vol-15.pdf.

5. H. Lauterpacht, *The Function of Law in the International Community* (Oxford: Clarendon Press, 1933), p. 437.

6. This assumption is reinforced by relevant treaties and other instruments that frequently use personal pronouns and/or refer to human beings. For example, article 57 of the 1863 Lieber Code provided that when "a *man* is armed by a sovereign government and takes the soldier's oath of fidelity, *he* is a belligerent; *his* killing, wounding, or other warlike acts are not individual crimes or offenses." *General Orders No. 100, Instructions for the Government of Armies of the United States in the Field* (emphasis added), http://avalon.law.yale.edu/19th_century/lieber.asp#art1. Article 72 provided that "all officers, when captured, must surrender *their* side arms to the captor. They may be restored to the prisoner in marked cases, by the commander, to signalize admiration of *his* distinguished bravery or approbation of *his* humane treatment of prisoners before *his* capture." In the 1868 Declaration Renouncing the Use, in Time of War, of Certain Explosive Projectiles, the state signatories agreed that, for the purpose of weakening the military forces of the enemy, "it is sufficient to disable the greatest number of *men*" (emphasis added): https://www.icrc.org/ihl/INTRO/130?OpenDocument. Article 13 of the 1949 Geneva Convention (I) for the Amelioration of the Condition of the Wounded and Sick in Armed Forces in the Field (Geneva Convention) applies to members of militias and organized resistance movements that are "commanded by a *person* responsible for *his* subordinates": https://ihl-databases.icrc.org/applic/ihl/ihl.nsf/Article.xsp?action=openDocument&documentId=CE8A59A191689791C12563CD00519F73, accessed 28 August 2020. Article 87 (3) of Protocol I Additional to the Geneva Conventions of 12 August 1949 (API) requires "any commander who is aware that subordinates or *other persons under his control* are going to commit or have committed breaches" of the Geneva Conventions or API, to initiate steps to prevent and/or punish the perpetrators: https://ihl-databases.icrc.org/applic/ihl/ihl.nsf/Article.xsp?action=openDocument&documentId=C203555D5F233D81C12563CD0051E1FE, accessed 28 August 2020.

7. T. Meron, *Bloody Constraint: War and Chivalry in Shakespeare* (Oxford University Press, 1998), p. 12.

8. H. Grotius, *On the Law of War and Peace* (1625), trans. A. C. Campbell (Kitchener: Batoche Books, 2001), p. 286, http://socserv2.socsci.mcmaster.ca/econ/ugcm/3ll3/grotius/Law2.pdf.

9. Grotius, *On the Law of War and Peace*, p. 286 (emphasis added).

10. Grotius, *On the Law of War and Peace*, pp. 319–24. Grotius's description of the importance of moderation resembles the modern principle of "military necessity" discussed below "[b]y way of conclusion to this subject it may be observed, that all actions no way conducive to obtain a contested right, or to bring the war to a termination, but calculated merely to display the strength of either side are totally repugnant to the duties of a Christian and to the principles of humanity." Grotius, *On the Law of War and Peace*, para. 9.

11. E. de Vattel, *The Law of Nations* (1758) (Philadelphia: T. and J. W. Johnson, Law Booksellers, 1844), section 137, http://www.loc.gov/rr/frd/Military_Law/Lieber_Collection/pdf/DeVattel_LawOfNations.pdf.

12. De Vattel, *Law of Nations*, sections pp. 137–38.

13. De Vattel, *Law of Nations*, section p. 137.

14. J.-J. Rousseau, *The Social Contract* (1762), trans. G. D. H. Cole, p. 8, http://www.ucc.ie/archive/hdsp/Rousseau_contrat-social.pdf.

15. Rousseau, *Social Contract*, p. 8.

16. Sources of Hague Law include, inter alia, the Lieber Code; the 1868 Saint Petersburg Declaration Renouncing the Use, in Time of War, of Explosive Projectiles Under 400 Grammes Weight; the 1874 Brussels Project of an International Declaration Concerning the Laws and Customs of War; the 1880 Oxford Manual on the Laws of War on Land; the 1899 Hague Convention (II) with Respect to the Laws and Customs of War on Land and its annex, Regulations Concerning the Laws and Customs of War on Land; the 1907 Convention (IV) Respecting the Laws and Customs of War on Land and its annex, Regulations Concerning the Laws and Customs of War on Land, 18 October 1907, and related Declarations; the Protocol for the Prohibition of the Use of Asphyxiating, Poisonous or Other Gases, and of Bacteriological Methods of Warfare, Geneva, 17 June 1925; and the 1980 Convention on Prohibitions on the Use of Certain Chemical Weapons.

17. Sources of Geneva Law include, inter alia, the Convention for the Amelioration of the Condition of the Wounded in Armies in the Field, Geneva, 22 August 1864; Convention (I) for the Amelioration of the Condition of the Wounded and Sick in Armed Forces in the Field, Geneva, 12 August 1949; Convention (II) for the Amelioration of the Condition of Wounded, Sick and Shipwrecked Members of Armed Forces at Sea, Geneva, 12 August 1949; Convention (III) Relative to the Treatment of Prisoners of War, Geneva, 12 August 1949; and Convention IV Relative to the Protection of Civilian Persons in Time of War, Geneva, 12 August 1949. The 1977 Additional Protocols to the Geneva Conventions of 1949 (API and APII) effectively combine Hague and Geneva Law, as they extend the protections of the conventions as well as develop the rules concerning the conduct of hostilities.

18. "Introduction to the Commentary on the Additional Protocols I and II of 8 June 1977," ICRC, https://www.icrc.org/ihl/INTRO/470.

19. J. Witt, *Lincoln's Code: The Laws of War in American History* (New York: Free Press, 2012), p. 196. "The more vigorously wars are pursued, the better it is for humanity. Sharp wars are brief." Art. 29, Lieber Code.

20. Witt, *Lincoln's Code*, p. 196 and nn. 177 and 196.

21. Art. 16, Lieber Code.

22. Art. 16, Lieber Code.

23. Art. 15, Lieber Code.

24. Declaration Renouncing the Use, in Time of War, of Certain Explosive Projectiles, Saint Petersburg, 29 November/11 December 1868, https://www.icrc.org/applic/ihl/ihl.nsf/Article.xsp?action=openDocument&documentId=568842C2B90F4A29C12563CD0051547C.

25. Rule 70, "Weapons of a Nature to Cause Superfluous Injury of Unnecessary Suffering," *ICRC Customary International Humanitarian Law Study*, https://www.icrc.org/customary-ihl/eng/docs/v1_cha_chapter20_rule70; art. 35, API.

26. The influence of the Lieber Code and the Saint Petersburg Declaration also can be seen in the unratified International Declaration Concerning the Laws and Customs of War (Brussels Declaration) of 1874 and the 1880 Oxford Manual of the Laws and Customs of War (Oxford Manual). For example, like the Lieber Code, the Brussels Declaration affirms that prisoners of war must be humanely treated (compare arts. 72–76 of the Lieber Code with art. 23 of the Brussels Declaration). Similarly, art. 9 (a) of the Oxford Manual, which prohibits the use of weapons

calculated to cause superfluous suffering or aggravated wounds, specifically refers to the Saint Petersburg Declaration.

27. See "History and Sources of the Law of Armed Conflict," in G. Corn et al. (eds.), *The Law of Armed Conflict: An Operational Approach* (New York: Wolters Kluwer, 2012), pp. 40–43.

28. H. Dunant, *A Memory of Solferino* (1862) (Geneva: International Committee of the Red Cross, 1986), pp. 13–128.

29. Dunant, *Memory of Solferino*, afterword by H. Haug, pp. 129–31.

30. Convention for the Amelioration of the Condition of the Wounded and Sick in Armies in the Field. Geneva, 6 July 1906, https://www.icrc.org/ihl/INTRO/180?OpenDocument.

31. Convention relative to the Treatment of Prisoners of War. Geneva, 27 July 1929, https://www.icrc.org/ihl/INTRO/305?OpenDocument.

32. Roberts and Guelff, *Documents on the Law of War*, 3rd ed. (Oxford University Press, 2000), p. 194.

33. Roberts and Guelff, *Documents on the Law of War*, p. 299.

34. Roberts and Guelff, *Documents on the Law of War*, p. 244.

35. Additional Protocol I, 1977 to the Geneva Conventions of 12 August 1949, and Relating to the Protection of Victims of International Armed Conflicts, https://www.icrc.org/ihl/INTRO/470 and Additional Protocol II, 1977 to the Geneva Conventions of 12 August 1949, and Relating to the Protection of Victims of Non International Armed Conflicts, https://www.icrc.org/ihl.nsf/INTRO/475?OpenDocument.

36. art. 36, Additional Protocol I.

37. arts. 48–59, Additional Protocol I.

38. arts. 85–87, Additional Protocol I.

39. As explained in Chapter 2, the creation of customary international law requires a combination of state practice and *opinio juris*. *North Sea Continental Shelf*, Judgment, ICJ Reports 1969, paras. 77–78. In the context of international humanitarian law, where multiple treaties codify legal obligations during armed conflict, the primary significance of a norm's customary character is that the norm binds states that are not parties to the instrument that restates the norm. T. Meron, *Human Rights and Humanitarian Norms as Customary Law* (Oxford: Clarendon Press, 1989), p. 3.

40. ICRC Introduction to *Convention (II) with Respect to the Laws and Customs of War on Land and Its Annex: Regulations Concerning the Laws and Customs of War on Land*, The Hague, 29 July 1899, https://www.icrc.org/ihl/INTRO/150?OpenDocument; Greenwood, "Historical Development and Legal Basis," in D. Fleck (ed.), *The Handbook of International Humanitarian Law* (Oxford University Press, 2009), p. 11; J. Kellenberger, foreword to J. Henckaerts and L. Doswald-Beck (eds.), *Customary International Humanitarian Law*, vol. 1, *Rules* (also referred to below as the ICRC Customary International Humanitarian Law Study), p. x.

41. *Legality of the Threat or Use of Nuclear Weapons*, Advisory Opinion of 8 July 1996, para. 79 (emphasis added).

42. Most provisions of the Geneva Conventions are considered to be declaratory of customary international humanitarian law. *Prosecutor v. Blagoje Simić et al.*, Decision on the Prosecution Motion Under Rule 73 for a Ruling Concerning the Testimony of a Witness, IT-95-9, 27 July 1999, para. 48.

43. Kellenberger, foreword, p. x.

44. "Introduction" Customary International Humanitarian Law Database, vol. 1, p. xxix, https://www.icrc.org/customary-ihl/eng/docs/home.

45. L. May and M. Newton, *Proportionality in International Law* (New York: Oxford University Press, 2014), pp. 171 and 177; ICRC Commentary to Art. 57, API, para. 2206, https://www.icrc.org/ihl/INTRO/470.

46. ICRC Commentary to Art. 57, API, para. 2206.

47. Legality of the Threat or Use of Nuclear Weapons, para. 95, http://www.icj-cij.org/docket/files/95/7495.pdf.

48. This principle is based on the concept that once a military purpose has been achieved, the further infliction of suffering is unnecessary. JSP 383, *The Joint Service Manual of the Law of Armed Conflict* (2004 ed.), Joint Doctrine and Training Centre, U.K. Ministry of Defence, paras. 2.4 and 2.4.1, https://www.gov.uk/government/publications/jsp-383-the-joint-service-manual-of-the-law-of-armed-conflict-2004-edition.

49. *The Public Committee Against Torture in Israel v. The Government of Israel*, Opinion of President (Emeritus) A. Barak, HCJ 769/02, 11 December 2005, para. 22.

50. Judgment, *Physicians for Human Rights v. IDF Commanders*, Opinion of President A. Barak, HCJ 4764/04, [2004] IsrLR 200, paras. 11–12.

51. Legality of the Threat or Use of Nuclear Weapons, para. 86.

52. Art. 14, Lieber Code.

53. *JSP 383, Joint Services Publication 383—the Manual of the Law of Armed Conflict Amendment 3* (September 2010) (22), para. 2.2.

54. The term "international humanitarian law" itself emerged from the influence of human rights doctrine on the law of armed conflict. *Prosecutor v. Duško Tadić a/k/a "Dule,"* Decision on Defence Motion for Interlocutory Appeal on Jurisdiction, No. IT-94-1, 2 October 1995, para. 87. Like human rights law, the rules of international humanitarian law rest on "the principle of respect for human personality," i.e., human dignity. ICRC Commentary to Common Art. 3 of 1949 Geneva Conventions (1952), p. 39. State practice vis-à-vis Common Art. 3, for example, calls "for treatment that respects a person's inherent dignity as a human being." ICRC Commentary to Common Art. 3 of 1949 Geneva Conventions (2016), para. 557.

55. The Legality of the Threat or Use of Nuclear Weapons, paras. 77 and 78, citing art. 23 (e) of *1907 Convention (IV) Respecting the Laws and Customs of War on Land and Its Annex: Regulations Concerning the Laws and Customs of War on Land*, which prohibits the use of arms, projectiles, or material calculated to cause unnecessary suffering, https://www.icrc.org/ihl/INTRO/195.

56. Art. 48, API. The principle of distinction "is the foundation upon which the codification of the laws and customs of war rests." International Committee of the Red Cross, "Protocol Additional to the Geneva Conventions of 12 August 1949, and Relating to the Protection of Victims of International Armed Conflicts (API), 8 June 1977: "Commentary" (ICRC, 2012), http://www.icrc.org/ihl.nsf/COM/470-750073?OpenDocument (accessed 22 March 2014), at para. 1863. This principle has become part of customary international humanitarian law. Rule 1, "The Principle of Distinction Between Civilians and Combatants" and "Rule 7, The Principle of Distinction Between Civilian Objects and Military Objective," ICRC Customary International Humanitarian Law Study, https://www.icrc.org/customary-ihl/eng/docs/v1_rul.

57. Art. 51 (4), API. The prohibition of indiscriminate attacks is also part of customary international humanitarian law. "Rule 11, Indiscriminate Attacks," and "Rule 12, Definition of Indiscriminate Attacks," ICRC Customary International Law Study, https://www.icrc.org/customary-ihl/eng/docs/home.

58. Art. 35 (2), API. This constraint on the means and methods of warfare also forms part of customary international humanitarian law. "Rule 70, Weapons of a Nature to Cause Superfluous

Injury or Unnecessary Suffering, ICRC Customary International Law Study. In *The Nuclear Weapons Case*, the International Court of Justice defined "unnecessary suffering" as "a harm greater than that unavoidable to achieve legitimate military objectives," para. 78. By prohibiting unnecessary suffering, international humanitarian law acknowledges that "*necessary suffering* to combatants is lawful, and may include severe injury or loss of life." W. H. Parks, "Conventional Weapons and Weapons Reviews," *Yearbook of International Humanitarian Law* (2005), 55, p. 140 (emphasis in original).

59. ICRC commentary to art. 51, API, para. 1957, https://www.icrc.org/applic/ihl/ihl.nsf/INTRO/470. The humanitarian character of the principles of the law of armed conflict applies to all forms of warfare and all kinds of weapons, *including future weapons*. Legality of the Threat or Use of Nuclear Weapons, para. 86.

60. Roberts and Guelff, *Documents on the Law of War*, p. 9.

61. In his Dissenting Opinion in the Legality of Threat or Use of Nuclear Weapons Advisory Opinion, Judge Shahabudeen makes a compelling argument that the prohibition on causing unnecessary suffering must apply to civilians as well as combatants (p. 404).

62. T. Meron, "The Martens Clause, Principles of Humanity, and Dictates of Public Conscience," 94 *American Journal of International Law*, 1 (2000), pp. 78–79, 87.

63. Legality of the Threat or Use of Nuclear Weapons, Advisory Opinion, ICJ Reports 1996 (Dissenting Opinion Judge Shahabuddeen), p. 405.

64. Legality of the Threat or Use of Nuclear Weapons (Dissenting Opinion Judge Shahabuddeen), p. 406.

65. Meron, "Martens Clause, Principles of Humanity, and Dictates of Public Conscience," p. 88. One example where the Martens Clause arguably delegitimizes a means or method of warfare is the use of nuclear weapons: Legality of the Threat or Use of Nuclear Weapons (Dissenting Opinion Judge Shahabuddeen), p. 411.

66. Legality of the Threat or Use of Nuclear Weapons (Dissenting Opinion Judge Weeramantry), pp. 490–91.

67. M. Rosenberg and J. Markoff, "At Heart of U.S. Strategy, Weapons That Can Think," *New York Times*, 26 October 2016, pp. 1 and 23.

68. Rosenberg and Markoff, "At Heart of U.S. Strategy," pp. 7–8.

69. "No-Strike and the Collateral Damage Estimation Methodology," CJCSI 3160.01A, *Chairman of the Joint Chiefs of Staff Instruction*, U.S. Department of Defense, 12 October 2012, Enclosure C, p. C-2, n. 7, citing JP 3-60, *Joint Targeting*, reference f.

70. K. Anderson and M. Waxman, "Debating Autonomous Weapon Systems, Their Ethics, and Their Regulation Under International Law," in R. Brownsword et al. (eds.), *The Oxford Handbook of Law, Regulation, and Technology* (Oxford University Press, 2017), pp. 1097, 1114.

71. A weaponeer is an "individual who has completed requisite training to determine the quantity and type of lethal or nonlethal means required to create a desired effect on a given target." "No-Strike and the Collateral Damage Estimation Methodology," CJCSI 3160.01, p. GL-11.

72. JP 3-60, Joint Targeting, p. viii.

73. JP 3-60, Joint Targeting, p. viii. See P. Margulies, "Making Autonomous Weapons Accountable: Command Responsibility for Computer-Guided Lethal Force in Armed Conflicts," in J. Ohlin (ed.), *Research Handbook on Remote Warfare* (Northampton: Edward Elgar, 2016), http://papers.ssrn.com/sol3/papers.cfm?abstract_id=2734900.

74. JP 3-60, Joint Targeting, p. II-5; "Operations Series, ADDP 3.14," *Targeting*, 2nd ed. Australia Department of Defence, 2009, para. 1.21, http://www.defence.gov.au/foi/docs/disclosures

/021_1112_Document_ADDP_3_14_Targeting.pdf. Australian targeting doctrine contains a fifth principle: legitimacy: "[a]ll legal obligations, domestic and international are understood and met" (para. 1.6).

75 JP 3-60, Joint Targeting, pp. II-1–II-2 and ADDP 3.14, *Targeting*, paras. 1.10–1.1.2.

76. JP 3-60, Joint Targeting, p. I-5.

77. *Joint Doctrine Publication 3-00*, 3rd ed., U.K. Ministry of Defence, October 2009, para. 337.

78. "No-Strike and the Collateral Damage Estimation Methodology," Chairman of the Joint Chiefs of Staff Instruction, U.S. Department of Defense, 12 October 2012, Enclosure A, p. A-6; *Joint Doctrine Publication 3-00*, para. 3B-8; ADDP 3.14, *Targeting*, para. 1.24.

79. "No-Strike and the Collateral Damage Estimation Methodology," Enclosure D, p. D-2.

80. "No-Strike and the Collateral Damage Estimation Methodology," pp. D-A-6–D-A-7.

81. "No-Strike and the Collateral Damage Estimation Methodology," pp. D-3 and D-A-2.

82. *Joint Doctrine Publication 3-00*, para. 338.

83. "ADDP 3.14," *Targeting*, para. 1.21.

84. "No-Strike and the Collateral Damage Estimation Methodology," p. D-1.

85. "No-Strike and the Collateral Damage Estimation Methodology," appendix B, Targeting Automation, p. B-1.

86. "No-Strike and the Collateral Damage Estimation Methodology," p. B-4.

87. "No-Strike and the Collateral Damage Estimation Methodology," p. B-4.

88. M. Waxman, "Detention as Targeting: Standards of Certainty and Detention of Suspected Terrorists," 108 *Columbia Law Review* (2008) 1365, 1394, n. 103, citing Christopher Greenwood, "The Law of War (International Humanitarian Law)," in M. Evans (ed.), *International Law*, 2nd ed. (Oxford University Press, 2003), p. 793.

89. *Prosecutor v. Tihomir Blaškić*, Judgment, IT-95-14-A, Appeals Chamber, 29 July 2004, para. 109. Article 52 defines "military objectives" as "those objects which by their nature, location, purpose or use make an effective contribution to military action and whose total or partial destruction, capture or neutralization, in the circumstances ruling at the time, offers a definite military advantage."

90. *Prosecutor v. Stanislav Galić*, Judgment, IT-98-29-A, Appeals Chamber, 30 November 2006, para. 130.

91. The ICRC commentary to art. 51 explains that military objectives principally include "the armed forces, their members, installations, equipment and transports," para. 1951, http://www.icrc.org/applic/ihl/ihl.nsf/Comment.xsp?viewComments=LookUpCOMART&articleUNID=4BEBD9920AE0AEAEC12563CD0051DC9E. Limited areas of strategic physical space, such as bridgeheads or mountain passes, may, in certain circumstances, qualify as military objectives (para. 1955).

92. S. Oeter, "Methods and Means of Combat," in D. Fleck (ed.), *The Handbook of International Humanitarian Law* (Oxford University Press, 2009), pp. 127–28. Attacks that employ certain means of combat that cannot discriminate between civilians and civilian objects and military objectives are "tantamount to direct targeting of civilians." *Prosecutor v. Pavle Strugar*, Judgment, IT-01-42-A, Appeals Chamber, 17 July 2008, note 689 (citing *Prosecutor v. Stanislav Galić*, Trial Judgment, note 101). Similarly, encouragement of soldiers to fire weapons for which they lack training may be indicative of the indiscriminate nature of an attack. *Prosecutor v. Pavle Strugar*, para. 274. Furthermore, the indiscriminate nature of an attack may be circumstantial evidence that the attack actually was directed against the civilian population. *Prosecutor v. Stanislav Galić* (Appeals Chamber), at para. 132.

93. Art. 57 (2) (a) (i), Additional Protocol I.

94. Art. 57 (2) (a) (ii), Additional Protocol I.

95. Rules 15–17, ICRC Customary International Law Study.

96. Art. 10, Protocol II to Convention on Prohibitions or Restrictions on the Use of Certain Conventional Weapons Which May Be Deemed to Be Excessively Injurious or to Have Indiscriminate Effects (CCW).

97. Y. Dinstein, *The Conduct of Hostilities Under the Law of International Armed Conflict*, 2nd ed. (Cambridge University Press, 2010), p. 139; W. Boothby, *The Law of Targeting* (Oxford University Press, 2012), p. 121.

98. Dinstein, *Conduct of Hostilities*, p. 139. Feasibility determinations depend on diverse factors such as access to intelligence concerning the target and the target area, availability of weapons, personnel and different means of attack, control (if any) over the area to be attacked, the urgency of the attack, and "additional security risks which precautionary measures may entail for the attacking forces or the civilian population." J. Wright, "'Excessive' Ambiguity: Analysing and Refining the Proportionality Standard," 94 *International Review of the Red Cross* (Summer 2012), 819, 827, citing N. Melzer, *Targeted Killing in International Law* (Oxford University Press, 2009), p. 365.

99. JSP383, Joint Service Manual of the Law of Armed Conflict, para. 5.32.4.

100. J. Beard, "Law and War in the Virtual Era," 103 *American Journal of International Law*, 3 (July 2009), 409, at 433–39.

101. Art. 57 (2) (a) (iii), Additional Protocol I. "Concrete and direct," JSP 383, Joint Service Manual of the Law of Armed Conflict, para. 5.33.3. For a discussion of the customary law basis of the rule of proportionality customary law, see *Prosecutor v. Zoran Kupreškić*, Judgment, IT-95-16-T, 14 January 2000, para. 524.

102. Art 51 (5) (b), Additional Protocol I. "Proportionality" JSP 383, Joint Service Manual of the Law of Armed Conflict, para. 2.6.1.

103. Y. Dinstein, "The Principle of Distinction and Cyber War in International Armed Conflicts," 17 *Journal of Conflict and Security Law*, 2 (2012), 261, 269.

104. A. Rogers, *Law on the Battlefield*, 2nd ed. (Manchester University Press, 2004), p. 20.

105. *U.S. Department of Defense Law of War Manual*, Office of General Counsel, 12 June 2015 (updated December 2016), section 5.12.3.

106. U.S. military doctrine defines "Collateral Damage Estimate" as "[a]n approximate calculation of potential collateral damage through analysis prior to target engagement." "No Strike and the Collateral Damage Estimation Methodology," *Chairman of the Joint Chiefs of Staff Instruction*, CJCSI 3160.01A, 12 October 2012, p. GL-4. Thus, collateral damage estimates do not predict the actual outcome of weapon use. Operational environments, weapon performance and accuracy of intelligence can contribute to collateral damage estimates that differ from actual results (p. D-2).

107. "No Strike and the Collateral Damage Estimation Methodology," p. D-2.

108. ICRC commentary to art. 57, API, para. 2208, https://www.icrc.org/applic/ihl/ihl.nsf/Comment.xsp?action=openDocument&documentId=D80D.

109. *Final Report to the Prosecutor by the Committee Established to Review the NATO Bombing Campaign Against the Federal Republic of Yugoslavia*, Office of the Prosecutor, United Nations International Criminal Tribunal for the Former Yugoslavia (2000), para. 48, http://www.icty.org/sid/10052.

110. ICRC commentary to art. 57, API, para. 2208.

111. *Prosecutor v. Stanislav Galić*, Judgment, para. 190.

112. "No responsible military commander would wish to attack objectives which were of no military interest." ICRC commentary to art. 57, API, para. 2195, https://www.icrc.org/applic/ihl/ihl.nsf/Comment.xsp?action=openDocument&documentId=D80D14D84BF36B92C12563CD00434FBD.

113. Oeter, "Methods and Means of Combat," pp. 189–90. Nor does the rule imply any prohibition of specific weapons. ICRC commentary to art. 57, API, para. 2201, https://www.icrc.org/applic/ihl/ihl.nsf/Comment.xsp?action=openDocument&documentId=D80D14D.

114. Oeter, "Methods and Means of Combat," p. 190.

115. "In considering whether commanders and others responsible for planning, deciding upon, or executing attacks have fulfilled their responsibilities, it must be borne in mind that they have to make their decisions on the basis of their assessment of the information from all sources which is available to them at the relevant time." *The Joint Service Manual of the Law of Armed Conflict*, U.K. Ministry of Defence, 2004, p. 85, https://www.gov.uk/government/publications/jsp-383-the-joint-service-manual-of-the-law-of-armed-conflict-2004-edition.

116. Colonel R. Jackson, Panel, "Autonomous Weaponry and Armed Conflict," Annual Meeting of American Society of International Law, Washington, D.C., April 2014.

117. M. Schmitt, Remarks During Panel "The International Legal Context" at "Autonomous Military Technologies: Policy and Governance for Next Generation Defense Systems," Chatham House, London, 24 February 2014; permission to cite provided in electronic mail message to author, 15 March 2014.

118. Jackson, Panel, "Autonomous Weaponry and Armed Conflict"; art. 8 (2) (b) (iv) of the Rome Statute of the International Criminal Court prohibits attacks where the anticipated civilian injury and damage is "clearly excessive" to the expected military advantage. No similar provision exists in treaty or customary law that criminalizes failures to take feasible precautions under arts. 57 (2) (a) (i) or (ii). I am grateful to Professor Robin Geiß for clarifying this point.

119. R. Clarke, *Against All Enemies: Inside America's War on Terror* (New York: Free Press, 2004), pp. 82–83.

120. The current legal standard for weapon systems, including those employing machine learning and artificial intelligence, is whether or not that system can apply the traditional principles of the law of the law of armed conflict, including minimizing death and injury to civilians and damage to civilian objects. E. T. Jensen, "The (Erroneous) Requirement for Human Judgment and (Error) in the Law of Armed Conflict," 96 *International Law Studies* 26, 57 (2020).

121. M. Cummings, "Man Versus Machine or Man + Machine?" *IEEE Intelligence Systems*, September/October 2014, 7, http://hal.pratt.duke.edu/sites/hal.pratt.duke.edu/files/u10/IS-29-05-Expert%20Opinion%5B1%5D_0.pdf. Peter Margulies, on the other hand, claims that machine recognition of human faces and landscape images have improved greatly, although it still requires "regular, frequent human monitoring and assessment." Margulies, "Making Autonomous Weapons Accountable."

122. B. Boothby, "How Far Will the Law Allow Unmanned Targeting to Go?" in D. Saxon (ed.), *International Humanitarian Law and the Changing Technology of War* (Leiden: Martinus Nijhoff, 2013), pp. 57–59 and 62.

123. During the trench warfare of the First World War, the "onus fell rather on the would-be prisoner to get his surrender accepted, something difficult to do when friend and enemy met so rarely face-to-face, when face-to-face encounters tended to provoke hair-trigger reactions,

and when a pacific shout from a dark dug-out in a foreign language might be misinterpreted." J. Keegan, *The Face of Battle* (New York: Penguin Books, 1978), pp. 282–83.

124 Boothby, "How Far Will the Law Allow Unmanned Targeting to Go?" p. 59.

125. M. Schmitt and J. Thurnher, "'Out of the Loop': Autonomous Weapon Systems and the Law of Armed Conflict," 4 *Harvard National Security Journal* (2013), 231, 266–67. M Sassóli, "Autonomous Weapons and International Humanitarian Law: Advantages, Open Technical Questions and Legal Issues to Be Clarified," 90 *International Law Studies* 308 (2014), 331–33.

126. Reliance on one's natural instincts, of course, can be fallible. Aristotle, *On Rhetoric: A Theory of Civic Discourse*, George A. Kennedy, trans., 2nd ed. (Oxford, Oxford University Press, 2007), p. 94.

127. Sassóli, "Autonomous Weapons and International Humanitarian Law," p. 334. ICRC commentary to art. 57, API, para. 2208, https://www.icrc.org/applic/ihl/ihl.nsf/INTRO/470.

128. Sassóli, "Autonomous Weapons and International Humanitarian Law," pp. 310–11.

129. Although algorithm-based artificial intelligence is the most common form in use today, "Statistical Machine Learning," whereby autonomous robots learn to modify their behavior by trial and error, is a significant area of research. L. Steels, "Ten Big Ideas of Artificial Intelligence," *Remarks to 25th Benelux Conference on Artificial Intelligence*, Delft Technical University, 8 November 2013; author Interview with Gianfranco Visentin, Head, Automation and Robotics Department, European Space Agency, Noordwijk, 4 November 2013; Margulies, "Making Autonomous Weapons Accountable."

130. R. Brooks, "A Brave New World? How Will Advances in Artificial Intelligence, Smart Sensors and Social Technology Change Our Lives?" Panel Discussion at World Economic Forum, 22 January 2015, http://www.weforum.org/videos/brave-new-world.

131. T. McHale, "Executive Summary for AR 15-6 Investigation, 21 February 2010, CIV-CAS Incident in Uruzgan Province," *Memorandum for Commander, United States Forces—Afghanistan/International Security Assistance Force*, Afghanistan, http://www.rs.nato.int/images/stories/File/April2010-Dari/May2010Revised/Uruzgan%20investigation%20findings.pdf.

132. Sassóli, "Autonomous Weapons and International Humanitarian Law," p. 310; Schmitt and Thurnher, "'Out of the Loop,'" p. 264.

133. Larry May and Michael Newton suggest that the time has arrived to consider, as lex ferenda, the lives of combatants as factors in a proportionality assessment. *Proportionality in International Law*, p. 151.

134. H. Natsu, "Nanotechnology and the Future of the Law of Weaponry," 91 *International Law Studies* (2015), 486, 501–2, and 507; Margulies, "Making Autonomous Weapons Accountable."

135. *U.S. Department of Defense Law of War Manual*, Office of General Counsel, 12 June 2015, para. 2.2.3.

136. *U.S. Department of Defense Law of War Manual*, para. 2.2.3.1.

137. ICRC commentary to art. 57, API, para. 2198, https://www.icrc.org/applic/ihl/ihl.nsf/Comment.xsp?action=openDocument&documentId=D80D14D84BF36B92C12563CD00434FBD.

138. T. McFarland, *Autonomous Weapon Systems and the Law of Armed Conflict: Compatibility with International Humanitarian Law* (Cambridge University Press, 2020), pp. 176–77.

139. W. Boothby, Presentation to Expert Meeting on Lethal Autonomous Weapon Systems, Convention on Certain Conventional Weapons, 13–17 April 2015, p. 3.

140. Boothby, *Law of Targeting*, p. 283.

141. C. Tams, "The Use of Force Against Terrorists," 20 *European Journal of International Law* (2009), 383, 389, and 392 (discussing jus ad bello and the "normative drift" with respect to the scope of the right of states to self-defense).

142. By mitigating human suffering and property damage, armed forces can accelerate recovery in postconflict situations. "No-Strike and the Collateral Damage Estimation Methodology," CJCSI 3160.01A, p. C-4.

143. Anderson and Waxman, "Debating Autonomous Weapon Systems," p. 1108.

144. Anderson and Waxman, "Debating Autonomous Weapon Systems," pp. 1109–10.

145. J. Waldron, *The Harm in Hate Speech* (Cambridge Mass.: Harvard University Press, 2012), p. 140.

146. Boothby, *Law of Targeting*, p. 284.

147. M. Newton, "Back to the Future: Reflections on the Advent of Autonomous Weapon Systems," 47 *Case Western Reserve Journal of International Law* (2015), 1, p. 16.

148. U.K. Government, "Statement to the Informal Meeting of Experts on Lethal Autonomous Weapon Systems, *Convention on Certain Conventional Weapons*, April 2015, para. 2 (emphasis added), http://www.unog.ch/80256EDD006B8954/(httpAssets)/3AA5E280106A73EFC1257E2900472797/$file/2015_LAWS_MX_UK_IHL.pdf.

149. A. Clare et al., "Assessing Operator Strategies for Real-Time Replanning of Multiple Unmanned Vehicles," 6 *Intelligent Decision Technologies* (2012), pp. 221–22.

150. Clare et al., "Assessing Operator Strategies," p. 221; Newton, "Back to the Future," pp. 21–22.

151. Such pressures are not a recent phenomenon. In 1841, for example, in correspondence with the government of the U.K. concerning "the Caroline Case," U.S. secretary of state Daniel Webster articulated a standard for the use of force in self-defense: "a show of necessity of self-defense, instant, overwhelming, *leaving no choice of means, and no moment of deliberation*." "British-American Diplomacy: The Caroline Case," Lillian Goldman Library, Avalon Project, 2008 (emphasis added), http://avalon.law.yale.edu/19th_century/br-1842d.asp. Although this standard derives from the jus ad bello context, it fairly describes armed conflict situations in which the need to return fire and/or attack will be immediate. K. Trapp, "Great Resources Mean Great Responsibility: A Framework of Analysis for Assessing Compliance with API Obligations in the Information Age," in D. Saxon (ed.), *International Humanitarian Law and the Changing Technology of War* (Leiden: Martinus Nijhoff, 2013), note 50.

152. Trapp, "Great Resources Mean Great Responsibility," p. 170.

153. Sassóli, "Autonomous Weapons and International Humanitarian Law," p. 310, citing R. Arkin, *Ethical Robots in Warfare*, Georgia Institute of Technology (20 January 2009), 2, http://www.cc.gatech.edu/ai/robot-lab/online-publications/arkin-rev.pdf.

154. E. Jensen, "The Future of the Law of Armed Conflict: Ostriches, Butterflies and Nanobots," 35 *Michigan Journal of International Law* (Winter 2014), 253, 300, citing Colonel (ret.) Thomas Adams, who contends that future autonomous weapons "will be too fast, too small, too numerous and will create an environment too complex for humans to direct". "Robots on Battlefield: Robotic Weapons Might be the Way of the Future, But They Raise Ethical Questions About the Nature of Warfare," *Townsville Bull* (Australia.), 18 September 2009, 210.

155. S. Sohm, "Obligations Under International Law Prior to the Use of Military Force: Current Developments Relating to the Legal Review of New Weapons and Methods of Warfare," 28 *Journal of International Law of Peace and Armed Conflict* (2015), 104–10, presented to Convention on Certain Conventional Weapons (CCW) Meeting on Lethal Autonomous Weapon

Systems, Geneva, 11–15 April 2016. Eric Talbot Jensen refers to the "vital signalling role" that international humanitarian law plays in the development of state practice, in particular vis-à-vis the development of new weapons. Jensen, "Future of the Law of Armed Conflict, pp. 253, 262.

156. Art 36, Additional Protocol I. Means of warfare refer to weapons while methods of warfare refer to how the weapon is used. Thus, an autonomous weapon system would be a means of warfare. Schmitt and Thurnher, "'Out of the Loop,'" p. 271.

157. For the purposes of compliance with art. 36, it is insufficient to rely on the promise of another state or the manufacturer of an autonomous weapon system that it can be used in compliance with international law, because that assessment may be incorrect. G. Giacca, Remarks to Panel "Challenges [of Autonomous Weapons] to International Humanitarian Law," Informal Expert Meeting on Lethal Autonomous Weapons, Convention on Conventional Weapons, Geneva, 13 April 2016, http://www.unog.ch/80256EE600585943/(httpPages)/37D51189AC4FB6E1C1257F4D004CAFB2?OpenDocument.

158. *A Guide to the Legal Review of New Weapons, Means and Methods of Warfare: Measures to Implement Article 36 of Additional Protocol I of 1977*, ICRC, Geneva, 2006, p. 4, https://www.icrc.org/eng/assets/files/other/icrc_002_0902.pdf.

159. Cf. Schmitt and Thurnher, "'Out of the Loop,'" p. 271, who argue that "the obligation to conduct legal reviews of new means of warfare before their use is generally considered . . . reflective of customary international law.

160. As of 2006, only nine states had informed the ICRC that they had "in place national mechanisms to review the legality of weapons." *Guide to the Legal Review of New Weapons, Means and Methods of Warfare*, note 8.

161. Parks, "Conventional Weapons and Weapons Reviews," p. 107. As Schmitt and Thurnher observe, all state parties to API are under a treaty obligation to art. 36 conduct legal reviews. "'Out of the Loop,'" 271.

162. Parks, "Conventional Weapons and Weapons Reviews," pp. 115–16.

163. Schmitt and Thurnher, "'Out of the Loop,'" p. 276.

164. *Guide to the Legal Review of New Weapons, Means and Methods of Warfare*, pp. 951–52.

165. Giacca, Remarks to Panel "Challenges [of Autonomous Weapons] to International Humanitarian Law." In addition, according to Giacca, novel uses of existing capabilities or technology may require legal review.

166. Parks suggests the rather vague criteria that legal reviewers have "some sense" how the new weapons work. Parks, "Conventional Weapons and Weapons Reviews," p. 100.

167. Comparisons of proposed new weapons to already existing weapon systems may inform a legal review. For example, although the drafting of DOD Directive 3000.09 was not a "legal review" in the context of article 36 of API, military lawyers with experience in article 36 reviews participated in the process, which included studies of the performance of older weapon systems such as the Patriot missile defense system and Aegis system. Jackson, Panel "Autonomous Weaponry and Armed Conflict."

168. *A Guide to the Legal Review of New Weapons, Means and Methods of Warfare*, pp. 1, 6, 22, and 26; Sohm, "Obligations Under International Law Prior to the Use of Military Force," 7 (CCW version).

169. *Guide to the Legal Review of New Weapons, Means and Methods of Warfare*, p. 955.

170. See Margulies, "Making Autonomous Weapons Accountable" ("Approval of an autonomous weapon system in the weapons review phase should be contingent on substantial ongoing human engagement with the weapon system").

171. *The Targeted Killing Case*, Judgment, Supreme Court of Israel, President A. Barak, 11 December 2005, para. 46.

172. Professor Jensen argues that "the incorporation of autonomous weapons into regular armed forces will diminish the role of humans in targeting decisions." "Future of Armed Conflict," p. 286.

Chapter 5

1. E. Benvenisti, "Human Dignity in Combat: The Duty to Spare Enemy Civilians," 39 *Israel Law Review*, No. 2 (2006), n. 12. See *Husayn Abu Zubaydah v. Poland*, para. 532, citing *Pretty v. the United Kingdom*, Judgment, ECtHR, Application No. 2346/02, 29 July 2002, paras. 61 and 65.

2. The preambles to the ICCPR and the ICESCR, for example, explain that the rights contained therein "derive from the inherent dignity of the human person." The American Convention on Human Rights recognizes that the essential rights of persons "are based upon attributes of the human personality" while the ICESCR requires that the right to education "shall be directed to the full development of the human personality and the sense of its dignity." Preamble, ACHR, and art. 13, ICESCR, 16 December 1966.

3. B. Beyer, "Economic Rights: Past, Present, and Future," in T. Cushman (ed.), *Handbook of Human Rights* (New York: Routledge, 2012), p. 297. See P. Carozza, "Human Dignity," in D. Shelton (ed.), *The Oxford Handbook of International Human Rights Law* (Oxford University Press, 2013), pp. 2 and 5 (observing that human dignity serves as a foundation for generic claims of human rights as well as a normative principle for the interpretation and application of specific rights).

4. "Man . . . can lose all so-called Rights of Man without losing his essential quality as man, his human dignity." H. Arendt, *The Origins of Totalitarianism* (New York: Harvest Books, 1976), p. 297.

5. J. Locke, "Concerning the True Original Extent and End of Civil Government," in *Two Treatises of Government*, paras. 22, 87 and 135, http://socserv2.socsci.mcmaster.ca/econ/ugcm/3ll3/locke/government.pdf.

6. *An Act Declaring the Rights and Liberties of the Subject and Settling the Succession of the Crown*, http://avalon.law.yale.edu/17th_century/england.asp.

7. *Declaration of the Rights of Man—1789*, http://avalon.law.yale.edu/18th_century/rightsof.asp. This declaration also emphasized the importance of the rule of law (art. 16). More than eighteen hundred years previously, in his oration in defense of Titus Annius Milo (referred to in Chapter 4 on international humanitarian law and autonomous weapon systems), Cicero argued in favor of the existence of law "not written, but born with us, . . . imbibed from nature herself." Part 4, para. 2, http://www.uah.edu/student_life/organizations/SAL/texts/latin/classical/cicero/promilone1e.html#cfour.

8. United States, Bill of Rights attached to the Constitution, https://www.law.cornell.edu/constitution/overview. Jean-Jacques Rousseau also advocated for the importance of "natural rights," at least for men. *The Social Contract (or Principles of Political Right)* (1762), trans. G. Cole, p. 22, http://www.ucc.ie/archive/hdsp/Rousseau_contrat-social.pdf. The concept of "natural rights" was rejected and famously mocked by Jeremy Bentham, who called the notion "nonsense on stilts." *Anarchical Fallacies: Being an Examination of the Declaration of Rights Issued During the French Revolution* (1843), art. 2, pp. 4–5, http://english.duke.edu/uploads/media_items/bentham-anarchical-fallacies.original.pdf. There Bentham also argued that all "rights" originate from laws made by governments.

9. H. Duffy, *The "War on Terror" and the Framework of International Law*, 2nd ed. (Cambridge University Press, 2015), p. 466.

10. C. Chinkin, "Sources," in D. Moeckli et al. (eds.), *International Human Rights Law* (Oxford University Press, 2010), p. 105.

11. Signed in San Francisco, 26 June 1945.

12. Art. 1 (3). Art. 1 (2) affirms the principle of equal rights and self-determination of peoples. Art. 13 (1) (b) charges the General Assembly with "assisting in the realization of human rights and fundamental freedoms for all."

13. M. Ishay, *The History of Human Rights: From Ancient Times to the Globalization Era* (Berkeley: University of California Press, 2004), p. 223.

14. No. 1021, Adopted by the General Assembly of the United Nations on 9 December 1948.

15. Adopted by the United Nations General Assembly on 16 December 1966, entered into force on 23 March 1976.

16. Adopted by the United Nations General Assembly on 16 December 1966, entered into force on 3 January 1976.

17. Chinkin, "Sources," p. 106.

18. Markus Schmidt opines that the "core" United Nations human rights treaties are: the ICCPR and the ICESCR (as well as their Optional Protocols), and the International Conventional on the Elimination of Racial Discrimination (ICERD), the Convention Against Torture and Other Forms of Cruel, Inhuman and Degrading Treatment (UNCAT), the Convention on the Elimination of All Forms of Discrimination Against Women (CEDAW) (as well as its Optional Protocol), the Convention on the Rights of the Child (CRC) (as well as its Optional Protocols), the International Convention on the Rights of Migrant Workers and Their Families (ICRMW), the Convention on the Rights of Persons with Disabilities (CRPD) (as well as its Optional Protocol), and the International Convention for the Protection of All Persons from Enforced Disappearances. M. Schmidt, "United Nations," in Moeckli, *International Human Rights Law*, p. 405. One might add to this list, inter alia, the 1951 Convention Relating to the Status of Refugees and the International Convention on the Suppression and Punishment of the Crime of "Apartheid."

19. Schmidt, "United Nations," pp. 404–9.

20. Schmidt, "United Nations," pp. 409–15.

21. T. Meron, *Human Rights and Humanitarian Norms as Customary Law* (Oxford: Clarendon Press, 1989), p. 9. For example, Common Article 3's requirement that civilians and persons hors de combat must be treated humanely "is an overarching concept," given expression by the detailed rules incorporated into modern international humanitarian law. "Commentary," *Rule 87. Humane Treatment*, ICRC Customary International Humanitarian Law Study, https://www.icrc.org/customary-ihl/eng/docs/v1_cha_chapter32_rule87.

22. A. Bianchi, "Human Rights and the Magic of Jus Cogens," 19 *European Journal of International Law* (2008) 3, 491, 495.

23. Chinkin, "Sources," pp. 460–73; D. Harris et al., *Law of the European Convention on Human Rights* (Oxford University Press, 2014); H. Steiner and P. Alston, *International Human Rights in Context*, 2nd ed. (Oxford University Press, 2000), pp. 787–937.

24. A. Drzemczewski and M. Ladewig, "Principal Characteristics of the New ECHR Control Mechanism, as Established by Protocol No. 11," 15 *Human Rights Law Journal* 81 (1994), 82.

25. B. Simma and P. Alston, "The Sources of Human Rights Law: Custom, Jus Cogens, and General Principles," 12 *Australia Yearbook of International Law* 82 (1988–89), 88–100. The

formation of customary international law will be addressed in Chapter 7, "Lethal Autonomous Weapon Systems and the Responsibility of States and Arms Manufacturers."

26. Chinkin, "Sources," p. 120. M. A. Glendon, *A World Made New: Eleanor Roosevelt and the Universal Declaration of Human Rights* (New York: Random House, 2001), p. 178.

27. Simma and Alston, "Sources of Human Rights Law," 90. Cf. the concurring opinion of U.S. Supreme Court Justice Breyer in *Kiobel v. Royal Dutch Petroleum Co., et al.*, where Breyer argued that acts of torture (prohibited, inter alia, by article 5 of the Universal Declaration) and genocide violate customary international law. 569 U.S. 108 (2013), p. 5. The *Kiobel* decision took a restrictive view of the ability of victims of violations of customary international law occurring outside the territory of the United States to seek damages in U.S. courts. Justice Roberts, pp. 1–14.

28. Chinkin, "Sources," pp. 119–22.

29. For example, General Comment 31 of the ICCPR's Human Rights Committee included the heading "The Nature of the General Legal Obligation Imposed on States Parties to the Covenant." U.N. Doc. CCPR/C/21/Rev.1/Add.13 (2004), https://www1.umn.edu/humanrts/gencomm/hrcom31.html.

30. L. Henkin, *How Nations Behave: Law and Foreign Policy* (New York: Frederick A. Praeger, 1968), p. 27. For example, in December 2015, the General Assembly passed a resolution condemning violence against and intimidation of human rights defenders. "General Assembly Adopts 64 Third Committee Texts Covering Issues Including Migrants, Children's Rights, Human Rights Defenders," 17 December 2015, http://www.un.org/press/en/2015/ga11745.doc.htm. In October 2013, the Security Council issued its seventh resolution addressing the empowerment of women and girls, gender equality, and the effects of violence against women in conflict and postconflict situations. S/Res/2122 (2013), http://www.un.org/en/ga/search/view_doc.asp?symbol=S/RES/2122(2013).

31. For example, on 9 April 2013, Professor Christof Heyns, United Nations Special Rapporteur on Extrajudicial, Summary or Arbitrary Executions, issued a report entitled "Lethal Autonomous Weapons and the Protection of Life," A/HRC/23/47, https://documents-dds-ny.un.org/doc/UNDOC/GEN/G13/127/76/PDF/G1312776.pdf?OpenElement.

32. Described in detail at http://www.ohchr.org/EN/HRBodies/UPR/Pages/UPRMain.aspx.

33. See, for example, the comprehensive "Report of the Detailed Findings of the Commission of Inquiry on Human Rights in the Democratic People's Republic of Korea," A/HRC/25/CRP.1, 7 February 2014.

34. Duffy, *The "War on Terror" and the Framework of International Law*, p. 466; U.N. Security Council Resolution 2122 (2013), p. 2. For example, the Torture Victim Protection Act of 1991 gives victims of torture or extrajudicial execution perpetrated by foreign nationals the right to sue those foreign individuals for damages in U.S. federal courts. H.R.2092, http://thomas.loc.gov/cgi-bin/query/z?c102:H.R.2092.ENR.

35. Art. 6.1, ICCPR.

36. Article 2, ECHR; article 4 (1), American Convention on Human Rights "Pact of San Jose, Costa Rica," article 4, African Charter on Human and Peoples' Rights.

37. *Case of Myrna Mack Chang v. Guatemala*, Judgment, Inter-American Court of Human Rights (Inter-Am. Ct. H.R.), 25 November 2004, para. 152.

38. Benvenisti, "Human Dignity in Combat, 83.

39. *Velasquez Rodriguez v. Honduras*, Judgment, Inter-Am. Ct. H.R, 29 July 1998, para. 188; *Myrna Mack Chang v. Guatemala*, paras. 152 and 153.

40. *Juan Humberto Sánchez v. Honduras*, Judgment, Inter-Am. Ct. H.R. (2003), para. 110.

41. *Juan Humberto Sánchez v. Honduras*, Judgment, para. 110; *The Massacres of El Mozote and Nearby Places v. El Salvador*, Judgment, Inter-Am. Ct. H.R., 25 October 2012, para. 146. According to article 1 of the ECHR, "[t]he High Contracting Parties shall secure to everyone within their jurisdiction the rights and freedoms defined in Section I of this Convention." The American Convention on Human Rights and the African Charter on Human and Peoples' Rights contain similar provisions. Article 1, African Charter on Human and Peoples' Rights (ACHPR); article 2, American Convention on Human Rights. The latter two instruments require state parties to undertake to adopt such "legislative or other measures" to give effect to the rights contained therein.

42. Art. 2, European Convention for the Protection of Human Rights and Fundamental Freedoms.

43. *Akpınar and Altun v. Turkey*, Judgment, European Court of Human Rights (ECtHR), Application No. 56760/00, 27 February 2007, para. 50.

44. *Case of Putintseva v. Russia*, Judgment, ECtHR, First Section, Application No. 33498/04, 10 August 2012, para, 42.

45. *McCann and Others v. the United Kingdom*, Judgment, ECtHR, Application No. 18984/91, 27 September 1995, para. 213. In *McCann*, U.K. soldiers shot dead three members of the Irish Republican Army on a street in Gibraltar. The soldiers feared that the IRA members carried a remote-control device for the purpose of exploding a car bomb. A majority of the ECtHR held that the U.K. was in breach of article 2 because the state could have planned and performed the operation without killing the suspects.

46. "A balance must be achieved between the aim pursued and the means employed to achieve it." *Case of Isayeva v. Russia*, Judgment, ECtHR, Application No. 57950/00, paras. 173 and 181, 24 February 2005.

47. C. Heyns, United Nations Special Rapporteur for Extrajudicial Executions, presentation to Annual Meeting of State Parties to Convention on Certain Conventional Weapons, 13–16 May 2014, p. 5, http://www.unog.ch/80256EDD006B8954/(httpAssets)/DDB079530E4FFDDBC1257CF3003FFE4D/$file/Heyns_LAWS_otherlegal_2014.pdf.

48. *McCann and Others v. the United Kingdom*, para. 194.

49. Heyns, presentation to Annual Meeting of State Parties to Convention on Certain Conventional Weapons, 13–16 May 2014, p. 6.

50. Heyns, presentation to Annual Meeting of State Parties to Convention on Certain Conventional Weapons, 13–16 May 2014, p. 6. The hostile intent of the target often plays a decisive role in the application of human rights law. The target's intention in the context of international humanitarian law, however, is irrelevant because the focus is on status or conduct (p. 6).

51. *Putintseva v. Russia*, para. 71. In *Putintseva*, the commandant of the detention facility entrusted care of the prisoner to a subordinate who, shortly before shooting the deceased, previously had a physical altercation with him. The ECtHR held that the Russian authorities failed to minimize possible recourse to lethal force and risk to the life of the deceased.

52. *Putintseva v. Russia*, para. 69.

53. *Case of Makaratzis v. Greece*, Judgment, ECHR, App. 50385/99, 20 December 2004, para. 58.

54. In *Makaratzis*, the ECtHR concluded that Greece's laws concerning the use of firearms by police were "obsolete and incomplete in a modern democratic society." Thus, the "chaotic"

shooting of the deceased while the police effected his arrest constituted a violation of his right to life (paras. 58 and 700).

55. *Case of Makaratzis v. Greece*, Judgment, at para. 70.

56. *McCann and Others v. the United Kingdom*, para. 193.

57. *Isayeva v. Russia*, para. 191.

58. *Juan Humberto Sánchez v. Honduras*, para. 112.

59. *McCann and Others v. the United Kingdom*, para. 194.

60. *Finogenov and Others v. Russia*, Judgment, ECtHR, Application No. 18299/03, 20 December 2011, paras. 208 and 209.

61. *Finogenov and Others v. Russia*, para. 243.

62. Art. 1, European Convention for the Protection of Human Rights and Fundamental Freedoms.

63. *Putintseva v. Russia*, para. 71.

64. Presentation to 2015 Meeting of Experts on LAWS, Convention on Certain Conventional Weapons, 16 April 2015, p. 10, http://www.unog.ch/80256EE600585943/(httpPages)/6CE049BE22EC75A2C1257C8D00513E26?OpenDocument.

65. Professor Heyns argued that the deployment of lethal autonomous weapons will eviscerate human hope for expressions of compassion or last-minute changes of mind about the use of force. "Dignity in many instances depends on hope, and high levels of lethal machine autonomy can do deep damage to our collective sense of worth." C. Heyns, "Autonomous Weapon Systems and Human Rights Law," Presentation Made at Informal Expert Meeting Organized by the State Parties to the Convention on Certain Conventional Weapons, Geneva, 13–16 May 2014, pp. 7–9, http://www.unog.ch/80256EDD006B8954/(httpAssets)/DDB079530E4FFDDBC1257CF3003FFE4D/$file/Heyns_LAWS_otherlegal_2014.pdf.

66. Preamble, *Basic Principles on the Use of Force and Firearms by Law Enforcement Officials*, Eighth United Nations Congress on the Prevention of Crime and the Treatment of Offenders, 7 September 1990, http://www.ohchr.org/EN/ProfessionalInterest/Pages/UseOfForceAndFirearms.aspx.

67. Preamble, *Basic Principles on the Use of Force*, paras. 9 and 16.

68. *The Massacres of El Mozote and Nearby Places v. El Salvador*, paras. 145–46.

69. Professor Heyns suggested that it may be necessary to develop a system for autonomous weapons to be used in law enforcement that is analogous to the article 36, API procedure. C. Heyns, presentation at Annual Meeting of State Parties to the Convention on Certain Conventional Weapons, p. 4.

70. *Makaratzis v. Greece*, para. 70 (observing that the police officers involved in the fatal shooting under review did not have sufficient time to evaluate all the parameters of the situation and carefully organize their operation).

71. "Both bodies of law take as their starting point the concern for human dignity, which forms the basis of a list of fundamental minimum standards of humanity." *Prosecutor v. Zejnil Delalić, et al.*, Judgment, IT-96-21-A, 20 February 2001, para. 149.

72. The preamble to APII recalls "that international instruments relating to human rights offer a basic protection to the human person," but a need exists to ensure a better protection for the victims of armed conflicts.

73. Meron, *Human Rights and Humanitarian Norms*, p. 9. For example, Common Article 3's requirement that civilians and persons hors de combat must be treated humanely "is an

overarching concept," given expression by the detailed rules incorporated into modern international humanitarian law. "Commentary," *Rule 87. Humane Treatment.*

74. Meron, *Human Rights and Humanitarian Norms*, p. 10.

75. "Necessitous circumstances, grave as they may be, do not overshadow human rights." *Prosecutor v. Lubanga*, Dissenting Opinion of Judge Pikis in the Judgment on the Release of Lubanga, ICC-01/04-01/06-1487 OA12, 21 October 2008, paras. 17–18. Diss. Op.

76. *Legality of the Threat or Use of Nuclear Weapons*, Advisory Opinion, International Court of Justice, 8 July 1996, para. 25. The principle of *lex specialis derogat lex generali* stands for the idea that because general rules may be interpreted in more than one way, we should interpret them in light of specific rules rather than vice versa. W. Abresch, "A Human Rights Law of Internal Armed Conflict: The European Court of Human Rights in Chechnya," 16 *European Journal of International Law* (2005), 741, 744. For a strong critique of *lex specialis* as an interpretive model for analysis of the relationship between international humanitarian law and international human rights law, see M. Milanović, "Norm Conflicts, International Humanitarian Law and Human Rights Law," in Orna Ben-Naftali (ed.), *Human Rights and International Humanitarian Law: Collected Courses of the Academy of European Law*, vol. 19/1 (Oxford University Press, 2010).

77. *Legal Consequences of the Construction of a Wall in the Occupied Palestinian Territory*, Advisory Opinion, International Court of Justice, 9 July 2004, para. 106. The court held that Israel, by constructing a wall that passed through occupied territory, breached various obligations under the applicable international humanitarian law and international human rights law (para. 137). Cf. *Case of Al-Jedda v. the United Kingdom*, Judgment, ECtHR, 7 July 2011, para. 105.

78. *Case Concerning Armed Activities on the Republic of the Congo (Democratic Republic of the Congo v. Uganda)*, Judgment, 19 December 2005, paras. 179 and 216–20. Professor Schabas interprets the court's language as treating international humanitarian and international human rights law "as two complementary systems, as parts of a whole." W. Schabas, "The Right to Life," in A. Clapham et al. (eds.), *The Oxford Handbook of International Law in Armed Conflict* (Oxford University Press, 2014), p. 5.

79. *Legal Consequences of the Construction of a Wall in the Occupied Palestinian Territory*, para. 368 (2).

80. Cf. art. 6, ECHR; art. 8, ACHR; art. 7, ACHPR.

81. *Case of Bámaca Velásquez v. Guatemala*, Judgment, Inter-Am. Ct. H.R., 25 November 2000, para. 209.

82. Art. 78 of Convention (IV) Relative to the Protection of Civilian Persons in Time of War, 12 August 1949. Persons interned pursuant to art. 78 need not be guilty of any violation of the laws of the occupying power. Nevertheless, that power may consider them dangerous to its security and thus entitled to restrict their liberty of movement. ICRC commentary to art. 78, para. 368 (1), http://www.icrc.org/applic/ihl/ihl.nsf/Comment.xsp?viewComments=LookUpCOMART&articleUNID=0DFFF94F559B0D17C12563CD0051C023. Cf. articles 40, 41, and 42.

83. F. Hampson, Written Statement, Appendix 3 to "Expert Meeting," *The Use of Force in Armed Conflicts: Interplay Between the Conduct of Hostilities and Law Enforcement Paradigms*, Geneva, ICRC, 2013, p. 78.

84. Unless a combatant is hors de combat, he or she can be made the object of attack by his or her adversary. JSP 383, *The Joint Service Manual of the Law of Armed Conflict*, U.K. Ministry of Defence, 2004, para. 5.5. See art. 23 (c), Regulations Respecting the Laws and Customs of War on Land, 1907 Hague Convention IV Respecting the Laws and Customs of War on Land (it

is forbidden to "kill or wound an enemy who, having laid down his arms, or having no longer means of defense, has surrendered at discretion").

85. *Isayeva v. Russia*, para. 181. The *Isayeva* case addressed the deaths of civilians as a consequence of the Russian military's bombing of a village in Chechnya during the Chechnyan internal armed conflict in 2000. In an effort to avoid the *ultra vires* application of international humanitarian law, the ECtHR disingenuously described the context of the events as "outside wartime" and implied that the Russian armed forces were a "law enforcement body" (para. 191). This jurisprudence raises the question whether the ECtHR disregards international humanitarian law, at least in internal armed conflict. Abresch, "Human Rights Law of Internal Armed Conflict," 746.

86. Hampson, Written Statement, p. 69.

87. *Case of Hassan v. The United Kingdom*, Judgment, ECtHR, Application No. 29750/09, 16 September 2014, para. 95 (referring to submission of third party Human Rights Centre of the University of Essex).

88. D. Jinks, "International Human Rights Law in Time of Armed Conflict," in Clapham et al., *Oxford Handbook of International Law in Armed Conflict*, pp. 3 and 4.

89. *Hassan v. the United Kingdom*, para. 104. This language appears to be an implicit rejection of a rigid application of the "lex specialis" terminology originally used by the International Court of Justice in the "Nuclear Weapons" Advisory Opinion, para. 25.

90. *Hassan v. the United Kingdom*, para. 104. Cf. *Serdar Mohammed v. Ministry of Defence*, Judgment, Case No. HQ12X03367, 2 May 2014, para. 288 (holding that in a situation where a more specialized body of international law also applies, provisions of the convention should be interpreted as far as possible in a manner consistent with that *lex specialis*).

91. Arts. 4 (A) and 21 of Geneva Convention III Relative to the Treatment of Prisoners of War of 1949 and arts. 43 and 78 of Geneva Convention IV Relative to the Protection of Civilian Persons of 1949.

92. *Hassan v.* The *United Kingdom*, Judgment, paras. 105–11. The court specified that its broad interpretation of a state's powers of detention under art. 5 of the ECHR—and the court's implicit deference to the laws of war in situations of capture or internment—could apply to an international armed conflict only where the safeguards provided by international humanitarian law and international human rights law coexist (para. 104). In a strongly worded dissent, however, five judges contended that the majority decision "effectively disapplies or displaces" the ECHR's fundamental safeguards for permissible detention "by judicially creating a new, unwritten ground for a deprivation of liberty and hence, incorporating norms from another and distinct regime of international law in direct conflict with the Convention provision." Partially Dissenting Opinion of Judge Spano, Joined by Judges Nicolaou, Bianku, and Kalaydjieva, para. 18. Effectively, the court incorporated the rules concerning capture and internment (from the law of armed conflict) into article 5 of the ECHR. C. de Koker, "A Different Perspective on Hassan v. United Kingdom: A Reply to Frederic Bernard," *Strasbourg Observers*, 14 October 2014, http://strasbourgobservers.com/2014/10/14/a-different-perspective-on-hassan-v-united-kingdom-a-reply-to-frederic-bernard/.

93. N. Melzer, *Interpretive Guidance on the Notion of Direct Participation in Hostilities Under International Humanitarian Law*, May 2009, http://www.icrc.org/eng/assets/files/other/icrc-002-0990.pdf.

94. *Interpretive Guidance*, at 77.

95. *Interpretive Guidance*, 82. The Israeli Supreme Court has taken a similar position with respect to the possible arrest of suspected terrorists, in particular under conditions of belligerent

occupation. Thus, in Israeli domestic law, "among the military means, one must choose the means whose harm to the human rights of the harmed person is smallest." *The Public Committee Against Torture in Israel v. the Government of Israel* ("Targeted Killing Case"), Judgment, HCJ 769/02, 11 December 2005, para. 40. Importantly, the court based its decision on "the rules of international law" as well as Israeli law (para. 61).

96. As one commentator observed, it is unsurprising that, in *Hassan*, the ECtHR rejected the United Kingdom's argument that the application of international humanitarian law in the circumstances excluded the authority of international human rights law. The majority decision, like *Interpretive Guidance*, strengthens the jurisdiction of international human rights law during armed conflict. S. Rau, *EJILTalk*, 18 September 2014, http://www.ejiltalk.org/the-grand-chamber-judgment-in-hassan-v-uk/. Professor Milanović refers to this jurisprudence as an example of the court's "interpretive self-empowerment." M. Milanović, "A Few Thoughts on Hassan v. United Kingdom," *EJILTalk*, 22 October 2014, http://www.ejiltalk.org/a-few-thoughts-on-hassan-v-united-kingdom/.

97. M. N. Schmitt, "The Interpretive Guidance on the Notion of Direct Participation in Hostilities: A Critical Analysis," 1 *Harvard National Security Journal* (2010), 5–44; W. H. Parks, "Part IX of the ICRC 'Direct Participation in Hostilities' Study: No Mandate, No Expertise, and Legally Incorrect," 42 *International Law and Politics* (2010), 769; K. Watkin, "Opportunity Lost: Organized Armed Groups and the ICRC 'Direct Participation in Hostilities' Interpretive Guidance," 42 *International Law and Politics* (2010), 641. For a more positive view, see the remarks of R. Goodman in "The Changing Character of the Participants in War: Civilianization of War-Fighting and the Concept of 'Direct Participation in Hostilities'" (U.S. Naval War College, International Law Conference 2010), http://www.usnwc.edu/Events/International-Law-Conference-2010.aspx, accessed 27 August 2012.

98. Customary International Humanitarian Law Database, https://www.icrc.org/customary-ihl/eng/docs/home.

99. The RTO Studies, Analysis and Simulation Panel (SAS), "NATO Policy on Non-Lethal Weapons" (Annex B to RTO-TR-SAS-040, Non-Lethal Weapons and Future Peace Enforcement Operations), December 2004, in (n. 65) 5-2, http://www.cso.nato.int/pubs/rdp.asp?RDP=RTO-TR-SAS-040.

100. H. Nasu, "Nanotechnology and the Future of the Law of Weaponry," 91 *International Law Studies* (2015), 486, 508–9.

101. For a discussion of the related issue of the capacity of autonomous weapon systems to recognize the intent of combatants to surrender, see R. Sparrow, "Twenty Seconds to Comply: Autonomous Weapon Systems and the Recognition of Surrender," 91 *International Law Studies* (2015), 699.

102. Schabas, "Right to Life," p. 7.

103. See Benvenisti, "Human Dignity in Combat," 86 (noting, similarly, that the principle of human dignity is not inconsistent with armed conflict, as conflict may be necessary to protect rights).

104. W. Boothby, *The Law of Targeting* (Oxford University Press, 2012), p. 409.

105. *Case of Lambert and Others v. France*, Judgment, ECtHR, Application No. 46043/14, 5 June 2015, para. 148. Margins of appreciation are not unlimited and "must always be viewed in light of the values underpinning the Convention, chief among them the right to life" (*Case of Lambert and Others v. France*, Joint Partly Dissenting Opinion of Judges Hajiyev, Šikuta, Tsotsoria, De Gaetano and Gritco, para. 7).

106. *Case of Lambert and Others v. France*, para. 3, citing *Case of Pretty v. the United Kingdom, ECtHR*, No. 2346/02, 29 April 2002, para. 65.

107. "Netherlands Termination of Life on Request and Assisted Suicide (Review Procedures)" (2002), https://www.government.nl/topics/euthanasia/contents/euthanasia-assisted-suicide-and-non-resuscitation-on-request; "The Belgian Act on Euthanasia of 28 May 2002, http://www.ethical-perspectives.be/viewpic.php?LAN=E&TABLE=EP&ID=59. In Colombia, the Constitutional Court authorized the practice of assisted suicide in 1997. However, no law exists that specifies the parameters for performing the procedure. P. Sierra Palencia, "Por Quinta Vez, Se Abre el Debate de la Eutanasia en el Congreso" (For the fifth time, debate about euthanasia begins in Congress), *El Heraldo*, 9 November 2014, http://www.elheraldo.co/nacional/por-quinta-vez-se-abre-el-debate-de-la-eutanasia-en-el-congreso-173293; Luxembourg Law of 16 March 2009 on Euthanasia and Assisted Suicide, http://www.luxembourg.public.lu/en/vivre/famille/fin-vie/euthanasie-soinspalliatifs/index.html. In South Africa, the Constitutional Court currently is reviewing a lower court order asserting a right to assisted suicide. "South African Court to Hear Landmark Assisted Suicide Case," BBC News, 2 June 2015, http://www.bbc.com/news/world-africa-32970801. In Switzerland, providing assistance to another's suicide is legal, as long as the assistance is not provided for "selfish motives." Article 115, Swiss Criminal Code, https://www.admin.ch/opc/en/classified-compilation/19370083/201501010000/311.0.pdf. In Uruguay, judges will not punish persons who assist the suicide of another, if the assistance was motivated by compassion and repeated requests of the victim. Article 17, Codigo Penal de Uruguay, https://en.wikipedia.org/wiki/Assisted_suicide#cite_note-McDougall_2008-20.

108. "The Belgian Act on Euthanasia of 28 May 2002," section 3, para. 1.

109. *Carter v. Canada* (Attorney General), 2015 SCC 5, [2015] (emphasis added).

110. *Carter v. Canada*.

111. *Case of Lambert and Others v. France*, Joint Partly Dissenting Opinion of Judges Hajiyev, Šikuta, Tsotsoria, De Gaetano and Gritco, para. 7.

112. See T. Jefferson, *Letter to David Harding*, 20 April 1824, http://tjrs.monticello.org/letter/428 ("In a republican nation whose citizens are to be led by reason and persuasion and not by force, the art of reasoning becomes of first importance").

113. Human dignity "cannot be gained or lost." W. Tadd et al., "Clarifying the Concept of Human Dignity in the Care of the Elderly: A Dialogue Between Empirical and Philosophical Approaches," 17 *Ethical Perspectives* 1 (2010), 253, 255.

114. P. Margulies, "Making Autonomous Weapons Accountable: Command Responsibility for Computer-Guided Lethal Force in Armed Conflict," in J. Ohlin (ed.), *Research Handbook on Remote Warfare* (Northampton: Edward Elgar, 2016).

115. Benvenisti, "Human Dignity in Combat," 109 (emphasis added).

Chapter 6

1. A. Cassese, *International Criminal Law*, 2nd ed. (Oxford University Press, 2008), p. 3. "The law is a living, growing thing. In no other sphere is it more necessary to affirm that the rights and duties of States are the rights and duties of men and that unless they bind individuals they bind no one." H. Shawcross, "Closing Speech," *The Trial of German Major War Criminals: Proceedings of the International Military Tribunal Sitting at Nuremburg Germany*, part 19, 16 July 1946–27 July 1946 (London: His Majesty's Stationery Office, 1949), p. 427.

2. B. Cheng, *General Principles of Law as Applied by International Courts and Tribunals* (London, Stevens and Sons, 1953), pp. 208 and 212. "Individual criminal responsibility reflects

the particular degree of blameworthiness of an act committed by a moral agent." H. Decoeur, "Avoiding Strict Liability in Mixed Conflicts: A Subjectivist Approach to the Contextual Element of War Crimes," 13 *International Criminal Law Review* (2013), 473, 480.

3. I am grateful to Louise Arbour for this point.

4. "Accountability of International Organizations," International Law Association, 1 *International Organization Law Review* 221, 225 (2004). This duty does not insist on perfection, "as there is no such thing as a perfect decision in war, where complexity, friction, uncertainty, the interlocking effects of the actions of independent individuals, and the enemy all affect the outcome of events." Gen. C. Campbell, "Army Action on the Re-Investigation into the Combat Action of Wanat Village, Wygal District, Nuristan Province, Afghanistan on 13 July 2008," Department of the Army, 13 May 2010, http://web.archive.org/web/20110716075735/http://usarmy.vo.llnwd.net/e1/wanat/downloads/campbellWanatReportRedacted.pdf.

5. S. Morse, "Law, Responsibility and the Sciences of the Brain/Mind," in *The Oxford Handbook of Law, Regulation and Technology*, R. Brownsword, E. Scotford, and K. Yeung (eds.) (Oxford University Press, 2017), p. 158.

6. *R. v. Finta*, [1994] (Supreme Court of Canada) 1 SCR 701, at 760. "In all advanced legal systems liability to conviction for serious crimes is made dependent, not only on the offender having done those outward acts which the law forbids, but on his having done them in a certain frame of mind or with a certain will." H. Hart, "Changing Conceptions of Responsibility," in *Punishment and Responsibility: Essays in the Philosophy of Law* (Oxford: Clarendon Press, 1963), p. 187.

7. B. Docherty, "Mind the Gap: The Lack of Accountability for Killer Robots," *Human Rights Watch*, 9 April 2015, https://www.hrw.org/report/2015/04/09/mind-gap/lack-accountability-killer-robots.

8. For example, the repression of piracy, committed at sea, contained an international dimension. W. Schabas, *An Introduction to the International Criminal Court*, 4th ed. (Cambridge University Press, 2011), p. 89.

9. London Agreement of 8 August 1945, http://www.icls.de/dokumente/imt_london_agreement.pdf; Special Proclamation by the Supreme Commander of the Allied Powers, 19 January 1946, https://www.loc.gov/law/help/us-treaties/bevans/m-ust000004-0020.pdf.

10. Charter of the International Military Tribunal, http://avalon.law.yale.edu/imt/imtconst.asp; Charter of the International Military Tribunal for the Far East, 19 January 1946, https://www.loc.gov/law/help/us-treaties/bevans/m-ust000004-0020.pdf.

11. Draft Law on the Specialist Chambers (English), https://www.docdroid.net/14op8/draft-law-on-the-specialist-chambers-eng.pdf.html.

12. Arts. 227–30, Versailles Treaty of 28 June 1919. Eventually, only a small number of individuals were prosecuted pursuant to these provisions. A. Cassese, *International Criminal Law*, pp. 317–19.

13. Arts. 1, 4–6, Adopted by the General Assembly of the United Nations on 9 December 1948.

14. Art. 4, Convention Against Torture and Other Cruel, Inhuman or Degrading Treatment (CAT), Adopted by General Assembly Resolution 39/46 of 10 December 1984. The CAT also provides that state parties should ensure the possibility of "universal" jurisdiction over alleged offenders present in their territories whom they do not intend to extradite (art. 5 [2]).

15. Articles 5–8, Statute of the International Criminal Court, Done at Rome 17 July 1998, https://www.icc-cpi.int/NR/rdonlyres/ADD16852-AEE9-4757-ABE7-9CDC7CF02886/283503/RomeStatutEng1.pdf.

16. The Security Council (UNSC) established the ICTY to prosecute persons responsible for serious violations of international humanitarian law committed in the territory of the former Yugoslavia after 1 January 1991. UNSC Resolution 827, S/RES/827, 25 May 1993, http://www.icty.org/x/file/Legal%20Library/Statute/statute_827_1993_en.pdf. The ICTR was established to prosecute persons responsible for genocide and other serious violations of international humanitarian law committed in the territory of Rwanda and Rwandan citizens responsible for genocide and other such violations committed in the territory of neighboring states, between 1 January 1994 and 31 December 1994. UNSC Resolution 955, S/RES/955 (1994), https://www1.umn.edu/humanrts/peace/docs/scres955.html.

17. Resolution 1595 (2005), S/RES/1595 (2005), https://www.treasury.gov/resource-center/sanctions/Programs/Documents/1595.pdf.

18. Security Council Resolution 1757 (2007), http://news.specialtribunalforlebanon.com/en/component/k2/225-security-council-resolution-1757?Itemid=213. In 2003, an agreement between the United Nations and the government of Cambodia facilitated the creation of the Extraordinary Chambers in the Courts of Cambodia for the purpose of prosecuting senior leaders of Democratic Kampuchea and those who were most responsible for the crimes and serious violations of Cambodian penal law, international humanitarian law and custom, and international conventions recognized by Cambodia that were committed during the period from 17 April 1975 to 6 January 1979. Agreement Between the United Nations and the Royal Government of Cambodia Concerning the Prosecution Under Cambodian Law of Crimes Committed During the Period of Democratic Kampuchea, http://www.eccc.gov.kh/sites/default/files/legaldocuments/Agreement_between_UN_and_RGC.pdf.

19. G. Werle, *Principles of International Criminal Law* (The Hague: T. M. C. Asser, 2005), p. 11.

20. "(1) Any person who commits an act which constitutes a crime under international law is responsible therefore and liable to punishment. (2) The fact that internal law does not impose a penalty for an act which constitutes a crime under international law does not relieve the person who committed the act from responsibility under international law. (3) The fact that a person who committed an act which constitutes a crime under international law acted as Head of State or responsible Government official does not relieve him from responsibility under international law (provided a moral choice was in fact possible). (4) The fact that a person acted pursuant to an order of his government or of a superior does not relieve him of responsibility under international law. (5) Any person charged with a crime under international law has a right to a fair trial on the facts and law. (6) Crimes Against International Law include crimes against peace (aggression), crimes against humanity and war crimes. (7) Complicity in the commission of a crime against peace, a war crime, or a crime against humanity as set forth in principle 6 is a crime under international law." International Law Commission, *Principles of International Law Recognized in the Charter of the Nürnberg Tribunal and the Judgment of the Tribunal,* International Law Commission, 1950, http://legal.un.org/ilc/texts/instruments/english/draft_articles/7_1_1950.pdf.

21. *Prosecutor v. Zejnil Delalić, et al.*, Judgment, IT-96-21-A, Appeals Chamber, 20 February 2001, para. 266 (holding that, for the purposes of determining superior responsibility, customary law specifies a standard of effective control).

22. Rule 156, J. Henckaerts and L. Doswald-Beck, *Customary International Humanitarian Law*, vol. 1, *Rules*, International Committee of the Red Cross (Cambridge University Press, 2005).

23. *Prosecutor v. Duško Tadić a/k/a "Dule,"* Decision on the Defence Motion for Interlocutory Appeal on Jurisdiction, IT-94-1-AR72, Appeals Chamber, 2 October 1995, para. 119.

24. *Prosecutor v. Stanislav Galić*, Judgment, No. IT-98-29-A, 2006, Appeals Chamber, para. 120. Previously, the International Criminal Tribunal for the former Yugoslavia held that the rules of treaty and customary international humanitarian law attempt to guarantee the "basic human rights" of life, dignity, and humane treatment of persons taking no active part in armed conflicts and that "their enforcement by criminal prosecution is an integral part of their effectiveness." *Prosecutor v. Zejnil Delalić, et al.*, Judgment, No. IT-96-21-T, 16 November 1998, para. 200.

25. Cassese, *International Criminal Law*, p. 99. Crimes against humanity are particular criminal acts "committed as part of a widespread or systematic attack directed against any civilian population, with knowledge of the attack." Art. 7, Rome Statute of the ICC. Art. 7 of the "Elements of Crimes" contained in the ICC statute clarifies that the attack against the civilian population must be carried out pursuant to a policy or plan of a state or organization, https://www.icc-cpi.int/NR/rdonlyres/336923D8-A6AD-40EC-AD7B-45BF9DE73D56/0/ElementsOfCrimesEng.pdf.

26. "The application and interpretation of law [by the court] must be consistent with internationally recognized human rights." Art. 21 (3), Rome Statute of the ICC.

27. *Prosecutor v. Thomas Lubanga Dyilo*, Judgment on the Appeal of Mr. Thomas Lubanga Dyilo against the Decision on the Defence Challenge to the Jurisdiction of the Court pursuant to article 19 (2) (a) of the Statute of 3 October 2006, ICC-01/04-01/06 (OA4), 14 December 2006, para. 37.

28. General Counsel of the United States Department of Defense, *Law of War Manual* 2015, section 1.9, http://www.defense.gov/Portals/1/Documents/pubs/Law-of-War-Manual-June-2015.pdf.

29. *Prosecutor v. Anto Furundija*, Judgment, IT-95-17/1-T, 10 December 1998, paras. 174–86 (defining the elements of the crime of rape).

30. *Prosecutor v. Ljube Boškoski & Johan Tarčulovski*, Judgment, IT-04-02-A, Appeals Chamber, 19 May 2010, para. 160.

31. *Prosecutor v. Zejnil Delalić, et al.*, Judgment, Appeals Chamber, paras. 192–98, 222–41, and 248–67.

32. Benton Heath describes how international criminal law is an attempt to enforce the community's most basic values via the threat of sanctions against persons bearing individual responsibility. "Human Dignity at Trial: Hard Cases and Broad Concepts in International Criminal Law," 44 *George Washington International Law Review* (2012), 317 and 354.

33. Every human being bears an obligation to respect "the dignity of humanity" that must be shown to every other human being. I. Kant, *The Metaphysics of Morals*, Mary Gregor (ed.) (Cambridge University Press, 2005), pp. 186 and 209.

34. D. Maxwell Fyfe, "Speech at the Close of the Case Against the Indicted Organizations" (19 August 1946), in *The Trial of German Major War Criminals: Proceedings of the International Military Tribunal Sitting at Nuremberg, Germany*, 1945–46, London, 1946, p. 3. Similarly, in the Judgment of the Cour de Cassation in the case of Klaus Barbie, M. Le Gunehec observed that the crime against humanity of persecution offends "the fundamental rights of mankind" and that such crimes "are aggravated by the voluntary, deliberate and gratuitous violation of the dignity of all men and women." *Prosecutor v. Duško Tadić a/k/a "Dule,"* Judgment, IT-94-1-T, 7 May 1997, para. 696, quoting A. Cassese, *Violence and Law in the Modern Age* (Cambridge: Polity, 1988), p. 112.

35. *Prosecutor v. Ferdinand Nahimana, et al.*, Judgment, ICTR-99-52-T, 3 December 2003, para. 1072. See also the Judgment on Appeal, para 986 (holding that "hate speech targeting a

population on the basis of ethnicity, or any other discriminatory ground, violates the right to respect for the dignity of the members of the targeted group as human beings").

36. *Prosecutor v. Zlatko Aleksovski*, Judgment, IT-95-14/1-A, Appeals Chamber, 24 March 2000, para. 185.

37. G. Fletcher, "What Is Punishment Imposed For?" in Russell Christopher (ed.), *Fletcher's Essays on Criminal Law* (Oxford University Press, 2013), p. 51.

38. *Prosecutor v. Zejnil Delalić, et al.*, Judgment, para. 200.

39. At the International Criminal Court, the tribunal can impose fines and or forfeiture of proceeds, property, and assets derived from crimes, but only "[i]n addition to imprisonment." Rome Statute, art. 2 (a) and (b).

40. S. Ratner and J. Abrams, *Accountability for Human Rights Atrocities in International Law: Beyond the Nuremberg Legacy*, 2nd ed. (Oxford University Press, 2001), p. 336.

41. Fletcher, "What Is Punishment Imposed For?" p. 52.

42. *Questions Relating to the Obligation to Prosecute or Extradite (Belgium v. Senegal)*, Separate Opinion of Judge Cançado Trindade, ICJ Reports 2012, 20 July 2012, para. 108, reprinted in A. Cançado Trindade, *The Construction of a Humanized International Law: A Collection of Individual Opinions* (1991–2013) (Leiden: Brill Nijhoff, 2015), p. 1568. *Case of Goiburú et al. v. Paraguay*, Judgment, Inter-American Court of Human Rights, 22 September 2006, paras. 158 and 164 (holding that continued impunity for persons responsible for gross violations of human rights constitutes a source of additional suffering and anguish for the victim's relatives and that "impunity fosters the chronic repetition of human rights violations and the total defenselessness of the victims and their next of kin, who have the right to know the truth about the facts").

43. In his closing speech at the end of the trial of the leading German war criminals, Sir Hartley Shawcross referred to that "natural justice which demands that these crimes should not go unpunished." "Speeches of the Chief Prosecutors at the Close of the Case Against the Individual Defendants," *The Trial of German Major War Criminals by the International Military Tribunal Sitting at Nuremberg, Germany*, London, 1946, p. 34 (26–27 July 1946). The preamble to the Rome Statute of the ICC emphasizes the determination of the drafters "to put an end to impunity for the perpetrators of these crimes and thus to contribute to the prevention of such crimes." The Commission of Inquiry on Human Rights in the Democratic People's Republic of Korea concluded that the perpetrators of crimes against humanity in North Korea enjoy impunity and recommended that those most responsible be held accountable by an international tribunal. Report, A/HRC/25/63, 7 February 2014, para. 85.

44. N. Roht-Arriza, "Introduction," in N. Roht-Arriza (ed.), *Impunity and Human Rights in International Law and Practice* (Oxford University Press, 1995), pp. 8–9. ("[T]he pursuit of accountability can be highly significant to the victims of atrocities—and their relatives and friends—by giving them a sense of justice and closure.") Ratner and Abrams, *Accountability for Human Rights Atrocities in International Law*, p. 155. Cf. Heath, "Human Dignity at Trial," 348 (arguing that international criminal law jurisprudence "maintains a delicate balance between the fight against impunity and the need to safeguard the defendant's rights—a balance the concept of dignity threatens to destabilize").

45. Art. 8 (2) (b) (xxi), "War Crime of Outrages upon Personal Dignity," *Elements of Crimes of the International Criminal Court*, p. 27, http://www.icc-cpi.int/NR/rdonlyres/336923D8-A6AD-40EC-AD7B-45BF9DE73D56/0/ElementsOfCrimesEng.pdf; *Prosecutor v. Germain Katanga and Mathieu Ngudjolo Chui*, Decision on the Confirmation of Charges, ICC-01/04-01/7, 30 September 2008, paras. 371, 376, 377, and 385; *Prosecutor v. Jean-Paul Akayesu*, Judgment,

ICTR-96-4-T, 2 September 1998, para. 597; *Prosecutor v. Zlatko Aleksovski*, Judgment, paras. 25 and 37; *Prosecutor v. Dragoljub Kunarac*, Judgment, IT-96-23-T & IT-96-23/1-T, 22 February 2001, paras. 408, 500–501, and 756.

46. *S. v. Williams and Others*, Judgment (CCT/20/94), [1995] paras. 11 and 89.

47. A. Duff, "Authority and Responsibility in International Criminal Law," in S. Besson and J. Tasioulas (eds.), *The Philosophy of International Law* (Oxford University Press, 2010), pp. 593–604. "Traditional" forms of justice also support these kinds of engagements between perpetrators and victims. P. Clark, "The Rules and Politics of Engagement," in P. Clark and Z. Kaufman (eds.), *After Genocide: Transitional Justice, Post-Conflict Reconstruction and Reconciliation in Rwanda and Beyond* (London: Hurst, 2009), pp. 300–301 and 314–15.

48. *Prosecutor v. Dragan Obrenović*, Sentencing Judgment, IT-02-60/2-S, 10 December 2003, paras. 145–46; *Report of the Truth and Reconciliation Commission of South Africa*, 29 October 1998, vol. 5, chap. 5, para. 101, chap. 9, paras. 33–37.

49. *Prosecutor v. Dragan Obrenović*, Sentencing Judgment, paras. 145–46.

50. Juan Mendez, then the special advisor on the prevention of genocide to the United Nations, observed in 2004 that the idea that criminal punishment plays a role in the prevention of crimes was "an act of faith." M. Mennecke, "Punishing Genocidaires: A Deterrent Effect or Not? *Human Rights Review*, July 2007, 319. In 2009, Mendez was more sanguine, remarking that "we have the expectation, and I would say the promise, that the [prosecutorial] actions we take with difficulty today will have a preventive effect in the future." "Justice as Prevention of Mass Atrocities," Presentation at the Carr Center for Human Rights, John F. Kennedy School of Government, Harvard University, 23 November 2009, http://www.youtube.com/watch?v=yQSLeru_n8o. No comprehensive data exists, yet, that clearly demonstrates the ability of international criminal courts to prevent and/or deter crimes. However, in very specific situations, the ICC may prevent/deter potential offenders from participating in or committing the crimes under the tribunal's jurisdiction. D. Saxon, "The International Criminal Court and the Prevention of Crimes," in S. Sharma and J. Welsh (eds.), *The Responsibility to Protect: Overcoming the Challenges to Atrocity Prevention* (Oxford University Press, 2015), pp. 122–23 and 139–46.

51. M. Langer, "The Diplomacy of Universal Jurisdiction: The Political Branches and the Transnational Prosecution of International Crimes," 105 *American Journal of International Law*, No. 1 (2011), 1, 47–48.

52. L. Kercher, *The Kenya Penal System: Past, Present and Prospect* (Washington, D.C.: University Press of America, 1981), p. 238.

53. Essentially, the prevention of crime requires three elements: (1) moral and legal norms for acceptable behavior, (2) institutions that make those norms credible, and (3) a culture that permits those norms to exist. Author interview with Matias Hellman, External Relations Advisor, Office of the President, International Criminal Court, The Hague, 1 April 2011, in Saxon, "International Criminal Court and the Prevention of Crimes," p. 120, n. 4.

54. *Armed Activities on the Territory of the Congo (Democratic Republic of the Congo v. Uganda)*, Judgment, ICJ Reports 2005, para. 211; *Prosecutor v. Duško Tadić a/k/a "Dule,"* Decision on the Defense Motion for Interlocutory Appeal on Jurisdiction," 2 October 1995, paras. 79–142.

55. Hence, art. 87 of API requires commanders who are aware that subordinates will commit or have committed grave breaches of the protocol to prevent the occurrence of additional crimes and/or punish the perpetrators. Individual criminal responsibility for failing to fulfill this obligation is enshrined in art. 28 of the Rome Statute of the ICC.

56. In the U.K. armed forces, "responsibility" entails a professional obligation held by a superior who ultimately takes credit for success and blame for failure. "Accountability" comprises a liability and an obligation to answer to a superior for the (im)proper use of authority and resources. "Army Doctrine Publications" Operations, Ministry of Defence, 2010, para. 0619, https://www.gov.uk/government/uploads/system/uploads/attachment_data/file/33695/ADPOperationsDec10.pdf.

57. Rule 139, ICRC Customary International Humanitarian Law Study, https://www.icrc.org/customary-ihl/eng/docs/v1_cha_chapter40_rule139; Common Art. 3 to 1949 Geneva Conventions; 2016 commentary to art. 3, Geneva Convention I, paras. 520–28, https://www.icrc.org/applic/ihl/ihl.nsf/Comment.xsp?action=openDocument&documentId=59F6CDFA490736C1C1257F7D004BA0EC; *Prosecutor v. Thomas Lubanga Dyilo*, Judgment Pursuant to article 74 of the Statute, ICC-01/04-01/06, 14 March 2012, paras. 1176 and 1222; *Prosecutor v. Thomas Lubanga Dyilo*, Decision on Sentence Pursuant to art. 76 of the Statute, ICC-01/04-01/06, 10 July 2012, para. 97; see L. Zegveld, *The Accountability of Armed Opposition Groups in International Law* (Cambridge University Press, 2002), pp. 111–32.

58. *Prosecutor v. Miroslav Kvočka, et al.*, Judgment, IT-98-30/1-T, 2 November 2001, para. 716; *Prosecutor v. Zlatko Aleksovski*, Judgment, IT-95-14/1-T, 25 June 1999, para. 88.

59. Maxwell Fyfe, "Speech at the Close of the Case Against the Indicted Organizations," p. 58.

60. A. Sen, *The Idea of Justice* (London: Penguin Books, 2010), p. 19.

61. Responsibility should not be confused with accuracy. A person acts responsibly if he or she accepts moral and legal integrity and makes a reasonable effort toward achieving them. The end result is secondary. R. Dworkin, *Justice for Hedgehogs* (Cambridge, Mass.: Harvard University Press, 2011), pp. 100 and 109.

62. *Prosecutor v. Ljube Boškoski & Johan Tarčulovski*, Judgment, IT-04-82-T, 10 July 2008, paras. 601 and 607–8. Similarly, when sentencing Sreten Lukić, former minister of interior for the Federal Republic of Yugoslavia, for his responsibility for, inter alia, crimes against humanity that occurred in Kosovo, the Trial Chamber recognized that Lukić acted "in the midst of a complicated situation, including the defense of the country against NATO bombing and some combat operations against the KLA." *Prosecutor v. Milan Milutinović, et al.*, Judgment, IT-05-87-T, 26 February 2009, para. 1201.

63. *Prosecutor v. Stanislav Galić*, Judgment, IT-98-29, Trial Chamber, 3 December 2003, para. 169.

64. *Prosecutor v. Momčilo Perisić*, Judgment, IT-04-81-A, Appeals Chamber, 28 February 2013, paras. 86–87.

65. *Prosecutor v. Zejnil Delalić, et al.*, Judgment, Appeals Chamber, para. 225 (emphasis added).

66. *Prosecutor v. Duško Tadić*, Judgment, IT-94-1-A, Appeals Chamber, 15 July 1999, para. 194.

67. *Prosecutor v. Zejnil Delalić, et al.*, Judgment, paras. 424 and 425.

68. *Prosecutor v. Mladen Naletilić, a.k.a. "Tuta" & Vinko Martinović, a.k.a. "Štela,"* Judgment, IT-98-34-A, Appeals Chamber, 3 May 2006, para. 114.

69. *Prosecutor v. Mladen Naletilić, a.k.a. "Tuta" & Vinko Martinović, a.k.a. "Štela,"* para. 114.

70. *Prosecutor v. Mladen Naletilić, a.k.a. "Tuta" & Vinko Martinović, a.k.a. "Štela,"* para. 114.

71. Rome Statute, art. 30.

72. *Prosecutor v. Germain Katanga and Mathieu Ngudjolo Chui*, Decision on the Confirmation of Charges, para. 529; *Prosecutor v. Abdallah Banda & Saleh Jerbo*, Corrigendum to Decision on Confirmation of Charges, ICC-02/05-03/09, Pre-Trial Chamber I, 7 March 2011, para. 153.

73. *Prosecutor v. Fatmir Limaj*, Judgment, IT-03-66-T, 30 November 2005, para. 509.

74. *Prosecutor v. Fatmir Limaj*, para. 509.

75. *Prosecutor v. Fatmir Limaj*, para. 509.

76. *Prosecutor v. Thomas Lubanga Dyilo*, Judgment Pursuant to article 74 of the Statute, para. 1011.

77. *Prosecutor v. Thomas Lubanga Dyilo*, para. 1018.

78. Rome Statute, art. 25 (3) (d); *Prosecutor v. Thomas Lubanga Dyilo*, Judgment Pursuant to article 74 of the Statute, para. 1018.

79. *Prosecutor v. Vujadin Popović, et al.*, Judgment, IT-85-88-T, 10 June 2010, para. 1027, citing *Prosecutor v. Momčilo Krajišnik*, Judgment, IT-00-39-A, Appeals Chamber, 17 March 2009, para. 215; *Prosecutor v. Radoslav Brđanin*, Judgment, IT-99-37-A, Appeals Chamber, 3 April 2007, para. 430; *Prosecutor v. Miroslav Kvočka, et al.*, Judgment, IT-98-30/1-A, Appeals Chamber, 28 February 2007, para. 97.

80. *Prosecutor v. Ferdinand Nahimana*, Judgment, ICTR-99-52-A, Appeals Chamber, 28 November 2007, para. 479.

81. *Prosecutor v. Ferdinand Nahimana*, para. 479.

82. *Prosecutor v. Ferdinand Nahimana*, para. 479. Article 25 of the Rome Statute does not recognize "planning" as a mode of liability. The drafters of article 25 wished to include modes of liability accepted by most major legal traditions and "planning" as a mode of liability does not commonly appear in the continental legal system. Email communication with Dr. Fabricio Guariglia, Senior Appeals Counsel, Office of the Prosecutor, International Criminal Court, 29 January 2012. However, most conduct recognized as "planning" at the ad hoc tribunals would incur liability under the broad categories of responsibility described in art. 25 (3) (c) and (d). "Forms of Responsibility in International Criminal Law," in G. Boas et al. (eds.), *International Criminal Law Practitioners Library*, vol. 1 (Cambridge University Press, 2007), p. 371.

83. *Prosecutor v. Ferdinand Nahimana, et al.*, Judgment, Appeals Chamber, para. 481; *Prosecutor v. Boškoski & Tarčulovski*, Judgment, IT-04-02-A, Appeals Chamber, 19 May 2010, para. 160.

84. *Prosecutor v. Ferdinand Nahimana*, para. 160.

85. *Prosecutor v. Ferdinand Nahimana*, para. 160.

86. *Prosecutor v. Laurent Gbagbo*, Decision on the Confirmation of Charges Against Laurent Gbagbo, ICC-02/11-01/11, 12 June 2014, para. 243.

87. *Prosecutor v. Radoslav Brđanin*, Judgment, IT-99-36-T, 1 September 2004, para. 269.

88. *Prosecutor v. Radoslav Brđanin*, para. 269.

89. *Prosecutor v. Momčilo Perisić*, Judgment, IT-04-81-A, Appeals Chamber, 28 February 2013, paras. 25–36.

90. *Prosecutor v. Nikola Šainović, et al.*, Judgment IT-05-87-A, Appeals Chamber, 23 January 2014, paras. 1617–50.

91. *Prosecutor v. Nikola Šainović, et al.*, paras. 1626 and 1649. Subsequently, the ICTY Appeals Chamber affirmed the Šainović holding in *Prosecutor v. Vujadin Popović, et al.*, Judgment, IT-05-88-A, Appeals Chamber, 30 January 2015, para. 1758, and *Prosecutor v. Jovica Stanišič & Franko Simatović*, Judgment, IT-03-69/A, 9 December 2015, paras. 104–6.

92. *Prosecutor v. Nikola Šainović, et al.*, para. 1649.

93. M. Milanović, "SCSL Appeals Chamber Affirms Charles Taylor Conviction," *EJIL: Talk!* 26 September 2013, http://www.ejiltalk.org/scsl-appeals-chamber-affirms-charles-taylors-conviction/.

94. Art. 25 (3) (f). The "attempt to commit a crime is a crime." *Prosecutor v. Germain Katanga & Mathieu Ngudjolo Chui*, Decision on the Confirmation of Charges, para. 460.

95. Art. 25 (3) (f).

96. *Prosecutor v. Abdallah Banda & Saleh Jerbo*, Corrigendum to Decision on Confirmation of Charges, para. 97.

97. *Prosecutor v. Abdallah Banda & Saleh Jerbo*, Corrigendum to Decision on Confirmation of Charges, para. 96. For example, in a case including charges of "attempted murder," "the provision of medical assistance to the wounded by a person other than the one responsible for causing the injuries qualifies as circumstances outside the perpetrator's control" (para. 99).

98. *Prosecutor v. Germain Katanga & Mathieu Ngudjolo Chui*, Decision on the Confirmation of Charges, para. 460.

99. ICRC commentary to art. 87, API, para. 3550.

100. *Prosecutor v. Fatmir Limaj*, Judgment, para. 76.

101. *Prosecutor v. Enver Hadžihasanović, et al.*, Decision on Joint Challenge to Jurisdiction, IT-01-47-PT, 12 November 2002, paras. 167–79.

102. Art. 7 (3), Statute of the ICTY, 25 May 1993, and art. 6 (3), Statute of the International Criminal Tribunal for Rwanda, 8 November 1994; *Prosecutor v. Momčilo Perisić*, Judgment, Appeals Chamber, para. 86.

103. Art. 28 (1) ICCSt.

104. *Prosecutor v. Jean Pierre Bemba Gombo*, Decision Pursuant to article 61 (7) (a) and (b) of the Rome Statute on the Charges of *Prosecutor v. Jean-Pierre Bemba Gombo* (Decision on Confirmation of Charges), ICC 01/05-01/08, 15 June 2009, para. 425. This standard requires more of an active duty on the part of the commander to take the necessary measures *to secure knowledge* of the conduct of his or her troops and to inquire, regardless of the availability of information at the time on the commission of the crime (para. 433).

105. *Prosecutor v. Enver Hadžihasanović & Amir Kubura*, Judgment, IT-01-47-T, 15 March 2006, paras. 76–77.

106. *Prosecutor v. Sefer Halilović*, Judgment, IT-01-48-T, 16 November 2005, para. 58.

107. *Prosecutor v. Sefer Halilović*, esp. para. 63 and n. 150.

108. *Prosecutor v. Sefer Halilović*, para. 63. The concept of superior is broader than immediate and direct command "and should be seen in terms of a hierarchy encompassing the concept of control." ICRC commentary to art. 86, API, para. 3544, https://www.icrc.org/applic/ihl/ihl.nsf/Comment.xsp?action=openDocument&documentId=BA2C2393DA08B951C12563CD00437A1C.

109. *Prosecutor v. Pavle Strugar*, Judgment, IT-01-42-A, Appeals Chamber, 17 July 2008, paras. 297–304; *Prosecutor v. Fatmir Limaj*, Judgment, para. 525.

110. *Prosecutor v. Zejnil Delalić et al.*, Judgment, Appeals Chamber, para. 226.

111. *Prosecutor v. Pavle Strugar*, Judgment, para. 299 (citing *Prosecutor v. Milorad Krnojelac et al.*, Judgment, IT-97-25-A, Appeals Chamber, 17 September 2003, para. 156, citing *Prosecutor v. Zejnil Delalić*, Judgment, Appeals Chamber, para, 239).

112. Art. 28 (1) (a) ICCSt.

113. *Prosecutor v. Jean Pierre Bemba Gombo*, Decision on Confirmation of Charges, para. 432.

114. Art. 28 (2) (a) ICCSt (emphasis added).

115. *Prosecutor v. Sefer Halilović*, Judgment, para. 63.

116. *Prosecutor v. Fatmir Limaj*, Judgment, para. 526.

117. *Prosecutor v. Vujadin Popović, et al.*, Judgment, para. 1044.

118. *Prosecutor v. Vujadin Popović, et al.*, para. 1044.

119. *Prosecutor v. Vujadin Popović, et al.*, para. 1045.

120. In modern warfare, the term "tactical level" refers to the "level at which activities, battles and engagements are planned and executed to accomplish military objectives assigned to tactical formations and units." Thus, a "tactical commander" exercises the authority "to assign tasks to forces under his command for the accomplishment of the mission assigned by higher authority." *NATO Glossary of Terms and Definitions*, AAP-06 (2014), 2-T-1–2-T-2, http://nso.nato.int/nso/zpublic/_branchinfo/terminology_public/non-classified%20nato%20glossaries/aap-6.pdf.

121. M. Schmitt, Remarks during panel discussion "The International Legal Context," at "Autonomous Military Technologies: Policy and Governance for Next Generation Defence Systems," Chatham House, London, 25 February 2014. Permission to cite provided in electronic mail message to author, 15 March 2014.

122. Rome Statute, art. 25 (3) (d); Prosecutor v. Thomas Lubanga Dyilo, Judgment Pursuant to article 74 of the Statute, para. 1018.

123. For example, when "determining whether an attack was proportionate, it is necessary to examine whether a reasonably well-informed person in the circumstances of the actual perpetrator, making reasonable use of the information available to him or her, could have expected excessive civilian casualties to result from the attack." *Prosecutor v. Stanislav Galić*, Judgment, para. 58.

124. Air Marshal (ret.) Sir Brian Burridge, former commander of U.K. forces in Iraq, Remarks during panel "The International Legal Context" at "Autonomous Military Technologies: Policy and Governance for Next Generation Defence Systems," Chatham House, London, 24 February 2014; permission to cite provided in electronic mail message to author, 6 March 2014.

125. Colonel R. Jackson, Special Assistant to Judge Advocate General of U.S. Army for Law of War Matters, Remarks in panel "Autonomous Weaponry and Armed Conflict," Annual Meeting of American Society of International Law, 10 April 2014, https://www.youtube.com/watch?v=duq3DtFJtWg&list=PLYp0ZUypbrnevQlBfMUSDG0IanrvJ3J6z&index=4; electronic mail message to author, 7 May 2014.

126. For discussions of the "predictability" challenges of autonomous weapon systems and the potential for "emergent behavior," see H. Liu, "Refining Responsibility: Differentiating Two Types of Responsibility Issues Raised by Autonomous Weapon Systems," in N. Bhuta et al. (eds.), *Autonomous Weapon Systems: Law, Ethics, Policy* (Cambridge University Press, 2016), pp. 325–44, and in the same volume: N. Jain, "Autonomous Weapons Systems: New Frameworks for Individual Responsibility" pp. 303–24.

127. I am grateful to Professor Geoffrey Corn for his insights on this topic.

128. M. Cummings, "Automation and Accountability in Decision Support System Interface Design," *MIT Human and Automation Laboratory* (2006), 10–11 and 18–19, http://web.mit.edu/aeroastro/labs/halab/papers/Cummings_JTS.pdf. Professor Cummings uses the term "moral buffer" to describe the sense of distance and remoteness that computer interfaces create for their users. It is this moral buffer that permits individuals "to morally and ethically distance themselves from their actions" while "operating" machines.

129. Electronic mail message to author, General B. A. Fabio Giunchi, Commander of Air Cooperation School, Guidonia Airport, Italian Air Force, 27 January 2015.

130. Cummings, "Automation and Accountability in Decision Support System Interface Design," p. 19.

131. This shift also undermines the ability of criminal law and the criminal justice system to supplement the moral standards acquired through education and other nonlegal processes. Saxon, "International Criminal Court and the Prevention of Crimes," p. 36.

132. In *Bloody Constraint: War and Chivalry in Shakespeare* (Oxford University Press, 1998), Professor Meron illustrates how one form of human reflection, conscience, works as a powerful instrument for ensuring accountability, when we pay attention to it (pp. 194–97). Adam Smith also described the important influence of "the tribunal" of man's conscience," and the power of this "supposed impartial and well-informed spectator, . . . the man within the breast, the great judge and arbiter of their conduct." *The Theory of Moral Sentiments* (1759), K. Haakonssen (ed.) (Cambridge University Press, 2004), p. 150.

133. J. Beard, "Law and War in the Virtual Era," 103 *American Journal of International Law* 3 (2009), 409, 436.

134. D. Stewart, "Maximising Compliance with IHL and the Utility of Data in an Age of Unlimited Information: Operational Issues," in D. Saxon (ed.), *International Humanitarian Law and the Changing Technology of War* (Leiden: Martinus Nijhoff, 2013), p. 185.

135. Beard, "Law and War in the Virtual Era," pp. 435–37.

136. Art. 86 (2) and 87, API.

137. The "failure to punish" prong common to the law of the ad hoc tribunals is replaced at the ICC by a "failure to repress" element, which encompasses the two distinct duties, arising at different stages of criminal conduct, to stop ongoing crimes and to punish subordinates after the commission of crimes. *Prosecutor v. Jean Pierre Bemba Gombo*, Decision on Confirmation of Charges, para. 439.

138. This premise should hold true regardless of whether courts apply the "had reason to know" standard of the ad hoc tribunals or the "should have known" standard of the ICC.

139. For example, during multinational NATO operations, the supreme allied commander for Europe (SACEUR) must "[e]stablish an intelligence architecture linking NATO Headquarters with national intelligence centers to provide the [joint force commander] with a common, timely and accurate picture of the situation during all phases of the campaign." "AJP-01D," *Allied Joint Doctrine*, North Atlantic Treaty Organization, 21 December 2010, at 0615 (e), https://www.gov.uk/government/uploads/system/uploads/attachment_data/file/33694/AJP01D.pdf.

140. K. Trapp, "Great Resources Mean Great Responsibility: A Framework of Analysis for Assessing Compliance with API Obligations in the Information Age," in Saxon, *International Humanitarian Law and the Changing Technology of War*, pp. 156 and 170.

141. Physical "remoteness" in this context refers to the geographical distance between the acts or omissions of a superior and the location of the criminal conduct. Temporal "remoteness" refers to the time elapsed between the accused's acts or omissions and the execution of the crimes. Trial Chambers at the ICTY and the ICC have held that: "[t]he more physically distant the superior was from the commission of the crimes, the more additional indicia are necessary to prove that he knew them." *Prosecutor v. Jean Pierre Bemba Gombo*, Decision on Confirmation of Charges, para. 484, citing *Prosecutor v. Milomir Stakić*, Judgment, IT-97-24-T, 31 July 2003, para. 460. In *Bemba*, the evidence established that Jean-Pierre Bemba, the president of the Mouvement de Libération du Congo (MLC), in his effective role as commander of MLC troops, communicated directly with his commanders in the field, had access to a regular reporting system, and regularly monitored international media reports about the events in the Central African Republic (paras. 486 and 488–89).

142. For example, in an iconic photograph taken in the White House "Situation Room" in Washington, D.C., on 1 May 2011, U.S. president Obama and members of his staff are seen intently watching "live updates" of Operation Neptune Spear, which resulted in the death of Osama Bin Laden in Pakistan. "Situation Room," http://en.wikipedia.org/wiki/Situation_Room. Moreover, the use of YouTube by all sides of the Syria conflict provides a graphic video record of events in Syria within minutes of their occurrence: https://www.youtube.com/results?search_query=syria+bread+line+air+strike; https://www.youtube.com/results?search_query=syria+rebels+linked+to+al+qaeda+apologize+for+beheading+fellow+fighter.

143. See *Trial of Bruno Tesch and Two Others* ("The Zyklon B Case"), Judgment, British Military Court, Hamburg, 1–8 March 1946 (the defendant Tesch and an employee were convicted for knowingly acting as agents—over several years—for the supply of Zyklon B gas from the German manufacturer to the Auschwitz concentration camp in Poland, where the gas was used to exterminate prisoners), http://www.loc.gov/rr/frd/Military_Law/pdf/Law-Reports_Vol-1.pdf. Temporal distance in another sense—the time between the alleged crimes and the commencement of prosecution—will not bar prosecutions of persons responsible for unlawful attacks employing autonomous weapon systems, as the imprescriptibility of war crimes, crimes against humanity, and genocide is part of customary law. B. Simma and A. L. Paulus, "The Responsibility of Individuals for Human Rights Abuses in Internal Conflicts: A Positivist View," 93 *American Journal of International Law* (April 1999), 302, 315.

144. Much of this "ceaseless flow of information" may consist of meaningless and irrelevant facts and figures. C. Garraway, "The Application of Superior Responsibility in an Era of Unlimited Information," in Saxon, *International Humanitarian Law and the Changing Technology of War*, pp. 201–5.

145. Y. Dinstein, *The Conduct of Hostilities Under the Law of International Armed Conflict*, 2nd ed. (Cambridge University Press, 2010), p. 139.

146. Cummings, "Automation and Accountability in Decision Support System Interface Design," p. 17.

147. P. Fiddian, "UAV Swarm Technology Trial Success," *Armed Forces International News*, 7 August 2012, http://www.armedforces-int.com/news/uav-swarm-technology-trial-success.html.

148. One notable exception to this attribute may be certain autonomous cyberweapons that, once released into the internet, may lack a specific deactivation mechanism, or are encrypted to prevent outside deactivation. M. Clayton, "More Telltale Signs of Cyber Spying and Cyber Attacks Arise in Middle East," *Christian Science Monitor*, 21 August 2012, http://www.csmonitor.com/USA/2012/0821/More-telltale-signs-of-cyber-spying-and-cyber-attacks-arise-in-Middle-East-video. Contrast this characteristic with the infamous "Stuxnet" malware, which was programmed to cease its operations in late June 2012. M. Clayton, "Stuxnet Cyberweapon Set to Stop Operating," *Christian Science Monitor*, 23 June 2012, http://www.csmonitor.com/USA/2012/0623/Stuxnet-cyberweapon-set-to-stop-operating.

149. C. Heyns, "Report of the Special Rapporteur on Extrajudicial, Summary or Arbitrary Executions," A/HRC23/47, 9 April 2013, para. 41, https://documents-dds-ny.un.org/doc/UNDOC/GEN/G13/127/76/PDF/G1312776.pdf?OpenElement.

150. G. Corn, "Autonomous Weapon Systems: Managing the Inevitability of 'Taking the Man Out of the Loop,'" draft paper presented to Conference on Autonomous Weapon Systems—Law, Ethics, Policy, Academy of European Law, European University Institute, Florence, 24 April 2014, 9–10 and 13 (concerning the duties of the "Compliance Commander" vis-à-vis autonomous weapon systems).

151. Corn, "Autonomous Weapon Systems." The control algorithms that constitute artificial intelligence for autonomous systems are created and tested by teams of humans. "Unmanned Systems Integrated Roadmap FY2013–2038," United States Department of Defense, p. 67, http://www.defense.gov/Portals/1/Documents/pubs/DOD-USRM-2013.pdf.

152. One definition of "strict criminal liability" refers to offences where, with respect to at least one element of the actus reus, "the offender's mental state is irrelevant." D. Prendergast, "The Constitutionality of Strict Liability in Criminal Law," 33 *Dublin University Law Journal* (2011), 285, 286.

153. S. Salako, "Strict Criminal Liability: A Violation of the Convention?" 70 *Journal of Criminal Law* (2006), 531 at 537 and 549.

154. *Prosecutor v. Mladen Naletilić, a.k.a. "Tuta," & Vinko Martinović, a.k.a. "Štela,"* Judgment, No. IT-98-34-A, 3 May 2006, para. 118. The chamber held that, consequently, in cases involving allegations of responsibility for grave breaches of the Geneva Conventions, the principle of individual guilt requires that the prosecution prove the accused's awareness of factual circumstances establishing the armed conflict's international character (para. 121). Nevertheless, as Henri Decoeur observes, the introduction to the chapter called "Article 8, War Crimes" in the "Elements of Crimes" of the ICC provides that "there is no requirement for awareness by the perpetrator of the facts that established the character of the conflict as international or non-international"; http://www.icc-cpi.int/NR/rdonlyres/336923D8-A6AD-40EC-AD7B-45BF9DE73D56/0/ElementsOfCrimesEng.pdf. Arguably, this provision, if it supersedes article 30 of the Rome Statute, permits conviction of an accused for war crimes although he or she lacks this particular mens rea. Decoeur, "Avoiding Strict Liability in Mixed Conflicts," 490–91.

155. H. Hart, "Punishment and the Elimination of Responsibility," in *Punishment and Responsibility: Essays in the Philosophy of Law* (Oxford: Clarendon, 1963), pp. 182–83.

156. *R. v. Finta* [1994], 815.

157. Human Rights Watch argues that significant challenges exist, under both direct and superior theories of criminal liability, to establish individual criminal responsibility for offences that occur upon the employment of LAWS. Docherty, "Mind the Gap."

158. H. Liu, "Refining Responsibility, p. 342.

159. This right is enshrined in numerous international human rights declarations and treaties. Art. 11 (1) UDHR; art. 14 (2), ICCPR; art. 8 (2), ACHR; art. 7 (1), AChHPR. The presumption of innocence is a "bedrock" "axiomatic and elementary" principle whose "enforcement lies at the foundation"" of criminal law. *In re Winship*, 397 U.S. 358 (1970), 363, citing *Coffin v. United States*, 156 U.S. 432 (1895), 453.

160. *Speiser v. Randall*, 357 U.S. 513, 525–26 (1958).

161. *In re Winship*, p. 372 (Justice Harlan concurring) (holding that "it is far worse to convict an innocent man than to let a guilty man go free").

162. G. Finch, "The Nuremberg Trial and International Law," 41 *American Journal of International Law* 1 (January 1947), 20, 36.

163. Finch argued, correctly, that the proposition that all criminals of a class must be punished, or none at all, is untenable. Finch, "Nuremberg Trial and International Law," p. 28.

164. For example, in September 2009, Colonel Georg Klein, a German commander serving in ISAF in Kunduz province in Afghanistan, ordered an airstrike on a fuel tanker that had been stolen by members of the Afghan Taliban. The strike allegedly killed over a hundred civilians. In April 2010, German prosecutors, citing Colonel Klein's lack of knowledge of the presence of civilians at the bombing site, declined to charge Colonel Klein for criminal responsibility for

the civilian deaths. S. Houlton, "German Prosecutors Drop Case Against Kunduz Airstrike Colonel," *DW*, 19 April 2010, http://www.dw.de/german-prosecutors-drop-case-against-kunduz-airstrike-colonel/a-5483181-1.

165. D. Saxon, "A Human Touch: Autonomous Weapons, DOD Directive 3000.09 and the Interpretation of 'Appropriate Levels of Human Judgment over the Use of Force,'" in Bhuta et al., *Autonomous Weapons—Law, Ethics, Policy*, pp. 196 and 200–201.

166. Following World War II, the lead U.S. prosecutor told the judges at the International Military Tribunal at Nuremberg that "[t]he real complaining party at your bar is Civilization. R. Jackson, "Presentation of the Case by the Prosecution" (21 November 1945), *Trial of German Major War Criminals*, part 1, 20 November 1945 to 1 December 1945) (London, 1946), p. 86.

167. J. van den Hoven et al., "Why the Future Needs Us Today: Moral Responsibility and Engineering Autonomous Weapon Systems," Presentation to 2015 Meeting of Experts on Lethal Autonomous Weapon Systems, Convention on Certain Conventional Weapons, April 2015, p. 2, http://www.unog.ch/80256EE600585943/(httpPages)/6CE049BE22EC75A2C1257C8D00513E26?OpenDocument.

168. "Tactical patience" refers to a commander's capacity to delay engagement and/or the use of force until he or she has a more complete awareness of the battlespace and specific situation. See General T. McHale, "Executive Summary for AR 15-6 Investigation, 21 February 2010 CIVCAS Incident in Uruzgan Province," Headquarters United States Forces—Afghanistan, p. 2, http://www.rs.nato.int/images/stories/File/April2010-Dari/May2010Revised/Uruzgan%20investigation%20findings.pdf.

169. P. Margulies, "Making Autonomous Weapons Accountable: Command Responsibility for Computer-Guided Lethal Force in Armed Conflict," in J. Ohlin (ed.), *Research Handbook on Remote Warfare* (Northampton: Edward Elgar, 2016).

170. *Physicians for Human Rights v. IDF Commander*, Separate Opinion of Justice D. Beinisch, HCJ 4764/04 [2004] IsrL 200, p. 227, http://elyon1.court.gov.il/Files_ENG/04/640/047/A03/04047640.a03.pdf.

171. *Physicians for Human Rights v. IDF Commander*, Separate Opinion of Justice D. Beinisch, p. 227.

172. M. Sassóli, "Autonomous Weapons and International Humanitarian Law: Advantages, Open Technical Questions and Legal Issues to Be Clarified," 90 *International Law Studies*, 308, 316, and 338.

173. Corn, "Autonomous Weapon Systems."

174. W. Fenrick, "The Prosecution of Unlawful Attack Cases Before the ICTY," 7 *Yearbook of International Humanitarian Law* (2004), 153, 156.

Chapter 7

1. *Legality of the Threat or Use of Nuclear Weapons*, Advisory Opinion, Dissenting Opinion of Judge Shahabuddeen, ICJ Reports 1996, p. 377 (observing that although no prohibition of the threat or use of nuclear weapons exists in international law, that does not conclude the question whether the threat or use of such weapons is lawful).

2. *Application of the Convention on the Prevention and Punishment of the Crime of Genocide*, Judgment, Preliminary Objections, Separate Opinion of Judge Weeramantry, ICJ Reports 1996, p. 645.

3. "Responsibility of States for Internationally Wrongful Acts," in *Draft Articles on Responsibility of States for Internationally Wrongful Acts with Commentaries*, International

Law Commission, 2001, http://legal.un.org/ilc/texts/instruments/english/commentaries/9_6_2001.pdf.

4. Statement by the Delegation of Ghana at the Convention on Conventional Weapons meeting "The Way Forward on Discussions [Regarding] Lethal Autonomous Weapons," 17 April 2015, http://www.unog.ch/80256EE600585943/(httpPages)/6CE049BE22EC75A2C1257C8D00513E26?OpenDocument. Also see for example, the Statement of Ecuador to Expert Meeting Concerning Lethal Autonomous Weapons, Convention on Certain Conventional Weapons, 13–17 April 2015, p. 2, http://www.unog.ch/80256EE600585943/(httpPages)/6CE049BE22EC75A2C1257C8D00513E26?OpenDocument.

5. J. Brunnée, "International Legal Accountability Through the Lens of the Law of State Responsibility," 36 *Netherlands Yearbook of International Law* (2005), 21, 23.

6. Seventy years ago, Professor Jessup observed, presciently, that the "embodiment in international law of the principle of the duty to respect the rights of man suggests new complications." *A Modern Law of Nations* (New York: Macmillan, 1948), p. 93. Jessup pondered whether "modernized international law" requires additional rules designed for the protection of special classes of individuals (p. 103).

7. The charter was not the first major international treaty to create state responsibilities for the protection of human dignity. The Treaty of Westphalia, for example, included provisions providing for the reparation of "any Prejudice or Damage" caused by the belligerent states and their allies during the Thirty Years' War. The purpose of the reparations was to reestablish, inter alia, the "Dignitys" of the state parties and their "Vassals, Subjects, Citizens, [and] Inhabitants." Treaty of Westphalia; 24 October 1648: Peace Treaty Between the Holy Roman Emperor and the King of France and their Respective Allies, section 6, https://is.muni.cz/el/1423/podzim2008/MVZ430/um/Treaty-of-Westphalia.pdf.

8. *Armed Activities on the Territory of the Congo (Democratic Republic of the Congo v. Uganda)*, Judgment, ICJ Reports 2005, paras. 220 and 245.

9. *Armed Activities on the Territory of the Congo (Democratic Republic of the Congo v. Uganda)*, Separate Declaration of Judge Tomka, para. 9.

10. *Armed Activities on the Territory of the Congo (Democratic Republic of the Congo v. Uganda)*, Separate Declaration of Judge Koroma, para. 6.

11. *Armed Activities on the Territory of the Congo (Democratic Republic of the Congo v. Uganda)*, Majority Opinion, para. 259.

12. *Velásquez Rodriguez v. Honduras*, Judgment, 29 July 1988, para. 155, http://www.corteidh.or.cr/docs/casos/articulos/seriec_04_ing.pdf.

13. *Velásquez Rodriguez v. Honduras*, paras. 151–53.

14. *Velásquez Rodriguez v. Honduras*, para. 154 (emphasis added).

15. *Case of Husayn (Abu Zubaydah) v. Poland*, Judgment, Application No. 7511/13, 24 July 2014, paras. 521–26; *Case of El Masri v. Former Yugoslav Republic of Macedonia*, Judgment, Application No. 39630/09, 13 December 2012, paras. 230–43.

16. *Abu Zubaydah*, paras. 531–34; *El Masri*, paras. 248–50.

17. *Abu Zubaydah*, para. 532; *El Masri*, para. 248 (emphasis added).

18. The court instructed Poland to, inter alia, conduct an effective and expeditious investigation into the applicant's detention (including his treatment by the CIA), prosecute those individuals responsible, recognize its violations of the applicant's rights, and compensate him for damage caused to his physical and mental health (paras. 563–68). The Inter-American Court of Human Rights ordered similar measures and reparations in the *Case of Myrna Mack Chang v.*

Guatemala, Judgment (Merits, Reparations and Costs), Inter-Am. Ct. H.R., 25 November 2003, paras. 275–92, and in the *Case of Maritza Urrutia Garcia v. Guatemala*, Judgment, Inter-Am. Ct. H.R., 27 November 2003, paras. 96–97, 129, 161–70, and 177.

19. *Application of the Convention on the Prevention and Punishment of the Crime of Genocide, Preliminary Objections*, Judgment, Separate Opinion of Judge Weeramantry, p. 641; S. Schmahl, "An Example of Jus Cogens: The Status of Prisoners of War," in C. Tomuschat and J. M. Thouvenin (eds.), *The Fundamental Rules of the International Legal Order: Jus Cogens and Obligations Erga Omnes* (Leiden: Martinus Nijhoff, 2006), p. 48. During the nineteenth century, states implicitly assumed legal obligations to take positive steps in furtherance of human dignity, in particular with respect to ending the slave trade. Art. 10, *Treaty of Peace and Amity Between His Britannic Majesty and the United States of America* (1814), http://avalon.law.yale.edu/19th_century/ghent.asp; additional article on the slave trade, *Treaty of Paris* (1815), http://napoleononline.ca/wp-content/uploads/2011/03/Treaty-of-Paris-1815.pdf.

20. D. Shelton, "Private Violence, Public Wrongs, and the Responsibility of States," 13 *Fordham International Law Journal* 1 (1989–90), 23.

21. United States Diplomatic and Consular Staff in Tehran, Judgment, ICJ Judgment 1980, paras. 63–68.

22. Done at Vienna on 18 April 1961, entered into force on 24 April 1964, http://legal.un.org/ilc/texts/instruments/english/conventions/9_1_1961.pdf.

23. United States Diplomatic and Consular Staff in Tehran, Judgment, para. 77 (emphasis added).

24. United States Diplomatic and Consular Staff in Tehran, Judgment, para. 91.

25. For a discussion of the failure of the International Court of Justice to clarify the theory of due diligence with respect to the responsibility of states, see A. Gattani, "Breach of International Obligations," in A. Nollkaemper and I. Plakokefalos (eds.), *Principles of Shared Responsibility in International Law: An Appraisal of the State of the Art* (Cambridge University Press, 2014), pp. 38–45.

26. Alabama Claims of the United States of America Against Great Britain, Award Rendered on 14 September 1872 by the Tribunal of Arbitration Established by Article I of the Treaty of Washington of 8 May 1871, http://legal.un.org/riaa/cases/vol_XXIX/125-134.pdf.

27. *Corfu Channel Case*, Judgment, 9 April 1949, ICJ Reports 1949, p. 22. Albania's obligations were based "on certain general and well-recognized principles, namely: elementary considerations of humanity, even more exacting in peace than in war; the principle of the freedom of maritime communication; and every State's obligation not to allow knowingly its territory to be used for acts contrary to the rights of other States."

28. *Corfu Channel Case*, p. 23.

29. *Corfu Channel Case*, p. 23. The 1907 Hague Convention (VIII) Relative to the Laying of Automatic Submarine Contact Mines prescribes several preventive measures for state parties. For example, anchored contact mines must become harmless as soon as they break loose from their mooring. Belligerents must "do their utmost" to render anchored automatic contact mines harmless within a limited time. Arts. 1 and 2, 18 October 1907, file:///Users/danielsaxon/Downloads/IHL-23-EN.pdf.

30. Settlement Agreement, on the Case Concerning the Aerial Incident of 3 July 1988 Before the International Court of Justice, https://www.icj-cij.org/files/case-related/79/11131.pdf.

31. Letter from W. Crowe, Chairman, Joint Chiefs of Staff, 18 August 1988, para. 9, attached to *Investigation Report: Formal Investigation into the Circumstances Surrounding the Downing of Iran Air Flight 655* on 3 July 1988; see part 4, A (6) and (11).

32. The conduct of state agents is considered an act of a state under international law. *Corfu Channel Case*, Judgment, p. 23; Draft Articles on Responsibility of States for Internationally Wrongful Acts, art. 3. Such "agents" would include persons or groups of persons who act on the instructions of, or under the direction and control of that state in performing the conduct.

33. The principle of state sovereignty implies responsibility, and this responsibility includes the duty of state authorities to protect the welfare of citizens. "The Responsibility to Protect: Report of the International Commission on Intervention and State Sovereignty," December 2001, para. 2.15, http://responsibilitytoprotect.org/ICISS%20Report.pdf.

34. *Legality of the Threat or Use of Nuclear Weapons*, Dissenting Opinion of Judge Weeramantry, p. 433.

35. B. Cheng, *General Principles of Law as Applied by International Courts and Tribunals* (London: Stevens and Sons, 1953), p. 170. Characterizations of acts of state as internationally wrongful are governed by international law, not domestic law; http://legal.un.org/ilc/texts/instruments/english/commentaries/9_6_2001.pdf. Thus, an internationally wrongful act of a state consists of an act or omission that (1) is attributable to the state under international law, and (2) constitutes a breach of an international obligation of the state (art. 2).

36. See "Poland's Position on Continuing the Discussions on Lethal Autonomous Weapon Systems within the CCW Framework," Convention on Certain Conventional Weapons, Annual Meeting of the States Parties, November 2015, http://www.unog.ch/80256EE600585943/(httpPages)/0D4B67A1E11A22BCC1257A410052DE38?OpenDocument.

37. See *Armed Activities on the Territory of the Congo (Democratic Republic of the Congo v. Uganda)*, Judgment, paras. 220 and 245 (concerning violations of international humanitarian law and international human rights law by Ugandan forces in the Democratic Republic of Congo); *Case of Velásquez Rodríguez v. Honduras*, Judgment, para. 155.

38. E. Roucounas, "Non-State Actors: Areas of International Responsibility in Need of Further Exploration," in M. Ragazzi (ed.), *International Responsibility Today: Essays in Memory of Oscar Schachter* (Leiden: Martinus Nijhoff, 2005), p. 403.

39. Art. 34, European Convention on Human Rights.

40. *Case of Bosphorous Hava Yollari Turizm Ve Ticaret Anonim Şirketi v. Ireland*, Judgment, Application No. 45036/98, 30 June 2005, paras. 139–40.

41. *Draft Articles on Responsibility of States for Internationally Wrongful Acts with Commentaries*, Commentary to art. 8.

42. In 2005, the Dutch Court of Appeal affirmed the conviction of Frans van Anraat for complicity in the commission of war crimes in Iraq. During the 1980s a company owned by Anraat exported precursor chemicals to the Hussein regime, which subsequently produced chemical weapons that were targeted against Iraqi Kurd communities. However, the Netherlands prosecuted Anraat as an individual, not as a business enterprise; http://uitspraken.rechtspraak.nl/inziendocument?id=ECLI:NL:GHSGR:2007:BA6734.

43. R. Wolfrum, "State Responsibility for Private Actors: An Old Problem of Renewed Relevance," in Ragazzi, *International Responsibility Today*, p. 43.

44. Art. 8, *Draft Articles on Responsibility of States for Internationally Wrongful Acts with Commentaries*.

45. United Nations "Guiding Principles on Business and Human Rights," arts. 11–21 (2011), http://www.ohchr.org/Documents/Publications/GuidingPrinciplesBusinessHR_EN.pdf.

46. United Nations "Guiding Principles on Business and Human Rights," para. 25.

47. A. Kasperson, Head of International Security at the World Economic Forum, Remarks, "Private Sector Perspectives on the Development of Lethal Autonomous Systems," Geneva, 12 April 2016.

48. A. Fursman, Remarks, "Private Sector Perspectives on the Development of Lethal Autonomous Systems," Geneva, 12 April 2016.

49. Human Rights Watch and Harvard Law School's International Human Rights Clinic have made a similar argument for grounding state responsibility for the use of autonomous weapon systems in the preventive principle. *Killer Robots and the Concept of Meaningful Human Control*, Memorandum to Convention on Conventional Weapons (CCW) Delegates, April 2016, pp. 15–16.

50. Award in the Arbitration Regarding the Iron Rhine (Ijzeren Rijn) Railway Between the Kingdom of Belgium and the Kingdom of the Netherlands, Decision of 24 May 2005, paras. 221–23, https://legal.un.org/riaa/cases/vol_XXVII/35-125.pdf.

51. United Nations Framework Convention on Climate Change, art. 2 (emphasis added), https://unfccc.int/resource/docs/convkp/conveng.pdf.

52. United Nations Framework Convention on Climate Change, art. 4 (c), principle 7, Declaration of the United Nations Conference on the Human Environment (Stockholm Declaration) (1972), http://www.unep.org/documents.multilingual/default.asp?documentid=97&articleid=1503.

53. *Gabčikovo-Nagymaros Project (Hungary/Slovakia)*, Dissenting Opinion of Judge Herczegh, ICJ Reports 1997, p. 185.

54. *Gabčikovo-Nagymaros Project (Hungary/Slovakia)*, Judgment, para. 140; Dissenting Opinion of Judge Oda, para. 33; P. Sands et al., *Principles of International Environmental Law*, 3rd ed. (Cambridge University Press, 2012), p. 201. This preference arises from the consideration that the correct objective of international environmental law is to prevent damage rather than simply provide victims with mechanisms to obtain compensation. T. Scovazzi, "Some Remarks on International Responsibility in the Field of Environmental Protection," in Ragazzi, *International Responsibility Today*, p. 212.

55. "Contingency Plans," art. 4 to annex 6 to the Protocol on Environmental Protection to the Antarctic Treaty: Liability Arising from Environmental Emergencies (1991), http://www.ats.aq/documents/recatt/Att249_e.pdf. "Each party shall require its operators to: (a) establish contingency plans for responses to incidents with potential adverse impacts on the Antarctic environment or dependent and associated ecosystems; and (b) co-operate in the formulation and implementation of such contingency plans."

56. *Pulp Mills on the River Uruguay (Argentina v. Uruguay)*, Judgment, ICJ Reports 2010, para. 197. "A state is . . . obliged to use all the means at its disposal in order to avoid activities which take place in its territory, or in any area under its jurisdiction, causing significant damage to the environment of another state" (para. 101).

57. *Draft Articles on Prevention of Transboundary Harm from Hazardous Activities*, International Law Commission, 2001, commentary to art. 3, "Prevention," para. 7. Art. 3 provides that "the State of origin shall take all appropriate measures to prevent significant transboundary harm or at any event to minimize the risk thereof"; http://legal.un.org/ilc/texts/instruments/english/commentaries/9_7_2001.pdf. Similarly, the 1992 Rio Declaration on the Environment

and Development concluded that states "should effectively cooperate to discourage or prevent the relocation and transfer to other States of any activities and substances that cause severe environmental degradation or are found to be harmful to human health." Principle 14, http://www.unep.org/documents.multilingual/default.asp?documentid=78&articleid=1163.

58. *Responsibilities and Obligations of States with Respect to Activities in the Area*, Advisory Opinion, 1 February 2011, International Tribunal for the Law of the Sea (ITLOS) Reports 2011, para. 117.

59. *Draft Articles on Prevention of Transboundary Harm from Hazardous Activities*, International Law Commission, commentary to art. 3, "Prevention," para. 11. "The higher the degree of inadmissible harm, the greater would be the duty of care required to prevent it" (para. 18).

60. C. Perrow, *Normal Accidents: Living with High Risk Technologies* (Princeton University Press, 1999), p. 36 (referring to the dangers of nuclear power plants).

61. Scovazzi, "Some Remarks on International Responsibility in the Field of Environmental Protection," in Ragazzi, *International Responsibility Today*, p. 211.

62. *Draft Articles on Prevention of Transboundary Harm from Hazardous Activities*, commentary to art. 3, "Prevention," para. 11.

63. *Draft Articles on Prevention of Transboundary Harm from Hazardous Activities*, commentary to art. 3, "Prevention," para. 11.

64. P. Margulies, "Making Autonomous Weapons Accountable: Command Responsibility for Computer-Guided Lethal Force in Armed Conflicts," in J. Ohlin (ed.), *Research Handbook on Remote Warfare* (Northampton: Edward Elgar, 2016), http://papers.ssrn.com/sol3/papers.cfm?abstract_id=2734900.

65. *Pulp Mills on the River Uruguay (Argentina v. Uruguay)*, Judgment, para. 197.

66. *Pulp Mills on the River Uruguay (Argentina v. Uruguay)*, Judgment, para. 197.

67. *Legality of the Threat or Use of Nuclear Weapons*, Advisory Opinion, para. 29.

68. Art. 9, "Generic Preventive Measures," Protocol on Explosive Remnants of War (Protocol V), 21 December 2001.

69. As amended on 3 May 1996 (Amended Protocol II), https://treaties.un.org/Pages/ViewDetails.aspx?src=TREATY&mtdsg_no=XXVI-2-b&chapter=26&clang=_en.

70. Article 35 (3) of API illustrates the reasonableness of applying, by analogy, principles of international environmental law to state responsibility for violations of international humanitarian law. "[i]t is prohibited to employ methods or means of warfare which are intended, or may be expected, to cause wide-spread long-term and severe damage to the environment."

71. ICRC commentary to art. 36, para. 1469.

72. ICRC commentary to art. 36, paras. 1476–78.

73. Perrow, *Normal Accidents*, pp. 7–23 and 330.

74. Remarks of Steven Goose, Human Rights Watch, to Informal Meeting of Experts on Lethal Autonomous Weapon Systems, Convention on Conventional Weapons, Geneva, 12 April 2016.

75. E. Barth Eide, Member of Managing Board of World Economic Forum, Remarks, "Private Sector Perspectives on the Development of Lethal Autonomous Systems," Geneva, 12 April 2016.

76. Sands et al., *Principles of International Environmental Law*, p. 201.

77. Social and Economic Rights Action Center (SERAC) and Center for Economic and Social Rights (CESR) / Nigeria, 155/96, African Commission on Human Rights, 27 October 2001, para. 52, http://www.achpr.org/files/sessions/30th/comunications/155.96/achpr30_155_96_eng.pdf.

78. *Maya Indigenous Communities of the Toledo District v. Belize*, Report No. 40/04, Case 12.053, 12 October 2004, para. 147.

79. *Maya Indigenous Communities of the Toledo District v. Belize*, Report No. 40/04, para. 147.

80. M. Düwell, "Human Dignity and the Ethics of Technology," in *The Oxford Handbook of Law, Regulation and Technology*, R. Brownsword et al. (eds.) (Oxford University Press, 2017), pp. 177 and 189.

81. Environmental Principles and Concepts," Organization for Economic Co-operation and Development, OECD/GD (95) 124, Paris 1995, para. 44; art. 2 (5) (a), United Nations Convention on the Protection and Use of Transboundary Water Courses and International Lakes, Amended 28 November 2003.

82. *Southern Bluefin Tuna Cases (New Zealand v. Japan; Australia v. Japan)*, Separate Opinion of Judge Treves, ITLOS, Order of 27 August 1999, para. 8.

83. See, for example, the Preamble to the Multilateral International Convention on Oil Pollution Preparedness, Response and Cooperation, No. 32194, Concluded at London on 30 November 1990: "MINDFUL of the importance of precautionary measures and prevention in avoiding oil pollution in the first instance."

84. Consolidated Version of the Treaty Establishing the European Community, 25 March 1957, art. 174 (ex art. 130r), http://www.refworld.org/docid/3ae6b39c0.html. The Stockholm Convention on Persistent Organic Pollutants recognizes the preventive and the precautionary approach to environmental protection. Preamble and art. 1, 22 May 2001.

85. Art. 3, "Principles" (3), United Nations Framework Convention on Climate Change, 1992. Furthermore, the language of the 1975 bilateral treaty between Argentina and Uruguay incorporates the spirit of the precautionary approach. Arts. 35–37, Statute of the River Uruguay, Signed at Salto on 26 February 1975.

86. *Tatar v. Romania*, Judgment, Application No. 67021/01, ECtHR, 27 January 2009, Press Release, file:///Users/danielsaxon/Downloads/003-2615810-2848789%20(2).pdf.

87. Judgment, ECtHR, Application, No. 59909/00, 26 March 2007, para. 119.

88. *Case of Di Sarno and Others v. Italy*, Application No. 30765/08, 10 April 2012, para. 106.

89. 25 November 2015, para. 214. In 1999, the Peruvian Ministry of Energy and Mines imposed administrative sanctions on Proaño Mining Company for "not implementing a precautionary and control program in the Mayoc sludge dump."

90. U. Beyerlin and T. Marauhn, *International Environmental Law* (Oxford: Hart, 2011), p. 59; Sands et al., *Principles of International Environmental Law*, p. 228; *Environmental Principles and Concepts*, OECD/GD (95) 124, Paris, 1995, p. 33.

91. Beyerlin and Marauhn, *International Environmental Law*, p. 58.

92. Art. 5 (b), United Nations Convention on the Protection and Use of Transboundary Water Courses and International Lakes. The Treaty on European Union stipulates that "environmental damage should as a priority be rectified at the source and that the polluter should pay." 7 February 1992 ("Treaty of Maastricht"), art. 130r. The Rio Declaration on Environment and Development supports "the approach that the polluter should, in principle, bear the cost of pollution." Principle 16, June 1992, http://www.unep.org/documents.multilingual/default.asp?documentid=78&articleid=1163; art. 3, International Convention on Civil Liability for Oil Pollution Damage, 1992, http://www.transportrecht.org/dokumente/HaftungsUe_engl.pdf; art. 42, Statute of the River Uruguay (Uruguay and Argentina), signed at Salto on 26 February 1975, http://www.internationalwaterlaw.org/documents/regionaldocs/Uruguay_River_Statute_1975.pdf.

93. *The Queen v. Secretary of State for the Environment, Minister of Agriculture, Fisheries and Food, Ex parte: H. A. Standley and Others Case* C-293/97, 29 April 1999 (holding that the polluter-pays principle should be applied proportionally, so that each polluter provides compensation only for the pollution it contributes).

94. Sands et al., *Principles of International Environmental Law*, p. 228.

95. States will not incur (or accept) legal responsibility for harm caused by third parties, unless it can be established that the state had an obligation to prevent the conduct and failed to fulfill its duty. Scovazzi, "Some Remarks on International Responsibility in the Field of Environmental Protection," pp. 215–16.

96. "F-35 Joint Strike Fighter (JSF)," Department of Defense Programs, p. 34, http://breakingdefense.com/wp-content/uploads/sites/3/2014/01/2013DOTE_F-35_report.pdf.

97. "F-35 Joint Strike Fighter (JSF)," p. 35.

98. "Building the F-35: Combining Teamwork and Technology," F-35 Lightning II, Lockheed Martin, https://www.f35.com/about/life-cycle/production.

99. "The F-35 Factory," F-35 Lightning II, Lockheed Martin, https://www.f35.com/about/life-cycle/production.

100. This phrase is the euphemism used in the U.S. Department of Defense Directive 3000.09 to describe incidents where autonomous weapon systems injure civilians. "Autonomy in Weapon Systems," 21 November 2012, 4 (a) (1) (c).

101. See Scovazzi, "Some Remarks on International Responsibility in the Field of Environmental Protection," p. 218.

102. In the environmental context a "[state or nonstate] operator that fails to take prompt and effective response action to environmental emergencies arising from its activities shall be liable to pay the costs of response action taken by Parties. . . . *Liability shall be strict*." "Liability," art. 6 to annex 6 to the Protocol on Environmental Protection to the Antarctic Treaty: Liability Arising from Environmental Emergencies (emphasis added). In certain situations, the annex sets a maximum amount of liability (art. 9).

103. Sands et al., *Principles of International Environmental Law*, p. 229.

104. The polluter-pays principle constitutes the fundamental principle for allocating costs of pollution prevention and control efforts. "Application of the Polluter-Pays Principle to Accidental Pollution," in *The Polluter-Pays Principle: OECD Analyses and Recommendations*, Environment Directorate, Organization for Economic Co-operation and Development, Paris, 1992, para. 2, http://www.oecd.org/officialdocuments/publicdisplaydocumentpdf/?cote=OCDE/GD(92)81&docLanguage=En. The principle obliges operators of hazardous installations to pay for reasonable measures to prevent and control accidental pollution, in state-imposed fees, taxes, etc. Accordingly, the costs of these measures will be reflected in the costs of goods and services that cause pollution during production and/or consumption. Recommendations of the Council Concerning the Application of the Polluter-Pays Principle to Accidental Pollution, Organization for Economic Cooperation and Development, C (89) 88/Final, paras. 4 and 5, http://acts.oecd.org/Instruments/ShowInstrumentView.aspx?InstrumentID=38&InstrumentPID=305&Lang=en&Book=False.

105. "Possible Outcome of 2019 Group of Governmental Experts and Future Actions of International Community on Lethal Autonomous Weapons Systems," Submitted by Japan, Group of Governmental Experts on Emerging Technologies in the Area of Lethal Autonomous Weapon Systems, Geneva, 22 March 2019, para. 20, https://www.unog.ch/80256EDD006B8954/(httpAssets)/B0F30B3F69F5F2EEC12583C8003F3145/$file/CCW_+GGE+.1_+2019_+WP3+JAPAN.pdf, accessed 5 August 2020.

106. Department of Defense Policy Directive 3000.09, entitled "Autonomy in Weapon Systems," http://www.dtic.mil/whs/directives/corres/pdf/300009p.pdf.

107. M. Meier, U.S. Delegation Opening Statement to Convention on Certain Conventional Weapons Meeting of Experts on Lethal Autonomous Weapon Systems, 13 April 2015, http://www.unog.ch/80256EDD006B8954/(httpAssets)/8B33A1CDBE80EC60C1257E2800275E56/$file/2015_LAWS_MX_USA+bis.pdf.

108. Department of Defense Policy Directive 3000.09, Section 4 (d).

109. The Directive includes a series of technical testing and training requirements to ensure that the weapons and their autonomous functions will perform as designed. For example, new autonomous systems must receive rigorous hardware and software testing in realistic conditions to ensure that they perform "as anticipated in realistic operational environments against adaptive adversaries" ("Policy," 4 a [1] [a] and [b]). Moreover, the validation and verification process must ensure that the new system will complete engagements in a timely manner "consistent with commander and operator intentions and, if unable to do so, terminate engagements or seek additional human input before continuing the engagement" (Enclosure 3, 1 a [2]).

110. To ensure such robustness, the Directive insists that the hardware and software of autonomous weapon systems must contain "appropriate" safety and "anti-tamper mechanisms" and "[h]uman machine interfaces and controls" ("Policy," 4 a [2] [a] and [b]). The term "human-machine interface" is the system of communication and distribution of functions, responsibilities, and expectations between computers and their human supervisors or operators. See generally M. Cummings, "Automation and Accountability in Decision Support Systems Interface Design," 32 *Journal of Technical Studies*, 1 (2006), 10, http://dspace.mit.edu/handle/1721.1/90321. The manner in which humans and machines interface with each other is just as important as the kinds of machines that are developed. Statement by United States representative to 2016 Informal Expert Meeting on Lethal Autonomous Weapon Systems, Convention on Conventional Weapons, 12 April 2016. Thus, the Directive provides that the human-machine interface should be easily understandable to trained operators, it should provide traceable information on the status of the weapon system, and it should provide clear procedures for trained operators to activate and deactivate functions of the weapons system ("Policy," 4 a [3] [a] [b] and [c]).

111. Author interview with Paul Scharre, coordinator of drafting process for Directive 3000.09, Washington, D.C., 9 April 2014; Directive 3000.09, "Policy," 4 a (3) (a) (b) and (c).

112. Author interview with Paul Scharre, coordinator of drafting process for Directive 3000.09. Furthermore, a second concern within the U.S. Department of Defense that motivated the production of Directive 3000.09 was perceived constraints to the research and development of new kinds of autonomous technologies. In the absence of government policy direction addressing the development and deployment of weapon systems with greater autonomy, researchers and developers were hesitant to develop autonomous functions that might be constrained by the complex legal, moral, and ethical challenges presented by these systems. Author interview with Paul Scharre. Thus, the Directive's guidelines were intended to provide clarity and encouragement so that researchers and developers could incorporate autonomous functions in weapons system within legal and ethical boundaries (electronic mail message from P. Scharre, 31 October 2014, copy in author's possession). Logically, a symbiotic relationship exists between modern armed forces, industry, and academic research centers. For example, in an effort to better inform future investments into robotics technology and better focus industry efforts to create robotic vehicles suitable for military missions, the U.S. Department of Defense

and a consortium of eighty defense contractors, "non-traditional contractors," and universities signed an agreement that enabled the defense industry to participate in the Department of Defense technology assessment process. *Unmanned Systems Integrated Roadmap FY2009–2034*, 6 April 2009, p. 3, file:///Users/danielsaxon/Downloads/ADA522247%20(1).pdf.

113. Statement of France to Informal Meeting of Experts on Lethal Autonomous Weapon Systems, Convention on Conventional Weapons, Geneva, 12 April 2016, http://www.unog.ch/80256EE600585943/(httpPages)/37D51189AC4FB6E1C1257F4D004CAFB2?OpenDocument.

114. Statement of France to Informal Meeting of Experts. Indeed, the Directive requires that training and doctrine for autonomous weapons ensure that operators and commanders understand the functioning, capabilities, and limitations of a system's autonomy. Directive 3000.09, "Responsibilities," section 8 (a) (6).

115. Directive 3000.09, Enclosure 3, "Guidelines for Review of Certain Autonomous or Semi-Autonomous Weapon Systems" (1) (b) (1). In addition, Directive 3000.09 describes who shall be responsible for, inter alia, the lawful design of semi-autonomous and autonomous weapons, their experimentation strategies, human-machine interfaces, operational standards, doctrine, training, hardware and software safety mechanisms, and employment against adversaries (Enclosure 4, "Responsibilities," parts 1–10).

116. Author interview with Paul Scharre.

117. Colonel R. Jackson, Panel, "Autonomous Weaponry and Armed Conflict," Annual Meeting of American Society of International Law (ASIL), Washington, D.C., April 2014.

118. Statement by United States representative to 2016 Informal Expert Meeting on Lethal Autonomous Weapon Systems, Convention on Conventional Weapons, 12 April 2016.

119. Jackson, Panel, "Autonomous Weaponry and Armed Conflict."

120. M. Cummings, "Man Versus Machine or Man + Machine?" unpublished draft, p. 12, copy in author's possession.

121. E. Jensen, "The Future of the Law of Armed Conflict: Ostriches, Butterflies and Nanobots," 35 *Michigan Journal of International Law* (Winter 2014), 253, 290.

122. Jackson, Panel, "Autonomous Weaponry and Armed Conflict."

123. J. Klabbers, *International Law* (Cambridge University Press, 2013), p. 45.

124. The experience of the U.S. government at the multilateral negotiations leading to the adoption of the Rome Statute of the ICC, the Landmines Convention, the Convention on Climate Change, and the Kyoto Protocol demonstrates that a dissident state—even the strongest—cannot assume it can dictate the outcome against the wishes of the majority. A. Boyle and C. Chinkin, *The Making of International Law* (Oxford University Press, 2007), p. 30. Consequently, the United States decided to be more proactive vis-à-vis the development and control of autonomous weapon systems so that it could control the narrative and outcome. Author interview with Thomas Nash, 29 January 2016.

125. "Constitutionalism . . . signifies not so much a social or political process, but rather an attitude, a frame of mind. Constitutionalism is the philosophy of striving towards some form of political legitimacy typified by respect for . . . a constitution." J. Klabbers, "Setting the Scene," in J. Klabbers et al. (eds.), *The Constitutionalization of International Law* (Oxford University Press, 2009), p. 10. For an argument that, owing to its fragmented characteristics, international law lacks an identifiable constitutional structure; see Boyle and Chinkin, *Making of International Law*, p. 100.

126. *Skinner v. Oklahoma ex rel. Williamson*, 316 U.S. 535 (1942), 546, Justice Jackson Concurring (holding that there are limits to the extent to which a legislatively represented

majority may conduct biological experiments at the expense of the dignity and natural powers of a minority).

127. "The right to self-determination, human dignity and protection of human rights are issues that concern the international community as a whole and constitute an international responsibility and an international obligation, they cannot be reduced to any bilateral *diferenda*." J. Sampiano, President of Portugal, Address at the International Court of Justice, 30 October 1997, http://www.icj-cij.org/presscom/index.php?pr=142&pt=1&p1=6&p2=1&PHPSESSID=5c407.

Conclusion

1. I. Berlin, "My Intellectual Path," in *The Power of Ideas*, H. Hardy (ed.) (Princeton University Press, 2000), p. 23.

2. L. Henkin, *How Nations Behave: Law and Foreign Policy* (New York: Frederick A. Praeger, 1968), p. 35.

3. B. Mitchell (ed.), *The Battle of Maldon and Other Old English Poems*, K. Crossley-Holland (trans.) (London: Macmillan, 1965), pp. 28–29, and 32. The Battle of Maldon took place in Essex, U.K., in August 901. A party of invading Danish Vikings defeated English warriors led by Byrhtnoth, who, under a duty to destroy the invaders, imprudently permitted the Danes to cross the Maldon River and engage the English in battle.

4. P. Mahon, *Royal Commission of Inquiry into and Report upon the Crash on Mount Erebus, Antarctica, of a DC10 Aircraft Operated by Air New Zealand Limited* (Wellington: P. D. Hasselberg, 1981), para. 398, http://www.erebus.co.nz/LinkClick.aspx?fileticket=PUWvCWDoUoE%3D&tabid=159.

5. H. Nye, "Dr. Will Roper on AI and Autonomy in the US Air Force," *Air Force Technology*, 3 December 2019, https://www.airforce-technology.com/features/dr-will-roper-on-ai-and-autonomy-in-the-us-air-force/, accessed 22 March 2020.

6. See *Barcelona Traction, Light and Power Company, Limited*, Judgment, ICJ Reports 1970, Separate Opinion of President Bustamente y Rivero, para. 4 (concluding that where the evolution of international economic law does not keep pace with the practicalities of transnational business, harm may occur to the "proper working of justice").

7. J. Waldron, "The Rule of International Law," 30 *Harvard Journal of Law and Public Policy* (2006), 15, 24–25.

8. S. Russell, "A Brave New World? How Will Advances in Artificial Intelligence, Smart Sensors and Social Technology Changer Our Lives?" Panel Discussion at World Economic Forum, 22 January 2015, http://www.weforum.org/videos/brave-new-world.

9. Law is most relevant precisely in the face of shifting political, social, economic, and military conditions that call for "fundamental assessments of human values and the purposes of society." *Shaw v. Director of Public Prosecutions*, House of Lords, Opinion of Viscount Simonds, 4 May 1961, p. 7.

10. H. Nasu, "Nanotechnology and the Future of the Law of Weaponry," 91 *International Law Studies* (2015), 486, 501–2; H. Eggen Røislien, "Thoughts on Autonomous Weapon Systems and Meaningful Human Control of Cyber," *Open Democracy: Free Thinking for the World*, 7 November 2014, https://www.opendemocracy.net/hanne-eggen-r%c3%b8islien/thoughts-on-autonomous-weapons-systems-and-meaningful-human-control-of-cyber.

11. Potentially, autonomous weapons technology can give persons more options to act legally and morally. J. Lanier, "The First Church of Robotics," *International Herald Tribune*, 9 August 2010, p. 6. However, it should not reduce the human *ability* to do the same.

12. The government of the Republic of Croatia contends that permitting "automated technical systems" to make fundamental moral judgments about the taking of life "would mark the end of humanity as such." "Opening Statement of the Republic of Croatia," Convention on Conventional Weapons, Informal Meeting of Experts on Lethal Autonomous Weapons, 13 April 1015, http://www.unog.ch/80256EE600585943/(httpPages)/6CE049BE22EC75A2C1257C8D00513E26?OpenDocument.

13. "Liberty and equality, spontaneity and security, happiness and knowledge, mercy and justice—all these are ultimate human values, sought for themselves alone; yet when they are incompatible, they cannot all be attained, choices must be made, sometimes tragic losses accepted in the pursuit of some preferred ultimate end." Berlin, "My Intellectual Path," p. 23.

14. "Only by being normative can law preserve a balance between its transformative force, which does not accept reality as it is, and its roots in social reality." B. Simma, "The Responsibility of Individuals for Human Rights Abuses in Internal Conflicts: A Positivist View," 93 *American Journal of International Law* (1999), 302, 307.

15. *Prosecutor v. Dražen Erdemović*, Joint Separate Opinion of Judge McDonald and Judge Vohrah, IT-96-22-A, Appeals Chamber, 7 October 1997, para. 75 (observing that "the law should not be the product or slave of logic or intellectual hair-splitting, but must serve broader normative purposes in light of its social, political and economic role"). "Moral and political considerations are not alien to law but part of it." Simma, "Responsibility of Individuals for Human Rights Abuses in Internal Conflicts," 308. For a different view, see J. Goldsmith and E. Posner, *The Limits of International Law* (Oxford University Press, 2005), p. 185 (arguing that states have no moral obligation to follow international law).

16. *Corfu Channel Case*, Judgment of 9 April 1949, Separate Opinion of Judge Alvarez, ICJ Reports 1949, p. 41.

17. One function of law is to establish "possible futures for society, in accordance with society's theories, values and purposes." P. Allott, "The Concept of International Law," 10 *European Journal of International Law* (1999), 31.

18. H. Grotius, *On the Law of War and Peace* (1625), A. C. Campbell (trans.) (Kitchener: Batoche Books, 2001), p. 172.

SELECTED BIBLIOGRAPHY

Books and Articles

Abresch, William. "A Human Rights Law of Internal Armed Conflict: The European Court of Human Rights in Chechnya" (2005) 16 *European Journal of International Law*, 4, 741–67.

Abtahi, Hirad, and Phillipa Webb (eds.). *The Genocide Convention: The Travaux Préparatoires* (Leiden: Martinus Nijhoff, 2008).

Achenbach, Joel. "After a Wait, Spacecraft Confirms That It Survived Its Close Pass of Pluto," *Washington Post*, 14 July 2015, http://www.washingtonpost.com/national/health-science/new-horizons-finally-makes-it-to-pluto-sees-craters-and-great-mounds/2015/07/14/9bcb0f04-2a1f-11e5-bd33-395c05608059_story.html?wpisrc=nl_evening&wpmm=1.

Ackerman, Evan. "Emergency Response Teams Combine Mobile Robots, Drones and Dogs," *IEEE Spectrum*, 6 May 2014, http://spectrum.ieee.org/automaton/robotics/military-robots/emergency-response-teams-combine-mobile-robots-drones-and-dogs.

———. "World's Largest Swarm of Miniature Robots," *IEEE Spectrum*, 5 May 2015, http://spectrum.ieee.org/automaton/robotics/artificial-intelligence/worlds-largest-swarm-of-miniature-robot-submarines.

Adams, Thomas. "Robots on Battlefield: Robotic Weapons Might Be the Way of the Future, but They Raise Ethical Questions About the Nature of Warfare," *Townsville Bull* (Australia), 18 September 2009.

Aguas, Jim. "The Notions of the Human Person and Human Dignity in Aquinas and Wojtyla" (June 2009) 3 *Kritike*, 1, 40–60.

Aircraft Weapon Systems, pp. 15-19–15-20, http://www.globalsecurity.org/military/library/policy/navy/nrtc/14313_ch15.pdf.

Akerson, David. "The Illegality of Offensive Lethal Autonomy," in D. Saxon (ed.), *International Humanitarian Law and the Changing Technology of War* (Leiden: Martinus Nijhoff, 2013), pp. 65–98.

Allott, Philip. "The Concept of International Law" (1999) 10 *European Journal of International Law*, 31–50.

Anderson, Kenneth, and Matthew Waxman. "Debating Autonomous Weapon Systems, Their Ethics, and Their Regulation Under International Law," in R. Brownsword et al. (eds.), *The Oxford Handbook of Law, Regulation, and Technology* (Oxford University Press, 2017).

Antebi, Liran. "Changing Trends in Unmanned Aerial Vehicles: New Challenges for States, Armies and Security Industries" (August 2014) 6 *Military and Strategic Affairs*, 2, 21–36.

Aquinas, Thomas. *The Summa Theologica*, II-II, Question 57, Art. 1, http://dhspriory.org/thomas/summa/SS/SS057.html#SSQ57OUTP1.

Arendt, Hannah. *The Life of the Mind* (New York: Harcourt, 1978).

——. *The Origins of Totalitarianism* (New York: Harcourt, 1968).

Aristotle. *Nichomachean Ethics.* W. D. Ross (trans.), book 3, (Oxford University Press, 2009).

——. *On Rhetoric: A Theory of Civic Discourse*, book 1, chapter 13, George A. Kennedy (trans.), 2nd ed. (New York: Oxford University Press, 2007).

Arkin, Ronald. *Ethical Robots in Warfare.* Georgia Institute of Technology (20 January 2009), 2, http://www.cc.gatech.edu/ai/robot-lab/online-publications/arkin-rev.pdf.

Asaro, Peter. "Determinism, Machine Agency, and Responsibility" (2014) 2 *Politica & Societa*, 265–92.

——. "On Banning Autonomous Weapon Systems: Human Rights, Automation and the Dehumanization of Lethal Decision-Making" (Summer 2012) 94 *International Review of the Red Cross*, 886, 687–709.

Augustine, Saint. *The City of God Against the Pagans*, W. M. Green (trans.) (Cambridge, Mass.: Harvard University Press, 1972), vol. 7, book 22.

Avery, Denis. *De Man Die Naar Auschwitz Wilde (The Auschwitz Volunteer)* (Antwerp: House of Books, 2011).

Baker, Herschel. *The Image of Man: A Study of the Idea of Human Dignity in Classical Antiquity, the Middle Ages, and the Renaissance* (New York: Harper and Row, 1961).

Baldwin, Thomas. "Identity," in R. Brownsword et al. (eds.), *The Oxford Handbook of Law, Regulation and Technology* (Oxford University Press, 2017).

Bamberger Robert J., et al. "Flight Demonstrations of Unmanned Aerial Vehicle Swarming Concepts" (2006) 27 *Johns Hopkins APL Technical Digest*, 1, 41–55, http://www.jhuapl.edu/techdigest/TD/td2701/Bamberger.pdf.

Barak, Aharon. *Human Dignity: The Constitutional Value and the Constitutional Right.* D. Kayros (trans.) (Cambridge University Press, 2015).

Baron de Jomini. *The Art of War*, G. H. Mendell and W. P. Craighill (trans.) (West Point: U.S. Military Academy, 1862), pp. 44–51, http://www.gutenberg.org/files/13549/13549-h/13549-h.htm#article_XII.

Beard, Jack M. "Autonomous Weapons and Human Responsibility" (2014) 45 *Georgetown Journal of International Law*, 617–81.

——. "Law and War in the Virtual Era" (2009) 103 *American Journal of International Law*, 409–45.

Bederman, David. *Custom as a Source of Law* (Cambridge University Press, 2010).

Bentham, Jeremy. *Anarchical Fallacies: Being an Examination of the Declaration of Rights Issued During the French Revolution* (1843), Art. II, http://english.duke.edu/uploads/media_items/bentham-anarchical-fallacies.original.pdf.

Benvenisti, Eyal. "Human Dignity in Combat: The Duty to Spare Enemy Civilians" (2006) 39 *Israel Law Review*, 2, 81–109.

Berlin, Isaiah. "My Intellectual Path," in H. Hardy (ed.), *The Power of Ideas* (Princeton University Press, 2000) 1-28.

Beyer, Gerald. "Economic Rights: Past, Present, and Future," in T. Cushman (ed.), *Handbook of Human Rights* (New York: Routledge, 2012), pp. 291–310.

Beyerlin, Ulrich, and Thilo Marauhn. *International Environmental Law* (Oxford: Hart, 2011).

Bianchi, Andrea. "Human Rights and the Magic of Jus Cogens" (2008) 19 *European Journal of International Law*, 3, 491–508.

Boas, Gideon. *Public International Law: Contemporary Principles and Perspectives* (Cheltenham: Edward Elgar, 2012).

Boas, Gideon, et al. "Forms of Responsibility in International Criminal Law," in G. Boas et al. (eds.), *International Criminal Law Practitioners Library*, vol. 1 (Cambridge University Press, 2007).

Bohn, Dieter. "Astro Teller: Google X 'Encouraged Too Much Attention' for Project Glass," *Verge*, 17 March 2015, http://www.theverge.com/2015/3/17/8235277/sxsw-astro-teller-google-x.

Boothby, William. "How Far Will the Law Allow Unmanned Targeting to Go?" in D. Saxon (ed.), *International Humanitarian Law and the Changing Technology of War* (Leiden: Martinus Nijhoff, 2013), pp. 43–63.

———. *The Law of Targeting* (Oxford University Press, 2012).

Bossuyt, Marc. *Guide to the "Travaux Préparatoires" of the International Covenant on Civil and Political Rights* (Dordrecht: Martinus Nijhoff, 1987).

Boyle, Alan, and Christine Chinkin. *The Making of International Law* (Oxford University Press, 2007).

Braudel, Fernand. *Capitalism and Modern Life: 1400–1800*, M. Kochan (trans.) (New York: Harper and Row, 1973).

Browning, Christopher R. *Ordinary Men: Reserve Police Battalion 101 and the Final Solution in Poland* (New York: Harper Collins, 1992).

Brunnée Jutta. "International Legal Accountability Through the Lens of the Law of State Responsibility" (2005) 36 *Netherlands Yearbook of International Law*, 21–56.

Byk, Christian. "Is Human Dignity a Useless Concept? Legal Perspectives," in M. Düwell et al. (eds.), *The Cambridge Handbook of Human Dignity: Interdisciplinary Perspectives* (Cambridge University Press, 2014), pp. 362–67.

Cameron, Edwin. "Dignity and Disgrace: Moral Citizenship and Constitutional Protection," in C. McCrudden (ed.), *Understanding Human Dignity* (Oxford University Press, 2013).

Cançado Trindade, Antonio. *The Construction of a Humanized International Law: A Collection of Individual Opinions* (1991–2013) (Leiden: Brill Nijhoff, 2015).

Carozza, Paulo. "Human Dignity," in D. Shelton (ed.), *The Oxford Handbook of International Human Rights Law* (Oxford University Press, 2013), pp. 345–59.

———. "Human Rights, Human Dignity and Human Experience," in C. McCrudden (ed.), *Understanding Human Dignity* (Oxford University Press, 2013).

Cassese, Antonio. *International Criminal Law*, 2nd ed. (Oxford University Press, 2008).

———. *Violence and Law in the Modern Age* (Cambridge: Polity, 1988).

Chantler, Robert. "Translator's Introduction" to V. Grossman, *Life and Fate* (London: Flamingo, 1985).

Charlesworth, Hilary. "Law-Making and Sources," in J. Crawford and M. Koskenniemi (eds.), *The Cambridge Companion to International Law* (Cambridge University Press, 2012), pp. 187–202.

Charney, Jonathan. "Universal International Law" (October 1993) 87 *American Journal of International Law*, 4, 529–51.

Chen, Stephen. "China Military Develops Robotic Submarines to Launch a New Era of Sea Power," *South China Morning Post*, 22 July 2018, https://www.scmp.com/news/china/society/article/2156361/china-developing-unmanned-ai-submarines-launch-new-era-sea-power.

Cheng, Bin. *General Principles of Law as Applied by International Courts and Tribunals* (London: Stevens and Sons, 1953).

Chinkin, Christine. "Sources," in D. Moeckli et al. (eds.), *International Human Rights Law* (Oxford University Press, 2010).

Clare, Andrew, et al. "Assessing Operator Strategies for Real-Time Replanning of Multiple Unmanned Vehicles" (2012) 6 *Intelligent Decision Technologies*, 3, 221–31.

Clark, Phil. "The Rules and Politics of Engagement," in P. Clark and Z. Kaufman (eds.), *After Genocide: Transitional Justice, Post-Conflict Reconstruction and Reconciliation in Rwanda and Beyond* (London: Hurst, 2009).

Clarke, Richard. *Against All Enemies: Inside America's War on Terror* (New York: Free Press, 2004).

Clayton, Mark. "More Telltale Signs of Cyber Spying and Cyber Attacks Arise in Middle East," *Christian Science Monitor*, 21 August 2012, http://www.csmonitor.com/USA/2012/0821/More-telltale-signs-of-cyber-spying-and-cyber-attacks-arise-in-Middle-East-video.

———. "Stuxnet Cyberweapon Set to Stop Operating," *Christian Science Monitor*, 23 June 2012, http://www.csmonitor.com/USA/2012/0623/Stuxnet-cyberweapon-set-to-stop-operating.

Cohen, Rachel. "Skyborg, Weapons Swarms, Satellites Chosen as First 'Vanguards,'" *Air Force Magazine*, 22 November 2019, https://www.airforcemag.com/skyborg-weapon-swarms-satellites-chosen-as-first-vanguards/.

"Conclusions," *The Church in the Actual Transformation of Latin America in Light of the Council*, II, Bogota, General Secretariat of Episcopal Conference of Latin America, 1968, citing Paul VI, Enc. Populorum progressio, No. 30.

Connors, Jane, and Schmidt, Markus. "United Nations," in D. Moeckli et al. (eds.), *International Human Rights Law* (Oxford University Press, 2014).

Corn, Geoffroy, et al. "History and Sources of the Law of Armed Conflict," in G. Corn et al. (eds.), *The Law of Armed Conflict: An Operational Approach* (New York: Wolters Kluwer, 2012).

Crawford, James. *Brownlie's Principles of Public International Law*, 8th ed. (Oxford University Press, 2012).

Cummings Mary. "Automation and Accountability in Decision Support Systems Interface Design" (2006) 32 *Journal of Technical Studies*, 23–31.

———. "Man Versus Machine or Man + Machine?" *IEEE Intelligence Systems*, September/October 2014, http://hal.pratt.duke.edu/sites/hal.pratt.duke.edu/files/u10/IS-29-05-Expert%20Opinion%5B1%5D_0.pdf.

Cummings, Mary, et al. "Boredom and Distraction in Multiple Unmanned Vehicle Supervisory Control" (2013) 25 *Interacting with Computers*, 1, 34–47.

Decoeur, Henri. "Avoiding Strict Liability in Mixed Conflicts: A Subjectivist Approach to the Contextual Element of War Crimes" (2013) 3 *International Criminal Law Review*, 473–92.

Defence and Security News—Russia, 23 April 2014, http://www.armyrecognition.com/april_2014_global_defense_security_news_uk/russian_army_to_use_unmanned_ground_robot_taifun-m_to_protect_yars_and_topol-m_missile_sites_2304143.html.

de Koker, Cedric. "A Different Perspective on Hassan v. United Kingdom: A Reply to Frederic Bernard" (October 2014) *Strasbourg Observers*, http://strasbourgobservers.com/2014/10/14/a-different-perspective-on-hassan-v-united-kingdom-a-reply-to-frederic-bernard/.

Del Vecchio, Giorgio. *General Principles of Law*, Felix Forte (trans.) (Boston University Press, 1956).

de Megrin, Ignacio. *Elementary Treatise on Maritime International Law* (1873).

de Vattell, Emer. *The Law of Nations* (1758) (Philadelphia: T. and J. W. Johnson, Law Booksellers, 1844), http://www.loc.gov/rr/frd/Military_Law/Lieber_Collection/pdf/DeVattel_LawOfNations.pdf.

Dinstein, Yoram. *The Conduct of Hostilities Under the Law of International Armed Conflict*, 2nd ed. (Cambridge University Press, 2010).

———. "The Principle of Distinction and Cyber War in International Armed Conflicts" (2012) 17 *Journal of Conflict and Security Law*, 2, 261–77.

Droege, Cordula. "Get Off My Cloud: Cyber Warfare, International Humanitarian Law, and the Protection of Civilians" (Summer 2012) 94 *International Review of the Red Cross*, 886, 533–78.

Drzemczewski, Andrew, and Jens Ladewig-Mayer. "Principal Characteristics of the New ECHR Control Mechanism, as Established by Protocol No. 11" (1994) 15 *Human Rights Law Journal* 81, 357–79 (excerpted in Steiner and Alston, p. 801).

Duff, Antony. "Authority and Responsibility in International Criminal Law," in S. Besson and J. Tasioulas (eds.), *The Philosophy of International Law* (Oxford University Press, 2010), pp. 593–604.

Duffy, Helen. *The "War on Terror" and the Framework of International Law*, 2nd ed. (Cambridge University Press, 2015).

Dunant, Henry. *A Memory of Solferino* (1862) (Geneva: International Committee of the Red Cross, 1986).

Dupré, Catherine. *The Age of Dignity: Human Rights and Constitutionalism in Europe* (Oxford: Hart, 2015).

Düwell, Marcus. "Human Dignity and Future Generations," in M. Düwell et al. (eds.), *The Cambridge Handbook of Human Dignity: Interdisciplinary Perspectives* (Cambridge University Press, 2014), pp. 551–58.

Dworkin, Ronald. *Justice for Hedgehogs* (Cambridge, Mass.: Harvard University Press, 2011).

Fackler, Martin. "Japanese Ace in World War II Is Pacifist Voice," *New York Times*, 4 April 2015, pp. A1 and A5.

Farmer, Ben. "Brimstone: British Missile Envied by the US for War on Isil," *Telegraph*, 1 October 2014, http://www.telegraph.co.uk/news/uknews/defence/11133680/Brimstone-British-missile-envied-by-the-US-for-war-on-Isil.html; "Brimstone," Royal Air Force, http://www.raf.mod.uk/equipment/Brimstone.cfm.

Feldman, David. "Human Dignity as a Legal Value: Part 2" (2000) *Public Law*, 61–71.

Fenrick, William. "The Prosecution of Unlawful Attack Cases Before the ICTY" (2001) 7 *Yearbook of International Humanitarian Law*, 153–89.

Fiddian, P. "UAV Swarm Technology Trial Success," *Armed Forces International News*, 7 August 2012, http://www.armedforces-int.com/news/uav-swarm-technology-trial-success.html.

Finch, George. "The Nuremberg Trial and International Law" (January 1947) 41 *American Journal of International Law*, 1, 20–37.

Finnis, John. *Natural Law and Natural Rights* (Oxford: Clarendon, 1980).

Fletcher, George. "What Is Punishment Imposed For?" in R. Christopher (ed.), *Fletcher's Essays on Criminal Law* (Oxford University Press, 2013), pp. 43–52.

Frith, Chris. "The Role of Metacognition in Human Social Interactions" (August 2012) 367 *Philosophical Transactions*, 1599, 2213–23, http://www.ncbi.nlm.nih.gov/pmc/articles/PMC3385688/.

Fuller, Lon. "Freedom—a Suggested Analysis" (June 1955) 68 *Harvard Law Review*, 8, 1305–25.

———. "Means and Ends," in K. Winston (ed.), *The Principles of Social Order: Selected Essays of Lon L. Fuller* (Durham: Duke University Press, 1981), p. 57.

Fussell, Chris. The Tim Ferriss Show, http://fourhourworkweek.com/2015/07/05/stanley-mcchrystal/.

Future Tech? Autonomous Killer Robots Are Already Here," NBC News, 15 May 2014, https://www.nbcnews.com/tech/security/future-tech-autonomous-killer-robots-are-already-here-n105656.

Garraway, Charles. "The Application of Superior Responsibility in an Era of Unlimited Information," in D. Saxon (ed.), *International Humanitarian Law and the Changing Technology of War* (Leiden: Martinus Nijhoff, 2013), pp. 187–206.

Gattani Ali. "Breach of International Obligations," in A. Nollkaemper and I. Plakokefalos (eds.), *Principles of Shared Responsibility in International Law: An Appraisal of the State of the Art* (Cambridge University Press, 2014), pp. 38–45.

Glendon, Mary. *A World Made New: Eleanor Roosevelt and the Universal Declaration of Human Rights* (New York: Random House, 2002).

Goebbels, Joseph. *Final Entries 1945: The Diaries of Joseph Goebbels*, Hugh Trevor-Roper (ed.) (New York: G. P. Putnam's Sons, 1978).

Goldsmith, Jack, and Posner, Eric. *The Limits of International Law* (Oxford University Press, 2005).

Gould, Joe. "U.S. Army Readying Unmanned Systems Doctrine," *Defense News*, 8 April 2015, http://www.defensenews.com/story/defense/land/army/2015/04/08/us-army-readying-unmanned-systems-doctrine/25473749/.

Greenwood, Christopher. "Historical Development and Legal Basis," in D. Fleck (ed.), *The Handbook of International Humanitarian Law* (Oxford University Press, 2009), pp. 1–42.

———. "The Law of War (International Humanitarian Law)" in M. Evans (ed.), *International Law*, 2nd ed. (Oxford University Press, 2003).

Gregg, Arron. "Swarming Drones Could Soon Be Real Weapons for the Military," *Washington Post*, 19 February 2019, https://www.latimes.com/business/la-fi-drone-swarms-20190219-story.html.

Grossman, Lt. Col. Dave. *On Killing: The Psychological Cost of Learning to Kill in War and Society* (Boston: Little, Brown, 1996).

Grotius, Hugo. *On the Law of War and Peace* (1625), A. C. Campbell (trans.) (Kitchener: Batoche Books, 2001).

"Ground Launched Small Diameter Bomb," *Army Technology*, https://www.army-technology.com/projects/small-diameter-bomb-glsdb/.

Haithcock, John Jr. TSM FATDS, Fort Sill, OK, Letter to the Editor, Field Artillery, January–February 2006, http://sill-www.army.mil/firesbulletin/archives/2006/JAN_FEB_2006/JAN_FEB_2006_FULL_EDITION.pdf.

Hambling, David. "If Drone Swarms Are the Future, China May Be Winning," *Popular Mechanics*, 23 December 2020, https://www.popularmechanics.com/military/research/a24494/chinese-drones-swarms/.

Hanson, Victor. *A War Like No Other: How the Athenians and Spartans Fought the Peloponnesian War* (New York: Random House, 2005).

Harris, David, et al. *Law of the European Convention on Human Rights* (Oxford University Press, 2014).

Hart, Herbert. "Changing Conceptions of Responsibility," in *Punishment and Responsibility: Essays in the Philosophy of Law* (Oxford: Clarendon, 1963).

———. "Punishment and the Elimination of Responsibility," in *Punishment and Responsibility: Essays in the Philosophy of Law* (Oxford: Clarendon, 1963).

Hastings, Max. *Nemesis: The Battle for Japan, 1944–45* (London: Harper Perennial, 2007).
Hatzfeld, Jean. *Into the Quick of Life: The Rwandan Genocide Survivors Speak* (London: Serpent's Tail, 2008).
———. *A Time for Machetes: The Rwandan Genocide; The Killers Speak* (London: Serpent's Tail, 2008).
Heath, Brenton J. "Human Dignity at Trial: Hard Cases and Broad Concepts in International Criminal Law" (2012) 44 *George Washington International Law Review*, 317–66.
Henkin, Louis. *How Nations Behave: Law and Foreign Policy* (New York: Frederick A. Praeger, 1968).
"Hero-400EC Extended Range Loitering System," Air Force Technology, https://www.airforce-technology.com/projects/hero-400ec-extended-range-loitering-system/.
Heyns, Christof. "Autonomous Weapon Systems: Living a Dignified Life and Dying a Dignified Death," in N. Bhuta et al. (eds.), *Autonomous Weapon Systems—Law, Ethics, Policy* (Cambridge University Press, 2016).
Higgins, Rosalyn. "Fundamentals of International Law," in R. Higgins (ed.), *Themes and Theories: Selected Essays, Speeches, and Writings in International Law* (Oxford University Press, 2009).
Holland, Thomas (ed.). "Letter, 11 December 1880," in *Letters to "The Times": Upon War and Neutrality with Some Commentary* (New York: Longmans, Green, 1914).
Houlton, Susan. "German Prosecutors Drop Case Against Kunduz Airstrike Colonel," *DW*, 19 April 2010, http://www.dw.de/german-prosecutors-drop-case-against-kunduz-airstrike-colonel/a-5483181-1.
Howard, Michael. *War in European History* (Oxford University Press, 2009).
Howard, Rhoda, and Jack Donnelly. "Human Dignity, Human Rights, and Political Regimes" (September 1986) 80 *American Political Science Review*, 3, 801–17.
Hughes, Robin. "Rafael Enhances SPICE 250 with Advanced Automatic Target Recognition Capability," *Jane's Missiles and Rockets*, 10 June 2019, https://www.janes.com/article/89149/rafael-enhances-spice-250-with-advanced-automatic-target-recognition-capability.
Hughes, Thomas. "Convergent Themes in the History of Science, Medicine and Technology" (July 1981) 22 *Technology and Culture*, 3, 550–58.
"India Buys Israeli 'SPYDER' Mobile Air Defence System," *Defence Industry Daily*, 19 August 2009, http://www.defenseindustrydaily.com/india-to-buy-israeli-spyder-mobile-air-defense-system-02702/.
Ishay, Micheline. *The History of Human Rights: From Ancient Times to the Globalization Era* (Berkeley: University of California Press, 2004).
Jain, Neha. "Autonomous Weapons Systems: New Frameworks for Individual Responsibility," in N. Bhuta et al. (eds.), *Autonomous Weapon Systems—Law, Ethics, Policy* (Cambridge University Press, 2016).
Jefferson, Thomas. *Letter to David Harding*, 20 April 1824, http://tjrs.monticello.org/letter/428.
Jensen, Eric T. "The (Erroneous) Requirement for Human Judgment and (Error) in the Law of Armed Conflict" (2020) 96 *International Law Studies*, 26.
———. "The Future of the Law of Armed Conflict: Ostriches, Butterflies and Nanobots" (Winter 2014) 35 *Michigan Journal of International Law*, 2, 253–317.
Jessup, Philip. *A Modern Law of Nations* (New York: Macmillan, 1949).
Jinks, Derek. "International Human Rights Law in Time of Armed Conflict," in A. Clapham et al. (eds), *The Oxford Handbook of International Law in Armed Conflict* (Oxford University Press, 2014), pp. 656–74.

Johnson, Matthew, et al. "Beyond Cooperative Robotics: The Central Role of Interdependence in Coactive Design" (May/June 2011) *IEEE Computer Society*, 81–88.

Kant, Immanuel. "The Contest of Faculties," in Hans Reiss (ed.), *Kant's Political Writings* (Cambridge, Mass.: Harvard University Press, 1970).

———. *The Groundwork of Metaphysics of Morals*, M. Gregor and J. Timmermann (eds. and trans.) (Cambridge University Press, 2011).

———. *The Metaphysics of Morals*, Mary Gregor (ed.) (Cambridge University Press, 2005).

Kateb, George. *Human Dignity* (Cambridge, Mass.: Harvard University Press, 2011).

Keegan, John. *The Face of Battle* (New York: Penguin Books, 1976).

Kellenberger, Jakob. "Foreword," in J. Henckaerts and L. Doswald-Beck, *Customary International Humanitarian Law*. Vol. 1, *Rules*, International Committee of the Red Cross (Cambridge University Press, 2005).

———. "Rule 156," in J. Henckaerts and L. Doswald-Beck, *Customary International Humanitarian Law*. Vol. 1, *Rules*, International Committee of the Red Cross (Cambridge University Press, 2005).

Kelsen, Hans. "What Is Justice?" in *What Is Justice: Justice, Law and Politics in the Mirror of Science: Collected Essays* (Berkeley: University of California Press, 1957).

Kercher, Leonard. *The Kenya Penal System: Past, Present and Prospect* (Washington, D.C.: University Press of America, 1981).

Killmister, Suzanne. "Dignity: Personal, Social, Human" (2017) 174 *Philosophical Studies*, 8, 2063–82.

Klabbers, Jan. *International Law* (Cambridge University Press, 2013).

———. "Setting the Scene," in J. Klabbers et al. (eds.), *The Constitutionalization of International Law* (Oxford University Press, 2009).

Klare, Michael. "Pentagon Asks More for Autonomous Weapons," Arms Control Association, April 2019, https://www.armscontrol.org/act/2019–04/news/pentagon-asks-more-autonomous-weapons.

Krishnan, Armin. *Killer Robots: Legality and Ethicality of Autonomous Weapons* (Surrey: Ashgate, 2009).

LaGrone, Sam. "Mabus: F-35 Will Be 'Last Manned Strike Fighter' the Navy, Marines 'Will Ever Buy or Fly,'" *U.S. Naval Institute News*, 15 April 2013, http://news.usni.org/2015/04/15/mabus-f-35c-will-be-last-manned-strike-fighter-the-navy-marines-will-ever-buy-or-fly.

Langer, Maximo. "The Diplomacy of Universal Jurisdiction: The Political Branches and the Transnational Prosecution of International Crimes" (2011) 105 *American Journal of International Law*, 1, 1–49.

Lanier Jaron. "The First Church of Robotics," *International Herald Tribune*, 9 August 2010, p. 6.

Lauterpacht, Hersch. *The Function of Law in the International Community* (Oxford: Clarendon, 1933).

———. *An International Bill of the Rights of Man* (1945) (Oxford University Press, 2013).

Letendre, Linelli, "Lethal Autonomous Weapon Systems: Translating Geek Speak for Lawyers" (2020) 96 *International Law Studies* 274, 278.

Levi, Primo. *The Drowned and the Saved* (New York: Vintage International, 1989).

Liddell Hart, Basil Henry. *History of the Second World War* (New York: G. P. Putnam's Sons, 1970).

Liu, Hin-Yan. "Refining Responsibility: Differentiating Two Types of Responsibility Issues Raised by Autonomous Weapon Systems," in N. Bhuta et al. (eds.), *Autonomous Weapon Systems: Law, Ethics, Policy* (Cambridge University Press, 2016).

Locke, John. "Concerning the True Original Extent and End of Civil Government," in *Two Treatises of Government*, http://socserv2.socsci.mcmaster.ca/econ/ugcm/3ll3/locke/government.pdf.

———. "Of Complex Ideas," in *An Essay Concerning Human Understanding* (1690), chapter 12, para. 2, ftp://ftp.dca.fee.unicamp.br/pub/docs/ia005/humanund.pdf.

Lubofsky, Evan. "A Smarter Undersea Robot: Engineers Seek to Correct a Curious Deficiency" (Winter 2016) 51 *Oceanus*, 2, http://www.whoi.edu/oceanus/feature/a-smarter-undersea-robot.

Lye, Harry. "Dr. Will Roper on AI and Autonomy in the U.S. Air Force," *Air Force Technology*, 3 December 2019, https://www.airforce-technology.com/features/dr-will-roper-on-ai-and-autonomy-in-the-us-air-force/.

Margulies, Peter. "Making Autonomous Weapons Accountable: Command Responsibility for Computer-Guided Lethal Force in Armed Conflicts," in J. Ohlin (ed.), *Research Handbook on Remote Warfare* (Northampton: Edward Elgar, 2016), http://papers.ssrn.com/sol3/papers.cfm?abstract_id=2734900.

———. "Sovereignty and Cyber Attacks: Technology's Challenge to the Law of State Responsibility" (2013) 14 *Melbourne Journal of International Law*, 496, 1–24.

Marks, Susan, and Azizi, Fiorentina. "Responsibility for Violations of Human Rights Obligations: International Mechanisms," in J. Crawford and A. Pellet (eds.), *The Law of International Responsibility* (Oxford University Press, 2010), pp. 725–38.

Marlantes, Karl. *Matterhorn* (London: Corvus, 2010).

———. *What It Is Like to Go to War* (New York: Grove, 2012).

May, Larry, and Michael Newton. *Proportionality in International Law* (New York: Oxford University Press, 2014).

McCullogh, Amy. "The Looming Swarm," *Air Force Magazine*, 22 March 2019, https://www.airforcemag.com/article/the-looming-swarm/.

McCullough, David. *John Adams* (New York: Simon and Schuster, 2001).

McDougal, Myers, and Norbert Schlei. "The Hydrogen Bomb Tests in Perspective: Lawful Measures for Security" (1955) 64 *Yale Law Journal*, 648–710.

McFarland, Tim. *Autonomous Weapon Systems and the Law of Armed Conflict: Compatibility with International Humanitarian Law* (Cambridge University Press, 2020).

McLuhan, Marshall. *Understanding Media: The Extensions of Man* (Cambridge, Mass.: MIT Press, 1994).

Melzer, Nils. *Targeted Killing in International Law* (Oxford University Press, 2009).

"Memorandum: The ICRC's Privilege of Non-Disclosure of Confidential Information" (October 2015) 895 *International Review of the Red Cross*, 433–44.

Mennecke, Martin. "Punishing Genocidaires: A Deterrent Effect or Not?" (July 2007) *Human Rights Review*, 319–39.

Meron, Theodor. *Bloody Constraint: War and Chivalry in Shakespeare* (Oxford University Press, 1998).

———. *Human Rights and Humanitarian Norms as Customary Law* (Oxford: Clarendon, 1989).

———. "The Martens Clause, Principles of Humanity, and Dictates of Public Conscience" (2000) 94 *American Journal of International Law*, 1.

Middlebrook, Martin. *The First Day on the Somme: 1 July 1916* (London: Penguin Books, 1984).

Milanović, Marko. "Norm Conflicts, International Humanitarian Law and Human Rights Law," in O. Ben-Naftali (ed.), *Human Rights and International Humanitarian Law: Collected Courses of the Academy of European Law*, vol. 19/1 (Oxford University Press, 2010).

Mill, John. "On the Liberty of Thought and Discussion," in *The Basic Writings of John Stuart Mill* (New York: Modern Library, 2002) 17–56.

Mitchell, Bruce (ed.). *The Battle of Maldon and Other Old English Poems* (London: Macmillan, 1974).

Mizokami, Kyle. "Gremlin Drone's First Flight Turns C-130 into a Flying Aircraft Carrier," *Popular Mechanics*, 21 January 2020, and DARPA, "Gremlins: Airborne Launch and Recovery of Unmanned Aerial Vehicles," https://www.popularmechanics.com/military/aviation/a30612943/gremlin-drone-first-flight/.

Morse, Stephen. "Law, Responsibility and the Sciences of the Brain/Mind," in *The Oxford Handbook of Law, Regulation and Technology*, R. Brownsword, E. Scotford and K. Yeung (Oxford University Press, 2017).

Moxley Sorrel, General G. *Recollections of a Confederate Staff Officer* (New York: Neale, 1905).

Nasu, Hitoshi. "Nanotechnology and the Future of the Law of Weaponry" (2015) 91 *International Law Studies*, 487–516.

"New Concept for Air Warfare, DARPA, Advancing System-of-Systems Open Architectures for Airborne Assets," *AUVSI News*, 31 March 2015, http://www.auvsi.org/blogs/auvsi-news/2015/03/31/darpasos.

Newton, Michael. "Back to the Future: Reflections on the Advent of Autonomous Weapon Systems" (2015) 47 *Case Western Reserve Journal of International Law*, 1, 5–23.

Nye, Harry. "Dr. Will Roper on AI and Autonomy in the US Air Force," *Air Force Technology*, 3 December 2019, https://www.airforce-technology.com/features/dr-will-roper-on-ai-and-autonomy-in-the-us-air-force/.

Oeter, Stefan. "Methods and Means of Combat," in D. Fleck (ed.), *The Handbook of International Humanitarian Law* (Oxford University Press, 2009), pp. 115–30.

Parks, William H. "Conventional Weapons and Weapons Reviews" (2005) 8 *Yearbook of International Humanitarian Law*, 55–142.

———. "Part IX of the ICRC 'Direct Participation in Hostilities' Study: No Mandate, No Expertise, and Legally Incorrect" (2010) 42 *International Law and Politics*, 769.

Perrow Charles. *Normal Accidents: Living with High Risk Technologies* (Princeton University Press, 1999).

Pico della Mirandola, Giovanni. *Oration on the Dignity of Man* (1486), A. Robert Caponigri (trans.) (Chicago: Henry Regnery, 1956).

Prendergast, David. "The Constitutionality of Strict Liability in Criminal Law" (2011) 33 *Dublin University Law Journal*, 285–318.

Raboin, Eric, et al. "Model-Predictive Asset Guarding by Team of Autonomous Surface Vehicles in Environment with Civilian Boats" (2015) 38 *Autonomous Robot*, 3, 261–82.

Ratner Stephen, and Jason Abrams. *Accountability for Human Rights Atrocities in International Law: Beyond the Nuremberg Legacy*, 2nd ed. (Oxford University Press, 2001).

Riza, Shane. *Killing Without Heart: Limits on Robotic Warfare in an Age of Persistent Conflict* (Washington, D.C.: Potomac Books, 2013).

Roberts, Adam, and Richard Guelff. *Documents on the Law of War*, 3rd ed. (Oxford University Press, 2000).

Roberts, Athena. "Traditional and Modern Approaches to Customary International Law: A Reconciliation" (2001) 95 *American Journal of International Law*, 757–93.

Rogers, Anthony. *Law on the Battlefield*, 2nd ed. (Manchester University Press, 2004).

Roht-Arriza, Naomi. "Introduction," in N. Roht-Arriza (ed.), *Impunity and Human Rights in International Law and Practice* (Oxford University Press, 1995).

Roland, Alex. "Technology and War: A Bibliographic Essay," in M. Roe Smith (ed.), *Military Enterprise and Technological Change: Perspectives on the American Experience* (Cambridge, Mass.: MIT Press, 1985), pp. 347–79.

Rosen, Michael. *Dignity: Its History and Meaning* (Cambridge, Mass.: Harvard University Press, 2012).

Rosenberg, Matthew, and John Markoff. "At Heart of U.S. Strategy, Weapons That Can Think," *New York Times*, 26 October 2016, https://www.nytimes.com/2016/10/26/us/pentagon-artificial-intelligence-terminator.html.

Roucounas Emmanuel. "Non-State Actors: Areas of International Responsibility in Need of Further Exploration," in M. Ragazzi (ed.), *International Responsibility Today: Essays in Memory of Oscar Schachter* (Leiden: Martinus Nijhoff, 2005), pp. 391–404.

Rousseau, Jean-Jacques. *The Social Contract* (1762), G. D. H. Cole (trans.), http://www.ucc.ie/archive/hdsp/Rousseau_contrat-social.pdf.

Salako, Solomon. "Strict Criminal Liability: A Violation of the Convention?" (2006) 70 *Journal of Criminal Law*, 531–49.

Sands, Philippe. *Principles of International Environmental Law* (Cambridge University Press, 2012).

Sassóli, Marco. "Autonomous Weapons and International Humanitarian Law: Advantages, Open Technical Questions and Legal Issues to Be Clarified" (2014) 90 *International Law Studies*, 308–40.

Saxon, Dan. "A Human Touch: Autonomous Weapons, DOD Directive 3000.09 and the Interpretation of 'Appropriate Levels of Human Judgment over the Use of Force,'" in N. Bhuta et al. (eds.), *Autonomous Weapons Systems—Law, Ethics, Policy* (Cambridge University Press, 2016).

———. "The International Criminal Court and the Prevention of Crimes," in S. Sharma and J. Welsh (eds.), *The Responsibility to Protect: Overcoming the Challenges to Atrocity Prevention* (Oxford University Press, 2015), pp. 122–46.

Schabas, William. *An Introduction to the International Criminal Court*, 4th ed. (Cambridge University Press, 2011).

———. "The Right to Life," in A. Clapham et al. (eds), *The Oxford Handbook of International Law in Armed Conflict* (Oxford University Press, 2014).

Schachter, Oscar. Excerpt from "Human Dignity as a Normative Concept," 77 *American Journal of International Law*, 848 (1983), in H. Steiner et al. (eds.), *International Human Rights in Context: Law, Politics, Morals*, 2nd ed. (Oxford University Press, 1996), p. 401.

Scharre, Paul. *Army of None: Autonomous Weapons and the Future of War* (New York: W. W. Norton, 2018).

Schmahl, Stephanie. "An Example of Jus Cogens: The Status of Prisoners of War," in C. Tomuschat and J. M. Thouvenin (eds.), *The Fundamental Rules of the International Legal Order: Jus Cogens and Obligations Erga Omnes* (Leiden: Martinus Nijhoff, 2005), pp. 41–68.

Schmitt, Michael. "The Interpretive Guidance on the Notion of Direct Participation in Hostilities: A Critical Analysis" (May 2010) 1 *Harvard National Security Journal*, 5–44.

———. "Rewired Warfare: Rethinking the Law of Cyber Attack" (2014) 96 *International Review of the Red Cross*, 893, 189–206.

Schmitt, Michael, and Thurnher, Jeffrey. "Autonomous Weapon Systems and LOAC" (2013) 4 *Harvard National Security Journal*, 231–81.

———. "Out of the Loop: Autonomous Weapon Systems and the Law of Armed Conflict" (2013) 4 *Harvard National Security Journal* 231–81.

Schrijver, Nico, and Larissa van den Herik. "Leiden Policy Recommendations on Counter-Terrorism and International Law" (2010) *Grotius Centre for International Legal Studies*, 706–26.

Scovazzi, Tullio. "Some Remarks on International Responsibility in the Field of Environmental Protection," in M. Ragazzi, *International Responsibility Today: Essays in Memory of Oscar Schachter* (Leiden: Martinus Nijhoff, 2005), pp. 209–22.

Seabrook John. "The Next Word: Where Will Predictive Text Take Us?" *New Yorker*, 14 October 2019, https://www.newyorker.com/magazine/2019/10/14/can-a-machine-learn-to-write-for-the-new-yorker.

Sebald, Winfred G. *On the Natural History of Destruction* (London: Hamish Hamilton, 2003).

Sen, Amartya. *The Idea of Justice* (London: Penguin, 2010).

Shelton Dinah. "Private Violence, Public Wrongs, and the Responsibility of States" (1989–90) 13 *Fordham International Law Journal*, 1–34.

Sheridan, Thomas B., et al. "Adapting Automation to Man, Culture and Society" (November 1983) 19 *Automatica*, 6, 605–12.

Shultziner, Doran, and Guy Carmi. "Human Dignity in National Constitutions: Functions, Promises and Dangers." Draft article in author's possession.

Sierra Palencia, Paula. "Por Quinta Vez, Se Abre el Debate de la Eutanasia en el Congreso" (For the fifth time, debate about euthanasia begins in Congress), *El Heraldo*, 9 November 2014, http://www.elheraldo.co/nacional/por-quinta-vez-se-abre-el-debate-de-la-eutanasia-en-el-congreso-173293.

Simma Bruno. "The Responsibility of Individuals for Human Rights Abuses in Internal Conflicts: A Positivist View" (1999) 93 *American Journal of International Law*, 302–16.

Simma, Bruno, and Alston, Philip. "The Sources of Human Rights Law: Custom, Jus Cogens, and General Principles" (1988–89) 12 *Australian Yearbook of International Law*, 82–108.

Simon, Herbert. *Reason in Human Affairs* (Stanford University Press, 1983).

Singer, Peter W. *Wired for War: The Robotics Revolution and Conflict in the 21st Century* (New York: Penguin, 2009).

Smith, Adam. *The Theory of Moral Sentiments* (1759), Knud Haakonssen (ed.) (Cambridge University Press, 2004).

Sohm, Stefan. "Obligations Under International Law Prior to the Use of Military Force: Current Developments Relating to the Legal Review of New Weapons and Methods of Warfare" (2015) 28 *Journal of International Law of Peace and Armed Conflict*, 104–10, presented to Meeting on Lethal Autonomous Weapon Systems, Convention on Certain Conventional Weapons, Geneva, 11–15 April 2016.

"South African Court to Hear Landmark Assisted Suicide Case," BBC NEWS, 2 June 2015, http://www.bbc.com/news/world-africa-32970801.

Sparrow, Robert. "Twenty Seconds to Comply: Autonomous Weapon Systems and the Recognition of Surrender" (2015) 91 *International Law Studies*, 699, 699–728.

"Spy Plane Causes Air Traffic Chaos," BBC NEWS, 6 May 2014, http://www.bbc.com/news/technology-27292440.

Srinivasan, Amia. "Busy Bodies: What Termites Are Teaching Us," *New Yorker*, 17 September 2018, 26–31.

Steiner, Henry, and Alston, Philip. *International Human Rights in Context*, 2nd ed. (Oxford University Press, 2000).

Stewart, Darren. "Maximising Compliance with IHL and the Utility of Data in an Age of Unlimited Information: Operational Issues," in D. Saxon (ed.), *International Humanitarian Law and the Changing Technology of War* (Leiden: Martinus Nijhoff, 2013), pp. 171–86.

Stone, Julius. *The Province and Function of Law* (Sydney: Associated General Publications, 1946).

Tadd, Winfred. "Clarifying the Concept of Human Dignity in the Care of the Elderly: A Dialogue Between Empirical and Philosophical Approaches" (2010) 17 *Ethical Perspectives*, 1, 253–81.

Talmon, Stefan. "Determining Customary International Law: The ICJ's Methodology Between Induction, Deduction and Assertion" (2015) 26 *European Journal of International Law* 2, 417–43.

———. "The Duty Not to "Recognize as Lawful" a Situation Created by the Illegal Use of Force or Other Serious Breaches of a Jus Cogens Obligation: An Obligation Without Real Substance?" in C. Tomuschat and J. M. Thouvenin (eds.), *The Fundamental Rules of the International Legal Order: Jus Cogens and Obligations Erga Omnes* (Leiden: Martinus Nijhoff, 2006), pp. 99–126.

Tams, Christian. "The Use of Force Against Terrorists" (2009) 20 *European Journal of International Law*, 2, 359–97.

Tomuschat, Christian. *Human Rights: Between Idealism and Realism* (Oxford University Press, 2014).

Trapp, Kimberly. "Great Resources Mean Great Responsibility: A Framework of Analysis for Assessing Compliance with API Obligations in the Information Age," in D. Saxon (ed.), *International Humanitarian Law and the Changing Technology of War* (Leiden: Martinus Nijhoff, 2013), pp. 153–70.

Tucker, Patrick. "Inside the Navy's Secret Swarm Robot Experiment," *Defence One*, 5 October 2014, http://www.defenseone.com/technology/2014/10/inside-navys-secret-swarm-robot-experiment/95813/.

U.S. Air Force 2030 Science and Technology Strategy, https://www.airforcemag.com/PDF/DocumentFile/Documents/2019/USAF%20Science%20and%20Technology%20Strategy.pdf.

Voyiakis, Emmanuel. "Do General Principles Fill 'Gaps' in International Law?" in G. Loibl and S. Wittich (eds.), *Austrian Review of International European Law*, vol. 14 (2009) (Leiden: Martinus Nijhoff, 2013), pp. 239–56.

Wagner, Markus. "Autonomy in the Battlespace: Independently Operating Weapon Systems and the Law of Armed Conflict," in D. Saxon (ed.), *International Humanitarian Law and the Changing Technology of War* (Leiden: Martinus Nijhoff, 2013), pp. 99–122.

Waldron, Jeremy. *Dignity, Rank and Rights* (Oxford University Press, 2012).

———. *The Harm in Hate Speech* (Cambridge, Mass.: Harvard University Press, 2012).

———. "The Rule of International Law" (2006) 30 *Harvard Journal of Law and Public Policy*, 15, 24–25.

Walzer, Michael. *Just and Unjust Wars: A Moral Argument with Historical Illustrations* (New York: Basic Books, 1977).

Watkin, Kenneth. "Opportunity Lost: Organized Armed Groups and the ICRC 'Direct Participation in Hostilities' Interpretive Guidance" (2010) 42 *International Law and Politics*, 641–95.

Waxman, Matthew. "Detention as Targeting: Standards of Certainty and Detention of Suspected Terrorists" (2008) 108 *Columbia Law Review*, 1365–430.

"Weapons from Israel," Maccabean Online, March 2009, http://www.freeman.org/MOL/pages/march2009/weapons-from-israel.php.

Weller, Jac. *Fire and Movement: Bargain-Basement Warfare in the Far East* (New York: Crowell, 1967).

———. *Wellington in India* (London: Longman/Camelot, 1972).

Werle, Gerhard. *Principles of International Criminal Law*, 2nd ed. (The Hague: T. M. C. Asser, 2009).

Werner, Debra. "Drone Swarm: Networks of Small UAVs Offer Big Capabilities," *Defence News*, 12 June 2013, http://www.defensenews.com/article/20130612/C4ISR/306120029/.

White, Lynn, Jr. *Medieval Technology and Social Change* (Oxford: Clarendon, 1962).

Wilamowitz-Moellendorf, Ulrich. *My Recollections: 1848–1914* (London: Chatto and Windus, 1930).

Wilson, J. R. "Interview with Brig. General Gary L. Thomas, U.S. Marine Corps Assistant Deputy Commandant for Aviation," DefenceMediaNetwork, 23 March 2012, http://www.defensemedianetwork.com/stories/interview-with-brig-gen-gary-l-thomas-u-s-marine-corps-assistant-deputy-commandant-for-aviation/3/.

Witt, John. *Lincoln's Code: The Laws of War in American History* (New York: Free Press, 2012).

Wolfrum, Rüdiger. "State Responsibility for Private Actors: An Old Problem of Renewed Relevance," in M. Ragazzi, *International Responsibility Today: Essays in Memory of Oscar Schachter* (Leiden: Martinus Nijhoff, 2005), pp. 423–34.

Wright, Jason. "'Excessive' Ambiguity: Analysing and Refining the Proportionality Standard" (Summer 2012) 94 *International Review of the Red Cross*, 886, 819–54.

Wright, Lord. Foreword, 15 *Digest of Laws and Cases, Law Reports of Trials of War Criminals*, xi (United Nations War Crimes Commission, 1948), http://www.loc.gov/rr/frd/Military_Law/pdf/Law-Reports_Vol-15.pdf.

Yearbook of the United Nations (1946–1947), Department of Public Information (Lake Success, N.Y.: United Nations Publications, 1947).

Zegveld, Liesbeth. *The Accountability of Armed Opposition Groups in International Law* (Cambridge University Press, 2002).

Zenne, M. "Death from a Swarm of Tiny Drones," *Daily Mail*, 20 February 2013, http://www.dailymail.co.uk/news/article-2281403/U-S-Air-Force-developing-terrifying-swarms-tiny-unmanned-drones-hover-crawl-kill-targets.html.

Zupan, Dan. "A Presumption of the Moral Equality of Combatants," in *Just and Unjust Warriors: The Moral and Legal Status of Soldiers*, D. Rodin and H. Shue (eds.) (Oxford University Press, 2008).

National Law and Policy

A. National Constitutions

Art. 9, 2009 Constitution of Plurinational State of Bolivia, https://www.constituteproject.org/constitution/Bolivia_2009.pdf.

Art. 1, 1988 Constitution of Brazil (Rev. 2014), https://www.constituteproject.org/constitution/Brazil_2014.pdf.

Art. 1, 1991 Constitution of Colombia (Rev. 2005), https://www.constituteproject.org/constitution/Colombia_2005.pdf.
Art. 2, 2011 Constitution of Hungary, https://www.constituteproject.org/constitution/Hungary_2011.pdf.
Art. 22, Constitution of Islamic Republic of Iran, http://www.iranonline.com/iran/iran-info/government/constitution-3.html.
Art. 10, Constitution of Kenya (Revised 2010), https://www.kenyaembassy.com/pdfs/The%20Constitution%20of%20Kenya.pdf.
Art. 54, Constitution of Kenya (Revised 2010), http://www.lcil.cam.ac.uk/sites/default/files/LCIL/documents/transitions/Kenya_19_2010_Constitution.pdf.
Art. 57, Constitution of Kenya (Revised 2010), http://www.lcil.cam.ac.uk/sites/default/files/LCIL/documents/transitions/Kenya_19_2010_Constitution.pdf.
Preamble, Constitution of India, http://lawmin.nic.in/olwing/coi/coi-english/Const.Pock%202Pg.Rom8Fsss(3).pdf.
Art. 5, 1852 Constitution of New Zealand (with revisions through 2014), https://www.constituteproject.org/constitution/New_Zealand_2014.pdf?lang=en.
Art. 34, Constitution of the Federal Republic of Nigeria, http://www.nigeria-law.org/ConstitutionOfTheFederalRepublicOfNigeria.htm#Chapter_4.
Art. 1, 1992 Constitution of Paraguay (Rev. 2011), https://www.constituteproject.org/constitution/Paraguay_2011.pdf?lang=en.
Constitution of the Republic of South Africa Act 200 of 1993, Chapter 2 (5), http://www.gov.za/documents/constitution/constitution-republic-south-africa-act-200-1993#Citizenship and Franchise.
Art. 32, 1948 Constitution of South Korea, https://www.icrc.org/ihl-nat.nsf/162d151af444ded44125673e00508141/aba339f342ad7493c1256bc8004c2772/$file/constitution%20–%20korea%20–%20en.pdf.
Art. 7, Constitution of Switzerland, http://www.legislationline.org/documents/section/constitutions.

B. National Legislation

Argentina, Codigo Electoral Nacional, Ley No. 19,495, capítulo 1, "Deber a Votar," artículo 12, http://infoleg.mecon.gov.ar/infolegInternet/anexos/15000-19999/19442/texact.htm.
Australia, Commonwealth Electoral Act 1918—Sect 245 (1), "Compulsory Voting," http://www.austlii.edu.au/au/legis/cth/consol_act/cea1918233/s245.html.
Belgium, The Belgian Act on Euthanasia of 28 May 2002, http://www.ethical-perspectives.be/viewpic.php?LAN=E&TABLE=EP&ID=59.
Germany, Art. 1, Bundesministerium der Justiz, "Basic Law for the Federal Republic of Germany in the Revised Version Published in the Federal Law Gazette Part III," classification no. 100-1, as amended by the Act of 21st July 2010 (Federal Law Gazette I), 944, http://www.gesetze-im-internet.de/englisch_gg/englisch_gg.html#p0014.
Luxembourg, Luxembourg Law of 16 March 2009 on Euthanasia and Assisted Suicide, http://www.luxembourg.public.lu/en/vivre/famille/fin-vie/euthanasie-soinspalliatifs/index.html.
Kosovo, Draft Law on the Kosovo Specialist Chambers (English), https://www.docdroid.net/14op8/draft-law-on-the-specialist-chambers-eng.pdf.html.
The Netherlands, "Netherlands Termination of Life on Request and Assisted Suicide (Review Procedures)" (2002), https://www.government.nl/topics/euthanasia/contents/euthanasia-assisted-suicide-and-non-resuscitation-on-request.

Peru, Ley Orgánica de Elecciones, “Ejercício del Derecho al Voto,” artículo 7, http://pdba.georgetown.edu/Electoral/Peru/leyelecciones.pdf.

Switzerland, Article 115, Swiss Criminal Code, https://www.admin.ch/opc/en/classified-compilation/19370083/201501010000/311.0.pdf.

United Kingdom, “Equal Franchise Act 1928,” http://www.parliament.uk/about/living-heritage/transformingsociety/electionsvoting/womenvote/parliamentary-collectionsdelete/equal-franchise-act-1928/.

United States, Bill of Rights attached to the Constitution, https://www.law.cornell.edu/constitution/overview.

———. *Torture Victim Protection Act of 1991*, H.R. 2092, http://thomas.loc.gov/cgi-bin/query/z?c102:H.R.2092.ENR.

———. Nineteenth Amendment to Constitution of the United States, https://www.congress.gov/constitution-annotated.

Uruguay, Article 17, Codigo Penal de Uruguay, https://en.wikipedia.org/wiki/Assisted_suicide#cite_note-McDougall_2008–20.

C. Government Statements of Policy and Law

Australia, “Operations Series, ADDP 3.14,” *Targeting*, 2nd ed. Australia Department of Defence, 2009, para. 1.21, http://www.defence.gov.au/foi/docs/disclosures/021_1112_Document_ADDP_3_14_Targeting.pdf.

European Union, Pilot Project EUROSWARM and SPIDER Completed,” *European Defense Agency*, 23 February 2018, https://www.eda.europa.eu/info-hub/press-centre/latest-news/2018/02/23/pilot-project-euroswarm-and-spider-activities-completed.

North Atlantic Treaty Organization, “General Petraeus Issues Updated Tactical Directive: Emphasizes ‘Disciplined Use of Force,’” ISAF News List, 2010-08-CA-004, 4 August 2010, http://www.isaf.nato.int/article/isaf-releases/general-petraeus-issues-updated-tactical-directive-emphasizes-disciplined-use-of-force.html.

United Kingdom, “Campaign Execution,” *Joint Doctrine Publication 3-00*, 3rd ed., U.K. Ministry of Defence, October 2009, 2.

———. *JSP 383: The Joint Service Manual of the Law of Armed Conflict*, U.K. Ministry of Defence, 2004, https://www.gov.uk/government/publications/jsp-383-the-joint-service-manual-of-the-law-of-armed-conflict-2004-edition.

———. “Operations,” Army Doctrine Publications U.K. Ministry of Defence, 2010, https://www.gov.uk/government/uploads/system/uploads/attachment_data/file/33695/ADP OperationsDec10.pdf.

———. “The U.K. Approach to Unmanned Aircraft Systems,” *Joint Doctrine Note 2/11*, 30 March 2011, paras. 205–6 and 508, www.gov.uk/government/uploads/system/uploads/attachment_data/file/33711/20110505JDN_211_UAS_v2U.pdf.

United States, Carter, Ashton. “Autonomy in Weapons Systems,” *Department of Defence Directive*, United States of America, Number 3000.09 (21 November 2012).

———. Chairman of U.S. Joint Chiefs of Staff, *Joint Fire Support, Joint Publication 3-09*, 12 December 2014, p. III-8.

———. Chairman, U.S. Joint Chiefs of Staff, *Joint Targeting, Joint Publication 3-60*, 31 January 2013.

———. *Department of Defense Law of War Manual*, Office of General Counsel, U.S. Department of Defense, June 2015, paras. 2.1.1 and 2.1.2, http://www.defense.gov/Portals/1/Documents/pubs/Law-of-War-Manual-June-2015.pdf.

———. "No-Strike and the Collateral Damage Estimation Methodology," CJCSI 3160.01A, *Chairman of the Joint Chiefs of Staff Instruction*, U.S. Department of Defence, 12 October 2012, Enclosure C, p. C-2, n. 7.

———. Summary of the "2018 Department of Defense Artificial Intelligence Strategy: Harnessing AI to Advance Our Security and Prosperity," https://media.defense.gov/2019/Feb/12/2002088963/-1/-1/1/summary-of-dod-ai-strategy.pdf.

———. Summary of the "2018 National Defense Strategy of the United States of America: Sharpening the American Military's Competitive Edge," https://dod.defense.gov/Portals/1/Documents/pubs/2018-National-Defense-Strategy-Summary.pdf.

Jurisprudence (Judgments, Decisions, Etc.)

A. International Courts

1. International Military Tribunal (IMT) at Nuremberg and Related Tribunals

Jackson, Robert. "Presentation of the Case by the Prosecution" (21 November 1945), *The Trial of German Major War Criminals: Proceedings of the International Military Tribunal Sitting at Nuremberg, Germany*, Part 1 (20 November 1945 to 1 December 1945), London, 1946.

Maxwell Fyfe, David. "Speech at the Close of the Case Against the Indicted Organizations" (19 August 1946), in *The Trial of German Major War Criminals: Proceedings of the International Military Tribunal Sitting at Nuremberg, Germany*, 1945–46, London, 1946.

Shawcross, Hartley. "Closing Speech," 27 July 1946, *The Trial of German Major War Criminals, Proceedings of the International Military Tribunal Sitting at Nuremberg, Germany*, part 19, 16 July 1946–27 July 1946. London, His Majesty's Stationery Office, 1949.

Trial of Bruno Tesch and Two Others ("The Zyklon B Case"), Judgment, British Military Court, Hamburg, 1–8 March 1946.

Trial of German Major War Criminals, Judgment, *Proceedings of the International Military Tribunal Sitting at Nuremberg, Germany*, 1 October 1946.

2. Permanent Court of International Justice (PCIJ)

Case of the S.S. Lotus, Judgment, Permanent Court of International Justice, Series A, No. 10, 1927.

Case of the S.S. Wimbledon, Judgment, Permanent Court of International Justice, Series A, No. 01, 1923.

3. International Court of Justice (ICJ)

Accordance with International Law of the Unilateral Declaration of Independence in Respect of Kosovo, Advisory Opinion of 22 July 2010 (Judge Cançado Trindade, Separate Advisory Opinion).

Application of the Convention on the Prevention and Punishment of the Crime of Genocide, Preliminary Objections, Judgment, 1996 (Judge Weeramantry, Separate Opinion).

Application of the Convention on the Prevention and Punishment of the Crime of Genocide (Bosnia and Herzegovina v. Serbia and Montenegro), Judgment of 26 February 2007 (Judge Weeramantry, Separate Opinion).

Armed Activities on the Territory of the Congo (Democratic Republic of the Congo v. Rwanda), New Application (2002), Jurisdiction and Admissibility, Judgment of 3 February 2006.

Armed Activities on the Territory of the Congo (Democratic Republic of the Congo v. Uganda), Judgment, ICJ Reports 2005.

Armed Activities on the Territory of the Congo (Democratic Republic of the Congo v. Uganda), Judgment, ICJ Reports 2005 (Judge Koroma and Judge Tomka, Separate Declarations).

Armed Activities on the Territory of the Congo (New Application: 2002) (Democratic Republic of the Congo v. Uganda).

Barcelona Traction, Light and Power Company, Limited (Belgium v. Spain) (New Application: 1962), Judgment of 5 February 1970, Second Phase (Judge Morelli, Separate Opinion).

Case Concerning Armed Activities on the Republic of the Congo (Democratic Republic of the Congo v. Uganda), Judgment of 19 December 2005.

Corfu Channel Case, Judgment of 9 April 1949 (Judge Alvarez, Separate Opinion).

Gabčikovo-Nagymaros Project (Hungary/Slovakia), Judgment, 1997 (Judge Herczegh and Judge Oda, Dissenting Opinions).

Legal Consequences of the Construction of a Wall in the Occupied Palestinian Territory, Advisory Opinion of 9 July 2004.

Legality of the Threat or Use of Nuclear Weapons, Advisory Opinion of 8 July 1996 (Judge Shahabudeen, Dissenting Opinion).

Legality of the Threat or Use of Nuclear Weapons, Advisory Opinion of 8 July 1996 (Judge Weeramantry, Dissenting Opinion).

Legality of the Threat or Use of Nuclear Weapons, Advisory Opinion of 8 July 1996.

Maritime Dispute (Peru v. Chile), Verbatim Record of 14 December 2012.

Military and Paramilitary Activities in and Against Nicaragua (Nicaragua v. United States of America), Merits, Judgment of 27 June 1986.

North Sea Continental Shelf Cases (Federal Republic of Germany v. Denmark and Federal Republic of Germany v. the Netherlands), Judgment of 20 February 1969.

Pulp Mills on the River Uruguay (Argentina v. Uruguay), Judgment, 2010.

Questions Relating to the Obligation to Prosecute or Extradite (Belgium v. Senegal), Judgment of 20 July 2012.

Reservations to the Convention on Genocide, Advisory Opinion of 28 May 1951 (Judge Alvarez, Dissenting Opinion).

Settlement Agreement, on the Case Concerning the Aerial Incident of 3 July 1988 Before the International Court of Justice.

South West Africa Case (Liberia v. South Africa), Judgment of 18 December 1966, Second Phase (Judge Tanaka, Dissenting Opinion).

South West Africa Case (Liberia v. South Africa), Judgment of 21 December 1962 (Judge Tanaka, Dissenting Opinion).

United States Diplomatic and Consular Staff in Tehran, Judgment, 1980.

4. Permanent International Criminal Court (ICC)

Prosecutor v. Abdallah Banda & Saleh Jerbo, Corrigendum to Decision on Confirmation of Charges, ICC-02/05-03/09, Pre-Trial Chamber I, 7 March 2011.

Prosecutor v. Jean Pierre Bemba Gombo, Decision Pursuant to Article 61 (7) (a) and (b) of the Rome Statute ("Decision on Confirmation of Charges"), ICC 01/05-01/08, 15 June 2009.

Prosecutor v. Laurent Gbagbo, Decision on the Confirmation of Charges Against Laurent Gbagbo, ICC-02/11-01/11, 12 June 2014.

Prosecutor v. Germain Katanga and Mathieu Ngudjolo Chui, Decision on the Confirmation of Charges, ICC-01/04-01/07, 30 September 2008.

Prosecutor v. Thomas Lubanga Dyilo, Judgment on the Appeal of Mr. Thomas Lubanga Dyilo Against the Decision on the Defence Challenge to the Jurisdiction of the Court Pursuant to Article 19 (2) (a) of the Statute of 3 October 2006, ICC-01/04-01/06 (OA4), 14 December 2006.

Prosecutor v. Thomas Lubanga Dyilo, Judgment Pursuant to Article 74 of the Statute, ICC-01/04-01/06, 14 March 2012.

5. International Criminal Tribunal for the Former Yugoslavia (ICTY)

Final Report to the Prosecutor (of the ICTY) by the Committee Established to Review the NATO Bombing Campaign Against the Federal Republic of Yugoslavia (2000).

Prosecutor v. Zlatko Aleksovski, Judgment, IT-95-14/1-A, Appeals Chamber, 24 March 2000.

Prosecutor v. Zlatko Aleksovski, Judgment, IT-95-14/1-T, 25 June 1999.

Prosecutor v. Tihomir Blaškić, Judgment, IT-95-14-A, 29 July 2004.

Prosecutor v. Ljube Boškoski & Johan Tarčulovski, Judgment, IT-04-82-T, 10 July 2008.

Prosecutor v. Ljube Boškoski & Johan Tarčulovski, Judgment, IT-04-02-A, Appeals Chamber, 19 May 2010.

Prosecutor v. Radoslav Brđanin, Judgment, IT-99-36-T, 1 September 2004.

Prosecutor v. Radoslav Brđanin, Judgment, IT-99-37-A, Appeals Chamber, 3 April 2007.

Prosecutor v. Zejnil Delalić, Judgment, IT-96-21-A, 20 February 2001.

Prosecutor v. Zejnil Delalić, et al., Judgment, No. IT-96-21-T, 16 November 1998.

Prosecutor v. Dražen Erdemović, Sentencing Judgment, Joint Separate Opinion of Judge McDonald and Judge Vohrah, IT-96-22-A, Appeals Chamber, 7 October 1997.

Prosecutor v. Anto Furundija, Judgment, IT-95-17/1-T, 10 December 1998.

Prosecutor v. Stanislav Galić, Judgment, IT-98-29-A, 30 November 2006.

Prosecutor v. Enver Hadžihasanović & Amir Kubura, Decision on Joint Challenge to Jurisdiction, IT-01-47-PT, 12 November 2002.

Prosecutor v. Enver Hadžihasanović & Amir Kubura, Judgment, IT-01-47-T, 15 March 2006.

Prosecutor v. Sefer Halilović, Judgment, IT-01-48-T, 16 November 2005.

Prosecutor v. Momčilo Krajišnik, Judgment, IT-00-39-A, Appeals Chamber, 17 March 2009.

Prosecutor v. Dragoljub Kunarac, Judgment, IT-96-23-T & IT-96-23/1-T, 22 February 2001.

Prosecutor v. Zoran Kupreškić, Judgment, IT-95-16-T, 14 January 2000.

Prosecutor v. Miroslav Kvočka et al., Judgment, IT-98-30/T, 2 November 2001.

Prosecutor v. Miroslav Kvočka, et al., Judgment, IT-98-30/1-A, Appeals Chamber, 28 February 2007, para. 97.

Prosecutor v. Fatmir Limaj, Judgment, IT-03-66-T, 30 November 2005.

Prosecutor v. Milan Milutinović, et al., Judgment, IT-05-87-T, 26 February 2009.

Prosecutor v. Mladen Naletilić, a.k.a. "Tuta" & Vinko Martinović, a.k.a. "Štela," Judgment, IT-98-34-A, Appeals Chamber, 3 May 2006.

Prosecutor v. Dragan Obrenović, Sentencing Judgment, IT-02-60/2-S, 10 December 2003.

Prosecutor v. Momčilo Perisić, Judgment, IT-04-81-A, Appeals Chamber, 28 February 2013.

Prosecutor v. Vujadin Popović, et al., Judgment, IT-85-88-T, 10 June 2010.

Prosecutor v. Vujadin Popović, et al., Judgment, IT-05-88-A, Appeals Chamber, 30 January 2015.

Prosecutor v. Nikola Šainović *et al.*, Judgment IT-05-87-A, Appeals Chamber, 23 January 2014.

Prosecutor v. Blagoje Simić et al., Decision on the Prosecution Motion Under Rule 73 for a Ruling Concerning the Testimony of a Witness, IT-95-9, 27 July 1999.

Prosecutor v. Milomir Stakić, Judgment, IT-97-24-T, 31 July 2003.
Prosecutor v. Jovica Stanišič & Franko Simatović, Judgment, IT-03-69/A, 9 December 2015.
Prosecutor v. Pavle Strugar, Judgment, IT-01-42-A, 17 July 2008.
Prosecutor v. Duško Tadić a/k/a "Dule," Decision on Defence Motion for Interlocutory Appeal on Jurisdiction, IT-94-1, 2 October 1995.
Prosecutor v. Duško Tadić a/k/a "Dule," Judgment, IT-94-1-T, 7 Trial Chamber, May 1997.
Prosecutor v. Duško Tadić a/k/a "Dule," Judgment, IT-94-1-A, Appeals Chamber, 15 July 1999.

6. International Criminal Tribunal for Rwanda (ICTR)

Prosecutor v. Jean-Paul Akayesu, Judgment, ICTR-96-4-T, 2 September 1998.
Prosecutor v. Ferdinand Nahimana, et al., Judgment, ICTR-99-52-T, 3 December 2003.
Prosecutor v. Ferdinand Nahimana, et al., Judgment, Appeals Chamber, ICTR-99-52-A, 28 November 2007.

7. European Court of Human Rights (ECtHR)

Case of Akpınar & Altun v. Turkey, Judgment, 1 March 2007.
Case of Al-Jedda v. the United Kingdom, Judgment, 7 July 2011.
Case of Bosphorous Hava Yollari Turizm Ve Ticaret Anonim Şirketi *v. Ireland*, Judgment, 30 June 2005.
Case of Christine Goodwin v. the United Kingdom, Judgment, 11 July 2002.
Case of Di Sarno and Others v. Italy, Application No. 30765/08, 10 April 2012.
Case of Finogenov and Others v. Russia, Judgment, 20 December 2011.
Case of Giacomelli v. Italy, Judgment, Application, No. 59909/00, 26 March 2007.
Case of Hassan v. the United Kingdom, Judgment, 16 September 2014.
Case of Hassan v. the United Kingdom, Partially Dissenting Opinion of Judge Spano, Joined by Judges Nicolaou, Bianku and Kalaydjieva, 16 September 2014.
Case of Husayn (Abu Zubaydah) v. Poland, Judgment, 24 July 2014.
Case of Isayeva v. Russia, Judgment, 24 February 2005.
Case of Khaled El Masri v. Federal Yugoslav Republic of Macedonia, Judgment, 13 December 2012.
Case of Kuznetsov v. Ukraine, Judgment, 29 April 2003.
Case of Lambert and Others v. France, Joint Partly Dissenting Opinion of Judges Hajiyev, Šikuta, Tsotsoria, De Gaetano and Gritco, 29 April 2002.
Case of Lambert and Others v. France, Judgment, 29 April 2002.
Case of Makaratzis v. Greece, Judgment, 20 December 2004.
Case of McCann and Others v. the United Kingdom, Judgment, 27 September 1995.
Case of M.S.S. v. Belgium and Greece, Judgment, 21 January 2011.
Case of Nachova and Others v. Bulgaria, Judgment, 26 February 2004.
Case of Pretty v. United Kingdom, Judgment, 29 July 2002.
Case of Putintseva v. Russia, Judgment, 10 August 2012.
Case of Tatar v. Romania, Judgment, 27 January 2009.

8. Inter-American Court of Human Rights

Case No. 10.506, Ms. X v. Argentina, Judgment of 15 October 1996.
Case of Bámaca Velásquez v. Guatemala, Judgment of 25 November 2000.
Case of Goiburú et al. v. Paraguay, Judgment, Inter-American Court of Human Rights, 22 September 2006.

Case of Juan Humberto Sánchez v. Honduras, Judgment of 7 June 2003.
(Case of) Kaliña and Lokono Peoples v. Surinam, Judgment, 25 November 2015.
Case of Maritza Urrutia Garcia v. Guatemala, Judgment, 27 November 2003.
(Case of) Maya Indigenous Communities of the Toledo District v. Belize, Report No. 40/04, 12 October 2004.
Case of the Mayagna (Sumo) Awas Tingni Community v. Nicaragua, Judgment of 31 August 2001.
Case of Myrna Mack Chang v. Guatemala, Judgment of 25 November 2004.
Case of Velasquez Rodriguez v. Honduras, Judgment of 29 July 1998.
The Massacres of El Mozote and Nearby Places v. El Salvador, Judgment of 25 October 2012.

9. African Commission of Human Rights

Social and Economic Rights Action Center (SERAC) and Center for Economic and Social Rights (CESR) / v. Nigeria, 155/96, African Commission on Human Rights, 27 October 2001, http://www.achpr.org/files/sessions/30th/comunications/155.96/achpr30_155_96_eng.pdf.

10. International Tribunal for the Law of the Sea

Responsibilities and Obligations of States with Respect to Activities in the Area, Advisory Opinion, 1 February 2011.
Southern Bluefin Tuna Cases (New Zealand v. Japan; Australia v. Japan), Separate Opinion of Judge Treves, ITLOS, Order of 27 August 1999.

11. International Arbitration Awards

Alabama Claims of the United States of America Against Great Britain, Award Rendered on 14 September 1872 by the Tribunal of Arbitration Established by Article I of the Treaty of Washington of 8 May 1871, http://legal.un.org/riaa/cases/vol_XXIX/125-134.pdf.
Award in the Arbitration Regarding the Iron Rhine ("Ijzeren Rijn") Railway Between the Kingdom of Belgium and the Kingdom of the Netherlands, Decision of 24 May 2005, http://legal.un.org/riaa/cases/vol_XXVII/35-125.pdf.

B. National Courts

1. Canada

Carter v. Canada (Attorney General), 2015 SCC 5, [2015], https://scc-csc.lexum.com/scc-csc/scc-csc/en/item/14637/index.do.
R v. Finta, [1994] (Supreme Court of Canada) 1 SCR 701, at 760.
R v. Morgentaler, [1988] 1 SCR 30, 164, http://scc-csc.lexum.com/scc-csc/scc-csc/en/item/288/index.do.

2. Germany

Judgment of the First Senate of 15 February 2006, 1 BvR 357/05, http://www.bundesverfassungsgericht.de/entscheidungen/rs20060215_1bvr035705en.html.

3. Israel

Adalah v. Minister of Defence, HCJ 8276/05 [2006] (2) IsrLR 352, Judgment, President (Emeritus) A. Barak, http://www.hamoked.org/files/2010/8299_eng.pdf.

Physicians for Human Rights v. IDF Commanders, HCJ 4764/04 [2004] IsrL 200, Judgment, Opinion of President A. Barak, http://elyon1.court.gov.il/Files_ENG/04/640/047/A03/04047640.a03.pdf.

Physicians for Human Rights v. IDF Commander, Separate Opinion of Justice D. Beinisch, HCJ 4764/04 [2004] IsrL 200, http://elyon1.court.gov.il/Files_ENG/04/640/047/A03/04047640.a03.pdf.

The Public Committee Against Torture in Israel v. the Government of Israel, Judgment, HCJ 769/02, Opinion of President (Emeritus) A. Barak, 11 December 2005.

The Public Committee Against Torture in Israel v. the Government of Israel, Judgment, HCJ 769/02, Separate Opinion of President D. Beinisch, 11 December 2005.

The Targeted Killing Case, Judgment, Supreme Court of Israel, President A. Barak, 11 December 2005.

4. The Netherlands

Criminal Proceedings Against Frans van Anraat, Judgment, Court of Appeal, ECLI:NL:GHS-GR:2007:BA6734, 8 June 2007, http://uitspraken.rechtspraak.nl/inziendocument?id=ECLI:NL:GHSGR:2007:BA6734.

5. South Africa

Dawood v. Minister of Home Affairs, Case CCT 35/99, Constitutional Court of South Africa, 7 June 2000.

The Minister of Home Affairs v. Watchenuka, Case No. 10/2003, Supreme Court of Appeal of South Africa, 28 November 2003.

National Coalition for Gay and Lesbian Equality v. Minister of Home Affairs, Case CCT 10/99, Constitutional Court of South Africa, 2 December 1999.

S. v. Makwanyane, Case No. CCT/3/94, Constitutional Court of South Africa, 6 June 1995.

S. v. Williams and Others, Judgment (CCT/20/94), [1995].

6. United Kingdom

Serdar Mohammed v. Ministry of Defence, Judgment, Case No. HQ12X03367, 2 May 2014.

Shaw v. Director of Public Prosecutions, House of Lords (4 May 1961), 7, http://zenithpubliclaw.blogspot.nl/2011/10/dpp-v-shaw-1962.html.

The Queen v. Secretary of State for the Environment, Minister of Agriculture, Fisheries and Food, Ex parte: H. A. Standley and Others Case C-293/97, 29 April 1999.

7. United States of America

Coffin v. United States, 156 U.S. 432 (1895).

Furman v. Georgia, Justice Brennan's concurring opinion, 408 U.S. 238 (1972).

Kiobel v. Royal Dutch Petroleum Co., Justice Breyer's concurring opinion, 569 U.S. 108 (2013).

Kiobel v. Royal Dutch Petroleum Co., Justice Roberts's opinion, 569 U.S. 108 (2013).

Obergefell v. Hodges, 576 U.S. 644 (2015).

The Paquete Habana, 175 US 677 (1900).

Skinner v. Oklahoma ex rel. Williamson, 316 U.S. 535 (1942), Justice Jackson Concurring.

Speiser v. Randall, 357 U.S. 513, 525–26 (1958).

Thirty Hogsheads of Sugar v. Boyle, 13 U.S. 191 (1815).

United States v. Windsor, 579 U.S. 744 (2013).

Wesberry v. Sander, 376 U.S. 1 (1964).

Whitney v. California, 274 U.S. 357 (1927), Justice Brandeis Concurring.
Winship, 397 U.S. 358 (1970).

International Instruments and Their Commentaries

A. Treaties and Covenants

Agreement Between the United Nations and the Royal Government of Cambodia Concerning the Prosecution Under Cambodian Law of Crimes Committed During the Period of Democratic Kampuchea, http://www.eccc.gov.kh/sites/default/files/legaldocuments/Agreement_between_UN_and_RGC.pdf.

Article 5 American Convention on Human Rights (ACHR), "Pact of San Jose, Costa Rica," http://www.oas.org/dil/treaties_B-32_American_Convention_on_Human_Rights.htm.

Article 5 (2), The Arms Trade Treaty (2013), https://unoda-web.s3.amazonaws.com/wp-content/uploads/2013/06/English7.pdf.

Charter of Fundamental Rights of the European Union, 2000/C 364/01, http://www.europarl.europa.eu/charter/pdf/text_en.pdf.

Charter of the International Military Tribunal (Nuremberg), http://avalon.law.yale.edu/imt/imtconst.asp.

Charter of the International Military Tribunal for the Far East, 19 January 1946, https://www.loc.gov/law/help/us-treaties/bevans/m-ust000004-0020.pdf.

Charter of the United Nations, Done in San Francisco, 26 June 1945, Entered into Force on 24 October 1945, http://www.un.org/en/sections/un-charter/preamble/index.html.

Consolidated Version of the Treaty Establishing the European Community, 25 March 1957, http://www.refworld.org/docid/3ae6b39c0.html.

Convention Against Torture and Other Cruel, Inhuman or Degrading Treatment or Punishment, 10 December 1984, http://www.ohchr.org/EN/ProfessionalInterest/Pages/CAT.aspx.

Convention on the Prevention and Punishment of the Crime of Genocide Adopted by the General Assembly of the United Nations on 9 December 1948, https://treaties.un.org/doc/Publication/UNTS/Volume%2078/volume-78-I-1021-English.pdf.

Convention on the Rights of Persons with Disabilities and Optional Protocol, 13 December 2006, A/RES/61/106, http://www.un.org/disabilities/default.asp?id=150.

"Elements of Crimes," International Criminal Court, 2011, http://www.icc-cpi.int/NR/rdonlyres/336923D8-A6AD-40EC-AD7B-45BF9DE73D56/0/ElementsOfCrimesEng.pdf.

European Convention for the Protection of Human Rights and Fundamental Freedoms and Its Fourteen Additional Protocols, http://www.echr.coe.int/Documents/Convention_ENG.pdf.

"Framework Agreement on Cooperation in the Field of Immigration Between the Kingdom of Spain and the Republic of Mali," Done in Madrid, 23 January 2007.

The Laws of War on Land, Done in Oxford, 9 September 1880.

https://www.icrc.org/applic/ihl/ihl.nsf/ART/140-80005?OpenDocument.

London Agreement of 8 August 1945, http://www.icls.de/dokumente/imt_london_agreement.pdf.

"Maipú Treaty for Integration and Cooperation Between the Argentine Republic and the Republic of Chile," Done in Buenos Aires, 15 June 2007.

Multilateral International Convention on Oil Pollution Preparedness, Response and Cooperation, No. 32194, Concluded at London on 30 November 1990, https://treaties.un.org/doc/Publication/UNTS/Volume%201891/volume-1891-I-32194-English.pdf.

Protocol on Environmental Protection to the Antarctic Treaty: Liability Arising from Environmental Emergencies (1991), http://www.ats.aq/documents/recatt/Att249_e.pdf.

Protocol for the Prohibition of the Use of Asphyxiating, Poisonous or Other Gases, and of Bacteriological Methods of Warfare, Geneva, 17 June 1925, https://www.icrc.org/ihl/INTRO/280?OpenDocument.

Slave Trade, *Treaty of Paris* (1815), http://napoleononline.ca/wp-content/uploads/2011/03/Treaty-of-Paris-1815.pdf.

Statute of the International Criminal Court, Done at Rome 17 July 1998, https://www.icc-cpi.int/NR/rdonlyres/ADD16852-AEE9-4757-ABE7-9CDC7CF02886/283503/RomeStatutEng1.pdf.

Statute of the International Court of Justice, http://www.icj-cij.org/documents/?p1=4&p2=2.

Statute of the River Uruguay (Uruguay and Argentina), Signed at Salto on 26 February 1975, http://www.internationalwaterlaw.org/documents/regionaldocs/Uruguay_River_Statute_1975.pdf.

Stockholm Convention on Persistent Organic Pollutants, 22 May 2001.

"Treaty Between Romania and the Italian Republic on Friendship and Collaboration," Done in Bucharest, 23 July 1991.

"Treaty Concerning Friendly Cooperation and Partnership in Europe Between Romania and the Federal Republic of Germany," Done in Bucharest, 21 April 1992.

"Treaty of Peace and Amity Between His Britannic Majesty and the United States of America," 1814, http://avalon.law.yale.edu/19th_century/ghent.asp.

Treaty of Westphalia; 24 October 1648: Peace Treaty Between the Holy Roman Emperor and the King of France and their Respective Allies, https://is.muni.cz/el/1423/podzim2008/MVZ430/um/Treaty-of-Westphalia.pdf.

United Nations Convention on the Protection and Use of Transboundary Water Courses and International Lakes, Amended 28 November 2003.

United Nations Framework Convention on Climate Change, 1992, https://unfccc.int/resource/docs/convkp/conveng.pdf.

Versailles Treaty of 28 June 1919, http://avalon.law.yale.edu/imt/partvii.asp.

1. American Convention on the Rights of Man (ACHR)

American Convention on the Rights of Man, 16 December 1966, http://www.ohchr.org/EN/ProfessionalInterest/Pages/cescr.aspx.

2. African Charter

African Charter on Human and Peoples' Rights, http://www.achpr.org/instruments/achpr/.

3. European Convention for the Protection of Human Rights and Fundamental Freedoms (European Convention on Human Rights)

European Convention on Human Rights, http://www.echr.coe.int/Documents/Convention_ENG.pdf.

4. Convention on Prohibitions or Restrictions on the Use of Certain Conventional Weapons Which May Be Deemed to Be Excessively Injurious or to Have Indiscriminate Effects (CCW)

Convention on Prohibitions or Restrictions on the Use of Certain Conventional Weapons Which May Be Deemed to Be Excessively Injurious or to Have Indiscriminate Effects, Protocol on Blinding Laser Weapons, Protocol IV (13 October 1995), http://www.unog

.ch/80256EDD006B8954/(httpAssets)/8463F2782F711A13C12571DE005BCF1A/$file/PROTOCOL+IV.pdf.

Art. 10, Protocol II to Convention on Prohibitions or Restrictions on the Use of Certain Conventional Weapons Which May Be Deemed to Be Excessively Injurious or to Have Indiscriminate Effects.

5. Conventions with Respect to the Laws and Customs of War on Land

The 1899 Hague Convention (II) with Respect to the Laws and Customs of War on Land and Its Annex: Regulations Concerning the Laws and Customs of War on Land, https://www.icrc.org/ihl/INTRO/150?OpenDocument.

The 1907 Convention (IV) Respecting the Laws and Customs of War on Land and its Annex: Regulations Concerning the Laws and Customs of War on Land, 18 October 1907 and Related Declarations, https://www.icrc.org/ihl/INTRO/195.

"General Commentary to 1899 Regulations," ICRC, https://www.icrc.org/ihl/INTRO/150?OpenDocument.

6. The Lieber Code

General Orders No. 100: The Lieber Code, 24 April 1863, http://avalon.law.yale.edu/19th_century/lieber.asp#sec1.

Art. 14, Lieber Code of 24 April 1863.

Art. 16, Lieber Code of 24 April 1863.

Art. 29, Lieber Code of 24 April 1863.

7. Geneva Conventions of 1949

Convention for the Amelioration of the Condition of the Wounded in Armies in the Field, Geneva, 22 August 1864, https://www.icrc.org/ihl/INTRO/120?OpenDocument.

Convention (I) for the Amelioration of the Condition of the Wounded and Sick in Armed Forces in the Field, Geneva, 12 August 1949, https://www.icrc.org/applic/ihl/ihl.nsf/INTRO/365?OpenDocument.

Convention (II) for the Amelioration of the Condition of Wounded, Sick and Shipwrecked Members of Armed Forces at Sea, Geneva, 12 August 1949, https://www.icrc.org/applic/ihl/ihl.nsf/INTRO/370?OpenDocument.

Convention (III) Relative to the Treatment of Prisoners of War, Geneva, 12 August 1949, https://www.icrc.org/applic/ihl/ihl.nsf/INTRO/375?OpenDocument.

Convention (IV) Relative to the Protection of Civilian Persons in Time of War, Geneva, 12 August 1949, https://www.icrc.org/ihl.nsf/INTRO/380.

a. Convention II

ICRC Introduction to *Convention (II) with Respect to the Laws and Customs of War on Land and Its Annex: Regulations Concerning the Laws and Customs of War on Land*, The Hague, 29 July 1899, https://www.icrc.org/ihl/INTRO/150?OpenDocument.

b. Convention III

Art. 3, Geneva Convention Relative to the Treatment of Prisoners of War (Third Geneva Convention), 12 August 1949.

Art. 4, Geneva Convention Relative to the Treatment of Prisoners of War (Third Geneva Convention), 12 August 1949.
Art. 9, Geneva Convention Relative to the Treatment of Prisoners of War (Third Geneva Convention), 12 August 1949.
Art. 10, Geneva Convention Relative to the Treatment of Prisoners of War (Third Geneva Convention), 12 August 1949.
Art. 11, Geneva Convention Relative to the Treatment of Prisoners of War (Third Geneva Convention), 12 August 1949.
Art. 21, Geneva Convention Relative to the Treatment of Prisoners of War (Third Geneva Convention), 12 August 1949.
Art. 56, Geneva Convention Relative to the Treatment of Prisoners of War (Third Geneva Convention), 12 August 1949.
Art. 72, Geneva Convention Relative to the Treatment of Prisoners of War (Third Geneva Convention), 12 August 1949.
Art. 75, Geneva Convention Relative to the Treatment of Prisoners of War (Third Geneva Convention), 12 August 1949.
Art. 79, Geneva Convention Relative to the Treatment of Prisoners of War (Third Geneva Convention), 12 August 1949.
Art. 123, Geneva Convention Relative to the Treatment of Prisoners of War (Third Geneva Convention), 12 August 1949.
Art. 125, Geneva Convention Relative to the Treatment of Prisoners of War (Third Geneva Convention), 12 August 1949.
Art. 126, Geneva Convention Relative to the Treatment of Prisoners of War (Third Geneva Convention), 12 August 1949.

c. Convention IV

Art. 43, Geneva Convention Relative to the Protection of Civilian Persons in Time of War (Fourth Geneva Convention), 12 August 1949.
Art. 78, Geneva Convention Relative to the Protection of Civilian Persons in Time of War (Fourth Geneva Convention), 12 August 1949.

8. Additional Protocols of 1977

a. Additional Protocol I (API)

Additional Protocol I, 1977 to the Geneva Conventions of 12 August 1949, and Relating to the Protection of Victims of International Armed Conflicts.
Art. 5, Additional Protocol I, 1977 to Geneva Protocol I Additional to the Geneva Conventions of 12 August 1949, and Relating to the Protection of Victims of International Armed Conflicts.
Art. 17, Additional Protocol I, 1977 to Geneva Protocol I Additional to the Geneva Conventions of 12 August 1949, and Relating to the Protection of Victims of International Armed Conflicts.
Art. 33, Additional Protocol I, 1977 to Geneva Protocol I Additional to the Geneva Conventions of 12 August 1949, and Relating to the Protection of Victims of International Armed Conflicts.
Art. 35, Additional Protocol I, 1977 to Geneva Protocol I Additional to the Geneva Conventions of 12 August 1949, and Relating to the Protection of Victims of International Armed Conflicts.

Art. 38, Additional Protocol I, 1977 to Geneva Protocol I Additional to the Geneva Conventions of 12 August 1949, and Relating to the Protection of Victims of International Armed Conflicts.

Art. 44, Additional Protocol I, 1977 to Geneva Protocol I Additional to the Geneva Conventions of 12 August 1949, and Relating to the Protection of Victims of International Armed Conflicts.

Art. 48, Additional Protocol I, 1977 to Geneva Protocol I Additional to the Geneva Conventions of 12 August 1949, and Relating to the Protection of Victims of International Armed Conflicts.

Art. 51, Additional Protocol I, 1977 to Geneva Protocol I Additional to the Geneva Conventions of 12 August 1949, and Relating to the Protection of Victims of International Armed Conflicts.

Art. 54, Additional Protocol I, 1977 to Geneva Protocol I Additional to the Geneva Conventions of 12 August 1949, and Relating to the Protection of Victims of International Armed Conflicts.

Art. 57, Additional Protocol I, 1977 to Geneva Protocol I Additional to the Geneva Conventions of 12 August 1949, and Relating to the Protection of Victims of International Armed Conflicts.

Art. 78, Additional Protocol I, 1977 to Geneva Protocol I Additional to the Geneva Conventions of 12 August 1949, and Relating to the Protection of Victims of International Armed Conflicts.

Art. 81, Additional Protocol I, 1977 to Geneva Protocol I Additional to the Geneva Conventions of 12 August 1949, and Relating to the Protection of Victims of International Armed Conflicts.

Art. 87, Additional Protocol I, 1977 to Geneva Protocol I Additional to the Geneva Conventions of 12 August 1949, and Relating to the Protection of Victims of International Armed Conflicts.

b. Additional Protocol II (APII)

Additional Protocol II, 1977 to the Geneva Conventions of 12 August 1949, and Relating to the Protection of Victims of Non-International Armed Conflicts.

9. ICRC Commentaries and Guides to the Geneva Conventions and Additional Protocols

"Commentary," *Rule 87: Humane Treatment*, ICRC Customary International Humanitarian Law Study, https://www.icrc.org/customary-ihl/eng/docs/v1_cha_chapter32_rule87.

A Guide to the Legal Review of New Weapons, Means and Methods of Warfare: Measures to Implement Article 36 of Additional Protocol I of 1977, ICRC, Geneva, 2006, p. 4, https://www.icrc.org/eng/assets/files/other/icrc_002_0902.pdf.

"Introduction to Convention (II) with Respect to the Laws and Customs of War on Land and Its Annex: Regulations Concerning the Laws and Customs of War on Land," The Hague, 29 July 1899, ICRC, https://www.icrc.org/ihl/INTRO/150?OpenDocument.

"Introduction to the Commentary on the Additional Protocols I and II of 8 June 1977," ICRC, https://www.icrc.org/ihl/INTRO/470.

ICRC Commentary to Common Art. 3 of 1949 Geneva Conventions, 1952.

ICRC Commentary to Art. 51, API, para. 1957, https://www.icrc.org/applic/ihl/ihl.nsf/INTRO/470.

ICRC Commentary to Art. 54, API, para. 2122, http://www.icrc.org/applic/ihl/ihl.nsf/Comment.xsp?viewComments=LookUpCOMART&articleUNID=C5F28CACC22458EAC12563CD0051DD00.

ICRC Commentary to Art. 57, API, para. 2206, https://www.icrc.org/ihl/INTRO/470.

10. International Covenant on Civil and Political Rights

Preamble, International Covenant on Civil and Political Rights, 19 December 1966, http://www.ohchr.org/en/professionalinterest/pages/ccpr.aspx.

Art. 4, International Covenant on Civil and Political Rights, 16 December 1966, http://www.ohchr.org/en/professionalinterest/pages/ccpr.aspx.

Art. 5, International Covenant on Civil and Political Rights, 16 December 1966, http://www.ohchr.org/en/professionalinterest/pages/ccpr.aspx.

Art. 6, International Covenant on Civil and Political Rights, 16 December 1966, http://www.ohchr.org/en/professionalinterest/pages/ccpr.aspx.

Art. 7, International Covenant on Civil and Political Rights, 16 December 1966, http://www.ohchr.org/en/professionalinterest/pages/ccpr.aspx.

Art. 13, International Covenant on Civil and Political Rights, 16 December 1966, http://www.ohchr.org/en/professionalinterest/pages/ccpr.aspx.

Art. 18, International Covenant on Civil and Political Rights, 16 December 1966, http://www.ohchr.org/en/professionalinterest/pages/ccpr.aspx.

Art. 19, International Covenant on Civil and Political Rights, 16 December 1966, http://www.ohchr.org/en/professionalinterest/pages/ccpr.aspx.

11. International Covenant on Economic, Social and Cultural Rights

International Covenant on Economic, Social and Cultural Rights, 16 December 1966, http://www.ohchr.org/EN/ProfessionalInterest/Pages/CESCR.aspx.

12. Vienna Convention on the Law of Treaties

Preamble, Vienna Convention on the Law of Treaties (1969), UNTS, vol. 1155.

Art. 1, Vienna Convention on the Law of Treaties (1969), UNTS, vol. 1155.

Art. 18, Vienna Convention on the Law of Treaties (1969), UNTS, vol. 1155.

Art. 26, Vienna Convention on the Law of Treaties (1969), UNTS, vol. 1155.

Art. 31, Vienna Convention on the Law of Treaties (1969), UNTS, vol. 1155.

Art. 38, Vienna Convention on the Law of Treaties (1969), UNTS, vol. 1155.

Art. 53, Vienna Convention on the Law of Treaties (1969), UNTS, vol. 1155.

B. Declarations, Principles, and Guidelines

An Act Declaring the Rights and Liberties of the Subject and Settling the Succession of the Crown, http://avalon.law.yale.edu/17th_century/england.asp.

Basic Principles on the Use of Force and Firearms by Law Enforcement Officials, Eighth United Nations Congress on the Prevention of Crime and the Treatment of Offenders, 7 September 1990, http://www.ohchr.org/EN/ProfessionalInterest/Pages/UseOfForceAndFirearms.aspx.

The 1874 Brussels Project of an International Declaration Concerning the Laws and Customs of War, https://www.icrc.org/ihl/INTRO/135.

Declaration of the Rights of Man—1789, http://avalon.law.yale.edu/18th_century/rightsof.asp.

1992 Rio Declaration on the Environment and Development, http://www.unep.org/documents.multilingual/default.asp?documentid=78&articleid=1163.

Declaration of the United Nations Conference on the Human Environment ("Stockholm Declaration") (1972), http://www.unep.org/documents.multilingual/default.asp?documentid=97&articleid=1503.

"Environmental Principles and Concepts," Organization for Economic Co-operation and Development, OECD/GD (95) 124, Paris, 1995, http://www.oecd.org/trade/envtrade/39918312.pdf.

Special Proclamation by the Supreme Commander of the Allied Powers, 19 January 1946, https://www.loc.gov/law/help/us-treaties/bevans/m-ust000004-0020.pdf.

"St. Petersburg Declaration Renouncing the Use, in Time of War, of Explosive Projectiles Under 400 Grammes Weight," 29 November/11 December 1868, http://www.icrc.org/ihl/INTRO/130?OpenDocument.

Universal Declaration of Human Rights, 10 December 1948, http://www.un.org/en/documents/udhr/.

C. United Nations Documents

"Agreement Regarding the Residence of Nationals of the States Parties to MERCOSUR," *Treaty Series: Treaties and International Agreements Registered or Filed and Recorded with the Secretariat of the United Nations*, vol. 2541, United Nations, 2008.

General Comment 31 of the ICCPR's Human Rights Committee addressed "The Nature of the General Legal Obligation Imposed on States Parties to the Covenant." U.N. Doc. CCPR/C/21/Rev.1/Add.13 (2004), https://www1.umn.edu/humanrts/gencomm/hrcom31.html.

Report of the Commission of Inquiry for the Democratic People's Republic of Korea, A/HRC/25/CRP.1, 7 February 2014, http://www.ohchr.org/EN/HRBodies/HRC/CoIDPRK/Pages/CommissionInquiryonHRinDPRK.aspx.

Report of the Special Rapporteur on Extrajudicial, Summary or Arbitrary Executions, Christof Heyns, A/HRC23/47, 9 April 2013.

Universal Periodic Review Process Conducted by the United Nations Human Rights Council, http://www.ohchr.org/EN/HRBodies/UPR/Pages/UPRMain.aspx.

D. United Nations General Assembly Resolutions

"The Crime of Genocide," Resolution 96 (I), Fifty-Fifth Plenary Meeting, 11 December 1946.

"General Assembly Adopts 64 Third Committee Texts Covering Issues Including Migrants, Children's Rights, Human Rights Defenders." 17 December 2015, http://www.un.org/press/en/2015/ga11745.doc.htm.

E. United Nations Security Council Resolutions

Resolution 827, S/RES/827, 25 May 1993, http://www.icty.org/x/file/Legal%20Library/Statute/statute_827_1993_en.pdf.

Resolution 955, S/RES/955 (1994), https://www1.umn.edu/humanrts/peace/docs/scres955.html.

Resolution 1595 (2005), S/RES/1595 (2005), https://www.treasury.gov/resource-center/sanctions/Programs/Documents/1595.pdf.

Resolution 1757 S/RES/1757 (2007), http://news.specialtribunalforlebanon.com/en/component/k2/225-security-council-resolution-1757?Itemid=213.
Resolution 2122 S/Res/2122 (2013), http://www.un.org/en/ga/search/view_doc.asp?symbol=S/RES/2122(2013).

F. United Nations Educational, Scientific and Cultural Organisation

Art. 1, UNESCO Convention Against Discrimination in Education, Paris, 14 December 1960, http://portal.unesco.org/en/ev.php-URL_ID=12949&URL_DO=DO_TOPIC&URL_SECTION=201.html.
Constitution of UNESCO, London, 16 November 1945, in the Royal Institute of International Affairs, *United Nations Documents, 1941–1945*, Oxford University Press, 1947.

G. North Atlantic Treaty Organization

AJP-3 (B), *Allied Joint Doctrine for the Conduct of Operations*, North Atlantic Treaty Organization, March 2011, para. 0424, http://www.cicde.defense.gouv.fr/IMG/pdf/20110316_np_otan_ajp-3b.pdf.
NATO Glossary of Terms and Definitions, North Atlantic Treaty Organization, NATO Standardization Agency, 2008, p. 2-T-3, https://fas.org/irp/doddir/other/nato2008.pdf.

H. European Union

Charter of Fundamental Rights of the European Union, 2000/C 364/01, http://www.europarl.europa.eu/charter/pdf/text_en.pdf.

I. Commentaries of International Law Commission

Draft Articles on Responsibility of States for Internationally Wrongful Acts, with Commentaries, International Law Commission, 2001, http://legal.un.org/ilc/texts/instruments/english/commentaries/9_6_2001.pdf.
Draft Articles on Prevention of Transboundary Harm from Hazardous Activities, International Law Commission, 2001, http://legal.un.org/ilc/texts/instruments/english/commentaries/9_7_2001.pdf.
Principles of International Law Recognised in the Charter of the Nürnberg Tribunal and the Judgment of the Tribunal, International Law Commission, 1950, http://legal.un.org/ilc/texts/instruments/english/draft_articles/7_1_1950.pdf.

Customary International Humanitarian Law and Commentaries

Commentary to Rule 54, "Attacks Against Objects Indispensable to the Survival of the Civilian Population," *ICRC Customary International Humanitarian Law Study*, https://www.icrc.org/customary-ihl/eng/docs/v1_cha_chapter17_rule54.
Committee on the Formation of Customary International Law, American Branch of the International Law Association: "The Role of State Practice in the Formation of Customary and Jus Cogens Norms of International Law" (19 January 1989).
Customary International Humanitarian Law Database, https://www.icrc.org/customary-ihl/eng/docs/home.
Rule 1, "The Principle of Distinction Between Civilians and Combatants," ICRC Customary International Humanitarian Law Study, https://www.icrc.org/customary-ihl/eng/docs/v1_rul_rule1.

Rule 7, "The Principle of Distinction Between Civilian Objects and Military Objective," ICRC Customary International Humanitarian Law Study, https://www.icrc.org/customary-ihl/eng/docs/v1_rul_rule7.

Rule 11, "Indiscriminate Attacks," ICRC Customary International Humanitarian Law Study, https://www.icrc.org/customary-ihl/eng/docs/v1_rul_rule11.

Rule 12, "Definition of Indiscriminate Attacks," ICRC Customary International Humanitarian Law Study, https://www.icrc.org/customary-ihl/eng/docs/v1_rul_rule12.

Rule 15, "Precautions in Attack," ICRC Customary International Humanitarian Law Study, https://www.icrc.org/customary-ihl/eng/docs/v1_rul_rule15.

Rule 16, "Target Verification," ICRC Customary International Humanitarian Law Study, https://www.icrc.org/customary-ihl/eng/docs/v1_rul_rule16.

Rule 17, "Choice of Means and Methods of Warfare," International Humanitarian Law Study, https://www.icrc.org/customary-ihl/eng/docs/v1_rul_rule17.

Rule 70, "Weapons of a Nature to Cause Superfluous Injury or Unnecessary Suffering," ICRC Customary International Humanitarian Law Study, htpp://www.icrc.org/customary-ihl/eng/docs/v1_cha_chapter20_rule70.

Rule 71, "Weapons That Are by Nature Indiscriminate," ICRC Customary International Humanitarian Law Study, http://www.icrc.org/customary-ihl/eng/docs/v1_rul_rule71.

Rule 113, "Treatment of the Dead," ICRC Customary International Humanitarian Law Study, https://www.icrc.org/customary-ihl/eng/docs/v1_rul_rule113.

Rule 139, "Respect for International Humanitarian Law," ICRC Customary International Humanitarian Law Study, https://www.icrc.org/customaryihl/eng/docs/v1_cha_chapter40_rule139.

Reports, Papers, and Additional Commentary

"Accountability of International Organisations." International Law Association, Berlin (2004), p. 5.

Anderson, Kenneth, and Waxman, Matthew. "Law and Ethics for Autonomous Weapon Systems: Why a Ban Won't Work and How the Laws of War Can." *American University Washington College of Law Research Paper* No. 2013-11 (Jean Perkins Taskforce on National Security and Law).

"Autonomous Weapons: Operationalizing Meaningful Human Control," *ICRC Humanitarian Law and Policy Blog*, Autonomous Weapons Series, Conduct of Hostilities, Law and Conflict, New Technologies, 15 August 2018, p. 6, https://blogs.icrc.org/law-and-policy/2018/08/15/autonomous-weapons-operationalizing-meaningful-human-control/.

Burridge, Brian, Air Chief Marshall (ret.) U.K. Army, "Military Capability Is Founded on a Body of Knowledge to Which Industry Is a Major Contributor" (2010), copy in author's possession.

Campbell Charles. "Army Action on the Re-Investigation into the Combat Action of Wanat Village, Wygal District, Nuristan Province, Afghanistan on 13 July 2008," Department of the Army, 13 May 2010, http://web.archive.org/web/20110716075735/http://usarmy.vo.llnwd.net/e1/wanat/downloads/campbellWanatReportRedacted.pdf.

Docherty, Bonnie. "Losing Humanity: The Case Against Killer Robots," *Human Rights Watch and International Human Rights Clinic* (Harvard Law School, November 2012), 1–49.

———. "Mind the Gap: The Lack of Accountability for Killer Robots," *Human Rights Watch and International Human Rights Clinic* (April 2015), 1–38.

———. "Shaking the Foundations: The Human Rights Implications of Killer Robots," *Human Rights Watch and International Human Rights Clinic* (Harvard Law School, May 2014), 1–27.

Foreword, Vol. 15, Digest of Laws and Cases, *Law Reports of Trials of War Criminals*, London, United Nations War Crimes Commission, 1949, xiii, http://www.loc.gov/rr/frd/Military_Law/pdf/Law-Reports_Vol-15.pdf.

Heyns, Christof. "Lethal Autonomous Weapons and the Protection of Life," A/HRC/23/47, 9 April 2013, https://documents-dds-ny.un.org/doc/UNDOC/GEN/G13/127/76/PDF/G1312776.pdf?OpenElement.

Hoagland, Bradley. "Manning the Next Unmanned Air Force: Developing RPA Pilots of the Future" (August 2013), Policy Paper, Centre for 21st Century Security and Intelligence, 1–26.

Hollis, Duncan. "The Fog of Technology and International Law," *Opinio Juris Blog*, 15 April 2015, http://opiniojuris.org/2015/05/15/the-fog-of-technology-and-international-law/.

Human Rights Watch and Harvard Law School's International Human Rights Clinic Killer Robots and the Concept of Meaningful Human Control, Memorandum to Convention on Conventional Weapons (CCW) Delegates, April 2016, 15–16.

"Investigation Report," Formal Investigation into the Circumstances Surrounding the Downing of Iran Air Flight 655 on 3 July 1988, U.S. Department of Defense, 19 August 1988.

Killer Robots and the Concept of Meaningful Human Control, Memorandum to Convention on Conventional Weapons (CCW) Delegates, Human Rights Watch, April 2016, 1–16.

Lynn, Willian J., III, and Nicholas Thompson. "The Pentagon's New Cyberstrategy," *Foreign Affairs*, 1 October 2010, http://www.foreignaffairs.com/discussions/news-and-events/foreign-affairs-live-the-pentagons-new-cyberstrategy.

Lyons, Jacques. ARIANE 5, *Flight 501 Failure, Report by the Inquiry Board*, 19 July 1996, https://www.ima.umn.edu/~arnold/disasters/ariane5rep.html.

Mahon Peter. *Royal Commission of Inquiry into and Report upon the Crash on Mount Erebus, Antarctica, of a DC10 Aircraft Operated by Air New Zealand Limited* (Wellington: P. D. Hasselberg, 1981), http://www.erebus.co.nz/LinkClick.aspx?fileticket=PUWvCWDoUoE%3D&tabid=159.

McHale, Timothy. "Executive Summary for AR 15-6 Investigation, 21 February 2010 CIVCAS Incident in Uruzgan Province," Memorandum for Commander, United States Forces—Afghanistan/International Security Assistance Force, Afghanistan, http://www.rs.nato.int/images/stories/File/April2010-Dari/May2010Revised/Uruzgan%20investigation%20findings.pdf.

McLurkin, James. "Speaking Swarmish: Human-Robot Interface Design for Large Swarms of Autonomous Mobile Robots" (2006) *Association for the Advancement of Artificial Intelligence*, 1–4.

Melzer, Nils. *Interpretive Guidance on the Notion of Direct Participation in Hostilities Under International Humanitarian Law*, May 2009, http://www.icrc.org/eng/assets/files/other/icrc-002-0990.pdf.

Milanović, Marko. "A Few Thoughts on Hassan v. United Kingdom," *EJIL: Talk!* 22 October 2014, http://www.ejiltalk.org/a-few-thoughts-on-hassan-v-united-kingdom/.

———. "SCSL Appeals Chamber Affirms Charles Taylor Conviction," *EJIL: Talk!* 26 September 2013, http://www.ejiltalk.org/scsl-appeals-chamber-affirms-charles-taylors-conviction/.

The Polluter-Pays Principle: OECD Analyses and Recommendations, Environment Directorate, Organisation for Economic Co-operation and Development, Paris, 1992, http://

www.oecd.org/officialdocuments/publicdisplaydocumentpdf/?cote=OCDE/GD(92)81&docLanguage=En.

Recommendations of the Council Concerning the Application of the Polluter-Pays Principle to Accidental Pollution, Organization for Economic Cooperation and Development, C(89)88/Final, http://acts.oecd.org/Instruments/ShowInstrumentView.aspx?InstrumentID=38&InstrumentPID=305&Lang=en&Book=False.

Report of the Truth and Reconciliation Commission of South Africa, 29 October 1998, http://www.justice.gov.za/trc/report/finalreport/Volume%201.pdf.

Report of the 2018 Session of the Group of Governmental Experts on Emerging Technologies in the Area of Lethal Autonomous Weapons Systems, 23 October 2018, CCW/GGE.1/2018/3, Para. 23 (f), https://undocs.org/en/CCW/GGE.1/2018/3.

Report of the 2019 Session of the Group of Governmental Experts on Emerging Technologies in the Area of Lethal Autonomous Weapons Systems, Geneva, 25 September 2019, CCW/GGE/3, https://undocs.org/en/CCW/GGE.1/2019/3.

"The Responsibility to Protect: Report of the International Commission on Intervention and State Sovereignty," December 2001, http://responsibilitytoprotect.org/ICISS%20Report.pdf.

Scharre, Paul. "Yes, Unmanned Combat Aircraft Are the Future," Centre for a New American Security, 11 August 2015, http://www.cnas.org/opinion/yes-unmanned-combat-aircraft-are-the-future#.VhJzG03smdJ.

"Stopping Killer Robots: Country Positions on Banning Fully Autonomous Weapons and Retaining Human Control," Human Rights Watch, August 2020, https://www.hrw.org/sites/default/files/media_2020/08/arms0820_web_0.pdf.

Rau, Simon. Comment on Cawthorne-Hill, L. "The Grand Chamber Judgment in Hassan v. UK," *EJILTalk*, 18 September 2014, http://www.ejiltalk.org/the-grand-chamber-judgment-in-hassan-v-uk/.

Røislien Eggen, Hanne. "Thoughts on Autonomous Weapon Systems and Meaningful Human Control of Cyber," *Open Democracy: Free Thinking for the World*, 7 November 2014, https://www.opendemocracy.net/hanne-eggen-r%c3%b8islien/thoughts-on-autonomous-weapons-systems-and-meaningful-human-control-of-cyber.

The RTO Studies, Analysis and Simulation Panel (SAS), "NATO Policy on Non-Lethal Weapons" (Annex B to RTO-TR-SAS-040, Non-Lethal Weapons and Future Peace Enforcement Operations, December 2004, http://www.cso.nato.int/pubs/rdp.asp?RDP=RTO-TR-SAS-040.

Townes, Charles. "Report of the Task Force on Space," 8 January 1969, in J. Logsdon (ed.), *Exploring the Unknown: Selected Documents in the History of the U.S. Civil Space Program* (Washington, D.C., 1995), vol. 1, Organizing for Exploration, http://history.nasa.gov/SP-4407/vol1/intro.pdf.

"Unmanned Systems Integrated Roadmap FY2009–2034," 6 April 2009.

"Unmanned Systems Integrated Roadmap FY2011–2036," U.S. Department of Defense, http://www.acq.osd.mil/sts/docs/Unmanned%20Systems%20Integrated%20Roadmap%20FY2011-2036.pdf.

Velez-Green, Alexander. "The South Korean Sentry—a 'Killer Robot' to Prevent War," *Lawfare*, 1 March 2015, https://www.lawfareblog.com/foreign-policy-essay-south-korean-sentry%E2%80%94-killer-robot-prevent-war.

Williamson, Gavin. "Defense in Global Britain," GOV.UK, 11 February 2019, https://www.gov.uk/government/speeches/defence-in-global-britain.

2010 Report on the Application of the European Union Charter of Fundamental Rights, European Commission, COM(2011) 160, http://ec.europa.eu/justice/fundamental-rights/files/annual_report_2010_en.pdf.

Conference Papers, Lectures, and Addresses

Article 36, Non-Governmental Organization, Remarks to the Meeting of Experts on Lethal Autonomous Weapon Systems, Convention on Certain Conventional Weapons, 12 April 2016.

Asaro, Peter. "Human Dignity and Autonomous Weapon Systems," Presentation to Conference on Autonomous Weapon Systems—Law, Ethics, Policy, European University Institute, Academy of European Law, 24 April 2014.

Barth Eide, Espen, Member of Managing Board of World Economic Forum, Remarks, "Private Sector Perspectives on the Development of Lethal Autonomous Systems," Geneva, 12 April 2016.

Boothby, William. "Possible Challenges to International Humanitarian Law," Presentation to Expert Meeting on Lethal Autonomous Weapons, Convention on Certain Conventional Weapons, April 2015, pp. 3–4, http://www.unog.ch/80256EDD006B8954/(httpAssets)/616D2401231649FDC1257E290047354D/$file/2015_LAWS_MX_BoothbyS+Corr.pdf.

Borrie, John. "On Safety Aspects of Meaningful Human Control: Catastrophic Accidents in Complex Systems," Conference in Weapons, Technology and Human Control, United Nations Institute for Disarmament Research, New York, 16 October 2014.

Brooks, Rodney. "A Brave New World? How Will Advances in Artificial Intelligence, Smart Sensors and Social Technology Change Our Lives?" Panel Discussion at World Economic Forum, 22 January 2015, http://www.weforum.org/videos/brave-new-world.

Burridge, Brian, Air Marshal (ret.), former commander of U.K. forces in Iraq. Remarks During Panel "The International Legal Context" at "Autonomous Military Technologies: Policy and Governance for Next Generation Defence Systems," Chatham House, London, 24 February 2014.

Concluding Remarks of Finland, 2015 Meeting of Experts on Lethal Autonomous Weapon Systems, Convention on Certain Conventional Weapons, 17 April 2015.

Corn, Geoffrey. Remarks at Autonomous Weapon Systems—Law, Ethics and Policy, Conference at European University Institute, Academy of European Law, 24 April 2014.

Fursman, Andrew. Remarks, "Private Sector Perspectives on the Development of Lethal Autonomous Systems," Geneva, 12 April 2016.

Gantz, Lt. General Benny. "The IDF in 2025," Address to the Begin-Sadat Centre for Strategic Studies, 9 October 2013, http://besacenter.org/new-at-the-besa-center/idf-chief-staff-benny-gantz-speaks-besa-center/.

Gao, F., et al. "Teamwork in Controlling Multiple Robots," Proceedings of the Seventh Annual ACM/IEEE International Conference on Human-Robot Interaction (2012), pp. 81–88, http://web.mit.edu/aeroastro/labs/halab/papers/hri167-gao.pdf.

Giacca, Gilles. Remarks to Panel "Challenges [of Autonomous Weapons] to International Humanitarian Law," Informal Expert Meeting on Lethal Autonomous Weapons, Convention on Certain Conventional Weapons, Geneva, 13 April 2016, http://www.unog.ch/80256EE600585943/(httpPages)/37D51189AC4FB6E1C1257F4D004CAFB2?OpenDocument.Goodman, R., in "The Changing Character of the Participants in War: Civilianization of War-Fighting and the Concept of 'Direct Participation in Hostilities'" (U.S. Naval War College, International Law Conference 2010), http://www.usnwc.edu/Events/International-Law-Conference-2010.aspx.

Goose, Stephen. Statement by Human Rights Watch to Informal Meeting of Experts on Lethal Autonomous Weapon Systems, Convention on Certain Conventional Weapons, 12 April 2016.

Governments of Belgium, Ireland, and Luxembourg, "Food for Thought Paper," Group of Governmental Experts on Emerging Technologies in the Area of Lethal Autonomous Weapon Systems, CCW/GGE.1/2019/WP.4, Geneva, 28 March 2019, para. 3, https://www.unog.ch/80256EDD006B8954/(httpAssets)/F3A850205D48D5A4C125841E00351CD7/$file/CCW_GGE.1_2019_WP.4.pdf.

Government of Israel, 2015 Meeting of Experts on Lethal Autonomous Weapons, Convention on Certain Conventional Weapons, 15 April 2015, http://www.unog.ch/80256EDD006B8954/(httpAssets)/AB30BF0E02AA39EAC1257E29004769F3/$file/2015_LAWS_MX_Israel_characteristics.pdf.

Government of Japan, "Possible Outcome of 2019 Group of Governmental Experts and Future Actions of International Community on Lethal Autonomous Weapons Systems," Group of Governmental Experts on Emerging Technologies in the Area of Lethal Autonomous Weapon Systems, Geneva, 22 March 2019, https://www.unog.ch/80256EDD006B8954/(httpAssets)/B0F30B3F69F5F2EEC12583C8003F3145/$file/CCW_+GGE+.1_+2019_+WP3+JAPAN.pdf.

Government of the United Kingdom, "Agenda Item 5 (b): Characterization of the Systems Under Consideration in Order to Promote a Common Understanding on Concepts and Characteristics Relevant to the Objectives and Purposes of the Convention," Group of Governmental Experts on Emerging Technologies in the Area of Lethal Autonomous Weapon Systems, Geneva, 25–29 March 2019, https://www.unog.ch/80256EDD006B8954/(httpAssets)/A969D779E1E5E28BC12583D3003FC0D9/$file/20190318-5(b)_Characterisation_Statement.pdf.

Hambling, David. "Change in the Air: Disruptive Developments in Armed UAV Technology," United Nations Institute for Disarmament Research, 2018, https://www.unidir.org/files/publications/pdfs/-en-726.pdf.

Hampson, Françoise. Written Statement, Appendix 3 to "Expert Meeting," *The Use of Force in Armed Conflicts: Interplay Between the Conduct of Hostilities and Law Enforcement Paradigms*, Geneva, ICRC, 2013.

Heyns, Christof. "Autonomous Weapon Systems and Human Rights Law," Presentation Made at Informal Expert Meeting Organized by the State Parties to the Convention on Certain Conventional Weapons, Geneva, 13–16 May 2014, http://www.unog.ch/80256EDD006B8954/(httpAssets)/DDB079530E4FFDDBC1257CF3003FFE4D/$file/Heyns_LAWS_otherlegal_2014.pdf.

———. Presentation to Annual Meeting of State Parties to Convention on Certain Conventional Weapons, 13–16 May 2014, http://www.unog.ch/80256EDD006B8954/(httpAssets)/DDB079530E4FFDDBC1257CF3003FFE4D/$file/Heyns_LAWS_otherlegal_2014.pdf.

———. Presentation to Convention on Certain Conventional Weapons Meeting of Experts on Lethal Autonomous Weapon Systems, 16 April 2015, http://www.unog.ch/80256EDD006B8954/(httpAssets)/1869331AFF45728BC1257E2D0050EFE0/$file/2015_LAWS_MX_Heyns_Transcript.pdf.

van den Hoven, Jeroen. "Why the Future Needs Us Today: Moral Responsibility and Engineering Autonomous Weapon Systems," Presentation to 2015 Meeting of Experts on Lethal Autonomous Weapon Systems at the Convention on Certain Conventional Weapons,

April 2015, http://www.unog.ch/80256EE600585943/(httpPages)/6CE049BE22EC75A2C1257C8D00513E26?OpenDocument.

ICRC Statement "Agenda Item 5 (c): Characterization: The Importance of Critical Functions," CCW GGE "LAWs," 25 March 2019, p. 2, https://www.unog.ch/80256EDD006B8954/(httpAssets)/7EA110E50853887DC12583CC003032E7/$file/ICRC+GGE+LAWS+ICRC+statement+agenda+item+5c+25+03+2019.pdf.

Jackson, Colonel R. Panel, "Autonomous Weaponry and Armed Conflict," Annual Meeting of American Society of International Law, Washington, D.C., April 2014.

Kasperson, Anja. Remarks, "Private Sector Perspectives on the Development of Lethal Autonomous Systems," Geneva, 12 April 2016.

Kellenberger, Jakob. "Keynote Address," International Humanitarian Law and New Weapon Technologies, 34th Round Table on Current Issues of International Humanitarian Law, San Remo, 8 September 2011, http://www.icrc.org/eng/resources/documents/statement/new-weapon-technologies-statement-2011-09-08.htm.

Kennedy, James, and Russell Eberhardt. "Particle Swarm Optimization," Neural Networks, Proceedings, IEEE International Conference, 1995, http://citeseerx.ist.psu.edu/viewdoc/download?doi=10.1.1.248.4138&rep=rep1&type=pdf.

Mauer, P. Remarks at Leiden University College, The Hague, 22 May 2014.

Meier, Michael. U.S. Delegation Opening Statement to Meeting of Experts on Lethal Autonomous Weapon Systems, Convention on Certain Conventional Weapons, 13 April 2015, http://www.unog.ch/80256EDD006B8954/(httpAssets)/8B33A1CDBE80EC60C1257E2800275E56/$file/2015_LAWS_MX_USA+bis.pdf.

Mendez, J. "Justice as Prevention of Mass Atrocities," Presentation at the Carr Center for Human Rights, John F. Kennedy School of Government, Harvard University, 23 November 2009, http://www.youtube.com/watch?v=yQSLeru_n8o.

Millar, Jason. Presentation to Convention on Certain Conventional Weapons Meeting of Experts on Lethal Autonomous Weapon Systems, 15 April 2015, p. 5, http://www.unog.ch/80256EDD006B8954/(httpAssets)/F483D421E67D230FC1257E2F0033E690/$file/Jason+Millar+-+Meaningful+Human+Control+and+Dual-Use+Technology.pdf.

Moyes, R. Remarks on "Towards a Working Definition of Lethal Autonomous Weapon Systems," Informal Expert Meeting on Lethal Autonomous Weapons, Convention on Certain Conventional Weapons, 12 April 2016, http://www.unog.ch/80256EE600585943/(httpPages)/37D51189AC4FB6E1C1257F4D004CAFB2?OpenDocument.

"Poland's Position on Continuing the Discussions on Lethal Autonomous Weapon Systems Within the CCW Framework," Convention on Certain Conventional Weapons, Annual Meeting of the States Parties, November 2015, http://www.unog.ch/80256EE600585943/(httpPages)/0D4B67A1E11A22BCC1257A410052DE38?OpenDocument.

Porter, Lisa. Statement Before the House Armed Services Committee on Emerging Threats and Capabilities, on "Department of Defense's Artificial Intelligence Structures, Investments and Applications," 11 December 2018, https://docs.house.gov/meetings/AS/AS26/20181211/108795/HHRG-115-AS26-Wstate-PorterL-20181211.pdf.

Presentation of Poland to Convention on Certain Conventional Weapons Meeting of Experts on Lethal Autonomous Weapon Systems, 14 April 2015, http://www.unog.ch/80256EDD006B8954/(httpAssets)/16BDFE48306133F6C1257E31002BA329/$file/2015_LAWS_MX_Poland_characteristics.pdf.

Russell, S. "A Brave New World? How Will Advances in Artificial Intelligence, Smart Sensors and Social Technology Changer Our Lives?" Panel Discussion at World Economic Forum, 22 January 2015, http://www.weforum.org/videos/brave-new-world.

Sampiano, Jorge. President of Portugal, Address at the International Court of Justice, 30 October 1997, http://www.icj-cij.org/presscom/index.php?pr=142&pt=1&p1=6&p2=1&PHPSESSID=5c407.

Schmitt, Michael. Remarks During Panel "The International Legal Context" at "Autonomous Military Technologies: Policy and Governance for Next Generation Defence Systems," Chatham House, London, 24 February 2014; permission to cite provided in electronic mail message to author, 15 March 2014.

Shapland, General John. Lecture to Conference on Air Defense in the Modern Era, Institute for National Security Studies, 18 March 2014, http://www.inss.org.il/index.aspx?id=4479&categoryid=59.]

"Statement of the Republic of Croatia," Convention on Conventional Weapons, Informal Meeting of Experts on Lethal Autonomous Weapons, 13 April 1015, http://www.unog.ch/80256EE600585943/(httpPages)/6CE049BE22EC75A2C1257C8D00513E26?OpenDocument.

Statement of Ecuador to Expert Meeting Concerning Lethal Autonomous Weapons, Convention on Certain Conventional Weapons, 13–17 April 2015, http://www.unog.ch/80256EE600585943/(httpPages)/6CE049BE22EC75A2C1257C8D00513E26?OpenDocument.

Statement of France to Informal Meeting of Experts on Lethal Autonomous Weapon Systems, Convention on Certain Conventional Weapons, 12 April 2016, http://www.unog.ch/80256EE600585943/(httpPages)/37D51189AC4FB6E1C1257F4D004CAFB2?OpenDocument.

Statement of Ghana on "The Way Forward on Discussions [Regarding] Lethal Autonomous Weapons," Convention on Conventional Weapons, 17 April 2015, http://www.unog.ch/80256EE600585943/(httpPages)/6CE049BE22EC75A2C1257C8D00513E26?OpenDocument.

Statement of Professor Christof Heyns to the 2015 Meeting of Experts on Lethal Autonomous Weapons at the Convention on Certain Conventional Weapons, 16 April 2015, http://www.unog.ch/80256EDD006B8954/(httpAssets)/1869331AFF45728BC1257E2D0050EFE0/$file/2015_LAWS_MX_Heyns_Transcript.pdf.

"Statement of South Africa," Meeting of Experts on Lethal Autonomous Weapon Systems, Convention on Certain Conventional Weapons, 13–17 April 2015, http://www.unog.ch/80256EE600585943/(httpPages)/6CE049BE22EC75A2C1257C8D00513E26?OpenDocument.

Statement of United Kingdom to Informal Meeting of Experts on Lethal Autonomous Weapons, Convention on Certain Conventional Weapons, 13–17 April 2015, http://www.unog.ch/80256EDD006B8954/(httpAssets)/1CBF996AF7AD10E2C1257E260060318A/$file/2015_LAWS_MX_United+Kingdom.pdf.

Statement (Oral) by United States representative to 2016 Informal Expert Meeting on Lethal Autonomous Weapon Systems, Convention on Certain Conventional Weapons, 12 April 2016.

Steels, Luc. "Ten Big Ideas of Artificial Intelligence," 25th Benelux Conference on Artificial Intelligence, Delft University of Technology, 8 November 2013.

Ulgen, Ozlem. "Autonomous Weapons and Human Dignity," Lecture at Winter Academy on Artificial Intelligence and International Law, Asser Institute, The Hague, 22 January 2020.

Waldron, Jeremy. "Dignity, Rank and Rights: The Tanner Lectures on Human Values," delivered at University of California, Berkeley, 21–23 April 2009, https://tannerlectures.utah.edu/_documents/a-to-z/w/Waldron_09.pdf.

Author Interviews and Electronic Mail Communications

Author Interview with Allen Borrelli, former U.S. Army Intelligence Specialist, The Hague, 15 July 2015.

Author interview with Dr. Jeffrey Bradshaw, Senior Research Scientist, Florida Institute for Human and Machine Cognition, Leiden, Netherlands, 10 June 2014.

Author interview with Colonel Hans Folmer, Commander of Cyber Command, Netherlands Ministry of Defence, 20 January 2015.

Author interview with Dr. Matthew Johnson, Researcher, Florida Institute for Human and Machine Cognition, Leiden, Netherlands, 10 June 2014.

Author Interview with Thomas Nash, 29 January 2016.

Author Interview with Paul Scharre, coordinator of drafting process for Directive 3000.09, Washington, D.C., 9 April 2014.

Author interview with Colonel Denny Traas, MSc, Chief Air Force Branch, Plans Directorate, Defence Staff, Netherlands Ministry of Defence, The Hague, 20 February 2015.

Author interview with Gianfranco Visentin (Head), Automation and Robotics Section, European Space Research and Technology Centre, European Space Agency, Noordwijk, Netherlands, 4 November 2013.

Electronic mail message from General B. A. Fabio Giunchi, Commander of Air Cooperation School, Guidonia Airport, Italian Air Force, 16 February 2015.

Electronic mail message from Dr. Fabricio Guariglia, Senior Appeals Counsel, Office of the Prosecutor, International Criminal Court, 29 January 2012.

Electronic mail message from Associate Professor Kevin Hamlen, University of Texas, Dallas, 28 May 2015.

Electronic mail message from Tom Keeley, 2 and 13 June 2014.

Electronic mail messages from Noga Nadler Mozes, Corporate Communications, Israel Aerospace Industries, 29 June 2015.

Electronic mail message from G. Santhanam, Senior Engineer at Google X, 31 May 2015.

Electronic mail message from Paul Scharre, 8 June 2020.

Statements and Communications of Arms Manufacturers

"Aviation Defence Equipment Technology: Rafael Spice 250," AirRecognition.com, 14 January 2015, http://www.airrecognition.com/index.php/focus-analysis-photo-report-aviation-defence-industry/aviation-defence-industry-technology/1424-rafaels-spice-250-precision-guided-glide-bomb-undergoing-adaptation-test-on-iafs-fighters.html.

"Brimstone Precision Attack Weapon Data Sheet," MBDA Missile Systems, https://www.mbda-systems.com/product/brimstone/.

"CARACAS (Control Architecture for Robotic Agent Command and Sensing)," Naval Drones, U.S. Office of Naval Research, Science and Technology, http://www.navaldrones.com/CARACAS.html.

Description of the M426S E-Scan IFF Interrogator, produced by SELEX ES, http://www.selex-es.com/-/m426s.

Egozi, Arie. "Israeli F-35s to Use Spice Bomb Kits," F-16.Net, 13 March 2013, http://www.f-16.net/forum/viewtopic.php?t=23226.

"Future Weapons Israel: Iron Fist APS," Discovery, https://www.youtube.com/watch?v=fI_cbAdCZCw.

"Future Weapons Israel Special Part V, Spyder ADS," Discovery, https://www.youtube.com/watch?v=YW8G-8uyqdA.

"Guardium Mark2 UGV: Field Proven UGV with Enhanced Combat Capabilities," GNIUS Unmanned Ground Systems, http://g-nius.co.il/pdf/brochures/GuardiumLS.pdf.

"Harpoon," WeaponSystems.net, http://weaponsystems.net/weapon.php?weapon=HH10+-+Harpoon.

"HARPY," Israel Aerospace Industries, http://www.iai.co.il/2013/36694-16153-en/IAI.aspx accessed 8 July 2015.

"IAI's MBT HARPY System," Israel Aerospace Industries, https://www.youtube.com/watch?v=AyKXUfOubH0 accessed 30 June 2015.

Israel Aerospace Industries, Harpy Loitering Weapon, http://www.iai.co.il/2013/16143-16153-en/IAI.aspx, accessed 30 June 2015.

Lockheed Martin, "Building the F-35: Combining Teamwork and Technology," F-35 Lightning II, https://www.f35.com/about/life-cycle/production.

Lockheed Martin, "F-35 Experience," Video in F-35's Capabilities: Multi-Mission Capability for Emerging Global Threats, https://www.f35.com/about/capabilities.

Lockheed Martin, "Multi-Mission Capability for Emerging Global Threats," F-35 Lightning II, https://www.f35.com/about/capabilities.

"Phalanx Close-In Weapons System," About.Com, United States Navy Fact File, http://usmilitary.about.com/library/milinfo/navyfacts/blphalanx.htm.

"Protector: Unmanned Naval Patrol Vehicle," Rafael Advanced Defence Systems, http://www.rafael.co.il/Marketing/288-1037-en/Marketing.aspx?searchText=autonomous.

Richardson, Jack. "The Coming Drone Swarm," *Defence Procurement International*, 16 February 2017, https://www.defenceprocurementinternational.com/features/air/drone-swarms.

Smalley, David. "LOCUST: Autonomous Swarming UAVs Fly into the Future," America's Navy, 4 April 2015, http://www.navy.mil/submit/display.asp?story_id=86558://.

"Spice: Precision Guided Weapon Kit," Rafael Advanced Weapon Systems, http://www.rafael.co.il/Marketing/332-891-en/Marketing.aspx.

"Spice: Smart, Precise-Impact and Cost-Effective Guidance Kits," Rafael: Smart and to the Point, http://www.rafael.co.il/marketing/SIP_STORAGE/FILES/4/924.pdf.

"SPYDER-SR ADS Short Range Air Defence System," Rafael Advanced Defence Systems Ltd., http://www.rafael.co.il/Marketing/186-704-en/Marketing.aspx.

"Successful Flight Demonstrations for HAROP Loitering Munitions," Israel Aerospace Industries, http://www.iai.co.il/2013/32981-46464-en/MediaRoom_News.aspx accessed 8 July 2015.

"Vehicle Management," in VCS-4586 Capabilities Guide, Lockheed Martin, p. 4, http://www.lockheedmartin.com/content/dam/lockheed/data/ms2/documents/cdl-systems/VCS-4586%20CAPABILITIES%20GUIDE-August2013.pdf.

Miscellaneous

Bellavia, David. Staff Sergeant David Bellavia, Induction into Pentagon Hall of Heroes, 26 June 2019, https://www.youtube.com/watch?v=zu3Gm5PGvRM.

"British-American Diplomacy: The Caroline Case," Lillian Goldman Library, The Avalon Project, 2008, http://avalon.law.yale.edu/19th_century/br-1842d.asp.

Campaign to Stop Killer Robots, http://www.stopkillerrobots.org/.

Cicero, "Oration for Titus Annius Milo," Society for Ancient Languages, section IV, http://www.uah.edu/student_life/organizations/SAL/texts/latin/classical/cicero/promilone1e.html#celeven.

"F-35 Joint Strike Fighter (JSF)," Department of Defense Programs, p. 34, http://breakingdefense.com/wp-content/uploads/sites/3/2014/01/2013DOTE_F-35_report.pdf.

Gates, Bill. EdX Course CS50x3 (Computer Science 50), Harvard College, Week 1 2015.

"History," Dictionary.com, http://dictionary.reference.com/browse/history.

International Committee for Robot Arms Control, http://icrac.net/who/.

"Law," Macmillan Dictionary, http://www.macmillandictionary.com/thesaurus-category/british/moral-rules-and-rules-of-behaviour.

Missile Defense Project, "Brimstone," *Missile Threat*, Center for Strategic and International Studies, published 6 December 2017, last modified 15 June 2018, https://missilethreat.csis.org/missile/brimstone/.

"RMC—About the Competition," 17 May 2015, http://www.nasa.gov/offices/education/centers/kennedy/technology/nasarmc/about.

"Situation Room," http://en.wikipedia.org/wiki/Situation_Room.

Strangeway, James. WWI War Diary Transcription of Acting Cpl. James Strangeway, S8922. No3 Section, 12th Platoon "C" Co. 2nd Battn. Rifle Brigade, https://www.forces-war-records.co.uk/library/document/1980/wwi-war-diary-transcription-of-acting-cpl-james-strangeway-s8922-no3-section-12th-platoon-c-co-2nd-battn-rifle-brigade/page-8/?searchCategory=war+diary&searchTag=wwi&searchPage=1&filterPagesOnSearchQuery=False&filterPagesOnSearchQueryExact=True.

INDEX

ACKNOWLEDGMENTS

Work on this book began at the University of Cambridge during the 2010–11 academic year, when I had the privilege to serve as the Leverhulme Visiting Professor in the Faculty of Law. Professors James Crawford, Roger O'Keefe, and Marc Weller gave me a home and encouragement to pursue my interest in the relationship between new technologies and international law, and the extraordinary students at Cambridge were a constant source of inspiration. Over time I received further insights and valuable advice and support from international law scholars, including Bill Boothby, Andrew Clapham, Kevin Jon Heller, Peter Marguiles, Tim McCormack, Mike Schmitt, Kimberly Trapp, and Wouter Werner. Paul Scharre helped me to understand more nuanced perspectives about the meaning of autonomy.

At the University of Leiden, William Schabas, Helen Duffy, and Robert Heinsch gave me helpful comments on earlier drafts. Larissa van den Herik kindly invited me to sit in during the discussions of the Joint Committee on Autonomous Weapon Systems that reported to the Netherlands Advisory Council on International Affairs. This book simply would not exist without the exceptional wisdom and guidance I received from Carsten Stahn. Jos Schaeken and Judi Denman, deans of Leiden University College, were always generous with their support as I juggled the demands of teaching with research and writing. Sam Gaunt and Emily Voorhies provided outstanding research and editorial assistance.

I was fortunate to have the help and encouragement of Bert Lockwood, Peter Agree, and Robert Lockhart in finding a home for this book at the University of Pennsylvania Press. Noreen O'Connor-Abel and Kathleen Kageff guided me through the copyediting and production process. I will be forever grateful to two anonymous reviewers whose wise and often razor-sharp comments on an earlier manuscript made this an immeasurably better book.

Last but not least, this book would not exist but for the love and support of Maritza and Fernando. They make life worth living.

CPSIA information can be obtained
at www.ICGtesting.com
Printed in the USA
JSHW021209220821
17984JS00008B/3